Distinctly Narcissistic: Diary Fiction in Quebec

THEORY / CULTURE

General editors: Linda Hutcheon and Paul Perron

Valerie Raoul

# DISTINCTLY NARCISSISTIC:
## Diary Fiction in Quebec

UNIVERSITY OF TORONTO PRESS
Toronto Buffalo London

© University of Toronto Press Incorporated 1993
Toronto Buffalo London
Printed in Canada
Reprinted in 2018
ISBN 0-8020-2882-9
ISBN 978-1-4875-8523-5 (paper)

Printed on acid-free paper

---

**Canadian Cataloguing in Publication Data**

Raoul, Valerie, 1941–
  Distinctly narcissistic:
  diary fiction in Quebec

(Theory/culture)
Includes bibliographical references and index.
ISBN 0-8020-2882-9

1. Narcissism in literature.  2. Canadian fiction (French) – Quebec (Province) – History and criticism.*  I. Title.  II. Series.

PS8191.N37R3 1993     c843.009'353     c93-093908-5
PR9192.6.N37R3 1993

---

This book has been published with the help of a grant from the Canadian Federation for the Humanities, using funds provided by the Social Sciences and Humanities Research Council of Canada.

# Contents

Acknowledgments   vii
Preamble   ix

PART ONE
**Identity and Difference**   1

1   Introduction: Diary Fiction in Quebec   3
2   Narcissism in Psychoanalytic Theory   14
3   Gender and Ethnicity   26

PART TWO
**Narcissism and Femininity (1870–1940)**   43

4   Femininity and Self-Denial:
    The Diary of Henriette Dessaulles   45
5   Phallic Women and Moral Narcissism:
    The Fictional Journals of Laure Conan   58

PART THREE
**Narcissism and Colonized Men (1940–1960)**   83

6   Masculine Misogyny and Cerebral Abstinence:
    Hertel, Baillargeon, Simard   85
7   The Phallic Mother, Impotent Men, and Madness:
    Loranger, Elie, Filiatrault   110

PART FOUR
**Gender Confusion and Self-Generation (1960–1990)**   133

8   Homosexuality, Androgyny, and Bi-Section:
    Pinsonneault, Blais, Richard, Tremblay, Monette   135
9   Self-Part(ur)ition or Giving Birth to the Book:
    Bessette, Godbout, Garneau, Amyot   167

PART FIVE
**Writing and Self-Esteem: From Mirror to Voice**   195

10  Separation and Survival:
    Women's Diary Fiction from Saint-Onge to Mailhot   197
11  Language and (R)evolution:
    Ducharme, Aquin, Brossard   221

CONCLUSION:
**Collective (Con)texts and (In)difference:**   251

12  Autism, Assimilation, or Babel: Noël   253

APPENDIX:
Diary Fiction in Quebec: Chronology and Classification   265

NOTES   267

BIBLIOGRAPHY   279

INDEX OF NAMES   299

GENERAL INDEX   305

# Acknowledgments

This book would never have been completed without grants from the Social Sciences and Humanities Research Council of Canada in 1984–5 and 1989, and the practical and moral support of my family, especially Yvon Raoul. I am also grateful to Françoise Maccabée Iqbal, Réjean Beaudoin, Ann Pearson, and Patricia Smart for their encouragement and helpful comments, and to Maureen Cromie, Emanuela Guerra, Deanne Achong, and Darlene Money for their work on the manuscript.

It is not without some trepidation that an immigrant from England, who finds Quebec fascinating, dares to write about it. I have the uncomfortable feeling that this is how a man must feel talking about women's writing. But there *are* some feminist men – and some bilingual English-Canadians, including myself, who would like to live in Quebec.

I have spent ten years thinking about identity and difference, separation and belonging, in connection with this project. The result is dedicated to my father, recently arrived from England, my mother-in-law in Montreal, and my daughter Mélanie, who looks like both her French and her English grandmothers.

In loving memory of my mother, Mabel Underwood, and my father-in-law, Alain Raoul

University of British Columbia
January 1993

PREAMBLE

# Literature as (re)membering: *'je me souviens'*

'.... the benefits of literature – the stirring of minds, the coherence of national consciousness ... the pride which a nation gains from a literature of its own and the support it is afforded in the face of the hostile surrounding world, this *keeping of a diary by a nation* which is something entirely different from historiography ... the narrowing down of the attention of a nation upon itself and the acceptance of what is foreign only in reflection, the birth of a respect for those active in literature ... the acknowledgment of literary events as objects of political solicitude ... the presentation of national faults in a manner that is very painful ... but also deserving of forgiveness ... all these effects can be produced even by a literature whose development is not in actual fact unusually broad in scope ...

A small nation's memory is not smaller than the memory of a large one and so it can digest the existing material more thoroughly. There are, to be sure, fewer experts in literary history employed, but literature is less a concern of literary history than of the people ... For the claim that the national consciousness of a small people makes on the individual is such that everyone must always be prepared to know that part of the literature which has come down to him, to support it, to defend it – to defend it even if he does not know and support it.'

FRANZ KAFKA's diary, 25 December 1911 (my emphasis)

# PART I

# IDENTITY AND DIFFERENCE

CHAPTER ONE

# Introduction:
# *Diary Fiction in Quebec*

'The strategic value of generic concepts ... clearly lies in the mediatory function of the notion of a genre, which allows the coordination of immanent formal analysis of the individual text with the twin diachronic perspective of the history of forms and the evolution of social life'.

FREDRIC JAMESON (1981), 105

## Precedent and procedure

This study of fictional journals produced in Quebec is a sequel, rather than a companion volume, to my previous work on the French diary novel, *The French Fictional Journal: Fictional Narcissism / Narcissistic Fiction* (1980). One criticism of that book (by a Canadian assessor) was that it failed to take into account examples of the subgenre concerned that were published in Quebec. At that time I considered the exclusion necessary, since if I included novels from Quebec, why should I not also extend the corpus (already large and unwieldy) to cover all diary fiction written in French, of whatever national origin? In fact, the theoretical approach adopted, producing as it did an abstract model for the structure and functioning of this type of text, was applicable to any diary novel written anywhere, at any time, and in any language. Three comparative studies of diary fiction published since then (by Lorna Martens 1985, H. Porter Abbott 1984, and Trevor Field 1989) all choose to ignore geographical and linguistic boundaries. The restriction to French examples was, for me, a pragmatic but ultimately arbitrary way of reducing the number of works involved, implying little emphasis on any specific 'Frenchness' illustrated by those I selected.

4 Identity and Difference

This aspect was actually limited to a perceived difference in the model, the *journal intime*, which evolved in France, as opposed to the anecdotal and frequently humorous one prevalent in the Anglo-Saxon tradition (Raoul 1980, viii). The approach adopted excluded any (problematic) consideration of why these divergent models should have emerged at different times and in different places – an aspect since then enlarged on by Martens, whose study is more diachronic.

In 1980 I could state firmly: 'Extra-literary elements, such as the author's biography or neuroses, the society to which he [sic] belongs, or the ideology he espouses, are not considered here' (viii). Deliberately refraining from any contextualization of the individual works, I proceeded to refer to them at random, as does Field (1988). The popularity of this type of fiction in France at certain times is noticeable in the chronological list of novels (Raoul 1980, 114–15), yet this aspect remained marginal. I also rigorously resisted the temptation (from the methodological standpoint adopted) to examine the relationship between the authors and their narrators, although gender identity emerged as a central preoccupation of the latter, especially in novels written by men depicting female narrators.[1]

Since 1980 I have been teaching Quebec civilization and women's studies courses, as well as literary theory. The focus of the present study is correspondingly very different from that of the previous one, although it builds on the model elaborated in it. I shall seek to address here some of the questions raised earlier but discarded or postponed because they did not fit into a structuralist framework. In what context does diary fiction emerge? Does the narcissism depicted in these contextualized fictional journals reflect the context – or distort, deflect, or modify it? Does the fictional diarist function as representative of a collective phenomenon, or is (s)he an exception? Previously, I minimized references to psychology, emphasizing the fact that a fictional character can have no unconscious, as has a 'real' diarist (Raoul 1980, 32), that any hidden depths are constructed by the author and destined not to remain hidden. I used the term 'narcissistic' loosely, to imply many types of self-reflexivity. I have since then discovered that the feminist post-Freudian theory of narcissism illuminates not only the relationship of narrative form to context, in the case of diary fiction in Quebec, but also the motivation and effects of my own abstract model for the relationship in this formal construct of the narcissistic self to time and to writing.

The model included three elements of the fictional journal in each of the essential dimensions, (divided) self, time, and writing, constituting a 'grammar' of this type of narration (Raoul 1980, 71-6). The 'self-as-diarist' was shown to be performing three separate roles, those of narrator, actor in what is narrated, and narratee, since the *intimiste* writes (initially, at least) for the self alone. These three roles correspond to the grammatical functions of subject (nominative case), direct object (accusative), and indirect object (dative). Each is also associated with a different tense, and a related series of chronological shifts and interweavings is thereby produced. The narrating self is situated in the present of narration, the narrated self is already in the past (however close), and the self who may reread what is written belongs to a hypothetical future. The grammatical category of voice is also present in three dimensions, since the narrated, past self is passive, and the future self-as-reader is anticipated as active, while the narrating self is engaged in the middle voice activity of writing (as defined by Barthes). The diarist simultaneously produces the journal and is produced by it, transformed by the diary-writing process. A fictional journal constitutes a portrayal of this mutual construction of self and text, through writing and over a period of time.

Kafka, in his own diary, maintained that the literature of a small nation functions as does a journal for an individual.[2] One assumption of the present study is that the model just described, which makes the diarist both producer and product of the text, is also applicable at the collective level, in a body of fictional texts. Speaking of the role of literature in Quebec, Réjean Robidoux claimed in 1968 that 'le fait collectif de conscience critique et créatrice est tout récent ... Il s'agit ... d'un phénomène d'action et de réaction qui se passe a l'intérieur et, si j'ose dire, entre nous' (101). Studies of Quebec literature of the 1960s, a period of great change, frequently recognize a quandary that seems to illustrate the collective 'middle voice' effect of literary production in a small but distinct cultural community: are the literary texts simply the product or reflections of cultural phenomena, or did they actually affect or effect social and political change? Since at that time Quebec texts were still read mainly by other members of the Quebec intellectual community, the diary function of communicating with the self (the same) seems to have been effective at the collective level. A closer look at Quebec diary fiction from 1878 to 1990 reveals, however, that this phenomenon is not limited to the 1960s.

6 Identity and Difference

**The Quebec corpus**

A further objection raised to my previous methodology, by Field (1989, 4–5), was that the term 'fictional journal' allowed me to include in my corpus not only novels or stories entirely or mainly in diary form, but also ones in which the journal is only a part of the text, even a relatively incidental element. I shall justify the same procedure here, on the grounds that my aim is not (as is Field's) to define and prescribe the parameters of a fixed entity labelled 'diary novel'. Intead, I am interested in the interaction of self, time, and writing in fictional texts (complete or partial) that exhibit characteristics enabling the reader to recognize the 'diary' model. For each case, I shall specify what these are. In establishing the Quebec corpus to be considered here, I have included some works that barely qualify as novels (such as those by Hertel and Baillargeon), and others that emphasize retrospection at the expense of immediacy (Simard's *Mon Fils pourtant heureux*, for example). In others the journal form provides a complement or counterpoint to different types of narration, as in *Angéline de Montbrun*, Filiatrault's *Chaînes*, or Aquin's *Trou de mémoire*. I have done so because these texts do illustrate the type(s) of narcissism associated with diary writing, which will be defined at the outset. I shall also allude to the function of references to diaries in novels that do not actually include even extracts (as in *Alexandre Chênevert*), if the journal element provides insight into how diary writing was perceived in Quebec at that time.

I shall not, however, include novels that may resemble diaries in their treatment of subjectivity or time, but that have no explicit references to writing (such as Choquette's *L'Interrogation*, Ducharme's *L'Avalée des avalés*, or Thériault's *Le Grand Roman d'un petit homme*).[3] Nor shall I discuss non-fictional journals, with the exception of two: one that will serve as a point of departure, Henriette Dessaulles's journal of 1874–81, and one, also by a woman, that will correspondingly provide some indications of what the intimate diary has become in Quebec, Nicole Brossard's *Journal intime*. Needless to say, I shall not repeat the discussion of the differences between real and fictional journals that I developed at length in *The French Fictional Journal* (3–25), except to point out modifications to those arguments that some Quebec examples provoke. The number of fictional texts by Quebec writers involving a diary in some form or other is surprisingly – and significantly

– high. The chronological list appended to this study makes no claim to exhaustivity, and not all the examples found will be discussed. It may be of use, however, to others doing research in this area.

It is significant that no diary fiction appeared in Quebec before 1878 (or if it did, it did not survive), when Laure Conan published her first story in diary form, 'Un Amour vrai'. The genre had existed in France since the beginning of the century and was well enough established by the 1850s for parodies to occur. But the novel itself did not develop in Quebec until the later part of the century, and there was never a wave of (mostly feminine) epistolary fiction, such as preceded the diary novel in Europe. One reason that fictional journals did not flourish sooner in Quebec is the opprobrium attached in the nineteenth century to the keeping of a journal in Catholic-dominated middle- and upper-class circles, as illustrated in the diary of Henriette Dessaulles, which was not published until 1971. The allowable exception was the 'spiritual' journal kept by some priests and nuns, but this type of diary, which is not for the self and about the self, does not qualify as a *journal intime*. Dessaulles records the popularity of diary writing among young girls at convent schools, but also the nuns' determined attempts to put an end to such a narcissistic activity, and the secrecy she needed to practise in order to preserve her journal. That no published examples of real intimate diaries written in Quebec were available to Conan as models is confirmed by the research of Françoise Van Roey-Roux (1983), Yvan Lamonde (1983), and Pierre Hébert (1988) on diaries in Quebec.

In literary histories of Quebec, Conan's *Angéline de Montbrun* (1881) is hailed as the first psychological novel, the first to be written by a woman and about a woman, the first to experiment with techniques of first-person narration, including both letters and a diary. I shall begin my analyses of individual novels by addressing the question of why this one was received with ambivalence and has fascinated critics ever since. Another enigma with respect to the evolution of diary fiction in Quebec is why the author abandoned this more modern form for the historical novel, and yet returned to it at the end of her life. Her anomalous novel is the only one of that period that still commands critical attention as a literary text, rather than as an example of ideology. It also represents a rare chronological coincidence with developments in France, since it was at that time that many real *journaux intimes* were posthumously published, and several relevant Russian texts were translated into French, and inspired a new wave of diary fiction. Angéline is depicted as being familiar with the life of Eugénie de Guérin, the author of one of the diaries published. Had Conan herself read French diary fiction? The question of influence is impossible to resolve. In any case, Conan's work is very different, as will be seen, from contemporary French examples of diary fiction.

The fact that it was a woman who first exploited the form in Quebec is not really surprising. It was also a woman, Madame de Souza, who produced the first 'genuine' diary novel in France, according to Field's criteria (1989, 34). As I have shown elsewhere,[4] Roquentin, in Sartre's *La Nausée*, was not the first or the only one to associate diary writing with girls. Male novelists frequently depicted female narrators as diarists, and male *intimistes* almost invariably comment on the effeminacy of diary writing as an activity. Male diarists in the French novel range from romantic, tubercular artist-heroes to priests and 'superfluous' or 'underground' men on the Russian model. 'Real men' do not keep diaries (Raoul 1989). That the intimate diary is perceived as a feminine form of narration will be central to the initial discussion of narcissism and of the relationship of narcissism to gender and ethnicity. The diary of Henriette Dessaulles and the fictional journals of Laure Conan will then be compared, in an attempt to establish how feminine narcissism functions in these texts, and to assess the ways in which it is modified when the text is a fiction.

What is more surprising is the absence of further examples of novels based on the diary model in the first part of the twentieth century. Raymond Turcotte was the first to turn his attention to this phenomenon in Quebec, in an important article published in 1969 entitled 'L'Apre Conquête de la parole.' He mentions two novels produced in the 1920s, *Journal d'un étudiant* (1925) by Jean Des Bois (Joseph Carre) and *Journal d'un vicaire de campagne* (1927) by Joseph Raiche. In spite of the Bernanosian title of the latter, both are justifiably relegated by Turcotte to the sub-category *'journal anecdotique,'* which has little literary interest. It was not until the 1940s that the form regained some popularity, but primarily as a vehicle for ideas, as in the examples provided by Pierre Baillargeon (*Les Médisances de Claude Perrin*, 1945) or François Hertel (*Journal d'Anatole Laplante*, 1947). In these fictional journals the diarist represents the intellectual and sees himself as universal. In the 1950s a more obviously narcissistic, individualistic type of diary becomes an essential element in several novels dealing with deranged male characters, notably Robert Elie's *La Fin des songes* (1950) and Jean Filiatrault's *Chaînes* (1955). These introduce into the Quebec corpus the diary-of-a-madman type of fictional journal illustrated earlier in France by Maupassant and Flaubert. The reasons for the madness, however, are specific to Quebec. Simard's *Mon Fils pourtant heureux*, published in 1956, shares the characteristics of the earlier ones. All the examples I have found of diary fiction written between 1920 and 1960 in Quebec (see the appendix) are by male authors, with the exception of *Mathieu* by Françoise Loranger (1949), which includes a diary attributed to a male narrator. Analysis of these texts depicting male narrators produces some points of comparison with the narcissism illustrated in the initial diaries by women.

The type of male character who is shown as preoccupied with an identity crisis related to self-perception, and engaged in a process of writing, emerges in the 1940s and 1950s as the alter ego of the previously proffered (and preferred) pioneer man-of-action model in the Quebec novel. The pioneer man-of-action placed the Quebec context firmly in a North American framework of conflict between man and nature, of conquest of the land. As many prominent critics have shown,[5] the new type of hero was urban and conquered, and defined as colonized rather than colonizer. In *Le Romancier fictif* (1980), André Belleau developed an analysis of the function of writing in the Quebec novel before the Quiet Revolution. Like Turcotte, he concludes his study at the point where literary self-consciousness clearly emerges, the '*roman du code*' and the '*roman de la parole*' giving way to the '*roman de l'écriture.*' The depiction of the artist/intellectual in the novel reflects the role of culture in the evolution of a collective identity, and the particular problems of defining culture in Quebec. Fictional journals depicting male narrators, prior to the turning point of 1966, which marks the beginning of the effects of the Quiet Revolution, focus on the Quebec male's questionable masculinity and its undermining by both pervasive religious and invasive colonizing influences. The psychoanalytic theory of narcissism will provide a framework for analysis of the parallels between the position of the colonized male and that of women, based on the designation of 'difference' or 'otherness' as a non-subject position in relation to the symbolic order. This approach implies a focus on the relationship between the sexes, as conveyed in the individual texts.

Before 1966, as well as diary fiction illustrating feminine and masculine types of narcissism, there is a third category of texts that go further in positing various modalities of gender confusion due to insufficient differentiation between self and other. These range from incestuous identification with the parent of the opposite sex (as in Filiatrault's *Chaînes*, which reverses the situation of *Angéline de Montbrun*) to male homosexuality (Pinsonneault, *Les Abîmes de l'aube*; Blais, *L'Insoumise*) and androgyny (Richard, *Journal d'un hobo*). Among the few Quebec novels of that period to depict sexual deviance, they represent one pole of the continuum of fears and desires experienced by the narcissistic individual: engulfment or assimilation by the other (obliteration of difference). Homosexuality reappears later in the fictional journals of Monette's *Le Double Suspect* (1980) and Tremblay's *Des Nouvelles d'Edouard* (1984), but the opposite pole of fragmentation or separation/segregation (the splendid isolation of independence) emerges at both the individual and collective levels in fictional journals after 1966.

The first examples of the modern diary novel appear in Quebec in the 1960s, when almost every major novelist experimented with the form: Blais, Ducharme, Godbout, Bessette, Aquin[6]. This phenomenon is related to the influence of the French *nouveau roman*, as many critics have pointed out,[7] but it is not attributable to that alone. The fictional journal emerges as a singularly appropriate medium for the textualization of the Quebec political situation at that time.[8] The emphasis in previous diary fiction on aspects of subjectivity in relation to difference from the other(s) is amplified by a new awareness of historicity, that is, relation to time, and difference from the previous self. Subjectivity is seen, finally, as dependent not only on the position(s) of self and other, but on language. There is a shift in the relative importance accorded to the imaginary (the origin) and the symbolic (the linguistic and social order through which the self is defined). The investigation of diary fiction in the 1960s will address an element that is prominent in the Quebec examples: the relationship of journal writing to primary narcissism and the need to escape from the dominance of the mother. This element produces a powerful image of giving birth to the self and to/through the book.

Both the self as constructed by language and self-conscious textuality are central in the works of Ducharme and Aquin, where the Quebec context is not simply a theme or a frame but the substance of the texts. Writing (literary production) becomes a weapon for individual and collective survival, replacing the cradle (reproduction). This shift has particular significance for women writers. In the 1960s, the fictional journal served to convey the dilemma of the traditional woman, for novelists such as Paule Saint-Onge and Yolande Chéné. In the 1970s and 1980s, women writers with a feminist consciousness experimented with the diary form to produce innovative texts that illustrate the parallels between gender identity and *québécitude*, between the feminine and the post-colonial as discourses of difference. For them the relationship between writing and reproduction as alternative, even rival, means to survival has further implications. By 'becoming the mother' of the text, the female subject emerges while remaining identified with the origin, achieving an apparent solution to the assimilation/separation dilemma. As at the time of Laure Conan, the double colonization of Quebec women appears to make them more powerful than men in that society in some important ways, as the imaginary phallic mother takes the place of the absent symbolic father. The stereotypes of gender relations in Quebec are called into question, however, when the fictional journal becomes part of post-modern experimentation with form. Both the narcissistic subject and the collective project of *survivance* appear in a new light.

**Dividing/devising the difference(s): An outline**

The theoretical approach used to focus the analyses of individual texts in this study is the psychoanalytic theory of narcissism, as revised by French feminist theorists (Kristeva, Irigaray, Kofman, Lemoine-Luccioni) in a Lacanian framework. Narcissism serves as a bridge between Lacanian and object relations theory.[9] Part 1 is devoted to the elucidation of the relationship between my model for the diary form, the theory of narcissism, and gender confusion in writing by men and women in the Quebec context. Some of the parallels between women and colonized men will be discussed, before the examination of individual texts. Part 2 begins with an analysis of the real diary of Henriette Dessaulles (1874-81), showing how 'femininity' is constructed. This construction, which prescribes self-abnegation in favour of marriage and motherhood, is then compared with a different type of self-denial, illustrated in Laure Conan's fictional journals published between 1878 and 1919. These reflect the moral narcissism and religious messianism prevalent in Quebec at that time and the feminization of Quebec culture that gives rise to powerful images of phallic mothers. Conan's female narrators reject marriage in favour of heroic martyrdom, however, and choose, as she did herself, the revenge of the pen over that of the cradle. These strong women can find no men to match them.

The image of apparently submissive but actually dominant women is accompanied by the absence or weakness of male figures, especially fathers. Diary fiction by male authors of the 1940s and 1950s, the focus of part 3, confirms an image of the Quebec male as impotent and sterile, if not castrated. The narrators perceive themselves as French, and as intellectuals or artists and therefore effeminate in the North American context – as in examples by Hertel, Baillargeon, and Simard. In the 1950s, novels by Loranger, Elie, and Filiatrault depict male narrators whose impotence, explicitly blamed on domination by the feminine, drives them to madness, which is itself represented as a feminine phenomenon.

The introjection of femininity by male narrators is related in diary fiction of the early 1960s to male homosexuality (already implicit in the earlier examples by men) and the ideal of androgyny, developed in Richard's diary of a hermaphrodite. Part 4 discusses these concepts as symptomatic of a narcissistic refusal to separate, a desire to remain 'one' and not 'bi-sected.' A second group of texts, which includes two of the most studied Quebec novels, Bessette's *Le Libraire* and Godbout's *Salut Galarneau!*, depict the opposite move, during the Quiet Revolution period, towards autonomy and individuation. The image that prevails is the feminine one of giving birth – to the book and to the self. Bisexuality is still central, as male narrators express their own desire to become the imaginary phallic mother, rather than the symbolic father. The same image is seen to have different implications for women writers, such as Geneviève Amyot.

Access to the symbolic order is associated with language and the law. Part 5 considers texts written by women in the 1960s and 1970s, in which female fictional diarists exploit this vehicle as a means to move away from the specularity of the narcissistic mirror to the projection of 'voice' (from Narcissus to Echo). The difficulty of the enterprise is illustrated more recently in Michèle Mailhot's *Le Passé composé* (1990). The problematic nature of the parallels between the position of women and that of men in a post-colonial context becomes apparent. Male authors such as Ducharme and Aquin also use the diary form in this period to attempt to subvert the rule of patriarchal language and law. Nicole Brossard's *Journal intime* adds a feminine and feminist perspective to their focus on the play of signifiers and provides a point of comparison with the other 'real' diary with which the study began. Finally, Francine Noël's *Babel: Prise deux* (1990) illustrates the possibilities of this narrative form to convey the multiplicity of otherness, the dangers of both assimilation and narcissistic withdrawal, and the problems of becoming the same in spite of a difference of language.

Throughout, the positive and negative aspects of narcissism will be taken into account, as developed by André Green in *Narcissisme de vie, narcissisme de mort* (1983). Narcissism, as both an individual and a collective phenomenon, is essential to survival, yet it can also lead to death. Whether it is a stage or a constant in psychic development is contentious, as is its association with femininity. This consideration of the functioning of narcissism in a specific context and in a particular type of text raises questions of wider importance for feminist and postcolonial studies.

As this brief outline indicates, my discussion of individual texts will follow a loosely chronological order and be framed by works by women. I shall focus on the role of gender identity in self-definition by both male and female narrators and its relevance to diary writing and to their *québécitude*. In doing so I hope to build on the feminist perception of Patricia Smart, whose work reveals in Quebec literature both illustrations of misogynist patriarchy and examples of women's survival of mythification (*Ecrire dans la maison du père*, 1988). The observations of Jean Larose (*La Petite Noirceur*, 1987), who laments the emasculation of Quebec men, will also be relevant. Reference to the psychoanalytic theory of narcissism, and feminist revisions of it, will enable a reassessment of the interplay of the imaginary and the symbolic orders in a particular type of fiction produced in a specific context. My hypothesis is that the male narrator in this sub-category of Quebec fiction faces the same dilemma as women everywhere: how to gain access to the symbolic order as a 'subject' and yet retain one's 'difference,' how to survive without becoming something else. These are questions central to the theory of narcissism, which I shall first review.

CHAPTER TWO

# Narcissism in Psychoanalytic Theory

'... the forms of human consciousness and the mechanisms of human psychology are not timeless and everywhere essentially the same, but rather situation specific and historically produced ...'

FREDRIC JAMESON (1981), 152

'Narcissism' is a term frequently used in everyday speech to designate a self-centred and self-indulgent type of behaviour or attitude that others do not usually find pleasant. As French psychoanalyst André Green comments in his study of narcissism: 'le narcissisme a mauvaise presse. Il est rare que narcissique soit un qualificatif laudatif' (1983, 17). The adjective form was also used extensively in the 1970s and early 1980s to describe a type of text in which fiction designates itself as such, rather than camouflaging its status, and narrative becomes the explicit theme as well as the necessary form and means of its message. In the latter case 'narcissistic' was generally deemed to be complimentary, indicating a degree of post-modern literary awareness not found in more naïve 'readerly' texts. Specularity – mirroring in all its possible modes – was hailed as inseparable from written accounts of post-humanist consciousness and the perception of reality as unknowable and unrepresentable – for example, by Dällenbach in *Le Récit spéculaire* (1977) and Hutcheon in *Narcissistic Narrative* (1980). In my 1980 study of the French fictional journal, I juxtaposed the psychological and textual dimensions of narcissism, using the subtitle 'Fictional Narcissism/Narcissistic Fiction.' My model for the structure and functioning of the diary novel established a link between the narrator's non-identity (the old-fashioned existential 'divided self' or the more recent disseminated or fragmented subject) and the auto-reflexivity of the diary, especially when it is a formally mimetic fiction.

Here, I shall extend that juxtaposition to investigate in greater depth the relationship between psychoanalytic concepts of narcissism, and diary writing as a symptom and product of narcissistic functioning. Further, diary writing as depicted in Quebec fiction will be examined in the light of a hypothetical collective parallel to individual narcissism, which must be justified. The use of gender as a link between the two will become clear as the discussion proceeds.

## Psychoanalytic theories of narcissism

The expression *narcissism* was first coined by Havelock Ellis in 1898 (Goldberg 1980, 11; Morrison 1986, 1) and also used by Paul Näcke in 1899 (Le Poulichet 1988, 76). Freud himself first mentioned it in 1905 (Rothstein 1980, 6) and 1911 (Le Poulichet 1976), and like the others he initially associated it with a type of auto-erotic fixation related to homosexuality. He did not develop the concept further until 1914, in his seminal paper 'On Narcissism: An Introduction' (reprinted in Morrison, 17–43). Freud's use of the term evolved and shifted, and various post-Freudian schools have developed divergent theories related to the concept. It currently denotes a wide range of behaviours and interpretations, which may sometimes appear contradictory. These include the distinction between primary and secondary narcissism, and various positions on the following issues: is narcissism a developmental stage or a permanent part of the individual psyche? is it normal and necessary or a pathological state? and are its effects positive or negative?

The body of research on narcissism, from both theoretical and clinical perspectives, is largest in the branches of psychoanalysis labelled object relations theory, ego psychology, or psychology of the self. The main proponents of these approaches are German-American or Anglo-Saxon: Heinz Kohut, Otto Kernberg, and Annie Reich, with contributions from Melanie Klein and D.W. Winnicott, as well as many others. The two major studies of narcissism in French are by Béla Grunberger (1971) and André Green (1983). I shall refer most extensively to the latter. Sarah Kofman (1980) and Julia Kristeva (1983) have both taken up some aspects of the existing theories from a feminist perspective. Current research on narcissism connects object relations theory to a

Lacanian framework, focusing particularly on the relationship between primary narcissism and the foundation of subjectivity through access to the symbolic order (see Le Poulichet 1988). Green goes so far as to claim that narcissism is 'la clé de voûte du système lacanien' (38), and Sylvie Le Poulichet states that, for Lacan, 'le moi n'est autre que cette captation imaginaire qui caractérise le narcissisme' (90).

## Primary narcissism

In psychoanalytic theory the development of self-awareness is associated with what Lacan calls 'the mirror stage' (Lacan 1966, 89–97; see Alford 1988, 168). The infant, on seeing the reflected image, recognizes both what he is (bounded by physical body limits) and what he is not: not the mother, who holds the child and may also be reflected, and who reflects him; and not *only* what appears in the image, which is where he is *not*. I use the masculine pronoun here advisedly, for up to this point the infant is supposed to have no gender identity, but is in fact perceived in psychoanalytic theory as masculine, regardless of sex: Lacan's 'homme-lette,' the formless human 'being,' before access to the symbolic order renders 'being' inaccessible. This pre-mirror state of non-subjectivity, prior to self-awareness, corresponding to Lacan's 'imaginary' stage, is also termed primary narcissism. For Freud or Lacan, individuation – a sense of unity and of separateness – does not occur at birth, with the cutting of the umbilical cord, but at the moment of psychic birth, of the realization that the sense of symbiotic union with an other indistinguishable from the self, of a consubstantial fusion, is indeed illusory/imaginary.

The subsequent nostalgia for an archaic state of blissful satisfaction and harmony with the whole is generally interpreted as a reluctance to face up to the reality of difference and non-coincidence with love objects. Primary narcissism belongs to the pre-Oedipal phase, before the intervention of the father that transforms the mother-child dyad into a triangular relation of rivalry. The 'Nom/Non du Père' will, in Lacanian terms, replace the imaginary by the symbolic, patriarchal system of language and law, Lacan's capitalized 'Other' (*'l'Autre'*), whose advent brings with it the unconscious and desire for the 'object' (*autre* with a small *a*), the 'other' who is desired because of the realization of lack, of wholeness lost. The phallus thus becomes the ultimate signifier of what is lost: completeness, conflated with transcendental meaning, absolute knowledge, and power.

Primary narcissism is therefore closely associated with the pre-Oedipal phallic mother, who is presumed to have a penis, and the realm of the imaginary, as opposed to the logocentric symbolic. Nostalgia for, or persistence of, a state of non-differentiation is generally perceived as regressive, infantile. It is also associated with the feminine, as Kristeva elaborates in her development of the concept of the 'semiotic chora' as a pre-Oedipal way of relating to the world and to others that may continue to co-exist alongside the symbolic (Kristeva 1974; see Weedon 1987, 88–90).

Narcissism, in this use of the term, does not, strictly speaking, allude to love of the self, since the sense of self does not yet exist: self and (m)other are one and the same. At the collective level, the nostalgia for a state of union with a collective whole appears in myths of a lost Golden Age or Eden, when all shared the same values, and individual differentiation and competitiveness were eclipsed by a sense of belonging and endeavour in a common cause; humans were at one with nature and the earth. Versions of this myth certainly appear in the history of Quebec nationalism, as indicated, for example, by Luc Bureau's title, *Entre l'Eden et l'Utopie: Les Fondements imaginaires de l'espace québécois* (1984). The wish to return to such a state is utopian at the collective level, and tends to be self-destructive for the individual, since the only actual escape from the conflicts of difference and the tensions of desire is death. André Green's study of narcissism is entitled *Narcissisme de vie, narcissisme de mort*. Primary narcissism is associated by him (36) with the wish to return to a state of being 'neuter' (*ne-uter*, that is, *neither* of the two, pre-choice), of returning to the womb (tomb) of non-selfhood, of union with the cosmic whole, or Nirvana: the absence of all desire, stasis. As such, it is governed by Thanatos, the death instinct, rather than Eros, the instinct of self-preservation through object-directed desire.

**Secondary narcissism**

As mentioned previously, 'narcissism' was first used to describe an auto-erotic attachment to one's own body, or part of it, or to a double of the self, a homo-erotic object (see Green 1983, 48; Freud, 1905 and

1911, on Schreber). These are categories of 'self-objects' associated with secondary narcissism, that is, narcissistic cathexes surviving or resurfacing beyond the Oedipal stage. In these instances an object exists, but its valuation by the self depends on its perception as connected to the self (the same) rather than on its being separate/different (other). Self-objects may take various forms: a part of the self, a double (reflection) of the self (as it was, is, or would like to be), or an extension of the self with which the self identifies excessively (child, loved one). The illusion of self-sufficiency is maintained by the fiction of fusion with the other.

At this point, I should clarify my use of the word *self*, since this is also a bone of contention among the various schools of thought represented in the theory of narcissism. In French 'le Moi' is used to refer to what Freud termed 'das Ich,' translated into English as 'ego': an element in the triangular relationship between id, ego, and superego, the conscious centre where conflicts between the other elements are resolved (or not). Self psychology goes beyond this specifically Freudian use of self (= ego) to a phenomenological concept that includes the 'whole self': not only the psychic elements, but the body. This self, termed in French 'le Soi,' may have a self-representation or image, whereas to speak of an image of the ego is meaningless. As Green explains (141–2), the ego is only a place, or 'instance,' that *has* representations of objects, but cannot itself be represented, except through the objects it chooses to invest. In this sense the self (ego) has been called the trace of all its previous narcissistic object choices, 'la sédimentation des investissements d'objets abandonnés' (Le Poulichet, 83).

The narcissistic self does not have an image of its self (ego) but rather of an ego ideal or ideal self, which precedes the superego. The latter is the consequence of introjection of parental and societal values, based on the name of the father. The former, on the other hand, has pre-Oedipal origins; it is a projection of the lost perfection of primary narcissism. Consequently, the result of intervention by the superego is Oedipal guilt, related to castration anxiety, whereas failure to correspond to the ideal self does not produce guilt, but *shame*. Guilt is related to having, or wanting to have, what is forbidden. Shame is related to being – or rather, failing to be – what one feels one should be. Shame is the effect of an affect, not of a transgression. As will prove important in analysing Quebec texts, the symptom of shame is not fear of castration, but acknowledgment of impotency (lack of the capacity to *jouir*, Green, 42). The cause is internal rather than external.

The cathexis of others as part of the self is always the result of a sense of lack, of deficiency or inadequacy. Paradoxically, the narcissist, who appears to overvalue his or her self, does so because of a fundamental disappointment regarding the self, due to what is termed a 'narcissistic injury' (Green, 17). The particular nature of this injury in the case of women and of 'colonized' men will be central in a later part of this discussion.

## Narcissistic personality disorders

In clinical practice personality disorders diagnosed as narcissistic are generally assigned to the 'borderline' category between neuroses and psychoses. The intensity and extent of the symptoms decide whether the behaviour concerned is relatively normal or pathological. Borderline is an apt metaphor for narcissistic problems of self-perception and definition, since these are related to frontiers: the boundaries of the self are not fixed or impermeable.

Specific traits or behaviour patterns associated with narcissism fall under the following headings (see Meissner, in Morrison 1986, 403–37):
- A sense of archaic grandiosity and omnipotence, which may develop into exhibitionistic megalomania. Everything else is subservient to the self, which seeks admiration.
- A corresponding, antithetical sense of helplessness, of impotence and passivity. The self is perceived as threatened by everything else; self-esteem is low.
- Lack of empathy with others. The narcissist frequently appears cold, self-engrossed, uninvolved with others, uncaring (Goldberg 1980, 12).
- A corresponding, antithetical exaggeration of empathy with an other, through over-identification. Self and other are confused, the tendency is to 's'aimer soi-même à travers un semblable' (Le Poulichet, 82).
- Arising from this confusion, fear of penetration, invasion, or engulfment by the 'vampiristic' other (Green, 160). Survival is perceived as threatened by assimilation or elimination.
- A corresponding, antithetical fear of loss of self-coherence through fragmentation or dispersal (diaspora), or separation within the self (Stolorow, in Morrison, 200).

– Disappointment with the self's failure to fulfil its own idealistic and unrealistic aspirations may lead to 'narcissistic rage' or, more often, severe depression, anxiety, or melancholia, characterized by a sense of emptiness.

All these symptoms are related to 'identity maintenance through mirroring in the object' (Morrison, 9). For Kernberg (in Morrison, 213–22) and many clinicians they are problems to be resolved by the establishment of a 'normal' assessment of the self in relation to others. Lou Andréas-Salomé (1921), Kohut (1977), and Green (1983), however, see narcissistic behaviours as necessary defence mechanisms essential to self-preservation. According to Stolorow (1975), 'Mental activity is narcissistic to the degree that its function is to maintain the structural cohesiveness, temporal stability and positive affective colouring of the self-representation' (179). This concept of the self as a representation constructed by the ego is the one that will prevail throughout this study, which will show the inevitability and benefits of narcissism, as well as its dangers.

At the collective level, similar behaviours may be perceived as indicative of collective narcissism, functioning in the interests of the self-representation of a national or ethnic identity whose survival is perceived as at stake. Freud himself emphasized that the survival instinct operates at both the individual and the collective level of the species; also in intermediate alliances, including ethnic groups, where narcissistic identification is strong: 'The ego ideal opens up an important avenue for the understanding of group psychology. In addition to the individual side, this ideal has a social side; it is also the common ideal of a family, a class or a nation' (Freud 1914, in Morrison, 43; cf. Green, 52).

## Moral narcissism

Several of the typical traits and behaviours enumerated above may be 'converted' to a cause, becoming what is termed moral narcissism. This has some similarities to moral masochism, as will be seen in an analysis of Laure Conan's *Angéline de Montbrun*, but it also has significant differences. In contrast with masochism, psychic pain is not a source of erotic gratification. On the contrary, moral narcissism is associated with desexualization (Green 1983, 158). It is a type of sublimation based on the withdrawal of desire from objects. It is directed instead at the self, whose superiority is demonstrated by its renunciation. The resulting asceticism may or may not have a religious dimension. Ultimately, moral narcissism tends towards Green's 'neutered' or neutral state (Green, 36, 53) of contemplative non-desire. According to Plotinus (see Hudot 1976 and Kristeva 1983, 134–9) the Narcissus myth may be interpreted as relating (to) the origins of philosophical reflexion. It is the basis of Derrida's *Psyché* (1987) and Gasché's study of Derrida, *The Tain of the Mirror* (1986).

However, moral narcissism may also take the form of subordination of immediate gratification to a collective cause, in which the individual contributes to a messianic endeavour (Green, 45, 187). In such instances, it is frequently associated with rebellion, rather than renunciation. Both share the element of moral superiority, of commitment to a cause; both are amply illustrated in the cultural history of Quebec, as discussed by Réjean Beaudoin in *Naissance d'une littérature: Essai sur le messianisme et les débuts de la littérature canadienne-française, 1850–1890* (1989).

## Narcissism and diaries

A third type of sublimation associated with narcissistic motivation, in addition to asceticism and rebellion, is artistic creativity, including writing (Green 1983, 50; Layton 1986, 19ff). Artists are typical of narcissistic personalities in their preference for being over having; also in their desire for immortality. Narcissists frequently have fantasies of self-engenderment (Green, 19, 111), of being reborn phoenix-like from the remains of their deficient self, through their own efforts (Green, 131, 169). This is the ultimate dream of self-sufficiency and continuity. The narcissistic interpretation of the value of art is that it is a process of self-production and self-reproduction, rather than production or representation of something else.

Many elements associated with clinical narcissism have specific relevance in the case of diary writing. The following will be of particular importance in subsequent analyses:
- Narcissistic withdrawal (Green, 41) into an enclosed space (refuge or prison: see Green, 69) of splendid or horrible isolation. This aspect is developed in Béatrice Didier's study of the *journal intime* under the heading 'le refuge matriciel' (1976, 87–115).

- The playing of subject and object roles by the self, depending on both empathy and its absence, projection, and introjection (see Didier, 116–37 and Raoul 1980, 35–45).
- A perception of time as discontinuous (see Layton 1985, 102, and Raoul 1980, 46–59); nostalgia for the past (unity) and fear of fragmentation in the present or future are accompanied by an attempt to impose coherence (see Didier, 159–75).
- The desire to control by 'seeing clearly': scopophilia, related to epistophilia (Green, 33); also the need for a witness to the 'truth,' even if it is a self-object in the form of a fetish, such as the diary, in which the self is exhibited.
- The use of language, not to communicate with others but to regulate self-esteem (Layton 1985, 103). This explains the paradoxical activity of writing for oneself alone.
- The frequent image of the (re)birth of the self through or as the book, central in many fictional journals.

At the collective level, parallels with the cultural history of Quebec are striking, as will become apparent in later analyses. Another important aspect of narcissistic self-perception that applies to diarists in general, and to those depicted in Quebec novels in particular, is gender confusion, which requires separate treatment.

**Narcissism and gender**

In his major essay on narcissism (1914), Freud expressed the view that women are more prone to narcissism than men: 'Women, especially if they grow up with good looks, develop a certain self-contentment which compensates them for the social restrictions that are imposed upon them in their choice of object. Strictly speaking, it is only themselves that such women love with an intensity comparable to the man's love for them. Nor does their need lie in the direction of loving, but of being loved; and the man who fulfils this condition is the one who finds favour with them' (Morrison, 31). Narcissism here designates the desire to be loved, rather than to love. Paradoxically, the self becomes the object of desire, but from the point of view of the other. The self does not function as an active subject, but as a willing object. This version of passive female sexuality in narcissistic women is illustrated by Annie Reich's account of one patient suffering from a narcissistic personality disorder who imagined, when being made love to by a man, that she was making love to herself (Reich 1953, 26). She was thus occupying, by her body, the passive object position, yet also, vicariously, by identification with her partner, his active subject position.

That women serve as objects in what Lacan and Luce Irigaray term a 'hommosexual' economy of exchange beween men is a central tenet of feminist theory, from Simone de Beauvoir to Irigaray's 'Des marchandises entre elles' (1977, 189–93). Beauvoir's opening assertion in *Le Deuxième Sexe* (1949, 1:16) was that 'woman' is defined as essentially 'other' in relation to man's central position as the subject of discourse. She is not only 'different' in a sense that might imply mutual complementarity, reciprocity, or dialogue between distinct but equal entities who could both occupy the subject position in turn. Rather, her difference is established from the outset as deviance, deficiency, and inferiority. Woman is defined in relation to man, while the reverse is not the case. Numerous studies of language (by Dale Spender for English, Marina Yaguello for French, for example) have since shown that the feminine is systematically construed as a diminished, pejorative, or ex-centric version of the masculine norm: the feminine is, in the phallocratic system, the unknown, that is, what the male speaker is not. Male logocentric autonomy is constantly contrasted with female anatomy, which belongs to the realm of the material and the imaginary, outside the symbolic order.

As Sarah Kofman points out, commenting on this essay by Freud (1980, 39), the fact that women are perceived as narcissistic and men as more inclined to over-investment of the object does not preclude masculine narcissism in a different form. On the contrary, men need the feminine object because of the positive self-image that the woman provides for them. In Virginia Woolf's famous words (1928), women have the mission to 'reflect men at twice their natural size.' Male subjectivity is founded on women's subjection. Without the feminine other in her place, the masculine sense of 'oneness' (unity and autonomy) is threatened. Beauvoir discusses the implications of this model of dual narcissism as the paradigm for 'normal' heterosexual relations, in the chapter on narcissism in *Le Deuxième Sexe* (2: 353–75).

Woman's relegation to the role of other in relation to a standard male model is based solely on one feature of her anatomy: her lack of a penis, which defines her as female. All her 'other' attributes – the fact that she can develop breasts and can bear children, which men cannot –

are irrelevant in this schema. Her acceptance of her disadvantaged position in the patriarchal order is attributed to penis envy. Once the girl discovers that she does not have a penis, and deduces that the mother does not either, she is assumed to perceive herself as deficient. This is a 'narcissistic injury' so profound that it easily accounts for the compensatory narcissism of women who invest their bodies as narcissistic objects, devoting their energy to their appearance (Le Poulichet, 82). For such women, the body is deemed to function as a substitute for the missing phallus, as does a child for the 'normal' mother, who displaces her desire for a penis onto her offspring – preferably a son, through whom she can vicariously acquire the missing organ. The fact that girls are assumed to be 'already castrated,' that is, to have nothing to lose, is for Freud the explanation for women's 'inferior' moral and cultural development (Freud 1925, in Strouse, 25). Boys should develop a stronger superego, because of their fear of castration at the Oedipal stage. The girl who refuses to admit that because she does not have a penis she is inferior is seen as denying her lack. She will identify with her father and continue to desire a female object, like the mother and herself. The relationship of female narcissism to female homosexuality and to a woman's rapport with her mother are aspects of psychoanalytic theory central to the revisions of Freudian theory suggested by feminist psychoanalysts such as Irigaray and Kristeva in France and, in American object relations theory, Nancy Chodorow (1978). Once more, there is opposition between being and having (the axes of metaphor and metonymy), in that the lesbian feminist woman does not desire to *be* her castrated mother and *have* (sexually) a double of her father; rather, she wishes to become (like) her father , while remaining a woman, that is, like her mother in the pre-Oedipal phase, when she was perceived as phallic, or complete.

In a Lacanian framework, this schema is complicated by the attempt to dissociate the phallus from the penis, to reduce men also to a state of lack. 'Masculine' and 'feminine' replace the biological terms of male and female, to be deployed as positions in relation to the symbolic order, regardless of anatomical sex. In theory, the name of the father may be represented by a woman, and femininity experienced by a man. In practice, the situation is further complicated by gender confusion, as primary narcissism re-emerges in the desire for the wholeness of the hermaphrodite, or androgyny. However, just as the theoretical designation of the phallus as a signifier without specific relevance to maleness is not ratified by a corresponding dissociation between political or economic power and gender, the realization that gender is a construct does not eliminate the force of gender-role distribution, and the conflicts that non-conformity to the norm produces.

These conflicts are apparent, when one considers more closely the parallel between 'woman as other' and 'the colonized male as other' in the Quebec context. The relationship to the mother is modified, as women appear to be more powerful. The apparent absence of the father, founder of the symbolic order, modifies the role of the imaginary. However, rather than a revalorization of women as non-castrated and non-inferior (even superior), this phenomenon produces in the colonized man a resentment of the 'castrating' phallic female, who is blamed for his own impotence. Since he is still a man (*not* castrated, like a woman), his sense of self-worth can only be re-established if the woman accepts her place as *his* other, putting him once more in the same category as the dominant, colonizing male. The function and effects of both individual and collective narcissism, and their depiction in fiction, involve a reconsideration of gender identity in relation to ethnicity.

CHAPTER THREE

# Gender and Ethnicity

'... the production of aesthetic or narrative form is to be seen as an ideological act in its own right, with the function of inventing imaginary or formal solutions to unresolvable contradictions.'

FREDRIC JAMESON (1981), 79

## The second (se)x

The question of whether the position of women in relation to men is comparable to that of other oppressed groups was raised by Simone de Beauvoir in the introduction to *Le Deuxième Sexe* (1949). She begins by claiming that neither category, gender or race, is immutable: 'Les sciences biologiques et sociales ne croient plus en l'existence d'entités immuablement fixées qui définiraient des caractères donnés tels que ceux de la femme, du Juif ou du Noir; elles considèrent le caractère comme une réaction secondaire à une situation' (1: 12). The particular situation shared by women and racial or ethnic groups defined as minorities, or as colonized, is that they are classified as *not* something else, which is dominant. As mentioned previously, they are relegated to the position of 'other' in relation to an oppressive 'one,' which exclusively occupies the subject role and is responsible for the classification. Reduced to passive 'object' status, the dominated category is 'l'inessentiel en face de l'essentiel' (16).

Beauvoir goes on to discuss the differences between the position of women and that of other dominated groups, in an attempt to explain why women have accepted the male view. She points out that they do not constitute a minority; nor were they once independent, and defeated at a certain point in time (19) In these two respects they may appear to resemble the working class. Yet women had not (in 1949) banded together to form a class, to say 'we,' like other groups: 'elles ne se posent pas authentiquement comme sujet' ... 'Elles n'ont pas de passé, d'histoire, de religion qui leur soit propre' (20), nor do they have their own geographical space. They have internalized the dependence produced by the stereotypical, modified master-slave relationship of the traditional heterosexual couple (22) and become collaborators in their own oppression: 'souvent (la femme) se complaît dans son rôle d'Autre' (23).

Women have frequently been content to accept the principle of 'l'égalité dans la différence' (26), the same one applied on racial grounds by segregationists. Here, Beauvoir emphasizes the similarities: 'qu'il s'agisse d'une race, d'une caste, d'une classe, d'un sexe réduits à une condition inférieure, les processus de justification sont les mêmes' (26). If inferiority cannot be assumed, as in the case of the Jews, the wish to keep the 'other' separate may become a desire to annihilate him (27). Difference will be tolerated as long as it stays 'in its place,' and fulfils the function of corroborating the strength of the Same.

## Oppressed women and colonized men

In his analysis of the stages of colonization, Albert Memmi (1972) portrayed the situation and the mentality of the colonized male in terms very similar to those used by Beauvoir to describe women. The following elements of comparison are particularly relevant to the discussion of the situation in Quebec:
- The colonized male, unlike some members of the working class, cannot usually 'passer dans le clan des privilégiés' (78), because he cannot change the colour of his skin. Nor can women change their sex. Although 'on ne naît pas femme,' femininity being produced by social conditioning, the anatomical difference is visibly verifiable. In the case of linguistic difference, the audible trace of origin (accent) may not be erasable. The relative importance accorded to the *visual*, as opposed to the *audible*, or otherwise perceptible differences, is an aspect taken up by feminist psychoanalytic theorists; it is related to narcissism (and the role of Echo in the myth) and will be discussed later.
- The attitude of the colonizer is paternalistic. He sees himself as nec-

essary to the colonized, indeed as a protector and benefactor (85). Men also have perceived themselves as defenders (rather than attackers) of women. Any change in this type of situation depends not only on the dependent party refusing to remain the victim, but also on the oppressor recognizing that his attitude is oppressive.
- The colonized are depersonalized by being referred to as a group, as 'they.' 'La marque du pluriel' (86–7) assists in their objectification, as is also the case for women. Individual members of an oppressed group will also refer to the group globally, as if they were not part of it, thus adopting the dominant view.
- Like women, the colonized tend to accept the image of themselves projected by the dominator, and eventually confirm it by their behaviour (88), seeing themselves as irremediably inferior. Traits may easily be assumed to be inherent, rather than circumstantial.
- According to Memmi, 'La carence la plus grave subie par le colonisé est d'être placé *hors de l'histoire et hors de la cité*' (92, his emphasis). Like women, he has not been 'sujet de l'histoire' (93) and has not participated in governing: 'éloigné du pouvoir, il finit en effet par en perdre ... le goût' (94–5). The past, rather than being part of an ongoing evolution, becomes a static museum of nostalgic folklore.
- As for women, the dominator will divide to rule. In particular, an élite of the colonized will be won over by special privileges. This aspect is developed by Frantz Fanon (1968/1976, 96). Similarly, as for women, individual success will be used to compensate for collective failure (see D'Allemagne 1966, 105).
- Like women, the colonized resort to 'les valeurs refuge' related to primary narcissism (family, religion, tradition, the private sphere), to maintain some sense of 'appartenance.' The colonized man becomes passive, like a woman: 'il restera englutiné à cette famille, qui lui offre chaleur et tendresse, mais qui l'absorbe et le castre' (Memmi, 97). Yet the difference remains between castration, as assumed by women in psychoanalytic theory, and impotence, as imposed on colonized men.
- Both women and colonized men are prepared to sacrifice themselves in the interests of group survival, 'réduisant la vie pour la sauver. Réaction spontanée d'auto-défense, moyen de sauvegarde de la conscience collective' (99). Their behaviour is characteristic of moral narcissism.

- Although 'le colonisé semble condamné à perdre progressivement la mémoire' (99), he becomes aware of the importance of remembering (Quebec's motto: 'Je me souviens') and focuses on the past. Women also have been the keepers of collective memories that serve to maintain a semblance of continuity and self-esteem (see Minh-ha 'Grandma's Story' in *Woman, Native, Other* 1989).
- After the stage of acceptance of their own inferiority, the colonized enter one in which their difference is positively valued. This is comparable to the moral superiority expressed by some contemporary radical feminists such as Mary Daly. It is illustrated by the messianism of late nineteenth- and early twentieth-century Quebec.
- The colonized are usually forced to become bilingual (Memmi, 102–3), using the mother tongue in the private sphere and the colonizer's language in the public one. Studies of women's use of language show a similar effect, due to awareness that the language (and associated behaviour) of public performance demands playing a masculine role, borrowing 'man-made language' (Spender 1980), in which the colonized/feminine is projected in pejorative terms.
- 'Success' for the colonized, as for women, is based on the abandonment of the characteristics that previously constituted the source of self-esteem (Memmi, 112). However, acceptance by the dominant group remains unguaranteed (114) and a sense of imitation/imposture or betrayal remains. The latter has commonly been diagnosed among prominent women. (In Quebec, it was illustrated in 1990 by the defection of Lucien Bouchard from the Conservative federal élite to form the Bloc québécois.)
- Resentment of this situation produces animosity towards the dominant group, provoking accusations of xenophobia/racism or man-hating (119), and a subsequent backlash (in 1990, anti-Quebec movements in English Canada, and attacks on feminists).
- Finally, 'le colonisé s'accepte et s'affirme ... Mais qu'est-il? Sûrement pas l'homme en général, porteur des valeurs universelles...' (120; cf. Ouellette-Michalska on universality, 1987, 19ff). He/she can only become universal by becoming part of or the same as the one, losing the differences that 'le constituent, constituent proprement son essence' (Memmi, 120; the problem of a belief in an essence of the self will continue to arise). This final act of collaboration, even if possible,

resembles a pyrrhic victory: 's'il cesse d'être cet être d'oppression et de carences, extérieures et intérieures, il cessera d'être un colonisé, il deviendra *autre* ...' (134).

Elisabeth Badinter analyses this aporia in regard to gender in *L'Un est l'autre* (1986), which provides a sequel to *Le Deuxième Sexe*. In her optimistic view, all may end up being neither dominant nor dominated: experience, however, so far shows that it is more likely that the dominated, once liberated, become dominant in their turn. The analysis of both Beauvoir and Memmi is based on an assumption of dualism as the only model for founding subjectivity: the subject can come into being only by opposition/assertion in relation to an other, subservient nonsubject. Psychoanalysis conforms to a similar model in positing a conscious ego as the site of conflict where the unconscious is tamed, and a symbolic order that must control the imaginary. Anthropology perpetuates the model, as shown by Minh-ha and Ouellette-Michalska, in the concept of culture as dominance over nature. This hierarchical arrangement sets up either/or categories that do not allow for alternative, pluralistic, or in-between solutions. The question Memmi attempted to answer in 1968 – 'Les Canadiens français sont-ils des colonisés?' – reveals the limitations of such 'zero sum' binary oppositions.

## The Québécois as colonized

Memmi's comments on this question arose from dialogue with prominent Quebec *indépendantistes*, in particular novelist Hubert Aquin and André D'Allemagne, then vice-president of the Rassemblement pour l'Indépendance Nationale. They followed De Gaulle's controversial 'Vive le Québec libre!' In the mind of these not-so-quiet 'revolutionaries' there was no doubt that Quebec experienced a colonized situation, in spite of its relative prosperity and the European origins of the majority of its population. When Pierre Vallières entitled his autobiography *Nègres blancs d'Amérique* (1968) and Michèle Lalonde proclaimed her refusal to 'speak white' (1970), they used a metaphor that was widely accepted. Memmi was himself amazed at the degree of recognition his description of *le colonisé* aroused in Quebec, especially his analysis of the resort to refuge values and the need to reject them in order to change. In the postwar period, the slogan of Quebec survival shifted from 'au pays du Québec rien ne doit changer,' as predicted at the end of *Maria Chapdelaine*, to Lesage's Liberals' 'Il faut que ça change!' of 1960. Duplessis was seen, in retrospect, as an archetypal 'roi nègre' (D'Allemagne 1966, 37), representative of colonized leaders trained, as Fanon (1968) explained, to serve as intermediaries, auxiliary administrators who left financial, industrial, and economic development to exploitative outside interests.

D'Allemagne's study, *Le Colonialisme au Québec* (1966), outlines the elements in Memmi's analysis that applied to the Quebec situation, emphasizing the role of religion as a refuge value, with its resulting narcissistic messianism. The collaboration of the clergy with the English (D'Allemagne, 18–19), while ensuring the prolongation of Catholicism as a 'national feature' until the 1960s, also contributed to an education system that discouraged francophones from engaging in business activities.[1] This ideology maintained self-esteem through a sense of moral superiority, in spite of evident inferior status in most other areas.

One significant difference in Quebec's situation from that of many other colonies was that 'depuis ses origines, le peuple québécois n'a jamais connu d'autre régime que le régime colonial' (D'Allemagne, 17), having passed straight from French rule to English conquest. The first real attempt on the part of the Québécois to be independent came with the rebellion of the Patriotes in 1837–8, but even this was part of a pan-Canadian attempt to defy Great Britain. Lord Durham's report following the failure of the rebellion (1838) explicitly recommended the assimilation of the French Canadians, since they were without a history or a literature of their own. This open statement of a previously camouflaged policy probably did as much as the brutal crushing of the rebellion to provoke a determination to resist. It resulted directly in François-Xavier Garneau's monumental *Histoire du Canada* (1845–8), which became the sacred text of French-Canadian refuge values, transforming the pre-conquest period of La Nouvelle France into a lost golden age of imaginary independence and exemplary heroic exploits. Defeat was turned into victory, as analyses of the evolution of nationalism in Quebec clearly show (Cameron 1974, Vincenthier 1983, Balthazar 1986).

The challenge to provide a history and a literature produced myth, in both categories, throughout the nineteenth century. The Métis rebellion led by Louis Riel in the West in the 1880s was strongly messianic in tone, aiming at the establishment of a utopian theocracy. The dream of a Catholic *Laurentie* propounded by right-wing Quebec nationalists before the Second World War was based on a similar ideology, related to Lionel Groulx's 'appel de la race' and 'notre maître le passé.' The future of French Canadians was believed to lie in a return to the past; the differences to be maintained were based primarily on the concept of origin. The expression that refers to a pure-blooded Québécois as *pure laine* evokes the national emblem, Saint John the Baptist's sheep, a symbol of docility and martyrdom (see D'Allemagne 21; Vallières 24; Larose 1987, 29–42) This attitude has obvious associations with femininity – resignation, moral virtue, passivity – reinforced by the cult of the Virgin Mary and its connection with leaders, such as Groulx, who wore the cassock and were dedicated to chastity and non-violence, that is, to non-virile behaviour (see Beaudoin, 55–7).

By 1966, D'Allemagne saw Quebec as already having abandoned its conservative refuge values, such as Catholicism and agriculturalism, in favour of political militancy. With the secularization of the education system and social services in the 1960s, the main specificity of the Québécois became linguistic. Prewar attempts to ensure *la survivance* by *la revanche des berceaux* – a high birth rate producing enough pure 'lambs' to maintain Quebec's proportion of the population of Canada – were transformed into a mission for writers, to redefine *la québécitude* in terms of language and literature rather than origin – what might be called a *revanche des stylos*. This represents a major shift from a feminine mode of reproduction to a masculine one of production, and from nature to culture; it also implies significant change in gender role perceptions in Quebec.

**Colonization and culture**

Bilingualism as described by Memmi (104) frequently produces people who speak two languages but do not fully master either of them. In the case of Quebec, the French spoken there has been affected by interference from the dominant language of North America, English (D'Allemagne 1966, 81–2, 87; see also Vachon 1974). A further complication of the Quebec situation is that the Québécois were not only politically subordinate to English Canadians and economically inferior to most other North Americans, but also culturally and linguistically inferiorized by comparison with France. Here again, the attempt at assimilation (that is, to speak 'standard' French) was superseded in the

1960s by a re-valuation of 'difference' in the debate over the use of *joual*. There are similarities to Jameson's remarks on the use of 'black language': 'the vernacular and its still vital sources of production ... are reappropriated by the exhausted ... speech of a hegemonic middle class' (1981, 87). Subsequent developments have produced a pragmatic compromise, closely related to the use of language to regulate self-esteem, rather than to communicate with an 'other.'

The wave of writing pouring from Quebec pens since the 1960s has, in fact, been largely addressed to the Québécois themselves, rather than to the rest of the world. This is typical of the 'decolonization' phase (Fanon, 169). The literary representation of self-recognition and self-affirmation during the Quiet Revolution years illustrates another observation by Jameson, that 'the literary work ... brings into being that very situation to which it is also, at one and the same time, a reaction' (1981, 82). Bernard states that 'the independence idea was first propagated by Quebec teachers, artists, poets, novelists, singers, journalists and other intellectual workers who, by 1966, were either converted to the idea or at least not actively opposed to it' (1978, 110–11). Writers who had consciously produced novels of propaganda for the notion of *la fidélité*, advocating the traditional refuge values as the means to survival, were replaced by a generation with equally utopian, messianic intent, who, having had contact with France and works such as Memmi's, took on the task of enlightening their fellow countrymen (see Robidoux and Renaud 1962). In 1966 D'Allemagne dedicated his book to 'tous les Québécois qui ont choisi de l'être.' Twenty years later, Gérard Bergeron cleverly entitled his analysis of the post-referendum situation in Quebec *A Nous Autres*, using a Quebec expression that poignantly underlines a collective sense of otherness, while also combining the designation of his addressee(s) with a toast to their future and the postcolonial resolve to be responsible for one's own destiny.

Memmi maintained that 'le surgissement de l'artiste colonisé devance un peu la prise de conscience collective dont il participe:' (104). In Quebec, *Refus global*, the manifesto of revolt signed by Borduas and other artists in 1948, certainly preceded a comparable manifestation in politics or literature. By 1968, Memmi could claim that 'on ne saurait surestimer ... la signification de la naissance d'une littérature canadienne-française' (141). Whether the close association of artists and writers with the independence movement may in fact have contributed to the loss of the referendum in 1980, an issue raised by Jean Larose (1987, 46, 54), is a point that will be discussed under the heading of gender relations in Quebec.

The fact that the term *canadien-français* was still used in the 1968 interview with Memmi, and that the discussion included the fate of francophones in Canada outside Quebec, indicates that the shift was not yet complete to a concept of Quebec as an entity containing the Québécois, the only group with hope of survival and a locus for separate development as a majority in their own territory (see D'Allemagne, 149–50). Memmi's concluding reference to young socialist *indépendantistes* ready to become martyrs to their cause (146) also indicates that utopian messianism was not dead at the time of the FLQ. Vallières saw his mission not only in terms of independence for Quebec, but as an attempt to produce 'un monde sans argent, sans haine et sans violence' (74). Post-referendum and post–Meech Lake Quebec presents a very different ideological picture. Before we can address the question of whether Quebec can still be considered colonized, a more detailed discussion is required of the relationship between narcissism, the colonized status of the Québécois, and gender definition and relations in Quebec.

## Gender distinctions in Quebec

As has been cited, the colonized male feels himself to be 'impuissant' (D'Allemagne, 104). Resorting to feminine refuge values, he is in many ways in the same position to the dominant group as women are to men. The colonizer treats him like a woman. This is particularly striking in the way in which the colonized are associated with nature, as opposed to culture (see Ouellette-Michalska 1987). The stereotypes of traditional Quebec civilization focus on images of snow/winter, a special relation to *la terre*, and 'spontaneous' recreational pursuits such as folk-dancing or singing, folk music and wood carving – activities not categorized as serious art. Like women, the Québécois were supposed to excel at performing rather than creating (see Filiatrault 1964, 181). D'Allemagne claimed that the English saw the typical French Canadian as 'léger, superficiel ... naïf ... résigné ... artiste et sentimental' (131–2) – characteristics that he summarized as typical of 'un grand enfant,' but that apply equally well to the traditional stereotype of femininity.

This schema is complicated by the fact that, for Anglo-Saxons, the French in general are associated with femininity. As Michèle Sarde convincingly demonstrates in *Regard sur les Françaises* (1983), French women represent the ultimate in femininity, being believed to excel in elegance (*le chic, la haute couture*) and all other forms of seduction: erotic – perfume, pornography – and also gastronomic. French men, while believed to be expert lovers – masters of the French kiss and the French letter – are nevertheless perceived as effeminate: small, unathletic, and associated with femininity by what Sarde terms a 'contagion': 'être sexué avant tout et associé avec l'amour et les relations avec les femmes ... il se trouve identifié à l'idée de la femme. Il se charge de féminité' (28–9). The phenomenal success of the film *La Cage aux folles* in North America is attributed by Sarde to the prior association of Frenchness with effeminacy.

To complicate matters further, the Québécois themselves share this prejudiced view of the French male, associating the French accent with homosexuality. According to Jean Larose, 'parler bien est souvent stigmatisé comme "tapette" au Quebec ... et "étudiant en lettres" signifie homosexuel dans le (dictionnaire) Bergeron' (1987, 25). In spite of clear evidence to the contrary, North Americans, including the Québécois, do not spontaneously associate the French with industry or technology. The French language has even been decried as inappropriate for the modern world (Bernard 1978, 26).

As Memmi emphasized, any colonization is both relative and specific. The Québécois male, inferiorized culturally by the French, may nevertheless gain some sense of superiority from his *américanité*. This is possible because, in North America, culture is devalued, being associated with women and effeminacy, in opposition to the pioneer man-of-action model. As Sarde argues, the difficulty experienced by French women in gaining access to the intellectual sphere is not shared to the same extent by American women. In fact, the stereotypes are reversed. Speaking of Claudine Hermann's image of women writers as 'des voleuses de langue,' Sarde claims that 'cette idée perd son sens aux Etats-Unis, oú la culture, tout au contraire, a été véhiculée par les femmes à l'époque oú les pionniers et les cow-boys avaient autre chose à faire qu'à jouer les instituteurs et préféraient à cet égard s'en remettre à leurs femmes ... associée aux femmes, la culture est méprisée' (22). This stereotype is confirmed, for example, by Roch Carrier, in the stories of his childhood where he associates the recognition of the value of education with his mother, and his father with resistance to it.[2] Education, for men of modest means, was also traditionally associated in Quebec with the seminary and the priesthood – the renunciation of virility, as illustrated in Ringuet's *Trente Arpents* (1936). In *La Petite Noirceur* (1987), Jean Larose shows how Denys Arcand's film *Le Déclin de l'empire américain* pits a group of intellectuals who talk a lot about sex against Mario, an uneducated rebel who actually indulges in it (13–14).

Larose also discusses the association between homosexuality and the identity of the Quebec male, in his discussion of the characters in the popular television comedy show 'Chez Denise' (90–2), and those in Michel Tremblay's plays (80). A frequent refrain in the latter is 'Chus pas capable!' Both women and men experience a sense of helplessness and hopelessness that leads them to seek escape through alcohol or other means, as evidenced in much Quebec fiction. The desire for a passive state of non-consciousness is associated with primary narcissism, as are 'feminine,' regressive values, and the imaginary order. Larose claims that the Québécois – and possibly all North Americans – have not collectively attained the symbolic order; they have been blocked in the imaginary stage associated with anal eroticism (17, 189), because of the power of the mother from whom they cannot separate.

This brings us to the question of the relation between the sexes in the Quebec context. It is undeniable that women have played an exceptionally important role in Quebec's history, especially in the pre-conquest 'mythical' period, which witnessed the exploits of Marie de l'Incarnation, Jeanne Mance, Marguerite Bourgeois, Mère d'Youville, and Madeleine de Verchères.[3] Whereas Quebec's male saints were martyrs, the female ones were women of action, and most chose not to be mainly mothers. Yet the centrality of the heroic mother figure (and the corresponding absence or weakness of the father) in Quebec literature has been much discussed (see Soeur Sainte-Marie-Eleuthère, *La Mère dans le roman canadien-français* 1964). Quebec has been described as a matriarchy, and Janine Boynard-Frot entitled her 1982 study of the Quebec novel *Un Matriarcat en procès*. Larose blames the failure of the referendum of 1980 on the 'Yvettes,' resurrected copies of Lemelin's 'Mère Plouffe' of the 1940s (Larose, 10, 45, 47).[4] Their anger was provoked by another strong woman, Lise Payette, representing an opposing feminist view, which was defeated by the older, mythical, anti-feminist femininity of the conservative phallic mothers. The latter are seen by Larose as fighting to preserve their influence, and reluctant to see either their sons or their daughters become 'liberated.' Larose even accuses Quebec male intellectuals of becoming feminists, in a paradoxical last-ditch attempt to exhibit some virility (168ff).

It appears that in Quebec the stereotypical gender roles (active = masculine, passive = feminine) are reversed, and that this is the cause of widespread misogyny, taking the form of resentment or violence against women. The latter is amply illustrated in Quebec fiction, which Patricia Smart (1988, 29–32) has shown to be frequently built on a foundation of matricide.[5] Novelist Jean Filiatrault had already remarked in 1964 that when Quebec women searched for a man in their bed, they found a child: they were imprisoned in the role of mother. And men, seeking to prove their virility through the conquest of a woman, frequently failed (as illustrated in Godbout's early novels).

This section began by positing an analogy between the situation of women and that of the Québécois. Larose also claims that a parallel exists between women's liberation and the liberation of Quebec. Yet his own remarks show that it is not so simple to combine the two. If it is essential for the Québécois male to assert his dominance over women in order to achieve the status of male subject, where does this leave the liberation of women in Quebec? In spite of their 'matriarchal power,' women in Quebec were the last in Canada to obtain the vote at the provincial level, in 1940. Did this have something to do with their Frenchness, as well as with the Church's resistance?[6] When equal educational opportunities were available to both sexes in English Canada, girls in Quebec were still being steered towards the *écoles ménagères* to hone their skills in domestic science.

The relationship of women to power, as represented by the phallus, is different from that of the colonized male. A man may be deprived of his 'rightful' position as putative father associated with the making of language and law; yet he still has the hope of replacing the current father figure. He is not castrated but made (temporarily) impotent. In the case of recourse to homosexuality to restore his self-esteem, the man does not actually become impotent, but sterile for other reasons. Female homosexuality, an important element in contemporary women's writing in Quebec, may convey the same implication for fertility, but represents a different challenge to the relationship between the imaginary and symbolic orders. While Larose makes many pertinent observations on these issues, his use of 'impotent,' 'castrated,' and 'homosexual' to describe the Quebec male, without making a distinction between them, leaves much to be investigated further.

One central aspect to be discussed is the different relationship to language between male and female writers, when they both belong to a colonized group. This is not unconnected to their different relationship to the question of fertility as physical reproduction or artistic production. A further element in the same chain is the gap between a concept of desire as product-oriented (related to 'having' on the metonymical plane) or process-oriented (related to *jouissance*, an aspect of 'being,' of transformation in the metaphorical dimension). I concluded my previous study of the French fictional journal with a discussion of the alternation of *récit* (story: past tense, third-person) and *discours* (ongoing dialogue using the first and second persons, in the present and future tenses). This distinction will be useful once more to define the change in the self-representation of Québécois men and women in diary fiction.

**The colonized colonizer**

It is ironic to maintain that Quebec women have suffered at the hands of a phallocratic system, while also claiming that the men in this 'distinct' society have been feminized: yet that is the case. There is a corresponding paradox in the relationship between Quebec and English Canada. The latter, though dominant in numbers and area, has a much weaker sense of national identity and is possibly in even greater danger of assimilation by the United States. D'Allemagne already pointed out in 1966 the irony that Canada is dependent on Quebec for its identity: 'C'est le cas paradoxal d'un colonisateur qui ne se définit guère que par rapport au colonisé' (25). That was before the federal policy of biculturalism and bilingualism promoted by the government led by Pierre Trudeau. Is there another dominant power that has accepted, even in theory, that the dominator should learn the language of the dominated, rather than the reverse? Larose refers to Canada as a 'caricature de l'impuissance québécoise' (198). It seems that there might have been the possibility of dialogue between two 'others,' resulting in mutually sustaining narcissism, both resisting a third-party oppressor.

Yet D'Allemagne also spoke of Confederation as a marriage that could be annulled, since both parties were not fully consenting (33). He perceived the colonial alliance as an improvement on imperial rape, but nevertheless asymmetrical. The marriage image was ubiquitous in the popular press throughout Canada in the second half of 1990, following the failure to reach agreement on the Meech Lake constitutional proposals.[7] From the English side, Quebec was perceived as the unfaithful and ungrateful wife who should not be allowed to leave with as big a share of the joint assets as she believes she is entitled to. From the French side, she had nothing to lose and should not have stayed in the relationship so long. Larose maintained even before Meech Lake that English Canadians 'veulent garder le Québec comme un homme qui se garde une belle femme' (300). As English Canada saw its own survival threatened by the possible departure of Quebec, the exasperated question echoed by André Bernard in 1974 was heard once more: What does Quebec want? This is itself a variation on Freud's famous *Was will das Weib?* – What does woman want? (However, in 1990–92 Quebec has asked the same question of English Canada, with similar exasperation.)

The first thing that Quebec wanted was greater control over immigration, to ensure that survival is not threatened from within. This was the theme of Lise Payette's controversial National Film Board documentary entitled *Disparaître* (1989). The latter caused alarm among feminists because of its support for a pro-natality policy, and among libertarians for its potentially xenophobic espousal of assimilation for immigrants, contrary to the mosaic model. As Larose also pointed out, for this to be successful the Québécois must be attractive enough to immigrants that they will wish to become like them, and thus compensate for the low birth rate: do the Québécois radiate 'assez de puissance immanente pour inspirer aux allophones de parler québécois?' (138). Just as Canada's survival appears to depend on its ability to retain Quebec, Quebec's survival hinges on control of its minorities, whether native, anglophone, or immigrant. Conflicts within Quebec – confrontation with the Mohawks at Oka, the unilingual signs legislation – illustrated the relativity of 'otherness'; the post-colonial, forced to become dominant in relation to another other, is redefined as the one, the standard of conformity rather than difference. It appears that the definition of Québécois, no longer based on origin, is now enforced in symbolic terms (language and law), that patriarchy is dropping its matriarchal disguise (see Smart, 29ff). As Madeleine Ouellette-Michalska pointed out, the 'nègres blancs' image was accepted because of the apparent (assumed) absence of 'nègres noirs' in Quebec in the 1960s, but the advent of Haïtian taxi drivers modified its appropriateness. On the other hand, 'Il ne vient à personne l'idée de se dire Indien ...' (1987, 149).

In these circumstances, can the Québécois still be considered colonized, or has Caliban turned into Prospero (see Dorsinville 1974)? Complaints of exploitation by American business interests have given way to the adoption of an American-style business ethic by the Québécois, possibly more successfully than by English Canadians. The arguments for independence expressed in 1992 were not utopian or messianic. They were based on strength rather than weakness, and the proclamation of difference was limited to the right to be American in French. Quebec continues to perceive a pressing need to liberate itself from Ottawa, while becoming increasingly invaded by American culture.

Language having become the only distinguishing feature of this 'distinct' society, its role in the 'survival' and 'self-esteem' central to narcissism is paramount. The relationship between language and ideology is thrown into relief. Does the use of French still produce *la différence*, or will French become the vehicle, in Quebec, of an American ideological clone? While language structures individual consciousness (and the unconscious is structured like a language), are individual languages not also modified by economic and political factors? French, even in France, is subject to Americanization, just as English was affected by Norman French in the Middle Ages. Belief in a *génie de la langue française* may be as essentialist as the belief in innate racial or sexual characteristics decried by Beauvoir.

Like women, the Québécois are faced with the opportunity for autonomy, at the risk of becoming 'the same': no longer by metonymical assimilation, incorporated into a larger whole, but through the metaphorical substitution of duplication. Fanon, speaking of other former colonies, called them 'le lieu vivant de contradictions qui menacent d'être insurmontables' (1976, 150). Fredric Jameson, discussing narrative form as symptomatic of the political unconscious, sees it also as a therapeutic means to invent 'imaginary or formal solutions to irresolvable contradictions' (see heading to this chapter). Like feminists, male Québécois writers have attempted to depict and solve a collective and individual dilemma through writing, usually in the only language available to them. Those who are sufficiently bilingual to have a choice have chosen to write in French, and by doing so have made their audience primarily their fellow Québécois.

Many critics have traced the evolution of narrative forms in Quebec in relation to Quebec's colonized status and nationalist aspirations. The insights of Arguin, Kwaterko, Pelletier, and Hébert are particularly relevant in looking at one specific type of narration: the fictional journal. While all types of first-person narration are bound to be narcissistic in some degree, the characteristics of this subgenre, as previously described, make it singularly appropriate to convey the conflicts involved. This is because of its intrinsic (incipient or self-conscious) concern for the definition and communication of subjectivity through language, and the relevance of gender distinction. For women, in Quebec and elsewhere, the intimate diary has long been a vehicle for narcissistic self-construction and deconstruction, as illustrated a century ago by Henriette Dessaulles and Laure Conan.

# PART II
# NARCISSISM AND FEMININITY (1870–1940)

CHAPTER FOUR

# Femininity and Self-Denial: *The Diary of Henriette Dessaulles*

> 'Le journal intime est toujours l'écho d'un malaise plus ou moins profond de l'individu en face de lui-même, des autres et de l'existence. C'est par ce malaise que se définit l'intimisme. Le journal est né de la prise de conscience de ce malaise.'
>
> ALAIN GIRARD (1963), 522

### Nineteenth-century women's diaries

Alain Girard, in his study of the development of the *journal intime* in France in the nineteenth century, included no detailed analyses of diaries by women, although he remarked, somewhat archly, that 'les femmes, quelle qu'en soit la raison, se révèlent volontiers à elles-mêmes dans un journal' (1963, 89). In fact, as Béatrice Didier subsequently pointed out in her book on the genre, proportionately women wrote more diaries than men: 'Si l'on compare le nombre de femmes diaristes au nombre de femmes écrivains, mettons même romancières, on voit que la proportion est très nettement supérieure à celle que l'on trouverait chez les hommes' (1976, 67). Although fewer diaries by women were published in the nineteenth century, this did not reflect the number that existed. More appeared by men, usually because the authors were prominent for some other reason. The first by women to be published were made public because of a connection between the author and a famous man – for example, those of Eugénie de Guérin, whose brother Maurice was well-known as a poet, and of Lamartine's mother. It has been only relatively recently that diaries by women have been considered of interest in their own right, because of what they reveal regarding both the lives of women and women's relationship to writing (see Raoul 1989).

The private nature of diary writing is the first aspect that made it appropriate for women, for whom public forms of writing were generally prohibited, or met with disapproval. Didier emphasizes this aspect: 'Les femmes se sont mises très tôt à tenir leur journal. On peut voir dans cette pratique le moyen pour elles de s'exercer à l'écriture, sans avoir à craindre l'affrontement avec un public ... pendant longtemps et pour beaucoup de femmes, ce fut le seul moyen d'expression possible' (40–1). Other elements of a practical nature that contributed to the popularity of diaries for women were the small and flexible time commitment involved in making short daily entries, and the everyday nature of what was expected to be recounted. In France, keeping a journal was perceived as a harmless, possibly beneficial, trivial pursuit for young girls awaiting marriage. Diary writing was not deemed to require a high level of education or intelligence, or a mastery of style and form. These derogatory stereotypes, which contributed to the exclusion of diaries from the literary canon, have more recently been re-evaluated as qualities, from both feminist and post-modernist perspectives.

The diary has been defined as apparently formless, making it a precursor of self-conscious modern fiction. The attempt to 'write the self' day by day already contained, implicitly, the problematic of subjectivity in relation to language/writing. This in itself explains why, as Judy Nolte Lensink has also claimed, 'in both form and content it comes closest to a feminine version of autobiography' (1987, 40; see also Juhasz 1980). An authentic *journal intime*, written *in medias res* and for no external reader, illustrates writing as narcissistic process serving to regulate self-esteem, rather than as product, aimed at communication with others. The fact that the diary may function as listener (albeit a self-object), and does become a product with the potential to be read, is often central in fictional journals.

The model of the typical diarist as a young girl is widespread in the nineteenth-century French novel (Raoul 1985), although actual examples of this type of diary were not published until the twentieth century, with the exception of Marie Bashkirtseff's journal (1887). These novels were mainly written by men, who frequently claimed in prefaces that the feminine style of the narrator was evidence for the (fictional) authenticity of the diary (Raoul 1985). The characteristics assumed to be feminine include incoherence, imprecision, repetition, lacunae, effusive expressivity, prosaic banality, bad spelling and bad grammar. As I have shown elsewhere (Raoul 1989), they are more justifiably associated with the genre of the *journal intime* than with the gender of the diarist. Real diaries by women rarely confirm them. The depiction of women diarists in fictions by men in the nineteenth century was based on projection, not knowledge of real models. Diary fiction became popular with women writers at the turn of the century, however, especially in Germany, and Lorna Martens shows that these examples reflected contemporary customs (1985, 173–4). In North America vast numbers of women kept diaries, as evidenced by several anthologies and studies. Susanna Moodie's journals have become the earliest English-Canadian texts by a woman to receive critical attention. In Quebec, however, there was ambivalence toward diary writing. A spiritual journal was considered a useful exercise for seminarians,[1] but did not conform to the model of the *journal intime*, since it was to be read by a confessor/mentor and to concern primarily the author's relationship to God. It was fashionable for girls in upper-class circles to keep a journal, but, as Henriette Dessaulles mentions in her diary (1989, 282, 314), the nuns at the convent schools confiscated and destroyed them. Many of these journals were also kept for amusement and to be shared with friends, rather than as an intimate means of introspection destined to remain secret. Those that were meant for the self alone usually remained just that, and were burned, as were Henriette Dessaulles's childhood diaries, which she began at age eight (287).

The ones she wrote from 1874 to 1881, at fourteen to twenty-one years of age, are paradoxically the best surviving example, to my knowledge, of a genre that is known to exist but, because of its nature, is rarely available for analysis – the nineteenth-century diary of a girl and young woman.[2] This one was not made public until 1971, twenty-five years after the author's death. According to Pierre Hébert (1985, 37n; 1988, 70–1), this journal is also exceptional in the body of autobiographical writings produced in Quebec in the last century, seeming almost to belong to the period of its publication, in its preoccupation with the construction of self through writing.

### The 'real' diary of Henriette Dessaulles

The 1971 version has since been superseded by Jean-Louis Major's critical edition (1989), which provides an impressive wealth of information about both the author and her diary. One aspect that is central to the present discussion is the question of authenticity. I am beginning my analyses of fictional journals in Quebec by considering a real one that preceded them, but cannot have been an actual model. I do not need to reiterate my previous arguments (1980) about the problematic differences between real, fake, and fictional journals, since this one illustrates them so well. Major's meticulous detective work on the manuscript reveals that Henriette Dessaulles's diary, like Anne Frank's, comes to us in adulterated form. Not only did the author copy out her original diary, with a view to a possible later (posthumous?) publication, probably twenty years after the last entry was originally written, she also expurgated large sections, and moved items from one year to another in an attempt to fill in the gaps. The chronology is questionable, as the notebook for part of one year (1878), which appeared to be missing in the 1971 version, has been redistributed, mostly into 1880–1 (Major 1989, 35–6). Yet, as Major claims, this does not affect the overall impression of authenticity. It even seems probable, as he shows, that Dessaulles deliberately retained earlier spelling and grammar mistakes, to maintain the validity of her diary as 'real' (Major, 74–5). She also left in disparaging remarks about her stepmother and criticism of religion, which one might have expected her to eliminate – leaving one wondering what was in the censored passages. Her restructuring of her own narrative seems to have respected the expectations of a reader engaged in the intimate contract (see Rousset *Le Lecteur intime* 1986).

Violation of the fine (and permeable) line between autobiography and fiction is further illustrated by the fact that Madame Saint-Jacques, formerly Henriette Dessaulles, also published in her lifetime (1908) anonymous extracts from her journal in which the names were changed.[3] These cover one episode, an abortive romance, and are presented as someone else's diary – that is, the frame becomes that of a fiction (Major, 15, 38). Ironically, the entire diary, as published posthumously, does read structurally like a novel – a romance with a happy ending, unlike the episode extracted by the author, which may be seen as a (reversed) *mise en abyme* of the main plot. The effect of overall coherence, so different from that produced by the more typical diaries of Marie Bashkirtseff or Anaïs Nin, is nevertheless the product of circumstances rather than design (as is also the case for Anne Frank's journal). The narrative covers a limited period, corresponding to the author's adolescence, intrinsically conveying the *Bildungsroman* model. The cast

Femininity and Self-Denial 49

of characters is limited, because of the diarist's milieu. Suspense and conflict are built in, since the narrator is mainly concerned with escaping from the clutches of a wicked stepmother into the arms of her prince (Maurice, the brother of her neighbour and best friend, Jos Saint-Jacques). Literary models are evident, yet the 'autobiographical pact' is maintained,[4] because of the diarist's genuine ignorance, at the time of writing, of subsequent events. Our knowledge that the author transcribed the original text after the death of Maurice – that is, when the happy ending had already been reversed – transforms the purpose of the diary's preservation. Yet the decision to publish it at some point, albeit in modified form, remains an additional, supplementary level of communication that does not supersede, in our reading of the diary, the sense of private recording and questioning by a real diarist writing primarily for herself.

Henriette Dessaulles's diary illustrates remarkably the construction of a female self: how one is not born a woman, but becomes one, as Simone de Beauvoir claimed. It also illustrates the ways in which fictional models structure all narration, as the narrator projects herself as heroine of her story and adapts it to various implied (projected) narratees. The model I developed for the fictional journal works for the non-fictional diary, except that the latter includes only the level of transition from *discours* (ongoing dialogue with the self, *in medias res*) to *récit* (third-person story, in the past). It does not include the frame of pre-established fictivity that, in a diary novel, defines this shift as a mimetic illusion, since the novel necessarily begins as *récit*, and becomes a *discours* on the nature of subjectivity and representation. The difference in the communication involved in a real and a fictional journal will be amply demonstrated in comparing Henriette Dessaulles's diary with the fictional journals produced by Laure Conan.

## Aspects of the diary form

The formal aspects of Dessaulles's journal, as available to us, are typical of the diary genre. The regularity and length of the entries varies and there are several gaps, but the impression of regular recording over a period of time is certainly conveyed. The dates vary in their degree of precision, but allusions to external events enable verification, as demonstrated by Major's analysis of the various years involved, with reference to political and social events corroborated by newspaper articles and church registries. The author may have later modified some redistributed entries to establish coherence, but there is no evidence of a conscious effort at the initial time of writing to link the entries. The young diarist resembles others of the period in her references to the physical aspects of the journal, such as how she procured the notebook, what kind of pen she is using, and so on. Although some of these references may be ambiguous (are the notebook and pen the originals or those used for recopying? [Major, 35–6]), the self-consciousness of the writing activity is underlined. Henriette Dessaulles's later expertise in graphology is not surprising.

She is also typical in her preoccupation with sincerity, with 'telling the truth' and the impossibility of doing so. Unlike some of her friends, whose diaries she mentions, she does not concentrate on anecdotal recording, nor does she show her journal to others. Hers is a genuine *journal intime*, focused on her own personal life and problems, and written initially for herself alone. She has a particular reason to need a journal to confide in, and to hide it, since her mother died when she was four and her stepmother is hostile. Her father, the mayor of Saint-Hyacinthe, is mostly absent. At the convent school where she becomes a boarder, diary keeping has to be clandestine, since, like mirrors (320), it is forbidden (282, 314).

Henriette consciously thinks of her journal, as do most *intimistes*, as a mirror, a means to see herself as an object, from outside (386). She also includes references to actually looking at herself in a mirror (222). She rereads what she has written with a critical eye, commenting on the style (116, 193, 243, 414–15) and to verify if it still seems true (573); she intends to reread her diary later, before destroying it (287). As in modern diary novels, the relationship between living and writing, and that between writing and reading, become explicit themes. This particular diary of a young woman in the mid-nineteenth century confirms all the clichés concerning *l'intimisme* that were later imitated and parodied in fiction. On the other hand, the 'story' told is not, as in the case of most early feminine diary fiction, that of a woman abandoned by a faithless lover (Martens, 101–2); it is modelled rather on the romance (see Ouellet 1988). This is, at least, the impression given by the wedding that terminates the diary. A closer look at the evolution of the narrator's depiction of herself as 'character,' however, reveals that this is not the only possible outcome – just as it was not, in fact, the final one.

## The female diarist as protagonist[5]

The first self-image Henriette projects is that of a rebel (144, 238, 354, 387). She dares to criticize what she calls 'les singeries' and 'les simagrées' of the religious practice around her, expressing her preference for the attitude of her father, a free-thinker who does not attend church, over that of her pious and zealous stepmother (see Verduyn 1983). Saint-Hyacinthe, a centre for liberal thought, was experiencing the effects of the Catholic revival that was sweeping Quebec. Henriette finds it ridiculous to offer wrinkled paper roses to a statue of Saint Joseph (141), and to confess to sins that she has not committed. She equally detests the strict rules governing the behaviour of a proper young lady (473). Imagining herself as a fearless adventurer, she confides to her diary that she would rather be battling robbers on the roof than entertaining old ladies in the drawing room (151). She even admits that she would love to smoke and swear ('sacrer'), but adds, comically, 'mais je ne sais pas et c'est défendu' (160, 559). The clothes she is expected to wear are as confining as a strait-jacket, and she laments the fact that she was not born a 'sauvagesse' (446).

It is hardly surprising that at this stage she confesses she would rather be a boy, that she is 'manquée' as a girl (244, 248, 257). Envy of the advantages of masculinity and a strong sense of narcissistic injury are evident in her resentment that she cannot, like Maurice, leave for Quebec to study law (437), that there are no opportunities for her to enlarge her physical and mental horizons (368, 534). Like a caged bird, she dreams of spreading her wings (178). At confession she has nothing to say: 'je ne pèche pas, c'est à peine si je vis. Et il y a eu des saintes et des héros et de grandes pécheresses!' (376). In spite of all obstacles, she is determined to take charge of her own life: 'qui m'éclairera? C'est moi toute seule, je réponds de moi!' (195). In this first part of the diary, Henriette accuses herself of being narcissistic in the obvious sense of being self-preoccupied: 'tu es remplie de toi ... tu te cherches, tu jouis de te découvrir, de parler de toi, de te poser en petite héroïne devant toi-même' (117). As she becomes attracted to Maurice, she is not sure that she wants to fall in love (186–8, 206, 228–9). She foresees the danger of being taken over by Maurice, of losing control of her own destiny, and is determined to resist: 'je ne veux pas pentoute. Amen' (324).

Her attitude towards herself and others changes gradually, however, between the ages of sixteen and eighteen. The first event that contributes to this change is a serious illness, during which her life is in danger: she is faced with the very real possibility that she will die young, like so many people around her (256, 259). While convalescing at Old Orchard, she experiences the episode that she was later to publish as a 'fiction': a young English musician, also sick, becomes enamoured of her. She refuses to take him seriously, since 'je suis une enfant – et c'est un Anglais' (262), yet she recognizes that her childhood is over. Now ready for the marriage market, the rebellious Henriette must become a demure Mademoiselle Dessaulles.

The horrible death of her favorite little half-sister, Rosalie (343–5), leads her to question even more the tenets of the Catholic faith, but also to be momentarily tempted by the mystical model provided in the lives of the saints. One other possibility is open to her: a religious vocation. *The Imitation of Christ* replaces Dickens as her bedside reading, but not for long. While the challenge of heroic sainthood appeals to her, the life she sees the nuns living definitely does not (434). From this point on, Maurice occupies more and more space in her life and in her diary, as do confrontations with her stepmother, who refuses to allow her to see him, probably preferring an alliance with a cousin (Major, 12).

In the last part of the diary, the model of the sentimental romance triumphs. Henriette completes her apprenticeship to become a 'madame' (603). She is obliged to accept that the only way to leave home, to escape from her stepmother, is to conform to her demands, to become enough like her that she will be allowed to marry Maurice. Reluctantly accepting the prescribed feminine role of virtue and submission, she asks herself why, in order to be 'bonne,' it is necessary to be 'sotte' (524). Yet she comes to condemn her previous self-preoccupation and rebellion; her earlier refusal to be a slave (232) is turned into willing submission to Maurice's orders. For him, she will accept the burden of domestic chores, previously detested (431–2). The girl who felt suffocated in her 'petites robes de tulle' (598) becomes 'cette heureuse petite fille en blanc qui attend Maurice, le coeur battant' (591). Maurice prefers her in white (487). Henriette envisages three possible futures for herself: early death, becoming a nun, or marriage. As she observes, whichever it is, she will be dressed in white (162). All three represent the end of her original dream of freedom and action, of life as a bright

Femininity and Self-Denial 53

tapestry, woven in the colors of her choice (428). The final section of her diary becomes an inventory of the moments spent with Maurice: 'C'est entendu avec moi-même que je ne parlerai que de Maurice, puisque lui seul m'intéresse' (487–8). The last pages provide a countdown to their marriage, when Henriette Dessaulles becomes Madame Maurice Saint-Jacques.

Parallel to this evolution in the type of heroine Henriette chooses to identify with, there is a shift in the implied narratee. Although the journal is written, initially, to be read only by herself, the diarist imagines various possible addressees and modifies her own role of projected interlocutor. At the beginning the diary serves as a friend and a confidante of her own age and sex; she addresses a double of herself. Yet this sympathetic friend tends to become a reassuring maternal figure. When the narrator addresses herself as 'tu,' it is to encourage and console in motherly tones. She justifies her own behaviour and opinions and seeks approbation. In the second stage, the diary replaces her ineffective confessor, M. Prince. Henriette admits that she would rather confess directly to God, as Protestants do (195), but also that she finds prayer difficult (541). The diary plays the role of judge, and the self-addressed 'tu' acquires the tone of a paternal upbraiding.

Throughout the journal Henriette excludes all members of her entourage as actual confidants, even Maurice. As she becomes more attached to him, however, she begins to address him in the diary. He progressively becomes the main narratee. In fact, the implied narratee undergoes a change of sex, as Henriette grows up, passing from her dead mother, to her stepmother, whose love she seeks, to her absent father, the priest and God, and finally Maurice. She progressively renounces herself or another female figure as judge, to seek and accept male approbation. Yet it is the 'feminine' qualities exhibited by Maurice (his gentleness and affection) that win her trust, whereas her stepmother is condemned and finally ignored because of her 'masculine' characteristics (violence, authoritarianism, and lack of sensitivity).

Maurice actually becomes the reader of the journal, when Henriette gives it to him shortly before their marriage. This self-disclosure is parallel to the gift of her body. The diary itself has become 'un ami un peu encombrant, dont l'utilité a cessé' (595), since she now has an actual other with whom to identify and communicate. Once she can talk freely to Maurice, the spoken word replaces writing (602), presence is stronger than absence. On her marriage, Henriette abandons her diary. The apparently narcissistic, masturbatory aspect of solitary diary writing (see Didier, 115) gives way to an apparently healthy and fulfilling relationship with a person of the opposite sex. For this reason, Mona Gautier-Cano (1987) claims that Dessaulles's diary illustrates the successful transposition of narcissism to other-directed object love, and Pierre Hébert (1987, 156) has interpreted it as showing the triumph of positivism.

**The feminine self-construed**

In a Freudian perspective, Henriette Dessaulles's diary represents the assumption of femininity by an initially bisexual subject, who after a period of maladaptation and conflict eventually accepts the prescribed feminine role of self-eclipse, defining herself as the object of Maurice's affections, as his wife and the mother of his children. From a feminist point of view, this scenario does not provide a euphoric happy ending, but illustrates that all the options open to women in a traditional, patriarchal framework involve the renunciation of autonomy, self-sacrifice in the name of an altruistic feminine ideal of devotion to others. However, in the context of object-relations theory of narcissism, Henriette's obsessive attachment to Maurice may appear as an example of narcissistic object choice in women, as discussed by Annie Reich (1953). Henriette does not initially want to marry Maurice: she wants to be him, that is, free, as he is. It is only on the painful realization that this is not possible that she accepts the alternative: metonymical association, by becoming part of him and living vicariously through him and their children. In this sense, Maurice literally replaces the diary as a self-object. Even her original desire to study becomes a wish to improve herself to better please Maurice, and she finally allows him to censor her reading (584–5) as well as keep her diary.

Union with Maurice, who represents feminine as well as masculine qualities, also fulfils, by substitution, the desire for symbiotic union with an 'other' (the lost mother). Maurice, who like her father is involved in liberal politics, becomes for Henriette a replacement for both parents, as well as a double/brother (his sister is her best friend), her 'other half' or alter ego. Throughout the journal, two series of images are striking by the dialectic they produce: on the one hand, those representing a desire for a secure refuge in an enclosed space; on the other, those portraying an equally pressing desire for escape from suffocation (see Raoul 1986). Leaving home to join Maurice provides a synthesis of the two.

Henriette experiences severe anxiety at the thought of losing Maurice. She believes that any infidelity on his part would kill her (534). A premonitory dream reveals her preoccupation with his possible disappearance, a foreboding that was justified, as he died in 1897, leaving her at the age of thirty-seven with five surviving children. Still recovering at the time from a long illness following a difficult birth and the later death of the child, Henriette was devastated (Major, 37–8). Maurice's sister Jos, her friend, died also the following year. According to Major, it was then that she returned to her diary, not to write a sequel, unfortunately, but to transcribe the original, as a tribute to Maurice and to relive her lost happiness. Publication was envisaged as a way to preserve *his* memory.

**Writing as salvation/survival**

Dessaulles does not appear to have entertained thoughts of immortality for herself through the publication of her journal, unlike her contemporary, Marie Bashkirtseff. Yet after Maurice's death she returned to writing, becoming one of the first women journalists in Canada as well as an expert graphologist. In addition to articles under the male pseudonym of Jean Deshaies, she produced a weekly women's column in *Le Devoir* called 'Lettre de Fadette,' from 1910–45, and also wrote children's stories. Her published writing is very different from that of the diary, reflecting the moralizing religiosity typical of 'women's literature' in Quebec at the time. She had indeed become, like her stepmother, 'fade' rather than subversive. Her metamorphosis recalls that of George Sand's 'petite Fadette,' who also went from rebel to paragon of conventional wisdom and virtue.

Like *La Petite Fadette*, Dessaulles's diary may be read as a 'conte de fées': allusions to this model abound in the journal (for example, 323, 331, 369, 402). Like Cinderella, the diarist is saved from a wicked stepmother by a handsome young man. Henriette may also be seen as a victim of the 'Cinderella complex' (Colette Dowling 1981), as an example of narcissistic object choice in women. Her family situation (absent/impotent father; dead/castrated mother; oppressive/phallic stepmother) provides a model significant, as we shall see, in Quebec diary fiction. Women's submission is reversed into matriarchal dominance through moral narcissism.

This phenomenon is illustrated strikingly in Laure Conan's fictional journals. Like Conan and her narrators, Henriette Dessaulles turned to self-reflexive/self-projecting writing because there was no man in her life for her to reflect (before and after Maurice). Married women, in nineteenth-century Quebec, did not write either fiction or diaries.[6] Dessaulles chose marriage and motherhood over writing, and returned to it only when the alternative was no longer available. In her later texts, personal narcissism is superseded by collective patriotism, an individual sense of superiority by one of moral righteousness. Her earlier intense desire to live becomes an individual and collective determination to survive, beyond an unbearable loss. The self-directed journal is converted to other-directed, polemical journalism. Addressing a conference on 'la langue française au Canada,' in a text published in 1913,[7] she paid tribute to 'l'influence des femmes canadiennes sur les lettres françaises depuis le commencement de notre vie nationale' (341) – not as writers, but as mothers, preservers and transmitters of 'la langue maternelle.' She quotes a letter from another woman to her son: 'Comprends bien, mon fils, que nous resterons français, à condition d'être supérieurs à ces brutes d'Anglais, qui veulent être nos maîtres' (342). She goes on to attribute French-Canadian survival to 'talent' and 'éloquence' rather than force, and identifies their source as feminine, justifying the choice of 'Vive la Canadienne!' as national anthem. Her closing remarks, however, include the statement that 'au Canada, les femmes ne sont pas féministes: elles ne veulent pas être traitées comme les hommes, mais autrement et mieux; elles y sont habituées' (348). Elsewhere, she is quoted as giving the following advice to a young woman: 'Soyez indépendante, mais gardez-vous bien de le paraître' (Couture 1966, 41). The ideology espoused by Fadette was that of the refuge values typical of a colonized society, whereas the Henriette of 1860–70 still felt the fervour of an ardent desire for independence, left over from 1838.

In the same address, Dessaulles referred to a 'brochure' by Laure Conan entitled 'Si les Canadiennes voulaient' [sic],[8] and praised *Angéline de Montbrun* as 'une exquise histoire d'âmes qui se racontent elles-mêmes, avec un sentiment vrai et profond, qui émeut' (343). Félicité Angers (Laure Conan) was recognized by Dessaulles, as by other contemporaries, as the first woman in Canada to 'ouvrir aux femmes ... le chemin des lettres: ceux qui écrivent savent qu'il n'est pas semé de roses' (343). Mme H.-D. Saint-Jacques (as the author is designated) did not say what she thought of the renunciation or condemnation of marriage, as depicted in Conan's fictional journals.

CHAPTER FIVE

# Phallic Women and Moral Narcissism: *The Fictional Journals of Laure Conan*

'Writing for publication represents entrance into the world of others, and by means of that passage a rebirth: access to the status of autonomous subject ... The question one must now ask is whether the story of a woman who sees conventional female self-definition as a text to be rewritten, who refuses the inscription of her body as the ultimate truth of her self, to become, if not a man, an exceptional woman (hence like a man), is a story significantly different from that of a man who becomes an exceptional man.'
NANCY K. MILLER, IN McCONNELL-GINET *Women and Language in Literature and Society* (1980), 266–7

## Fictivity

Henriette Dessaulles's rewriting of her nevertheless undoubtedly authentic diary, and her publication of an extract in a fictional frame, serve to highlight some of the problems involved in distinguishing between fiction and autobiography. These are particularly complex in the case of a diary, where 'fake' is a third category to be considered, as I have discussed elsewhere (Raoul 1980, 3–11). Arguments may be based on the reading pact involved or on intrinsic formal aspects of the text: in either case marginal, overlapping, and indeterminate cases remain and frequently provide the most interesting aspects of the debate (see Lejeune 1975, 1980, and 1986).

Félicité Angers, a woman fifteen years older than Dessaulles and personally known to her,[1] produced the first diary fiction in Quebec and became famous as Laure Conan, the first Canadian professional woman writer. She did this by avoiding the conventional female roles of wife and mother (whether willingly or not), or nun, although she spent a large part of her life in a convent. Her fiction was lauded at the time because of its religious and patriotic propaganda message; yet she was also derided for her 'masculinity' and assumed to be compensating, by writing, for an inability to be a 'real woman.'[2] This information is relevant here, not only because it confirms the lack of choice available to someone like Dessaulles, but because it is considered an important element in the evaluation of her fiction by many critics who read it as thinly disguised autobiography, even 'imposture.'[3] Brochu goes so far as to ask regarding *Angéline de Montbrun*: 'S'agit-il bien d'un roman?' (1963, 115). No one has suggested, however, that parts of her fictional journals might actually be drawn from real diaries kept by her. Passages such as descriptions of nature set in her home region of La Malbaie, or expressions of sympathy for those condemned to spend loveless lives performing menial tasks, are interpreted as references to the author's life, but not as self-plagiarism comparable to that of Dessaulles or Valéry Larbaud.[4]

The latter is unlikely, since Conan's fictional journals do not read like real diaries, in spite of their dated entries. The formally mimetic code is established, but in a frame and with other novelistic characteristics that designate the text as fiction. A comparison of Conan's first text, 'Un Amour vrai' (published in 1878) and Dessaulles's extract, 'L'Amour passa' (an episode of 1875 published in 1908) reveals some obvious distinguishing features.[5] Both are accounts of the refusal of a young French-Canadian woman to marry an anglophone Protestant. The attitude and tone of Dessaulles's narrative is that of the everyday, and she leaves Henry Robinson with some pangs of regret but no great drama, accepting the strictures of her society. Conan's heroine, Thérèse Raynal, in contrast, is depicted as dramatizing the situation to the maximum. She agrees to marry Francis Douglas, but only because of a secret pact with God that in exchange for his conversion she will die on the wedding day. The story and the message are conveyed not only through extracts from Thérèse's diary, but by letters and further information, whose source is revealed as Thérèse's stepmother (both Thérèse and Francis are orphans). The diary is incorporated into the plot, since Francis adds a postcript to it, to be found by the editor. The latter is represented as writing ten years later, after Francis has died as a monk at the Grande Chartreuse.

The 'truth' of the 'amour vrai' here has nothing to do with historical events – although there was a real diary in nineteenth-century France that could have served as a model, had Conan known of it: that of Elisabeth Leseur, whose atheist husband was actually converted and became a monk on reading her diary after her death (see Girard 1963, 112–13 and Didier, 67). Thus the events recounted do not in themselves mark the text as fiction; it is rather the melodramatic way they are presented, and the mixture of diary, letters, and narration by an 'editor.'

Some critics have claimed that all Conan's fiction, including her historical novels, conveys the same message of self-denial and religious sublimation (for example, Dionne 1976). Here, the focus will be on her use of the diary form, in relation to the narcissism involved in such a choice. I shall return to a comparison with her less well-known diary narratives (including 'L'Obscure Souffrance' and 'La Vaine Foi' published in 1919) after a more detailed consideration of *Angéline de Montbrun*. This novel is one of the most enigmatic works of fiction ever produced in Quebec, as suggested by the divergent conclusions drawn from it. I shall begin my analysis by indicating some of the surprisingly numerous points of overlap between this overtly fictional journal and the diary of Henriette Dessaulles.[6]

## Henriette Dessaulles and Angéline de Montbrun

The most obvious resemblance between the two texts is that the diarist in both is a young nineteenth-century female belonging to a social milieu in which girls were educated but not expected to work outside the home, except to 'help the poor' on a voluntary basis. The assumption in both cases is that the diarist is defined by her relationship to her father, and that the major change in her life will occur when she marries, to be re-defined as her husband's wife. In both, the only acceptable alternative to this is a religious vocation, which would define her in relation to God, as the bride of Christ. Both diarists reject this alternative. Both become ill, with what may be psychosomatic symptoms, and come close to death. For both, religious questions are extremely important, and faith in God is brought into question when a family member dies. However, Dessaulles criticizes the practice of religion but ultimately continues to believe in God (as does Mina, Angéline's alter ego in Conan's text), whereas Angéline is depicted as less concerned with the external appearances of faith and closer to actually losing it.

Both diarists become involved with a young man called Maurice, who is the brother of their best friend (Jos Saint-Jacques, Mina Darville). Both Maurices are studying to become lawyers. Henriette and Angéline are both avid readers, although Henriette, like Mina, reads novels, whereas Angéline has been 'protected' from them by her father. Both have a strong sense of patriotism and of the need to resist 'les Anglais' (*Angéline*, 30). Whereas Henriette is courted by an anglophone and refuses him, in Conan's text it is Mina who is unsuccessfully pursued by an amorous Anglican minister (19, 31).

Henriette's childhood is marked by the death of her mother and the subsequent imposition of an unloving and unlovable stepmother. Her father, as mayor of Saint-Hyacinthe and a prominent public figure, was not often available, yet she remained closely attached to him. Angéline has also lost her mother as a young child (and Mina has lost both her parents). For Henriette, obstacles to her union with Maurice come from her stepmother. For Angéline they come, initially, from her father. Although both Maurices have more liberal views than the parent opposed to them, they appear to be less forceful characters than the diarists themselves. Henriette becomes progressively more sure that she wishes to marry her Maurice. Angéline apparently becomes less and less sure, to the point that she refuses to do so. Mina shares Henriette's fondness for the Cinderella model (53, 72), but with less happy results.

Some of the similarities are no doubt coincidental. Was the name Maurice very popular at that time? It happens also to be the name of Eugénie de Guérin's brother, the poet Maurice de Guérin, and this may account for Conan's use of it.[7] There is no mention of Eugénie de Guérin in Dessaulles's diaries. Other elements are circumstantial in the case of Dessaulles (the death of her mother and Maurice's profession), whereas in a fiction they must be assumed to be incorporated for some purpose. Neither Henriette nor Angéline considers writing as a career, although both Dessaulles and Conan actually became writers. At the time of writing her diary Dessaulles could not know that this would happen; the fact that it later became possible was due in part to the precedent set by Félicité Angers, who by publishing *Angéline de Montbrun* under the pseudonym of Laure Conan and in spite of many scruples (Smart 1988, 44–6) found a solution not envisaged by her fictional diarist.

Henriette Dessaulles kept her journal from an early age and terminated it on her marriage, when her need for a confidant was filled by Maurice. She returned to writing when he died. Angéline de Montbrun is depicted as having no urge to write, until the death of her father and the disappearance of Maurice and Mina create a void in her life. While Dessaulles's diary is forward-looking, anticipating future possibilities, Angéline's is retrospective. This is possible, within the fiction, because of the formal relationship of her diary to the other parts of the novel. In the case of Dessaulles, novelistic elements intruded into the diary, as Henriette, unaware of the future, assigned herself roles as heroine and addressed hypothetical readers. In *Angéline de Montbrun* the diary is incorporated into a text pre-defined as a novel; the movement is from *récit* to the representation of *discours* in a simulated situation, rather than the reverse. Whereas Dessaulles's diary finally conforms to the Cinderella model, ending with a marriage, Conan's novel evolves from fairy tale to hagiography.

### Angéline's diary: Formal aspects

The diary in *Angéline de Montbrun* occupies half the book – the last ninety pages in a total of one hundred and ninety (Fides 1967). The preceding sections are composed primarily of correspondence (eighty-five pages), in which Angéline is seen from the outside and from various points of view: those of her friend, Mina; Mina's brother, Maurice, who wishes to marry Angéline; and her father, Charles de Montbrun. Only two of thirty-one letters are written by Angéline herself, and these reveal little about her. This rare example of epistolary fiction in Quebec has mostly been disregarded by critics as of little interest, with the notable exception of Patricia Smart (1988), who emphasizes the role of Mina as Angéline's alter ego, representing a rebellious double in the letters, a situation reversed in the journal. Critical attention to the narrative techniques of the novel has tended to focus on the short third-person summary of intervening events (85–8): the father's accidental death shortly before the wedding was to take place, followed by Angéline's illness and Mina's entry into the convent, Angéline's loss of her beauty through a fall, and the subsequent cooling of Maurice's love that leads her to break off their engagement. These three pages serve as a pivot between the 'earthly Paradise' depicted in the letters (which anticipate its continuation) and 'Paradise lost,' the dominant theme of Angéline's journal, which finally represents the attempt to earn a place in heaven.

No editorial frame is needed here, as the letters themselves provide the expository information necessary later to understand references in the diary. The apparently omniscient narrator of the bridging section does not use the first-person pronoun, nor explain how the letters and the diary come to be available for publication. As Rosmarin Heidenreich has pointed out (1979, 41), there is a tension in the third-person section between two voices, one of them impersonal and 'objective,' the other personally involved and sympathetic. As in Sartre's *La Nausée*, the reader is left not knowing whether Angéline is dead – though in the diary she claims that she will destroy it before disappearing (165) – or whether an intradiegetic character (possibly Angéline herself) might be responsible for the transformation of letters and diary into a novel. The few footnotes (59, 104, 126, 151) include one explaining who someone was (104), inferring the control of a character who is part of the fiction. The occasional use of initials or suspension marks rather than full names conforms to a traditional technique for creating an impression of non-fiction in a fictional context (for example, 62, 179; see Raoul 1980, 15–18).

Internal references to the diary and the diary-writing process are few in this instance, indeed the only explicit ones are to the diarist's regret at not having kept a journal before (131) and her intention to follow the example of Véronique Désileux, another lonely and ugly woman, and later destroy her own journal (165). The notion of keeping a diary is nevertheless pervasive: Mina mentions that Angéline's mother also left a notebook, the source of information on her first day as a wife (25). The diary code is sufficiently well established that the reader accepts these 'feuilles détachées' (89; torn out but not destroyed?) as authentic, that is, written by Angéline in ignorance of the outcome, and for her eyes alone. Although she plans to leave her house to Maurice, as a constant (ambivalent) reminder of her (111), and is tempted to write to him (140), nowhere does she mention the possibility of giving or leaving him her diary. Indeed, she does not want him to see it (101). References to Eugénie de Guérin (50, 117), who continued to address her journal to her beloved brother, Maurice, even after his death, recall this model of devotion to the dear departed, expressed by means of a diary.

The journal entries are regular and dated. They cover the period from 7 May to 7 November of an unspecified year, three years after her father's death, which occurred on 20 September.[8] The diary starts one week after her return to her home, Valriant, for the first time since her illness. Occasional longer entries interrupt the flow of regular, short, reflective ones. The distribution is as follows:

| 1 = number of pages | | | | 2 = number of entries | | |
|---|---|---|---|---|---|---|
| 3 = number of longer entries | | | | 4 = letters | | |

|    | May | June | July | August | September | October | November |
|----|-----|------|------|--------|-----------|---------|----------|
| 1: | 13  | 13   | 14   | 14     | 18        | 13      | 15       |
| 2: | 11  | 7    | 17   | 19     | 16        | 11      | 3        |
| 3: | 1   | 0    | 1    | 3      | 3         | 1       | 1        |
| 4: | 1   | 2    | 0    | 1      | 1         | 1       | 2        |

Six of the longer entries provide further information about the past, from Angéline's perspective. These are not in chronological order, but related, as in real diaries, to specific reminders that evoke the occasion.[9] The order is: (1) her father's death (20 May); (2) the night before (7 July); (3) an accident on horseback, when she was saved by Maurice (4 August); (4) her reactions after the death of her father (17 August); (5) Maurice's concern for her when she was ill (1 September); (6) her breaking off of their engagement (6 October). Three of the longer entries are not primarily narrative in function: one (15 August) expresses her inner conflict; a second (19 September) discusses her father's character; a third (25 September) comments on the historian Garneau and conveys her patriotism. The letters include four to Mina, one from Véronique Désileux, one from a missionary who knew her father, and a final one from Maurice, followed by Angéline's answer, which concludes the book.

As many critics have pointed out, nothing happens in this last part of the novel, which serves to review the past and re-affirm her decision not to marry Maurice. In this sense, as Heidenreich claims (44), the dates are largely irrelevant. The main function of the diary in the economy of the fiction is to enable the reader to identify with Angéline, who in the previous sections appeared only as an object of admiration, desire, or pity. The re-invoking of past happiness in the journal underlines the narrator's present misery and sense of loss, and her conviction that she has no future. This use of the diary as elegy and post-mortem does not prevent it from also being the vehicle of a transformation of the narrator, through writing. All the essential dimensions of the journal (self-perception and projection, the passing of time, and the production of a text through writing) are illuminated in this example by the theory of narcissism.

## Narcissistic identification: Self/Other confusion

François Gallays (1985) has shown convincingly, using concepts developed by André Green and Guy Rosolato, that the relationship between Angéline and her father is typical of narcissistic identification. It is necessary to recapitulate the much quoted characteristics of their mutual mirroring, as described by Mina and Maurice in their letters, before considering further symptoms of narcissism illustrated in Angéline's journal.

The striking resemblance between Charles de Montbrun and his daughter is repeatedly emphasized. Both like to contemplate their own reflection in each other's face or portrait (27). As Mina says, 'il y a de bons miroirs ici' (75). Angéline looks nothing like her mother (17); she is made in her father's image, both physical and 'moral' (39). According to him, she shares his character, although there is little in the first part to demonstrate this, apart from her desire to 'démondaniser' Mina. Charles is represented as an authority figure, whereas Angéline is docile and obedient (16, 27). He wears 'magic armour' (75) that makes him the undesiring object of the desire of others: Gallays connects this to the 'carapace narcissique' (Gallays, 15). Angéline, on the other hand, is not impervious to Maurice's seduction: she does not laugh at his declaration of love, as her father expects (33, 34), and learns to blush like the heroine of one of the novels she has never read (19, 36).

Angéline and her father are always together (for example, 15), and plan to remain so even after her marriage (38). Since Angéline's mother died when Angéline was very young (39, 154), he has filled the function of both father and mother (see Smart 1988, 52 and Blodgett 1988, 17, on the 'vaginal father'). Their symbiotic union may be seen as a prolongation of the primary narcissism experienced by an infant in relation to the mother. Angéline's total absorption in her father is reflected in the scene where she admires the swan admiring itself in the pool (32–3, 37), wishing that Mina could join her, but ignoring Maurice (who is admiring her but has forgotten her father). M. de Montbrun has the ambivalent role of providing both paternal discipline and maternal comfort and affection: he represents both the Law and a refuge from it. The references to Angéline as made in her father's image and being, so to speak, born from him (as Eve from Adam) are part of a web of allusions to Valriant as the Garden of Eden (see Heidenreich, 14, 42). These contribute to the later confusion in the journal between the father and God, the heavenly Father ('Elle vit en lui un peu comme les saints en Dieu,' [16]). Charles, in God's image, appears as all-powerful creator and sustainer of Angéline's universe, which Maurice and Mina seek to enter. Parentless themselves, they are enchanted by the projected image of blissful harmony, unaware that the intrusion of their desire will destroy it (152).[10]

The exclusive dyadic obsession of father and daughter has been the basis of many analyses attributing the main interest of Conan's novel to its implication of incest. Gallays goes the furthest in interpreting the entry in Angéline's journal describing the night before her father's death (7 July, 120–3; Gallays, 15) as a seduction scene, lacking only sexual consummation, which is conveyed at the symbolic level. Like Cotnam (1973), Gallays sees the desire of Angéline for her father as the source of later feelings of guilt. This explanation seems to me to neglect other aspects of narcissism, as they are revealed in Angéline's journal, and to confuse guilt and shame. If their relationship is seen as modelled on primary narcissism, they do not desire each other, but themselves as a unit: they are already united, and only fear separation. The explicit provocation of the scene in question is their contemplation of Tintoretto's picture of his dead daughter (121, cf. 69). This is one of the many 'too close' relationships mentioned in the novel, which Gallays enumerates (14–15). They include Marie de l'Incarnation and her son, Eugénie de Guérin and her brother, and the twin orphans, Paul and Marie. One might add a more obvious one, that of Maurice and Mina; Mina expresses jealousy of her brother's love for Angéline (67). The web of narcissistic relationships, in which each subject only ever desires the 'same' (a double or self-extension) is part of a system of both gender and generation confusion in *Angéline de Montbrun*.

### Gender and generation / denial of difference: 'C'est pareil'

As previously mentioned, Charles is both father and mother, male and female. As well as his obviously manly characteristics of authority and physical strength (25, 67), and his less obvious 'virile parole' (45) and 'virilité chrétienne' (75), he has an artistic side and is capable of 'la tendresse de la femme' (37). Angéline herself, although her femininity is emphasized by Maurice's perception of her as a 'flower' (in her white muslin dress [16], like Henriette Dessaulles), first appears in a 'costume d'amazone' (15) and is a physically strong (84), sports-loving outdoor person (128). When Maurice asks Charles whether he regrets not having a son, the predictable reply is that Angéline is everything he could wish for (28): that is, both son and daughter to him. She mentions that she received an 'éducation virile' (141). Maurice and Mina are also ambivalent. Maurice is effeminate – a 'poltron' (28) and a 'poète' (29; cf. 167), with his 'nerfs de vieille duchesse' (38). Mina, conversely, is the only one to resist, initially, the charm of 'le montbrunage' (Smart, 59–61) and to express an energetic, positive love of 'les saines jouissances de la vie' (65).

Several critics have remarked on the homosexual overtones of M. de Montbrun's asking Maurice if he has 'quelque objection à *m'épouser* [sic]?' (38) and Maurice's declaration of devotion to him (40). The relationship between Angéline and Mina also has an intensity that would be suspect today. Not only does Mina admit that she feels slighted by Angéline's preference for the men (69), but she sends her friend 'mille tendresses trop tendres' (21) and Angéline replies: 'Si vous saviez comme je vous désire' (46).[11] As Smart has shown, Angéline and Mina function as two sides of the same person, with a role reversal in the middle of the book, and Mina's friend Emma provides a third facet of one female figure. In fact, the names Emma and Mina both function as reversals of the initials *A.M.*

The gender of the loved one is ultimately of little importance in the economy of desire established by Conan, since even marriage is only envisaged if the partners remain pure, that is, chastely disincarnate.[12] The father's own marriage was desexualized, as Angéline's mother's account reveals (25). One is almost surprised that this couple managed to produce a child, and not at all that she should be named 'Angéline' and dedicated to the Virgin Mother. Charles's use of gloves to work in the fields (68) is part of the armour that preserves him from the contamination of contact with the flesh. That desire is repressed between Angéline and her father is evident. Charles' apparently unmotivated 'accidental' death – he catches his gun in a tree and it goes off, killing him (86) – may be read as a symbolic masturbatory ejaculation in response to the recognition of his own desire the night before.[13] In Eden, the wages of sin (carnal knowledge entailing creation, that is, rivalry with God) is death (156), the ultimate castration.

Angéline later wonders whether her father 'loved her too much' (160). Within the context of Conan's novel, it is not incest that she has in mind, but preference for another human being over God. She never recognizes her own devotion as excessive. If anyone is guilty, on this count, it is the father, rather than the daughter, as Heidenreich (44) and Smart (48) have mentioned, and as Angéline herself intimates ('Remettez-lui les peines qu'il a pu mériter,' [160]). Angéline's suffering is, in my view, caused by another dilemma, related to the primary narcissism of generation (self-reproduction) rather than the forbidden object relation evoked by incest. Charles is her father, therefore her life implies his death, since reproduction eventually entails the superfluity and elimination of the origin(al). At forty-two, Charles is already preoccupied with his own death (39) and accepts Maurice as a future husband for Angéline, to replace him when he will no longer be there (39). Yet on his deathbed he neglects to 'bequeath' her to her fiancé, as Maurice mentions in his final letter (183), recommending her, rather, into the care of God, the eternal father-figure (95).

The central question, as Blodgett (19) puts it, is 'Can Maurice become the father?' The answer is that he cannot; he is still like a child (78) and wishes that his father were there to speak for him (16). Nor can Mina become the mother, although she mothers Maurice (49) and would like to marry Charles. Models for mothers are lacking: Mina wishes she had a fairy godmother (53). The model available is a God-like androgyne, whose only fault is that he is mortal and not replaceable. Maurice cannot become the father, because he has no authority, in spite of his study of law (20). Both Mina and Angéline like strong men (20, 30, 72). Charles warns Maurice that he will have to command his wife (44), and

Maurice envisages ordering Angéline to change her mind (80), but when the time comes to act to ensure that the wedding takes place, or to insist on seeing Angéline, he fails. He fails because, unlike Charles, he is not her 'pair' (peer/equal). Above all, he sees only Angéline's beauty, her body; he does not love her for her spiritual qualities, her soul (37). Unlike Charles, he recognizes the positive power of carnal desire, but he expresses it only through his singing (see Belle-Isle 1978). Maurice may end up a 'father,' if his dream of becoming a Jesuit priest is fulfilled (56), as is Mina's corresponding premonition (64) of becoming an Ursuline (sister/mother?). However, he cannot father a child, any more than Angéline can become a mother, except symbolically, as godmother to an Indian convert (173). She finally returns Maurice's mother's ring to him (77, 170). Maurice may have changed by the end, but at the crucial moment he is not worthy of Angéline; and she is right, within her frame of reference, to fear that she may one day blush with shame (in contrast to her previous reasons) for ever having loved him (187).[14] Like Mina, Angéline finds no accessible man her match (77).

The only person who can become the father is Angéline, because she *is* still like him (110). To do so, she must remain 'de Montbrun' (cf. Blodgett, 29), faithful to the name of the father. She must learn to command, which she initially finds hard (52). As Madeleine Gagnon first pointed out (1972, 65), she becomes a buyer and giver of property, acting as an autonomous legal subject. She also passes on her own name, Angéline, to the Indian girl (173). The marriage does not take place, because she, in place of her father, is not willing to sign the contract. Charles was afraid of losing his 'treasure,' Angéline (18). Now in possession of herself, Angéline decides not to give herself away – except in the diary, to herself. The diary replaces her father as confidant, but she is no longer sure of his approval. In fact, she is sure of his disapproval (116, 137), because she is no longer the same: nothing is the same, and that is the reason for the journal. In it she can confess her shame and console herself for her loss – that is, be her own father (and mother).

### Narcissistic injury and shame: 'Séparés'

Much has been made by critics of the fact that the Valriant to which Angéline returns at the beginning of her diary is Paradise lost, and that

Angéline (in the second version)[15] has suffered a 'fall' (Heidenreich, 42; Blodgett, 22). For Heidenreich and others, the enigma posed by the journal is what the sin is that leads to her expulsion from Eden. Discussion centres on a passage where Angéline refers to 'la honte insupportable de la première souillure' (119). It is significant that the word used is 'honte': shame, not guilt. Adam and Eve were expelled from Eden because of their desire to be equal to God, by disobediently acquiring knowledge. As mentioned above, the 'wages of sin is death' (156), and it is the godlike father who dies. Angéline, who has always been obedient, would like to die but is not allowed to (93). Her shame bears more similarity to the awareness of sexuality that led Adam and Eve to cover themselves. Angéline in fact becomes aware of herself as a (rejected) feminine sexual object when she loses her beauty – and veils her face (93). Her fault was to have believed that the innocence (that is, unconditional love) of childhood could continue. According to André Green, the narcissist 'n'a pas commis d'autre faute que d'être resté fixé à sa mégalomanie infantile' (183). Angéline's sense of invulnerability depended on her inclusion in the father's narcissistic projection of omnipotence. Since the father is encoded as God, it is not surprising that he is subsequently conflated with 'our Father in Heaven' (especially by the use of pronouns with ambiguous reference; see Heidenreich, 44 and Gallays, 13). Yet the fact that Angéline cannot be sure that he is in heaven gives her father's death Nietzschean implications (Heidenreich, 45): Is God dead? Her belief in an omniscient and omnipresent father-figure is shaken. Valriant becomes hell (separation from God [180]), or at least purgatory (a waiting place).

It is tempting to accept the view that Angéline's 'disfigurement' provides a pretext for her not to marry Maurice (Cotnam, 157), that it enables her to continue to be obsessed with her father, who is now an admissible object of adoration, since carnal knowledge is no longer a threat. Yet I have to agree with Jean-Cléo Godin, in his article on 'l'amour de la fiancée' in this novel (1964), that the text does not support this interpretation. Angéline's recollection of Maurice's devotion after the death of her father seems to show her willingness at that time to transfer her faith to him: 'Je croyais en lui' (145). Although she postpones the wedding, she still believes before her 'fall' that Maurice will replace her father. She does love him, although she may hope that his love will indeed be pure, that is, unwavering and non-sexual, as her

## Phallic Women and Moral Narcissism 71

father's was (or appeared to be). This attitude is common among bereaved widows, as Rosenblatt shows (1963, 378) – and it has frequently been pointed out that Angéline acts like a widow. Her 'accidental' deformity provides a test for Maurice. If he is good enough to replace Charles, he will still love her, for her soul rather than for her body: the loss of her outward beauty should make little difference. The narrator of the events tells us that Angéline was *surprised* that Maurice's love should cool (88). The narcissistic injury that she receives is not so much the actual loss of her good looks, by which she set little store, but the loss of Maurice's love (see Godin, 14). As Mina said earlier (58), when one is not loved one does not feel lovable, and ceases to love oneself. Angéline has lost the mirror that sustained her self-esteem, and been provided with another that re-defines her as imperfect, as damaged goods. She can only be pitied (88, 101), so she begins to pity herself.

The journal becomes an alternative 'mirror of the soul,' by which she can project, at least to herself, a more favourable image, having first recognized the negative one produced by her separation from Maurice. This separation from the father-substitute brings her back to her father: the resemblance is re-established, first as her face is disfigured and veiled, as his is by death (96), then as the moral resemblance is reaffirmed. Perfection, for both, proves impossible, because of death: however, they may both still aspire to become 'angels' (66, 160; Mina also becomes one [102]).

Angéline wishes to continue to obey her father's orders and turn to God for solace. This is not easy, however, as the death of the father represents, for her, the death of God. It is the end of oneness, the realization of separation: 'Maintenant je sais ce que c'est que la séparation' (48). One might say that 'c'est pareil' becomes 'séparés.' Enclosed in the space they previously shared, surrounded by objects, including their portraits, whose presence confirms his absence and the disfigurement suffered by them both, Angéline exhibits all the symptoms of narcissistic withdrawal, including lack of faith in God. These are closely linked to the melancholic depression associated with mourning, and analysed by Kristeva in relation to feminine narcissism in *Soleil noir* (1987):[16] 'Ma dépression signale que je ne sais pas perdre ... toute perte entraîne la perte de mon être ... et de l'Etre lui-même ... La dépression est le visage caché de Narcisse' (14–15). The 'perte de l'être' implies denial of God. As Kristeva adds, 'La mélancolie s'affirme, si l'on peut dire, dans le doute religieux' (18). The paternal phallus is redefined as lack.

## Moral narcissism: The solution for survival

The loss of belief in wholeness may lead to suicide (Kristeva 1987, 30), or to what André Green calls an 'anorexie de vivre' (23). It is accompanied by a fear of further fragmentation, as the self-representation is shattered. Angéline's journal bears the title 'Feuilles détachées': the entries are fragments, discarded by the trunk that survives ('l'arbre dépouillé tient toujours à la terre' [185]). Re-integration cannot be achieved through memory, which suffers 'une carence de la séquentialité,' paralysed by 'un passé qui ne passe pas' (Kristeva 1987, 29, 70). Time becomes decentred: '...un passé hypertrophié, hyperbolique, occupe toutes les dimensions de la continuité psychique. Et cet attachement à une mémoire sans lendemain est sans doute aussi un moyen de capitaliser l'objet narcissique, de le couver dans l'enclos d'un caveau personnel sans issu' (Kristeva 1987, 71). Kristeva's reference to a 'caveau' echoes surprisingly Maurice's question to Angéline: 'Votre coeur est-il donc tout entier dans son (?) cercueil?' (182). The image of narcissistic withdrawal as incubation ('couver') is one that recurs constantly in diary fiction. According to Kristeva, it conveys 'par-delà la défaillance paternelle, l'adhésion symbolique à notre mère perdue' (1987, 35). This is corroborated in the novel by Angéline's gradual turning away from paternal figures to maternal ones, as Heidenreich and Smart have shown. Even the 'vide océanique' of which Kristeva speaks (1985, 40) is experienced by Angéline (171) but becomes a positive feminine image of re-integration into the cycle of nature (Heidenreich, 55; Smart, 74–6).

While some critics claim that Angéline is simply waiting for death (for example, Brochu 1965, 128), others see her diary as an account of her 'lente remontée vers la vie' (Poulin, 126). Both impressions are possible, because her 'salvation' is dependent on an oxymoron: death is life/life is death (as indicated in the novel's epigraph from Lacordaire: 'L'avez-vous cru que cette vie fût la vie?'). This inversion is brought about through Angéline's evolution from primary narcissism (oneness with the parent), through the failure of narcissistic object choice (Maurice), to moral narcissism (God). These three stages may also be seen as the repression of (incestuous) desire, the suppression of (disappointed) object love, and the sublimation of desire through belief in an (illusory) ideal. Whereas desire was non-existent or denied at the first level, it is dominant at the second and third ones: as Angéline's health improves, she recognizes her own frustration. It is separation (temporal and spatial) from the object(s) of desire that brings awareness of desire, and the reverse, as André Green states: '... le désir est ce qui induit la conscience de séparation spatiale et celle de la dyschronie temporelle avec l'objet' (1983, 20). The only way to remove the shame of loss is 'un nouveau renoncement qui appauvrira les relations d'objet pour la seule gloire du narcissisme' (Green, 183).

### The triumph of virginity: 'C'est paré'

By transferring her desire to God, Angéline attempts to find a remedy for her humiliation, a means to turn defeat into victory. Parenthood as model is replaced by that of the virgin martyrs (175). When she refers to those who arrive in heaven 'ensanglantés' and who are 'not to be pitied' (186), the allusion is to the wounds sustained in defending virginity, not the one inflicted when it is lost, as Gallays (23) suggests. These injuries are narcissistic in another sense – a source of pride and self-satisfaction. They are part of the price to pay for entry to heaven, which must be earned, as the Poles or the young widow earn theirs (167, 176). Angéline is also paying for her father to be there (172), and her suffering may be seen as a sacrifice to expiate his guilt, allowing at-one-ment, on the model of Christ. In the logic of this perspective, the more one suffers, the better it is. This is not necessarily masochistic, as some critics, notably Cotnam, have claimed, since the aim is not eroticized pain, but the stoical elimination of feeling, the deliberate desexualized deferral of fulfilment. This is related to what André Green terms 'le neutre,' which advocates self-denial, self-effacement, and the voluntary renunciation of desire, to achieve a serenely superior state of self-sufficiency characteristic of the 'elect' (1983, 38–9, 45). Thus the narcissistic armour can be reinstated, albeit at the level of the imaginary. Union with the other is replaced by denial of need for the other. 'Séparés' is converted to 'c'est paré.'

Christian religious belief is a form of moral narcissism closely associated with femininity in Freudian theory.[17] For Freud it represents a refusal to accept the reality principle of separation and desire, in favour of illusory fulfilment of the wish for an enduring state of non-separation with an idealized parent. As Green has stated (40–1), narcissism does not accommodate itself to reality. It chooses the imaginary order of the pre-Oedipal stage over the symbolic order based on the phallus as lack. In this, it served the cause of survival for Quebec, as one of Memmi's refuge values that enable the colonized to preserve their self-esteem (see chapter 3). Defeat and loss of *la patrie* were reinterpreted after the failure of the 1838 rebellion as 'exile' – not from France, the uncaring and unfaithful mother (as Maurice mentions [67, 82]), but as exiles in their own land (Conan quotes Crémazie on this [67]), who compensate for dispossession by laying claim to a heavenly utopia.

Several critics have mentioned the patriotic allusions in *Angéline de Montbrun*,[18] especially the long diary entry devoted to the historian Garneau (161–4), another father-figure whose tomb is to be honoured. In Quebec, as in Angéline's story, the father fails, the mother is absent (in heaven), and the son(s) are impotent. They do not match their ancestors: Maurice wishes his father were there to speak for him (16), and Mina finds that contemporary men do not deserve the admiration won by the heroes of history (30). It is left to the daughters and the clergy (dressed as women; see Smart, 52) to proclaim a victory based on moral superiority, self-denial, and deferral, rather than on the patriarchal values of power and possession.

In this perspective, Maurice and Mina are in the first part insufficiently religious, royalist (66), non-materialistic (70–1), and attached to the land (the colonized refuge values). They represent the exogamous threat of the city (Darville) and France: Mina admires 'le tricolore' (31), and Maurice, a secret Bonapartiste (67), goes to France to study. It is Charles's death, in the case of Mina, and Angéline's 'sacrifice' for Maurice, that will 'save' them from 'this world.' The belief that 'this world is not our home,' echoed in a song quoted in Angéline's journal (165), has been analysed as part of a larger feminization of culture in nineteenth-century North America.[19] Rosenblatt's sociological study of grief in nineteenth-century American diaries shows, however, that while lip-service was paid to the belief in an afterlife and eventual reunion, few of those moved to express their loss in a journal were really convinced that their lost loved one was, so to speak, safely stored in the vault of heaven, rather than irremediably unavailable (Rosenblatt, 134). Angéline similarly has difficulty believing that her father can see (98) or hear her (89, 124).

## The diary as substitute and survival mechanism

This is the source of tension in Angéline's journal, as Smart (71) has shown. While trying to look up to heaven, the diarist remains fixated on 'la terre' and the tomb. Henriette Dessaulles's diary showed how one becomes a woman; Laure Conan apparently intended to show in Angéline's diary how one becomes a sexless angel. One is reminded of Virginia Woolf's famous comment on the 'Angel in the House' (1979). Either way, the female subject is defined in relation to a male Other, and in terms of self-sacrifice and renunciation rather than entitlement. Like Henriette, Angéline compares herself to a caged bird (125), though her words could also apply to her sense of being potentially an angel: 'se sentir des ailes et ne pouvoir les déployer' (125). Angéline's dilemma is that she wanted to become a woman and, perceiving this option as removed, is left with the alternative of becoming a saint (like the mother figure to whom she turns for advice [179]) or continuing to act as she has been doing while writing her journal, that is, like a man, defined by herself, in relation to the world. The Cornelian tone of her decision to choose to end her writing project (to do what?) conveys the controlling, phallic aspect of sublimated femininity.

Remaining true to 'herself,' that is, to her father's image of her, in her daily life may in fact no longer be necessary, since she has now produced a moral self-portrait, in the journal, to supersede the physical one at Valriant. Her unbound diary demonstrates her father's view that physical beauty is to the soul only what a book's binding is to its content (141). The whole novel is permeated with the presence of representations (letters, likenesses), which substitute for the presence of the characters concerned. Conversely, God, who appears to be absent, exerts power through the 'real presence' of the Catholic communion (139, 175, 178, 180), to which Francis' conversion in 'Un Amour vrai' was also attributed. The sacrifice of all hope of worldly happiness at the end of Angéline's diary is represented by the burning of Maurice's letters and portrait, just as, in 'Un Amour vrai,' Francis gives up the portrait and hair of Thérèse. The diary may be interpreted as a fetish that has replaced both Angéline's father and Maurice as a self-object (Blodgett, 13, 27), but its ending (if not destruction) shows her recognition that writing about herself does not bring her closer to God. Speaking of Christian diarists, Girard states ironically that 'il faut sans doute être déjà très avancé dans la voie de la sainteté pour s'oublier en parlant de soi' (575–6).

Keeping a diary at a time of bereavement is an ambivalent solution, as Rosenblatt shows: 'A diary may both hinder and facilitate griefwork' (40). It may be therapeutic, but it also serves to prevent forgetting – not so much because it may be reread (Angéline regrets not keeping one before, for that reason [131]), but because at the time of writing one relives past experiences. The 'we-there-then' of memory is placed in stark contrast with the 'I-here-now' of the time of writing, especially when, as in this case, the place is ostensibly the same. Charles's wish that Angéline never forget him is obeyed (17, 91, 93, 119), and his portrait is the only one she keeps. Yet she has reduced her grief to manageable proportions and re-established her self-esteem, by its embodiment in the journal. As Kristeva puts it: 'La perte, le deuil, l'absence déclenchent l'acte imaginaire et le nourrissent ... (mais) ... c'est de désavouer ce chagrin mobilisateur que s'érige le fétiche de l'oeuvre' (1987, 18). Green comments that narration is 'le support du narcissisme' (71). The diary, for Angéline, replaces all her absent potential narratees – including her mother and God, when she could not pray (137, 144, 170). Writing for oneself, according to Kristeva, 'Je fais exister par l'artifice des signes et pour moi-même ce qui s'est séparé de moi' (1987, 34). The polyvalence of signs (such as the pronouns used by Angéline) and the power of prosody allow Angéline herself to regain control, to become a creator/generator (see Kristeva 1987, 109). Aesthetic effect clearly takes over from the illusion of spontaneity in passages such as 6 July (119; rhythmic repetition) and 28 September (165; a series of rhetorical questions). The incorporation of numerous quotations, criticized by Casgrain (1884, 10), may also be seen as an attempt by Angéline to establish a dialogue/polylogue in her isolation. The diary ends when communication is re-established with others (the priest, the nun, Maurice), albeit through letters or a grille (179). The reversal of roles between Angéline and Mina is complete when Mina refuses to see Angéline, alleging illness (179). Writing is more effective than the cloister in combatting death. Writing is also an accessible and effective means to arouse sympathy in others, as Angéline remarks (149) – a narcissistic aim, recognized by Kristeva: 'La création littéraire est cette aventure du corps et des signes qui porte le témoignage de l'affect: de la tristesse, comme marque de la séparation et comme amorce de la dimension du symbole ... Elle transforme l'affect dans les rythmes, les signes, les formes. Le "sémiotique" et le "symbolique" deviennent les marques

communicables d'une réalité affective présente, sensible au lecteur ... et néanmoins dominée, écartée, vaincue' (Kristeva 1985, 32–3). The journal is addressed, by the 'editor,' to others who have 'suffered' (88). If this were a twentieth-century novel, we would expect Angéline to admit to being the editor, to her rebirth as author: the text would reflect the transformation of Félicité *Angers* into Laure Con/an (the *an*onymous feminine?). Kristeva's explanation of the literary work of art as communication of the 'réalité affective' of the author may seem to echo the accusations of 'disguised autobiography' cited earlier: but in a Lacanian framework, the question is not so much 'who speaks?' in a 'fictional' journal, as 'whose desire is spoken?' The constant recognition by modern women readers of something of their own experience in Conan's novel is due, ironically, to what is there/theirs in spite of her intention.

## Conan's other fictional journals: 'A travers les ronces' and 'L'Obscure Souffrance'

In the year following the appearance of *Angéline de Montbrun* Laure Conan published 'A travers les ronces' in *Nouvelles Archives Canadiennes* (1883, 340–61). This is another short fictional journal, prefaced by a letter from the author: at least, one assumes so, since the letter itself is unsigned, but the name 'Laure Conan' is appended to the entire text. The letter (340–1) is addressed to a Madame S.S., once more deploying the 'discreet initials' technique that ostensibly signals nonfiction in a fiction, but actually conveys the fictional code. The writer claims to have come into possession of a diary, of which this is extracts, by some unexplained 'circonstances un peu particulières.' She describes it as an 'entretien d'une âme avec elle-même' but warns her audience not to expect 'ce qui fait le charme du roman.' The diarist, Valérie B., is the only one of Conan's fictional 'intimistes' to be married, but her life is 'aride et monotone,' 'sans sympathie et sans joie.' Like the others, however, she triumphs through self-sacrifice, by resigning herself, with difficulty, to a 'vie ordinaire.' The letter ends with an appeal to the reader: 'Donnez-lui un peu de sympathie et gardez-moi votre bonne amitié.' The apparent distinction between diarist and author serves to conflate them, and recalls Angéline's envy of the writer who can 'inspire sympathy.'

The diary reads like an abbreviated version of Angéline's, without the melodramatic events and ubiquitous quotations that marked the latter. The first part (May to September of one year) uses similar imagery to evoke spring and regret for the past, when earthly happiness seemed attainable. The second part follows an interval of four years. The narrator, like Henriette Dessaulles, has reread her 'cahiers de jeune fille' (354). They ended with hope: 'Faut-il que l'avenir ressemble au passé?' (354), but she now recognizes that there is no change. She has lost all her illusions regarding marriage as a state of bliss. On the eve of *la Toussaint*, the feast of the dead, Valérie abandons her dream of earthly love to seek it instead in God, by means of 'la piété, cette vie des femmes' (352).

One passage in particular recalls *Angéline de Montbrun*, when God is described in terms of a maternal, all-loving, and consoling father (350). This passage and several others from 'A travers les ronces' reappear in 'L'Obscure Souffrance,' published with 'La Vaine Foi,' another fictional diary, in 1919. These two later works echo the earlier period and may date from it; their later publication reveals that Conan had not entirely changed her perspective, in spite of the intervening historical novels. 'L'Obscure Souffrance' is in fact a rewriting and expansion of 'A travers les ronces,' in which the shadowy, oppressive male figure is no longer a husband but a violent, alcoholic father. Conan had published a Temperance pamphlet entitled 'Aux Canadiennes' in 1913. Faustine, the diarist, wishes that her father were dead, and stays with him initially only because she promised her dying mother not to abandon him. She has also, like Dessaulles, had to put up with a disagreeable stepmother. Given the opportunity to move out to live with a motherly aunt, and having some hope of marriage, she nevertheless, on the advice of a priest, chooses the path of self-sacrifice and filial devotion to duty, and returns to her father.

Many elements that are textually the same in 'A travers les ronces' and 'L'Obscure Souffrance' were also present in Angéline's journal.[20] Vegetative imagery is particularly noticeable, culminating in the metaphor of radical pruning as essential to growth: 'On n'appauvrit pas un arbre en arrachant ses feuilles flétries' (*TR*, 356; *OS*, 21). The bitter choice of the phallic tree as model of survival reappears, triumphing over the feminine and vulnerable flower representing a lost dream: 'Entre fleurs avortées et fleurs flétries, la différence est-elle si grande?' (*TR*, 357). 'L'Obscure Souffrance' also shares with the earlier text the artificial linking of the diary entries, and both include a greater emphasis than *Angéline de Montbrun* on the diary-writing activity. Faustine consciously uses the journal as a pastime and as a means to confess, to herself at least, what she cannot confide to anyone else (47). Actual confession to a priest precedes her decision to end the diary, as she finally perceives it as self-indulgent wallowing in regrets and useless dreams. The feminine Faust comes to answer the questions : 'Qui suis-je? d'où viens-je? où vais-je?' (9) in terms of a dominant other, whether it is her father or God. Like Angéline, she is appalled at her own pride in having wanted anything else, covered with shame (34, 46) at not being what she should be, and determined to reconstitute an ideal self as heroic martyr, even if it is only in 'la vie domestique' (54). Her suffering, like Angéline's, will save her father.

## 'La Vaine Foi' (1919)

A similar scenario unfolds in 'La Vaine Foi,' which is based on the same situation as 'Un Amour vrai.' Marcelle is courted by an anglophone Protestant, Benedict Osborne, who thinks that religion, for them both, is 'de nom seulement.' On witnessing the death of an unbeliever who seeks faith at the last minute (a Monsieur *Durville*, recalling the Darvilles of *Angéline de Montbrun*; like Maurice he sings), the diarist realizes the truth of his judgment and sets out to change it. She condemns her own feminine narcissism – her enjoyment of admiration and of her own beauty (79), her 'culte du moi' (78). Inspired by a friend who becomes a nun, Marcelle opts for an 'Invisible Beauté.' Like Angéline she comes to regard the beauty of the soul as a more reliable investment (87), although another minor character echoes Véronique Désileux's remarks on the tragedy of ugliness for a woman.

Marcelle's father, like Angéline's, dies (on 21 September, one day later), but although as charming as M. de Montbrun, he has not been an exemplary Christian. It is left to Marcelle, as to Thérèse in 'Un Amour vrai,' to earn the salvation of a man she loved (her father rather than her fiancé, this time) by sacrificing herself (100). In keeping with the less dramatic tone of the later fictions, she becomes a 'Petite Soeur des Pauvres,' rather than dying. The importance of a name is emphasized once more, through the 'regeneration' of baptism, the 'divine adoption' (91). Those with faith 'ont en eux le ciel' (101) and no longer need ask why they live and die (101). Although, like Angéline, she plans to destroy her journal, Marcelle finally decides to leave it as a 'consolation' for her mother (as the stepmother in 'Un Amour vrai' received Thérèse's).

Marcelle shares the scepticism regarding the durability of men's love expressed by Angéline and Faustine (66), and their refusal to believe that this life can be all there is (67). Like Alissa in Gide's *La Porte Etroite* (see M.-L. Wittenberg 1972) and the Princesse de Clèves (see M.J. Green 1987), she refuses the 'female plot' of marriage as the ultimate happy ending. This was the model in Henriette Dessaulles's diary, and in most nineteenth-century diary fiction by women; Martens does recall one French example with a somewhat similar message, though written by a man – Octave Feuillet's *Journal d'une femme* 1878: '... the heroine renounces the man she loves out of a refined sense of moral scrupulousness; she suffers unspeakably in order to triumph morally ... It is taken for granted that marriage to the right man would mean ultimate happiness for the heroine ... woman's truest nature fulfills itself in her role as wife and mother' (Martens, 102). The main reason for the refusal of Conan's heroines is that the men available are not worthy of them. As Maïr Verthuy has pointed out: 'Le rôle de la Québécoise serait moins de se préserver du mariage avec l'ennemi que de se préserver du mariage tout court, puisque aucun Canadien français n'est digne d'elle' (1986, 401). Men do not share the same aspirations as women, and are not perceived as capable of lasting love. This is strikingly similar to the point of view expressed in Madame de Lafayette's novel. Some of Conan's male characters do show signs of 'improvement,' but only on following the example of a heroic woman who is then no longer available to them. As in *La Princesse de Clèves*, desire is predicated on the inaccessibility of the object, and these women refuse to become objects of consumption or consummation. The ideal husband, as Faustine portrays him, would make his wife feel beautiful ('L'Obscure Souffrance,' 25) and have wings to carry her to heaven. Real men, on the other hand, are earthbound and severe in their judgment of a woman's face.

## Feminine narcissism

Belle-Isle remarked in 1978 that 'L'oeuvre de Laure Conan est très souvent marquée de ce contentement narcissique que ressent la femme devant la reconnaissance de sa "puissance"' (466). Le Moine had claimed earlier that 'Dans l'univers de Laure Conan l'initiative revient à la femme et non à l'homme' (31). In her play of 1886, *Si les Canadiennes le voulaient*, Conan certainly proclaimed that the future of French Canada lay in the hands of its women, not only because of *la revanche des berceaux*, but because men needed leadership. In her fictional journals, women's power may be seen as that of refusing to grant sexual satisfaction to men, rendering them impotent; yet it is also the men's impotence that diverts women's libido into sublimation.

Conan seems to have shared the view expressed by Mina, quoting Madame de Staël: 'une femme qui meurt sans avoir aimé a manqué la vie' (*Angéline de Montbrun*, 77). Henri d'Arles concluded his 1914 study of Conan's works by also quoting Madame de Staël, wondering if for Conan herself 'la gloire' represented 'le deuil éclatant du bonheur' (1919, 38). The many critics who have referred to Conan's supposed physical ugliness (for example, Dumont 1960, 6) seem to imply that her heroines' refusal of men is based on a prior refusal by men of the author, as a woman. However that may be, she projects female characters who prefer to renounce love rather than risk the humiliation of being no longer loved. Their initial feminine narcissism, based on their physical attraction, gives way to the moral narcissism of moral superiority. Not being sought by a man may even become, paradoxically, a sign of success ('Eugénie de Guérin n'a jamais été recherchée,' [*AM*, 50]). All women, for Conan, are torn between the need to be loved ('Je suis une femme qui a besoin d'être aimée' [*AM*, 127]) and the refusal to accept a love that is less than perfect ('Etre aimée comme devant ou malheureuse à jamais' [*AM*, 140]).

This 'all or nothing' attitude is typical of narcissists, in response to narcissistic injury. Conan's fictional journals are encoded as a 'cry from the heart.' Brochu says of 'L'Obscure Souffrance': 'C'est le cri pur de la souffrance, de la honte, du désespoir, de la révolte contre Dieu, qui alterne avec l'expression de la résignation' (1963, 118). This is true of them all. Didier mentions that the emphasis on emotivity, on the expressive function in diary writing, is related to nineteenth-century concepts of femininity: 'Le journal, et d'une façon plus générale l'écriture féminine à cette époque, sont conçus comme une traduction scripturale du *cri*' (41). Faustine sums up the image of the diary as a heartfelt cry to the ideal listener, in her imagined scene with God: 'Le plus tendre des pères ne s'offense pas quand son enfant, trouvant la soumission trop difficile, se jette entre ses bras et lui crie: mon père' (350).

The keeping of a private diary, in these terms, is a vestige of primary narcissism, a last attempt to communicate with the perfect other, who is a double or part of the self. The perception of the diary as a cry for help from the helpless contributes to the image of diary writing as passive and fluid, qualities associated in the nineteenth century with femininity, which caused Amiel, the most famous French diarist, to tell himself 'Tu t'es laissé devenir une femme' (Didier, 106). Yet all Conan's diarists are depicted as using the diary as a means to emerge from the impossible situation of being 'une femme,' after which they abandon it for some form of self-sacrifice involving a choice and active involvement on their part – even if the result is death or the being 'buried alive' that Marcelle envisages, like Mina, in the convent. The paradox of their situation is that all forms of action open to them involve self-abnegation, but this self-denial ultimately becomes self-glorification.

Celibacy was in fact almost a prerequisite for diary writing in the nineteenth century (see Girard, 112–13 and Didier, 74), and not only for women. In the case of Conan's female diarists, one is reminded of the cries of Echo, who in the myth is ignored and abandoned by Narcissus and loses her own image as well as his. Both become disincarnate. Yet the concept of self that is valorized by Conan is based on connectedness to an other: autonomy, attainable through the journal, is renounced as unfulfilling. Time as passing dates, as history, necessarily leads to death and extinction. The timelessness of eternity (of heaven, of the finished text) is deemed preferable. Myth – the imaginary, structured by origin and telos – is mightier than the symbolic order of power politics. In Conan's universe, women choose to remain women, without being subservient to men, by rejecting the male order of 'reality.' We shall now turn to some fictional journals produced in Quebec by male authors in the 1940s, and see how their narcissism compares to that depicted by Laure Conan.

# PART III

# NARCISSISM AND COLONIZED MEN (1940–1960)

CHAPTER SIX

# Masculine Misogyny and Cerebral Abstinence: *Hertel, Baillargeon, Simard*

'Freud discerned similar mental structures in (a) femininity and Christian "illusion"; (b) masculinity and Jewish renunciation of wish; and (c) the human ideal (which is the masculine ideal) and the postreligious, psychoanalytic "scientific attitude." One can see that these three groups constitute a critical hierarchy ...'

JUDITH VAN HERIK (1985), 2

## From communion to individuality

The years following the publication of Conan's last fictional journals in 1919 saw the flowering of the diary novel in France. Between 1920 and 1940 most major authors produced at least one work in this form, including Bernanos, Duhamel, Gide, Martin du Gard, Mauriac, Romains, and Sartre (see Raoul 1980, 114–15). Yet the same period in Quebec produced very few mediocre examples of marginal interest, such as Des Bois's *Journal d'un étudiant* (1925) and Joseph Raiche's *Journal d'un curé de campagne* (1927). Turcotte justifiably assigns both of these to the category of 'fourre-tout anecdotique.' They provoke him to ask whether, even in this form, diary fiction in Quebec serves to 'décanter le dépaysement et l'impotence' (1969, 16). That this should be the case is not surprising if this generation of young men can be assumed to resemble Conan's Maurice Darville. There was a shift during this period, however, in the nature of the predominant religiosity. Still aligned with patriotism, Catholicism in Quebec espoused an ideology similar to that of the right-wing Action française movement, associated with Barrès and his 'culte du moi.' The concept of the self was changing, as shown by Pierre Hébert in his study of real diaries in Quebec.

There were still traces of nineteenth-century messianism in the nationalism of Lionel Groulx or Henri Bourassa, and the utopian dream of theocracy (La Laurentie) favoured by the young intellectuals of La Relève in the 1930s.[1] Yet the aim was to establish a new (old) 'mère-patrie' firmly located in this world rather than the next. Visits to France and greater exposure to French texts contributed to the displacement of the more sentimental and feminine aspects of the Catholic zeal displayed by Casgrain or Conan and typical of North America (Douglas 1977). The mystical virgin martyr is superseded as model by a male intellectual hero who rationalizes and ultimately questions his religious belief.

According to Van Herik's analysis of Freudian theory (1985), this corresponds to a shift from an emphasis on the feminine or imaginary (wish-fulfilment), pietistic side of Christianity, to the severe, patriarchal phallogocentrism represented by the Judaic tradition, based on the Word and the Law. The parallel modification of the concept of self is from communion or connectedness, associated with nostalgia for primary narcissism, to the primacy of differentiation. Separation is no longer perceived as disastrous, but as a hierarchically superior sense of autonomy. There is a move to individual self-definition, beyond adhesion to the group. Self-conscious analysis of the self and the world replaces intuitive identification with others. The symbolic order, based on the 'Nom/Non du Père' dominates emotional attachment to a reassuring mother-figure. As Hébert (1988) puts it, the self is no longer 'occulté' through an ethic of self-abnegation and collectivity, but 'affirmé' as the centre of the universe. One example given by him is François Hertel's concept of the self, as developed in his *Journal philosophique et littéraire* published in 1961.

Hertel (Rodolphe Dubé, 1905–85)[2] was also the author of two fictional journals. He wrote the first, *Le Beau Risque* (1939), when he was a Jesuit priest; the second, *Journal d'Anatole Laplante* (1947), when he had left the priesthood and spent some time in France. A comparison of the two throws light on the emergence of the cerebral, misogynist, male self in the Quebec context and the particular type of narcissism involved.

**Hertel, *Le Beau Risque* (1939): 'The (Catholic) young man'**

This novel presents three levels of narration. On the first, a nameless

## Masculine Misogyny and Cerebral Abstinence 87

editor claims in an *avant-propos* that the manuscript was found in a parcel left by a 'vieux camarade de collège,' Father Henri Berthier, who has gone to the Far East as a missionary. Whether this voice can be attributed to Hertel is complicated by a dedication from 'F.H.' to a friend who is a missionary in China, 'R.P. Léo-Paul Bourassa S.J.' The manuscript is described as 'une sorte de journal rétrospectif, composé aux heures perdues' (7). The combination of 'journal' and 'rétrospectif' is an apparent contradiction in terms. The diary model is further problematized by the fact that the 'diarist,' 'oublieux de lui-même ... raconte l'histoire d'un autre ... d'un petit gars de chez nous.' In fact, Berthier's account is that of his relationship with a pupil, Pierre Martel (an echo of Hertel?), who kept a diary on Berthier's advice: '... tenez un journal où vous consignerez, chaque soir si possible, victoires et défaites' (21). The retrospective narrative is interspersed with extracts from the diary written by Pierre and finally given by him to Berthier, who therefore functions as reader of Pierre's text as well as narrator/commentator on the events from his own perspective.

Berthier is attracted to this adolescent, in the all-male world of the 'collège': 'Qu'est-ce qui m'attire en lui? Une physionomie d'adolescent tourmenté ... Assez grand pour son âge, il est aussi nerveux que musclé' (13). We learn that Pierre is disappointed in his father, who is 'mondain' and may be 'le principal obstacle à l'ascension de son fils vers la virilité' (28). The only quality he appreciates in his son is his ability to play hockey. His disapproval of Pierre's taste for reading, and poetry in particular, will be compensated for by the encouragement of Berthier, who becomes the boy's 'spiritual father.' The relationship is obviously one of narcissistic object choice for Berthier, who sees in Pierre a double representing himself at that age. In the epilogue, he maintains that his only duty is to 'tenter chaque jour, en reculant chaque jour d'un pas, de reconquérir les lambeaux de sa jeunesse' (131). The underlying implication of homosexual desire is apparently just as unconscious as that of incest in *Angéline de Montbrun*.[3]

Pierre hides his journal from his mother (45). Rather than a 'spiritual' record of the progress of his relationship with God, it becomes an account of his intellectual development and of his disillusionment with women. Only his sister, Claire, is untainted by sexuality and remains 'l'idéale jeune fille, celle à qui je les compare toutes' (79). Frustrated by her lack of education ('Je ne suis qu'une fille. On ne m'a pas ouvert les beaux livres' [88]), Claire succumbs to an illness as arbitrary as Angéline de Montbrun's: 'cette syncope soudain, cette embolie du pauvre *cerveau glacé*' (108, my emphasis). Whereas Pierre owes his evolution to books and Berthier, 'Claire a poussé seule ... à travers la désolation des herbages revêches' (an echo of Conan's 'A travers les ronces'). She represents the Eternal Feminine: 'L'âme des aïeules peut-être, cette âme qui ne se transmet pas au moyen des mots comme les âmes des hommes ... chantait spontanément dans la sienne' (108–9).

For Pierre to attain the status of 'un homme,' which he finally achieves (130), words are essential, both those he reads and those he writes: 'Il me semble que je deviens meilleur quand j'écris. Cette fièvre me délivre des autres' (44). Like Maurice Darville, he wishes to remain pure, that is, chaste, and all women are therefore perceived as a threat: 'L'âme féminine est si roublarde, sous ses airs ingénus' (117). It is by celibacy and by writing his diary – which once more acquires the masturbatory function spoken of by Didier (1976, 115) – that he will resist his father. The latter believes that poets are useless, 'jamais ils ne réalisent quoi que ce soit' (49). Through literature, Pierre will combat the Americanization of Montreal (44, 80–1), with its English signs and posters, by seeking French models: 'Je voudrais être français ... il me semble qu'on vit là-bas. Ici on tâtonne' (44). Yet the combination of Frenchness and celibacy smacks of impotence: 'notre congénitale impuissance' (65). His disappointment with the flesh is inextricably entwined with an inability to 'jouir de la vie' (76); he shares the generalized French-Canadian 'honte d'être ce que nous sommes' (114). However, on the death of his sister and of his grandfather, who represented the past (the ideology of Conan), he feels reborn: 'Je suis un jeune homme. Je suis le jeune homme ... Je vais à la vie ... Je nais ... de toutes ces cendres qui se refoidissent derrière moi. Le passé est bien mort' (119).

Dessaulles's diary and Conan's fictional journals demonstrated how one becomes a woman, or an angel. In *Le Beau Risque* Hertel provides a case study for the development of the young Catholic male Québécois, a double of himself. In the later semifictional writings of Anatole Laplante, written after he himself had reverted to secular life and turned to existentialism, he depicts a man of forty. Still obsessed by Pascal's wager regarding the existence of God, but less inclined to consider Catholic faith a 'beau risque,' he is concerned with a definition of the self that is far removed from the earlier one.

### Hertel, *Journal d'Anatole Laplante* (1947)

Pierre Martel was in search of an 'âme soeur' (114) and tired of his journal once he perceived it only as a means to 'me trouver en présence d'un "moi" que je voudrais meilleur, plus fort' (114). In the *Journal d'Anatole Laplante* and the preceding volumes that introduced the same characters (*Mondes chimériques* [1940] and *Anatole Laplante, curieux homme* [1944][4]), Hertel exploits the concept of *dédoublement* by creating two characters: Anatole Laplante and a fantastic, surrealistic projection of his 'imaginary self' named Charles Lepic. In the *Journal d'Anatole Laplante*, Laplante claims to have been 'born' (as a writer) through his meeting with Lepic: 'J'ai eu un ami, Lepic ... Aimer, être aimé, l'amour? Des mots ... qui recouvrent le néant du désir charnel ... La confiance seule est durable ... c'est l'amitié' (21). Once more, heterosexual relations are rejected in favour of an (imaginary) homosexual friendship. Lepic is in fact depicted as 'doux comme une femme et fort comme un homme' (26), an androgyne reminiscent of Charles de Montbrun. Like Angéline de Montbrun, Laplante believes that one must be loved in order to fulfil one's potential, and he attributes his 'emergence' to the mirror image provided by Lepic: 'Que m'a apporté cet ami ... il m'a apporté moi-même' (21). Told by Lepic to choose between thought and action, he makes the right decision, choosing *both*, because of his new-found confidence, his narcissistic 'soif de grandeur' (22).

This passage, entitled 'Naissance au journal philosophique,' follows two prefatory letters: one from Lepic to Laplante, and Laplante's answer. The rest of the 'journal' is divided into two parts. The first, like Berthier's, is labelled 'Journal rétrospectif.' In it, the narrator recounts his life, from age five in 1910 (corresponding to Hertel's age) to 1924, recognizing that, through memory, 'on s'est organisé une histoire cohérente' (25). As a child he loved nature, which is once more construed as the 'feminine': 'J'aimais la nature, comme on aime une femme, sans comprendre pourquoi on aime ces *choses*' (my emphasis). He adds, 'Maintenant je ne les aime plus guère' (26). Thirty years later, he feels some nostalgia for his lost sensuality: 'je savais alors communier à l'existentiel, co-naître, comme je ne le sais plus aujourd'hui' (26). However, the loss of 'animality' (27) is the price of becoming a man. The change is effected (as Van Herik also explains) by a 'dressage,' which forces the acceptance of 'renunciation' of wish-fulfilment as representing, paradoxically, a force of 'volonté' (27). The moral narcissism of *Angéline de Montbrun* is exposed for what it is: *orgueil* posing as humility, humiliation disguised as triumph.

Laplante explains how he resolved to become a poet, with his mother's help: she was good in French and 'bien élevée,' whereas his father was not (29–30). He also mentions that he would have liked to read Lamartine's *Jocelyn* (a fictional journal in verse in which the diarist is a priést), but it was on the Index of books forbidden by the Church (29). The shift from the sensual to the symbolic order is seen as inevitable: 'Il est un temps pour naître à soi-même par le monde ambiant et un autre pour renoncer à ce monde en s'exprimant' (31). His first attempts at writing use 'des pseudonymes prudents' (34) and are accompanied by a desire for God: 'Plus tard on parvient à être heureux par la mort des désirs. A vingt ans, seul le désir de Dieu peut assouvir la soif de désirer' (35). In the rest of the 'Journal,' this evolution towards the state that Green calls *le neutre* is equated with the power of thought. The mind is desexualized but nevertheless encoded as masculine.

## The male self as French intellectual

For Laplante, as for Hertel, man is characterized by his ability to think: 'Le cerveau bien lubrifié pense juste et se rend compte à tous les instants des insuffisances de l'agir humain, cette grimace extérieure où la personne croit s'engager profondément, alors que la personne est forclose et centrée sur soi et que l'acte qui, seul, compte est l'acte intime' (38). The 'acte intime' that counts, for Hertel as for his fictional diarist, is not sexual. In his own *Journal philosophique et littéraire* he claims explicitly that sex had little importance for him, and that he believed Freud's ideas to be those of an 'obsédé sexuel' (1961, 43). For him, 'forniquer requiert un effort trop considérable' (27) and 'l'amour littéraire est un mythe fallacieux' (25–6).[5] The intimacy he refers to is that of introspection, based on *dédoublement* and typical of the *journal intime*. The self analyses the self, and 'Réfléchir, c'est conquérir,' as Laplante puts it (63). Here he echoes Plotinus' conception of Narcissus as the archetypal reflective Thinker whose self-contemplation entails disincarnation (see Hudot 1976 and Kristeva 1983, 142ff).

Yet Laplante recalls Pascal's dictum that 'qui veut faire l'ange fait la bête.' The 'homme de pensée' who tries to 'jouer à l'ange' (another reminder of *Angéline de Montbrun*), to be a pure spirit (54, 58), forgets that man is inseparable from time and space and from his own body (135). Our most sublime thoughts are at the mercy of our digestive system: 'Nos pensées les plus hautes sont engagées dans une aventure ... avec le navet que nous digérons' (133–4). This rapprochement was already suggested earlier, when Laplante warns any potential readers: 'Pardonnez-moi, lecteurs bénévoles, de vous faire assister à ma digestion cérébrale. Je ne vous ferai grace d'aucun borborygme' (95). The metaphor of books/thought as food for the mind, of cogitation as digestion, is parallel to that of writing as (pro)creation, excremental purge, or masturbatory wasting of seed. While the last two images are implied at several points throughout Laplante's notebook, it is creation that is the aim. The writer/poet is able to 'singer Dieu' by creating through the Word (45), which is thought incarnate (92). The illusory desire for union with God and for access to 'le Ciel' (as in *Angéline de Montbrun*) is abandoned in favour of faith in the self. Heaven and hell are within us, and the author is God. In the Pirandellian Conclusion appended to Laplante's journal, Hertel explains that he is about to murder Laplante and Lepic, the products of his 'cerveau,' who represent his 'âme' (144). They will not 'see God,' because he did not make them immortal; yet they will not die, because they are idea(l)s, and 'l'esprit est indestructible' (146). He ends by addressing God: 'Ils sont nés de moi, mais ils viennent de vous. Ce sont les seuls fils que je reconnaisse. J'ai pu les tuer sans vous offenser, parce que je les ai faits d'esprit et que l'esprit est indestructible' (146). The author and God are one – the father, or source of creation – and the only immortality is intellectual and literary rather than spiritual. Contrary to Angéline de Montbrun, Laplante sees 'se fondre en Dieu' as self-assassination. Whereas Angéline rejoiced that 'l'arbre dépouillé tient toujours à la terre,' perceiving self-immolation/voluntary castration as a source of spiritual strength, Laplante hypothesizes that 'Dieu ne veut point pour amis des impuissants, des ébranchés' (90). For him, sexual abstinence is nevertheless part of the glorification of the mind or 'esprit.'

This type of 'esprit' is associated throughout Laplante's journal, as also in Hertel's, with France. France is the source of Cartesian thought, a 'paradis perdu' representing the triumph of 'la justesse, l'équilibre et la mesure' (49). It is a model for the world: 'C'est en France que se compose, jour après jour, l'art de vivre ... tous les pays sont des colonies spirituelles de la France' (47). Having arrived at middle age, Laplante exclaims: 'De ma maturité je m'enivre comme d'un vin. C'est un grand vin français qui ne fait point tourner la tête, mais qui irrigue le cerveau généreusement' (38). The French also have laughter on their side (wit, the other meaning of *esprit*), '... vaccin contre la plus dérisoire des démences humaines: le culte de soi' (40). Like Pierre Martel, Laplante would rather live in France. In Quebec he feels isolated, and 'La solitude, même quand elle est aimée, pèse sur le dos comme un gros mouton' (16). This reminder of Saint John the Baptist with his sheep, the emblem of Quebec, is only one of many elements in Laplante's journal that reappeared in Jean Larose's *La Petite Noirceur* (1987). Both works convey the message of the superiority of French (and masculine) abstract symbolic thought over Canadian/Anglo-Saxon 'physical' pragmatism and iconic visual imagery, associated with the feminine 'imaginary' order.[6] As discussed in chapter 3, this perception is at odds with the American one of physical force and practical technology (accompanied by anti-intellectualism) as typifying masculinity, and spirituality or artistic inclination as feminine. In both *Le Beau Risque* and the *Journal d'Anatole Laplante* the diarist's father disapproves of literary activity for his son and would prefer him to excel in sports and study science, while the mother is more encouraging, on the American model.

### The wandering Jew and the 'Canadien errant'[7]

In his *Journal philosophique*, Hertel admits that 'On ne veut pas étudier des hypothèses où l'on cesserait d'être des fils de Dieu, des élus' (1961, 10). The Québécois, as discussed in chapter 3, perceived themselves in the nineteenth century as a people with a messianic mission and a promised land, implying a comparison with the Jews. In the 1930s and early 1940s, when antisemitism was strong in Quebec, the analogy was less popular (see Teboul 1975 on images of the Jew in Quebec). Hertel uses it in the *Journal d'Anatole Laplante* to convey the sense of exile experienced by those Québécois, like himself, who wished to define themselves as French. From New Zealand, the end of the world that provides refuge to this Irish Jew (!), Lepic, Laplante's double, writes to him advising him to remain in Quebec, although it is the only place where Descartes is not recognized as a great philosopher (13), and al-

Masculine Misogyny and Cerebral Abstinence 93

though he is afraid that all Jews may eventually be banned (9). Laplante replies that Lepic was right to leave: 'C'était ton droit de Juif errant ... Mon destin à moi, c'est d'être crucifié sur place' (14). According to Lepic, Quebec has a great past and possibly a great future, but the present is impossible: 'Je suis la vie; ton pays, c'est la mort' (9). Only nations with great self-confidence, like England and France, can accept minorities such as Jews, but if he went there he would become an 'homme,' like them, losing his 'fantaisie' (9–10). Hertel, after publishing this novel, did in fact return to France, to stay there in exile for most of his life. This occurred after he had admitted his complete loss of faith in Catholicism, over which Laplante still hesitates; Hertel concluded, like Laplante, that Quebec was 'en partance vers la totale noirceur' (15).

In a passage on Claudel in Laplante's *Journal* there is a further illuminating comment on the relationship between Catholic Christianity and Judaism, which reflects Van Herik's conclusions regarding Freud's distinction between them. Whereas Lepic, although supposed to be Jewish, identifies with Christianity because of the importance it gives to the imaginary ('moi, qui suis avant tout un chrétien,' [11]), Claudel, the Catholic poet and playwright, is represented (by Lepic, quoted by Laplante) as writing in the Judaic tradition, returning to the Old Testament (44) in which the word creates and imposes order (45). Laplante, the intellectual, also chooses order and renunciation over intuitive wish-fulfilment. Whereas Lepic decides to remain (literally) marginal, to *not* become 'un homme' (in spite of his phallic name), Laplante's efforts are towards identification with the universal and prescriptive (although his name associates him with nature and the feminine). Even when he claims that he wants to 'livrer aux hommes une pensée à moi' (15) and that he is 'la voix anonyme de tous ceux qui ne sauraient s'exprimer' (15), one has the impression that he is, rather, the 'porte-voix' of a 'universal' accumulation of metaphysical reflection. The ubiquitous use of 'on,' 'nous,' and 'l'homme' attests to this. Here universal means French, although Laplante also dreams of a universal language (127).

'Réfléchir, c'est conquérir' (63), and the man who reflects cannot remain innocent. He must judge, and in doing so forfeits the capacity to create intuitively, by the imagination (92). He loses his 'animality' and 'il ne s'aime plus lui-même' (51). Rather, he is tired of himself, 'on voudrait se divorcer ... se fuir ... On ne veut pas s'avouer qu'on est faible et désemparé ... que la vie est une noyade perpétuellement en

cours' (52). The allusion to drowning recalls one version of the Narcissus myth. Yet, as Hertel remarks in his *Journal* (1961, 73), self-preoccupation may not necessarily have an 'aboutissement narcissiste,' if it leads to the recognition that one is not 'beau,' and that one is 'banal' (cf. *Journal d'Anatole Laplante*, 52). In spite of this, the intellectual self reemerges as superior, because of its effort (typified by Anatole Laplante) to 'voir clair' and to 'se maîtriser' (42). On the one hand, 'je me résigne à n'être qu'un homme' (38); on the other, 'c'est en se penchant sur soi qu'on a plus de chances de rencontrer Dieu' (52).

According to Laplante, artists are a special category, who remain self-satisfied and self-sufficient; they are 'des êtres lunaires,' 'des êtres d'exception' (60), wreaking havoc among the ordinary mortals around them: 'Quand l'être lunaire est homme son inconscience nous paraît monstrueuse. Quand il est femme on se croit d'abord dans le registre du normal' (60). Once more, femininity is associated with narcissism (in a negative sense), with 'inconscience,' and with dissociation from the real ('Les êtres lunaires existent fort peu,' [61]). Lepic is an 'être lunaire.' Laplante, however, by switching his allegiance from Quebec to France, becomes 'un homme de pensée,' and author of his *Journal*.

## The diary as autobiographical essay

The *Journal d'Anatole Laplante* is typical of the *journal intime* in its preoccupation with the indefinability of the self ('Qui suis-je?' [22]), and with its *dédoublement*; also in its fragmentary nature and in its recognition that the present is non-existent, being only a pivot between past and future, which are both imaginary. Otherwise, it does not follow the model of dated diary entries, with emphasis on the time of narration. The last section of part 1 and the whole of part 2 are presented as discussions of specific topics, from 'Claudel' to 'Le gouffre intérieur.' The first part ends with a 'Lettre ouverte aux hommes d'ordre (Extrait du testament d'Anatole Laplante),' the second with a 'Confession philosophique' beginning ' J'aurai bientôt cent ans. Les années passent si vite ...' (131). As Van Roey-Roux says of Hertel's 'non-fictional' *Journal philosophique*, which adopts a similar format, 'Si cette oeuvre offre le caractère discontinu du journal, elle ne fournit aucune date. L'aspect hétéroclite de l'ensemble ne permet pas d'y voir des mémoires ni une autobiographie. Il s'agit tout au plus d'un essai, au sens large du

terme' (1983, 32-3). Yet the 'essai' also would have to be redefined, to include this type of pot-pourri. There is a sense in which it is closer to the diary (or notebook) because the thoughts expressed remain, precisely, at the stage of 'essai': they are not coherently developed to a logical conclusion. The text represents an initial attempt at writing, rather than the polished result of several drafts.

The fact that Hertel returns to several of the same themes in his own *Journal* and still regards his ideas as incipient, rather than fully developed, implies a decision on his part to refuse to conclude, and an imprisonment in a web of associations, which are also typical of the *journal intime*. Hébert does include the *Journal philosophique* in his study of the diary in Quebec. The reason, as mentioned above, is that the 'moi' is 'affirmé' in a way new to Quebec. The relationship of fiction to non-fiction, in the case of the 'notebook' form, is once more problematized because the 'moi' in question seems to be the same, whether it is attributed to Hertel or Laplante/Lepic. Some passages are virtually interchangeable. This is all the more obvious, since in both cases the narrator, while claiming to be unique, indeed a rare case in Quebec, also announces that he represents not only all French-Canadians but man. Man, here, is meant to be read as universal, but is actually encoded as specifically excluding women.

Turcotte designates the type of text represented by the *Journal d'Anatole Laplante* as a 'journal-essai' (1969, 23ff). The other example he mentions is *Les Médisances de Claude Perrin*, published two years earlier by Pierre Baillargeon. The two works have a great deal in common, for both are based on a narcissistic conception of male intellectual superiority predicated on misogyny.[8]

### Baillargeon, *Les Médisances de Claude Perrin* (1945/1973): The fictional journal as self-portrait

The similarities between the works include a preface apparently by the author, although Baillargeon does not claim to know his admittedly fictional narrator. Here, the preface attempts to distance the 'editor' from Perrin, and to justify the publication of 'ce qui n'était pas d'abord sûrement destiné à l'être' (9). Some ambiguity remains as to whether the referent is Baillargeon's 'novel' or Perrin's notebook. Excuses are proffered for Perrin's cynicism that do not apply to the author:

Baillargeon was not one month away from death and had not previously been denied publication. Yet critics read the text as at least semi-autobiographical, and all at the time equated the fictional narrator with the author.[9] Like Hertel's Laplante, Perrin also appears in other works, in this case particularly *Commerce* (1947). Though written after the *Médisances*, *Commerce* represents Perrin in an earlier period, when he is supposed to have run a bookstore with his wife – although there was no mention of this in the *Médisances*. This provides an example of what Hertel posited at the end of the *Journal d'Anatole Laplante*, that is, resurrecting a fictional character who had previously been killed off, thus demonstrating his immortality.

The form adopted in this novel is close to that of Hertel's: the narrator, who is a writer, keeps a notebook in which he recounts his memories of the past and current reflections on life, the self, and writing. Neither uses dates, nor conforms to the chronology usual in a journal intime (Genette's 'narration intercalaire,' in which time of narration and time of what is narrated alternate[10]). Both are more concerned with ideas than specific events, although the 'story' is more developed in the *Médisances* and there is more emphasis on the narrative situation. In both, the writer claims to be writing primarily for himself alone, although Perrin also mentions a potential readership (29, 63). Both speak as individuals who are exceptions in their milieu (*Médisances*, 123) and yet representative of the Quebec intellectual who has gone to France. Both question traditional French-Canadian ideology and have nationalist leanings.

Neither has any time for women, though they have played a bigger role in Perrin's life. Perrin, like Laplante, tends to express himself in pithy aphorisms and maxims: both are 'moralistes,' but whereas Laplante's model was Pascal, Perrin's is Montaigne. His text correspondingly comes closer to the 'self-portrait' as described by Michel Beaujour (1980). While both narrators devote part of their notes to a retrospective life-story and refer to this text as their testament, Perrin is actually depicted as retiring to the country to complete a last work before his imminent demise. His potential narratees are also 'real,' within the fiction – his estranged wife, Gilberte, and his daughter, Paule, who accompanies him. Like Laplante, he has an imaginary 'légataire universel,' who resembles Hertel's Pierre Martel: 'Il est né, il grandira, il deviendra un jeune homme' (29). Like Laplante and Lepic for Hertel, this implied reader substitutes for the son (double or self-extension) he never had. Perrin is depicted as a failed writer, and this failure is related to his family situation as well as to the fact that he is French-Canadian. A closer look at these two aspects of his 'diary' establishes a pattern of impotence related to narcissism that was confirmed two years later by Hertel's Anatole Laplante.

## Writing for the self and self-esteem

Like Laplante, Perrin asks himself, 'Que suis-je?' (65), and his notes are an attempt to answer that question. He claims that from an early age he perceived himself as destined to become a writer (44). This aim persisted, in spite of the prevailing belief that writing could not be a means to make a living (45) and that writers are a luxury, rather than a necessity, to a society (46). The sense of 'l'oeuvre ... à accomplir' (53) gave purpose to his life, and enabled him to abandon medical school, which his mother persuaded him to begin. So far he has never actually published anything, only filled numerous notebooks with reflections and ideas towards a result that is always deferred.

Now that he has been given only a month to live (his illness remains vague, although the local inhabitants assume that he has T.B.), Perrin has his last chance to express 'ce que moi seul je pouvais dire' (62). Once more he finds that the result is banal, and probably not worth publishing. His reason for continuing is no longer the desire to be read. When his daughter asks what he is doing, he replies: 'Rien. J'écris. A qui? A personne' (25). He claims now to write 'par jeu,' and to try to write well only because every game has rules (29). He also admits that he continues in order to 'oublier de vivre péniblement' (31), to forget 'la pensée de la mort' (61): 'mes malheurs, je compte m'en dépiquer par le récit que j'en ferai.' This therapeutic exercise will never become a 'text' (44): 'ceci n'est qu'une divagation, un bavardage, le mouvement de ma main, un ouvrage manuel' (59).

Perrin is accompanied by his grown-up daughter, Paule, and wonders if she will read his notes. This is doubtful, as he considers her 'illettrée' (27). He himself regrets that his father, who died when he was six, did not write anything. The first reference to his wife, Gilberte, explains that she does not read what he writes, because she writes herself (30). This is subsequently construed as the main reason for

Perrin's own lack of success, as well as the cause of their separation. Marriage itself was a terrible mistake (29) that he still regrets (141), although he mysteriously mentions in passing that he did fall in love with his wife, several years after the wedding (167). As long as she supported him morally, by reading his work, and he supported her financially, they got along; but 'le mari et la femme peuvent s'empêcher réciproquement. C'est le grand problème de la vie conjugale' (170). Gilberte began to write herself, with his guidance, and in order to make money for him to be able to stay at home and write. Unexpectedly, she achieved fame and fortune with two highly successful books. Perrin cannot judge what she has written, as he has not read it (171). There is evidently not room in a marriage for two writers: one must be a reader, and neither of them is willing to assume that role. Having also inherited his mother's money, Perrin no longer needs to write for a living (he has been translating from English), nor to seek the opinion of others: 'Je n'écrivais plus pour m'exprimer, mais pour me corriger' (172). The diary/notebook form suits him because he is in effect his own reader, and engaged in a dialogue with himself.

Perrin is convinced that 'le style, c'est l'homme' and that 'le style mène à l'idée du lecteur' (29). It is therefore for an imaginary reader, a younger version of himself (63), that he wishes to leave a self-portrait in words. It is not a 'confession,' but 'des confidences' (55), since he tends to 's'excuser' or 'se plaindre' rather than 'se juger.' The idea of confession is too closely associated with the religion he rejects. The visiting priest is told that he has not confessed for thirty years – not because he is not a practicing Catholic, but because he 'has not sinned'! (50). Like Laplante, Perrin is unwilling to trade 'le bonheur terrestre' for an imaginary 'bonheur céleste' (52), or to believe that renouncing all desire is a source of strength. Ironically, however, he does seem to have renounced marital happiness and professional success, in favour of an elusive vocation as writer. He also shares with Laplante the belief that reason is not a source of error (51), but rather the only means not to be taken in by the imaginary (163). Baillargeon is quoted in Gaulin's introduction to the novel (xviii), declaring that the French Canadians' belief in their innate superiority is an excuse not to prove themselves superior in anything in practice. Perrin's dream was to 'exprimer, au besoin inventer, les sentiments obscurs et les pensées nouvelles des Canadiens' (44). So far, according to him, they had not made much effort to 's'exprimer' (150): 'Quand c'est à peine si l'on peut être, le moyen d'être écrivain?' (126). Their problem is that they are neither French, nor Canadian (126). French logic has been debased in Quebec by the pernicious influence of English, a language that is 'floue' (82). The result is a meaningless expression such as 'un pays libre au sein d'un empire' (41). Perrin has, himself, had to sell his 'esprit à des Anglais' (167), by working as a translator for an advertising company (146, 161). He predicts that French-Canadian literature may one day become more important than French literature, in North America, but adds that 'jusqu'ici nous avons failli à notre tâche. Les Américains se sont inspirés mieux que nous de la littérature française' (161).

Baillargeon refers to French models in his preface to Perrin's notes, mentioning Gide, but not Sartre (as Hertel does two years later). Yet Perrin echoes *La Nausée* (1939) when he reflects on the choice between 'vivre' and 'écrire' (as does Godbout's Galarneau twenty years later). Hertel's Laplante refuses to choose beween action and thought. Perrin abolishes the living/writing dichotomy by claiming that 'l'écrivain écrit toujours. Vivre est son premier jet' (119–20). The diary may seem to represent the in-between stage. Yet Perrin judges the authors of *journaux intimes* severely: 'Leurs oeuvres sont tellement longues qu'elles en sont moins précieuses que le temps qu'il faut mettre à les parcourir' (63). This judgment is from the point of view of a reader, and we know that Perrin does not like reading. His own diarylike notes seem to indicate that this kind of writing is worth the time and effort, for the writer. Although he announces his preference for brevity and concision, and his notes are scattered with aphorisms, he also includes meandering passages of apparently formless memories and meditations. These are as much a part of his actual self-portrait as the cynical and sarcastic epigrams conveying his diabolical side, which is emphasized by Baillargeon in his preface.

After a month of being too ill to write, Perrin appends a postscript to his last notebook, having reread it. Like Quebec, he sees himself as being too concerned with 'conservation,' with memories, aiming to 'survivre' rather than 'vivre.' Yet he has expressed himself, simply by writing (183), although the result is neither the collection of maxims that he wished to produce, nor the 'story' that would have made this text a good novel. He concludes that by writing anything – even an 'objective' description of a village – an author reveals (creates?) 'himself.' The text ends with Perrin's description of the village of Saint-Larron, where he has come to die. The name, alluding to the anonymous petty criminal crucified with Christ, is obviously significant: Laplante also will refer to being 'crucifié sur place.' Perrin began his notebook by remarking that the old *habitants* no longer cultivate the earth, they have become 'incultes.' Now he explains that they have been transformed from 'brutes' into pure 'esprit.' His own metamorphosis has been in reverse, as he now sees the body as essential. The village is a museum, but one in which he belongs, since he recognizes it as his own environment, the mould that formed him. In this, he is distinct from 'le métèque, le juif, l'étranger en général' (192–3). The outsider has to try to conform to a foreign mould, he is 'régi par le pays qui n'est pas le sien,' he can never 'être maître' (193). Yet staying always in one place is to vegetate and to renounce the rest of the world. Perrin wanted to 'posséder la terre,' in the sense of the whole world. He has travelled, especially in France. Now he has returned to his origins, because 'le village est une voie. C'est le passage de la vie à la mort ... Une de ses caractéristiques est son incapacité à croître, l'impuissance de ses habitants, qui, au lieu de se multiplier, se succèdent' (193–4). Self-replacement is not the same thing as fecundity.

Earlier Perrin mentions that the forests around the village belong to Jews (17). Is this to be read as an echo of the prevailing anti-semitism and a prediction of the coming movement to be 'maîtres chez nous'? Or as a more surprising prophecy of current questions regarding multiculturalism and renewal in relation to survival, as taken up in a more recent diary novel, Francine Noël's *Babel: Prise deux* (1990, see chapter 12)? The explicit connection made in this work between impotence and gender rivalry is also surprisingly modern. The concerns that emerged in the mid-1940s in these works by Hertel and Baillargeon make them a link between the traditional ideology still dominant until the Second World War, and the changes that occurred in the late fifties, as the Quiet Revolution began. One example of diary fiction published as late as 1956 still conveyed the same image of the Quebec male as impotent intellectual, and has received more critical attention. Jean Simard's *Mon Fils pourtant heureux* provides many points of comparison with the earlier ones.

## Simard, *Mon Fils pourtant heureux* (1956): Similarities in form and situation

Belleau, who discusses this novel in *Le Romancier fictif* (1980, 96–108), quotes Pierre de Grandpré: 'Le roman de Simard est à ranger sous la rubrique de l'*essai* autant que parmi les romans' (99). Like Laplante and Perrin, Simard's narrator, Fabrice Navarin (an unmarried classics professor whose name echoes that of Duhamel's Salavin) fills a notebook with his reflections on life. However, more than in the two previous examples, the narration is contextualized. As in the others, the narrative begins as an account of the past. In addition, here all the protagonists are treated as characters, 'as if' in a novel. The narrator's parents are even referred to as 'Monsieur and Madame Navarin.' Subsequently, however, there is a self-conscious shift from this *journal rétrospectif* to a 'real' diary format, in which the narrator's apparent control of the *récit* gives way to a fragmentary and disrupted *discours* of the present rather than the past, emphasizing the distinction between the two. The shift occurs when the retrospective account reaches the death of Fabrice's father, at the age of fifty-three (147). We know that Fabrice is now a man of forty – middle-aged, like Laplante and Perrin. His father left a diary, as Angéline's mother did, and Perrin wished his father had done. Fabrice's account is interrupted by extracts from his father's notebook, which the son subsequently continues. He abandons the tone of his previous narrative for one more like his father's, conforming more closely to what is expected in a *journal intime*.

Whether the entire book can be considered a diary is a question raised by Fabrice himself at the outset. There is no editorial frame; the text begins with the heading 'Chapitre 1,' rather than a date, and the narrator's announcement, 'Je me nomme Fabrice Navarin.' The interrogative 'who am I?' characteristic of the diary form is conflated with the statement central to the retrospective autobiography: 'This is who I am.' The latter begins three paragraphs later: 'Un de mes premiers souvenirs d'enfance c'est celui de la grande messe ...' (10). The intervening preamble constitutes a self-reflexive commentary on the act of narration exceptional in the Quebec novel at that time (see Belleau, 102). Fabrice first states his purpose: 'J'entreprends, à quarante ans avec la connivence de l'insomnie, de noircir chaque soir quelques pages de ce cahier' (9). The anxiety indicated by his insomnia, and the regular daily recording proposed, both correspond to the diary model. Yet he adds immediately: 'Non pas qu'il s'agisse d'un "journal," au sens précis, biographique du terme; mais d'une tentative de compréhension. Je veux faire le point, jeter quelque clarté sur ce qui m'arrive' (9). Fabrice apparently equates the 'precise' meaning of 'diary' with a factual account of daily events; but Simard was surely aware that 'tentative de compréhension' and 'faire le point' are expressions typical of the rhetoric of the *journal intime*. 'Jeter quelque clarté sur ce qui m'arrive' is exactly what Roquentin sets out to do in Sartre's *La Nausée*, also denying the model while adopting it. The present tense of 'arrive' belies the distance of a retrospective account aimed at explaining the past. As Jacques Michon has pointed out (1979, 5), Simard's novel is an example of self-conscious narration in the tradition of Mauriac, Green, and Bernanos, all of whom wrote fictional journals.

The past occupies the text up until page 196, when Fabrice draws attention to his change in perspective: 'Jusqu'à maintenant, le récit s'est déroulé à l'imparfait, au passé antérieur et au plus-que-parfait. Mais le conte a rejoint le narrateur, et me voici acculé tout à coup au temps présent, au passé immédiat.' It is at this point that he switches to his father's notebook and begins to provide dates:

> J'ai contracté, moi aussi, l'habitude de consigner jour après jour, comme autant de pièces versées au dossier, réflexions, fragments de conversations, lettres, voire parfois des rêves ... Je les crois capables de m'enseigner quelque chose sur moi-même ... Il s'agit désormais, au point où j'en suis, non plus de dégager des souvenirs longtemps ensevelis; mais, interrogeant les traces toutes fraîches de mon passage, de voir clair en tout cela. De quoi est fait mon existence? Quel est mon ressort? ... Quel est mon but? ... Questions redoutables, auxquelles il faudra pourtant répondre un jour, si je veux découvrir ... la trame véritable de ma vie, l'étoffe dont je suis fait. (196-7)

More 'modern' in some ways than the previous narrators (he has some notions of psychoanalytic theory), Fabrice nevertheless seeks like them to know his 'real' self, to uncover the meaning of life, to define his own, unique essence. For him these questions also still remain connected to the concept of religious faith. Chapter 13, which consists mainly of extracts from his father's diary, begins: 'Je pense bien que mon père avait la foi' (143). Fabrice's own diary leads to a reaffirmation of allegiance to the Catholic Church, after a period of lack of faith associated with his stay in France. His reconversion is attributed (as in Hertel's *Le Beau Risque*) to the intervention of a male friend, Gérard, a double who becomes a missionary. As in the other texts treated in this chapter, male bonding is the counterpart to a rejection of women; here this is explicitly inseparable from the narrator's recognition of his own femininity and his analysis of the role models provided by his father and his mother.

## Gender and generation: Synchronic and diachronic difference or sameness

The distribution of power and resentment between women and men is traced back to Fabrice's grandparents. On his mother's side, the family was ruled by a matriarch resembling Queen Victoria. The younger men treated her like 'de jeunes lévites autour d'un prélat' (19). Fabrice adds that 'il y avait, en vérité, quelque chose de sacerdotal dans la façon dont cette femme autoritaire exerçait, sur la famille toute entière, les prérogatives de son matriarcat' (20). The parallel between the priesthood or the ministry and the mother-figure is reminiscent of the 'feminization of America' as described by Douglas (1977) and reflected in the works of Laure Conan. The grandmother here – a formidable forerunner of the Yvettes – is represented as reigning with a 'poigne de fer' over her sons-in-law. The latter aquiesce willingly, because she appears to support them: 'Cette femme impérieuse, nullement féministe, s'avérait toujours, vis-à-vis de ses filles, la championne de l'autorité masculine ... elle prêchait l'abnégation, l'obéissance. Elle exceptée, elle ne concevait point que les femmes prétendissent à l'émancipation. Les hommes étaient les maîtres ... On devait s'en remettre à eux pour tout – ou à elle, qui savait se faire leur interprète' (22–3). The narrator's hostility towards this phallic mother-figure is evident, especially in his image of her as an ostrich (29). Unlike Fabrice and his father, who suffer from insomnia, the grandmother escapes from reality by sleeping.

Fabrice's grandfather is also stereotypical. An irresponsible spendthrift, he is content to leave authority in the hands of his wife, while maintaining his self-esteem by beating the children and projecting himself as a 'maître du langage' (26), especially by reading aloud (24–5). A prototype of the 'beau parleur' later embodied in Gabrielle Roy's Azarius, he is also in one respect a parodic echo of Charles de Montbrun. Like him he dies in a bizarre incident while out shooting, but: 'Non pas d'un coup de carabine maladroit, comme il eût été naturel; mais d'une angine de poitrine ... à l'issu d'une partie de cartes' (27).

There are further echoes of *Angéline de Montbrun* in the evocation of Fabrice's mother, Stéphanie de Valauris, a name acquired as an improvement on her family's original one, Boisdon (30, 40). Like Angéline and Henriette Dessaulles, as a girl her world was confined to convent school, church, and charitable works; she also wore white dresses (34) and limited her expectations to 'mariage, monde, mari' (32). Like Angéline, she was over-attached to her father (48). Totally ignorant regarding sexual relations (43) and horrified by marriage, she attempted unsuccessfully to return to her parents' home (59). Her mother gave her the same advice as Conan's narrators would: 'Crois-tu vraiment, ma fille, qu'on soit sur la terre pour être heureuse? On y est pour faire son devoir, voilà tout! La vie n'est pas un roman' (60).

If marriage represents happiness in the novel, in this case neither the marriage nor the novel conforms to the model. Fabrice's father's diary, like Perrin's, attributes all his problems to the fatal mistake of getting married. He is depicted as having done so only because his inseparable male alter ego had already succumbed (35), and sees the married man as a martyr or conscript (46). Like Hertel's Laplante he dislikes both women and nature (41, 95–6). Fabrice interprets his father's violence towards his wife as compensation for his physical smallness (56, 77). M. Navarin is a government employee (they live in Quebec City), whose only passions are history (401) and listening to himself talk (40, 138). His narcissism is negative. As Fabrice puts it, 'Monsieur Navarin ne s'aime pas. Mais on peut se haïr et quand même ne se préoccuper que de soi, se préférer toujours à l'interlocuteur' (40).

In his journal, M. Navarin reveals his regret that his relationships with both his wife and his son have been a failure (146): his wife is frigid, his son a disappointment, neither an athlete nor a brilliant student (105). Like Laplante and Perrin, and typical of their generation of educated Québécois, Fabrice's father combines a 'coeur janséniste' with a 'tête voltairienne' (15). On reading his posthumous diary, Fabrice is moved by a 'son de vérité, d'authenticité' that he had not heard from his father before: 'Cet homme était donc *malheureux*, lui aussi?' (144–5).

This variation on the title ('Mon père pourtant malheureux') underlines the imbricated roles of father and son: 'Il souffrait discrètement ... ne se confiant qu'à ce cahier – comme je le fais moi-même, son fils, vingt-cinq ans plus tard. Ah! quand les pères ont mangé des raisins verts ...' (145).

Although Fabrice now identifies with his father – who after all was pleased to have a son, a 'diplôme de virilité' (62) – he previously preferred the feminine world (139). For his mother, the child replaced her husband (the lost phallus [60]); she would have preferred a daughter, but a son will do if he is in her image (66). She chooses a novelistic name, Fabrice (66), and would not mind if he became a priest (76). Her son is 'englué dans le marais de son amour insatisfait' (68) and their relationship is marked by an unhealthy 'coquetterie' (78). At the time of writing, however, Fabrice has realized that it is necessary for children to 'kill' the internalized parent in order to survive – and this is in effect the function of his narrative.

## The impotent man's dream of paternity

Fabrice's notebook represents his attempt to escape from the 'climat d'irréalité' (102) associated with his mother. She is not, in his view, an innocent victim. Rather, she is as guilty as his father, 'en ce qu'elle nous avait donné, à tous les deux, les plus mauvaises habitudes: à son mari, celle du despotisme, à son fils celle de la sujétion.' She failed in her role of 'régulatrice': 'C'est la femme qui fait un foyer' (102). It is his mother whom he blames for his own effeminacy.

At the beginning of his narrative, Fabrice comments on his over-meticulous handwriting, describing it as 'proprette': 'Je ressemble à ma mère' (10). His accusation that she cared too much about keeping the pots clean to be a good cook implies a parallel with his writing. The first part of his account does not conform to the 'real' journal model, because he must be in control, of both his writing and his story. As Belleau shows, 'si Fabrice Navarin ne s'aime pas, son discours s'aime bien' (98). Although at the outset he claims that his text is not a diary, 'parce que celui-ci est complaisant, narcissique, trop littéraire' (9), it nevertheless becomes one, in spite of the narrator. He finally recognizes that the 'miroir de Socrate' inevitably serves as 'le bassin de Narcisse' (195). His 'tentative d'objectivation' (195) becomes an 'acte d'accusation ou de plaidoyer'; objective self-reflection is not possible, because 'je suis dans la nécessité de me *réaliser*' ([sic], 195). Rather than an autonomous subject projecting an authentic self-image, the writer is himself formed by the act of writing, 'realizing,' as in Lacan's mirror stage, that he both is and is not the mirror image that is an object to others. The last part of his account, which adopts the diary model, formally conveys the unconscious excluded or repressed in the previously 'controlled' narrative. Of course, from the perpective of the text as novel, this aspect is also produced by the author's control. It serves as an ironic commentary on Fabrice's contention that this is neither a diary nor a novel (195). It is also not impossible, bearing in mind the model of *La Nausée*, that Belleau could be right when he suggests that the entire text might be the 'notes for a novel' that Fabrice mentions (1980, 96).

The shift from *récit* to *discours* corresponds to the recognition by Fabrice of his own femininity, not only as an element of his childhood as a 'fils à maman' (112), but as ongoing. His mother had defended him against his father's anger (127), and he in turn wished to kill his father because of his attacks on her (77). Now the father is dead, but Fabrice still has not resolved the problem of the internalized mother. The diary plays once more the role of 'return to the womb,' as Fabrice plunges into his own 'lac intérieur,' becoming 'scaphandrier de soi-même' (10). His aim is to 'tuer, en dedans de soi, la plupart des souvenirs toxiques' (10). These are associated with the 'abject,' the 'pouvoirs de l'horreur' that Kristeva (1980) ascribes to birth and the mother as origin/receptacle. More recent diary novels (see chapter 9) show that the intro-spection of the *journal intime* ultimately represents re-production of the self, brought forth from one's own inner regions, rather than from the mother's.

These inner regions are conveyed in Simard's novel by the image of a marshy bog (10) or a cavelike labyrinth. The allusions to Theseus, as in Butor's *L'Emploi du temps*, involve trying various possible solutions to the maze, and finding both the way in and the way out. One possibility, as in Butor's novel, is salvation through another woman, that is, not the mother. Fabrice's attempts in this direction have failed so far. He recognizes that he is Narcissus rather than Don Juan; or rather, that the two are the same, both seeking only self-reflections (140, 177, 178). Fabrice's friend, Gérard, is also referred to as a 'fil d'Ariane' (110, 116). He proposes the alternative (homosexual) solution of platonic male friendship and religious sublimation. The notebook itself is also posited as a 'fil d'Ariane' (9), a means to 'voir clair' (196).

The attraction shared by Gérard, God, and the journal is that they provide a listener (13, 137, 156). Although he writes with no particular reader in mind, for himself, Fabrice admits that like Pascal (18) he would secretly like to be read. He resembles his father in one important respect: he loves to talk. His mother, however, had nothing to say (138). With Gérard he experiences the only relationship in his life in which dialogue is possible, as represented by the epistolary mode. There is neither 'bourreau' nor 'victime' (122); both can speak and listen. But this double (he calls himself Gérard's shadow [110]) is also now dead (158–9).

The notebook 'dossier' includes letters from and to Gérard, written during Fabrice's stay in France, which proves (as for Laplante and Perrin) a 'chemin de Damas' (see Belleau, 104). It is in Paris that he finally admits: '*je ne suis pas heureux!*' [sic]. Europe brings him the realization of his own abjectness and the experience of shame: 'Ma vie n'était qu'un vaste échec, un tissu de mécomptes, une non-réussite, un mensonge ... je n'étais en réalité qu'un pauvre type hésitant, inquiet, impropre à la joie, inadéquat, assurément inférieur à cette humanité inflexible et joyeuse que je voyais défiler sur les grands boulevards ...' (199). Once more, the male Québécois is defined by his inability to 'jouir,' to remain 'inflexible' – by his impotence. He suffers from a 'déficience de caractère nationale,' a 'maladie de la personnalité' (207) that goes back to the battle of the Plains of Abraham: 'Le Canadien se martyrise délicieusement' (180).

The dreams recounted in the final, fragmentary journal entries convey the recognition of impotency and the need to move beyond masturbation (an obsession at the *collèges* in both Perrin's and Fabrice's recollections). In one dream (208–9) Fabrice sees a girl in white, like a bride, attacked by a snake, which she welcomes; Fabrice cuts it up, recognizing his own self-castration. In another (209–210), a snakelike hand emerges from the bedroom wall and takes a shoe: Fabrice seizes it in his own hand. Diary writing, as mentioned previously, is often perceived as analogous to masturbation, as a bad habit to be replaced by interaction with an other. Fabrice's diary ends with two relevant developments. The first is his confession to a priest (217) and return to the Church, although he is not sure if he has faith (207–8), following what he terms a 'ravissement' (216): a spiritual communication with God, who once more appears as a sublime parent-figure and ideal listener. This second 'chemin de Damas' is conveyed as a dawn, as in many other diary novels (cf. *Les Abîmes de l'aube, Salut Galarneau!*). It is a rebirth, through a decision to choose life over death. It is followed by his admission to a desire to become a father – to have a son who would be happier than he has been, 'mon fils pourtant heureux' (228). The model to imitate is Albert, the Frenchman without parents, who in spite of his 'vie épouvantable' manages to be 'heureux ... parce qu'il vit, voilà tout' (226–7).

The final line echoes the title of the book and its epigraph, from Pierre Jean Jouve:

> Toi qui connais bien l'acte de pleurer
> Engagé dans la confusion de la mentale douleur
> 'vers le milieu du chemin de ta vie qui t'es trouvé dans la forêt obscure'
> Mon fils pourtant heureux ...

Fabrice is Simard's 'fils pourtant heureux,' as Laplante and Lepic are Hertel's only sons. He is also the imaginary reader of his father's journal, as dreamed by Baillargeon's Claude Perrin. Survival is perceived in terms of continuity, of reproduction of the *same*: 'C'est comme les parents, les enfants ...' (227). Fabrice, who is exempted from military service on medical grounds (to his mother's shame), recalls looking at pictures of Napoleonic battles with his father: 'Mon père et moi, aussi couards l'un que l'autre, nous excitant sur ces images guerrières, tels des impuissants sur un livre pornographique!' (118). Gérard's prediction that the battle might not be over (201), which may be interpreted as a reference to the conquest (Fabrice's father liked to walk with him on the Plains of Abraham), seems to have little chance of fulfilment, as long as the sons are like Fabrice. His retreat into the religion that he had abandoned marks a return to feminine refuge values, rather than a desire to fight for change.

### The Father, the Son, and the Holy Spirit/Word

In *Psyché: Invention de l'autre* (1987), Derrida discusses Cicero's reply to his son's request for knowledge: 'Invente-t-on un enfant? Si l'enfant *s'invente*, est-ce comme la projection spéculaire du narcissisme parental ou comme l'autre ...?' (14). He goes on to ask who is excluded in this dialogue between father and son. In these novels, produced in Quebec in the 1940s and 1950s, it is women who are excluded. Not only are they not legitimate heirs (like Perrin's daughter), their exclusion provides the necessary foundation for phallogocentric thought. As Wladimir Granoff comments in *La Pensée et le féminin* (1976), they also represent a constant threat to the fragile edifice of male 'culture,' by their physicality and 'naturalness,' that is, their sexuality: 'la femme, comme être sexué ... et dans ce qu'on pourrait appeler son fonctionnement même ... ne porte-t-elle pas témoignage d'une possibilité permanente d'un retour du tout à l'incertitude ... à la déstabilisation du champ stabilisé?' (255). The stereotypes of women illustrated in the novels discussed in this chapter are prevalent throughout Western literature, and certainly not unique to Quebec or to all 'colonized' communities. Yet in Quebec it was definitely the feminine that provided the refuge values necessary for survival. Nevertheless, identification with the feminine is perceived by the Quebec male intellectual in these texts as the source of his weakness, and his resentment is directed towards women rather than the dominant culture. Fabrice Navarin is, typically, tempted to suicide and in danger of madness, because of his non-virile and therefore, in patriarchal terms, deficient self-representation. Like the diarists imagined by Hertel and Baillargeon, he survives through writing, by re-producing a male self through the Word, re-affirming the primacy of mind over mat(t)er. Yet Fabrice still feels that 'un homme parfaitement normal, s'il existe, n'éprouve sûrement pas la démangeaison d'écrire' (176–7), that the 'orgie verbale' of diary writing is a 'vice de vieux adolescents inconsolables' (177). Some other fictional diarists of 1950s Quebec are portrayed as overwhelmed by their apparent inability to be 'normal,' or to 'grow up,' and their diaries serve to depict more extreme versions of a narcissism of death or madness rather than positive self-esteem. We shall turn to these in the next chapter.

CHAPTER SEVEN

# The Phallic Mother, Impotent Men, and Madness: *Loranger, Elie, Filiatrault*

'Un fait constant de notre histoire ... c'est l'influence de la femme et particulièrement de la mère dans l'évolution de notre peuple et de notre culture.'
SOEUR SAINTE-MARIE-ELEUTHÈRE (1964), 1

'L'abjection ... est une précondition du narcissisme ... l'abjection sexuelle, morale, religieuse comme un effondrement des lois paternelles – un univers de pères désavoués, factices ou morts, où règnent, fétiches féroces ... des matrones en vertige de pouvoir.'
JULIA KRISTEVA (1980), 22, 27

## Male impotence and the phallic mother

We have seen that the dominant ideology in late nineteenth- and early twentieth-century Quebec confirmed the 'feminization of America,' as discussed by Ann Douglas (1977), and also Soeur Sainte-Marie-Eleuthère (1964) and Julia Kristeva.[1] Two versions of feminine power are provided. The first, illustrated by Henriette Dessaulles's diary, is the moralizing mother-figure associated with Catholic pietism and the clergy. The second, propagated by Laure Conan in her fictional journals, is the desexualized virgin martyr. Both female models are presented as superior to men because of a greater capacity for self-sacrifice and 'faithfulness,' that is, unconditional love based on identification with the other. Both include elements of narcissistic renunciation of desire and sublimation through Memmi's conservative refuge values (see chapter 3). The latter are associated with Lacan's imaginary, which belongs to the pre-Oedipal narcissistic stage prior to differentiation from the mother and assimilation to the patriarchal symbolic order. According to psychoanalytical theory, full access to the symbolic – language and law – depends on the intervention of a third party – the father – which tends to be lacking in the Quebec context.

Diary fiction discussed so far by male authors of the 1940s and early 1950s depicted male narrators who reject the feminine, which they associate with sentimental religiosity on the one hand, and with bodily pleasures (including sex and contact with nature) on the other. Their moral narcissism takes the form of cerebral idealism, excluding heterosexual relations and sublimating homosexual ones to the platonic exchange of ideas. The projection of imaginary male doubles – ideal readers or listeners – culminates in the desire for a son – self-regeneration – that is, a wish to become the father. This is accomplished, however, only at the level of the imaginary, for actual procreation is impeded by misogyny, founded in fear of the mother.

The sense of infantile helplessness, of impotence and uselessness, experienced by these men is attributed less to their status of colonized and disempowered males than to the disproportionate power of women in a colonized society. The fact that older women are perceived as powerful is interpreted by the male narrators as a cause of their own powerlessness. Yet the earlier female narrators saw themselves as acceding to power and rejecting men of necessity, since the latter had abdicated or been defeated. A role reversal appears to occur, as women come to represent the law, and men the repressed that threatens to erupt in social rebellion (alcohol, '*le sacre*'), violence, or madness, as in the case of the poet Nelligan.[2] Yet this reversal is only apparent, and gives rise to intense conflict in both categories, for both men and women continue to compare themselves to dominant transcultural norms of masculinity and femininity, that is, women persist in seeking a dominant male (a resurrection of the dead father) and men an indulgent, caring female (a substitute for the lost mother). Both are marked by nostalgia for narcissistic non-differentiation with a nurturing parent, who may be replaced by the diary. Both project their ideal self in their journal, and are painfully aware of their inability to conform to it: men because they are not dominant, women because they are not indulgent.

Mothers as well as fathers place their hopes and self-projections in a child, but for women the child is real. This was illustrated in the attitude of Stéphanie de Valauris, the mother in Simard's *Mon Fils pourtant heureux* (1956). Other examples of diary fiction in the same period bear similarities to Fabrice Navarin's account of a crisis approaching madness, and the concomitant temptation to commit suicide. Three of these illustrate the relationship of narcissism as a borderline personality disorder (which may become psychotic) to diary writing and to the survival/self-elimination dilemma experienced by the male subject when relegated to a 'feminine' position of marginality. Françoise Loranger's *Mathieu* (1949), although written by a woman, depicts a male narrator. The outcome in this novel is positive. In Robert Elie's *La Fin des songes* (1952) and Jean Filiatrault's *Chaînes* (1955) the fictional diarists' writing proves ineffectual as therapy, and both end their lives with their diaries. All three texts include diary extracts as part of a longer third-person narrative. All three introduce male narrators younger than those discussed in the last chapter. These diarists do not look back on their lives; rather, they are concerned with the future, and whether it is worth living. None of these novels exhibits the ambivalence regarding autobiographical narration that was central in those by Hertel, Baillargeon, and Simard. These narrators are projections of what the authors are *not*: the novels serve as successful catharsis, even when the narrator's journal is depicted as failing in that purpose. A closer analysis of these three texts will provide the basis for a re-evaluation of the interconnection of male impotence, madness, and the phallic mother.

## Loranger, *Mathieu* (1949): The diary in the novel

Although they are not dated, Mathieu's *cahiers* consist of fragmentary reflections based on recent events, on the diary model. They incorporate poems by the diarist in which he expresses in literary form the ideas and feelings that preoccupy him. They also include imaginary dialogues, an acting-out of the diarist's role-playing as addresser, addressee, and object of the exchange. This element of drama is present throughout the novel, and links the main narrative to the diary exerpts. These are samples, since Mathieu mentions that he has other notebooks (132). The main part of the text consists of third-person narration, with a high proportion of dialogue and interior monologue conveying Mathieu's thoughts. Parts of the latter, like the diary extracts, are printed in italics, and represent an inner voice (conscience or demon [9, 119]) that comments critically on Mathieu's behaviour and attitude. The text is divided into three parts, each encompassing a notebook (pages 60–70 in part 1,

132–140 in part 2, and 250–6 in part 3). While these passages form a small portion of the whole novel (22 pages of 338), they play a central role in the action and in both the development and the interpretation of Mathieu's borderline personality.

The first notebook appears as an enigma. Etienne Beaulieu, a rich industrialist, finds it in his limousine (59–60), and we read it through his eyes (60, 70–1). Like him, we do not know that it is written by Mathieu, although we have more reason than he does to suspect that this is the case. We follow his attempts to discover who, among the group of young actors who have used his car, may be the author. The question 'who am I?' central to all intimate diaries (Mathieu himself asks it on page 322) is formulated first, in this instance, as 'who is he?' (60, 101). Etienne's observation of various suspects who might be sufficiently ugly, morose, and miserable to own the diary, which is black, conspicuously excludes Mathieu as a possibility. This error is based on two significant misconceptions: first, that the author is an actor (Mathieu is only an observer of the troupe); second, that he is, from outside, either as repulsive as he believes himself to be, or as interesting as Etienne finds him in the notebook. These elements become central to Mathieu's ultimate metamorphosis.

Loranger, who subsequently devoted herself to writing for the theatre, exploits the presentation of plays and the self-projection of actors as the central metaphor in this novel. Etienne and Mathieu are both potential writers: Etienne imagines stories about other people (124); Mathieu analyses everyone, including himself. Faced with the choice between living and analysing (a variation on 'vivre/écrire') they choose analysis and control. Both, however, will be forced to become actors, to participate in relations with others, and to recognize their detachment as false. They are also obliged to experience the problematic nature of judgment, when the spectator's viewpoint shifts from external to internal, and also to a different vantage point. Mathieu's brief experience as a drama critic concretely illustrates this.

In his notebooks Mathieu assumes that he is both judge and judged. His self-accusation doubles as self-defence. While revealing himself as *abject* (a word he uses often, for example, on 64, 140, and 175), he also gains the sympathy of a potential reader. His implied reader is first God (a role adopted by others, as we shall see), then Danielle, Etienne's niece and the troupe's leading actress, whom Mathieu begins to love:

'Danielle seule comprendrait ...' (204). His worst fear is that his first lost notebook could fall into the hands of someone close to him (132), that is, his mother, with whom he lives. The second notebook is not lost, but taken by Etienne, who sees it in Mathieu's pocket while Mathieu is attempting to blackmail him (122). The handwriting confirms that Mathieu is indeed the author, and this knowledge transforms Etienne's reaction to Mathieu's 'abjection,' just as Danielle's reading of both notebooks (314) later persuades her to 'save' him. Etienne justifies his act of giving Danielle the notebooks to read, because they are the only means to know Mathieu 'tel qu'il est' (314). This is the function the diary serves in the novel: to provide an inner view that is assumed to be more sincere or authentic than the cynical, sarcastic, negative persona that Mathieu projects to his mother and his friends. In response to Danielle's hesitation ('Mathieu détesterait qu'on lise ce qu'il a écrit pour lui, pour lui seul!'), Etienne replies: 'Ecrit-on jamais uniquement pour soi? Il y a dans ces cahiers, certaines recherches de style qui me font croire ...' (314). His unfinished sentence implies that Mathieu's secret desire is to be read, indeed to become a writer. The notebooks reveal him as an avid reader of poetry and a perceptive critic of plays – the reason Etienne finds him a job as theatre critic, to everyone's surprise. The illicit readers of the journal plan either to return it to its owner or burn it (318). The moment of its return by Danielle (336–7) also serves to modify her relationship with Mathieu and his own self-perception.

The notebooks play an extensive part in the story as objects of exchange. In this *Mathieu* is reminiscent of *Les Faux-Monnayeurs*: in addition, Etienne recalls Gide's Edouard in several respects. The diary as object also serves as a representation of Mathieu: 'Les pages étaient couvertes d'une écriture renversée, nerveuse qui par endroits sortait des lignes comme si rien n'avait pu la contenir. Elle ne se lisait pas facilement à cause des nombreuses ratures qui accrochaient le regard' (59). This description of the physical appearance of Mathieu's notes, which we can only imagine through Etienne's eyes, serves to confirm diary writing as expressive at both the conscious and unconscious levels. The key words here are 'contenir' and 'ratures.' Mathieu's personality disorder is associated with his mother, the source of constraint, and with his perception of himself as a 'raté,' a failure. The diary, as a means to go beyond restraint and to erase and start over again, is the first step in his transformation.

The third notebook is the only one not read by someone else within the fiction, and it ends with Mathieu's decision to abandon diary writing. An external reader is no longer necessary, since Mathieu is now able to see himself clearly. He has given up the dark glasses that he previously wore constantly. These both distorted his view of others and prevented them from seeing him. The diary, in this text, is part of an extended network of allusions to projection, perception, and mirroring. The mirror motif occurs several times (for example, on 114, 117, 181, 270, and 287). Several references to Sartre include the concept of 'les autres' as reflecting/refracting the self-image: 'Le regard des autres est à mon visage le plus implacable des miroirs' (65). Yet Mathieu's assumptions regarding others' perception of him are proved wrong. Etienne is also aware that the self-portrait provided in the journal may be distorted: 'Il se pouvait bien que mon héros ait fait à son sujet un peu de littérature ...' (76). Both self and others are exposed as representations, although the concept of a true self remains.

Like Fabrice Navarin, Mathieu comes close to madness and suicide. Like him, he is saved by his journal. Several elements present in Simard's novel are already developed more fully in Loranger's: the mother, the friend who plays God, the suicide attempt. Here they are aspects of a plot that plays out to the full the pre-Oedipal drama associated with narcissism as both a mental disorder and a survival mechanism.

## Abjection and the phallic mother

Kristeva, in *Pouvoirs de l'horreur: Essai sur l'abjection* (1980), makes the connection between borderline narcissistic disorders and the function of the mother: 'L'abject nous confronte ... dans notre archéologie personnelle, à nos tendances les plus anciennes de nous marquer de l'entité maternelle avant même que d'exister en dehors d'elle grâce à l'autonomie du langage' (20). According to Kristeva, the 'abject' is what is excluded by the symbolic order; it pulls us back to 'là où le sens s'effondre' (9) and fills us with horror. It is intimately associated with negative aspects of the maternal womb as origin and source of disgust. Critical comment on *Mathieu*[3] focuses on the relationship between Mathieu and his mother, Lucienne Normand. The latter vies with Anne Hébert's sadistic mother-figure in *Le Torrent* (1950) as the most horrific in any Quebec novel. Whereas Fabrice Navarin's mother's affection in *Mon Fils pourtant heureux* was shown to have a negative, oppressive effect in feminizing the son, Mathieu's mother's disappointment in her offspring turns love to hate and drives him to his borderline state. His inability to identify with either mother or father produces a generalized misanthropy that leaves only the self as object, although the narcissism involved is negative.

Lucienne sees herself as a victim, but this interpretation is not corroborated by either the impersonal narrator or Mathieu. Rather, she is presented as the perpetrator of suffering, literally with a vengeance. An ugly rich girl (9), she married 'le beau Jules,' a seductive philanderer who after three years ran off with an American (96), leaving her with Mathieu, who unfortunately did not inherit his father's looks. Mathieu's negative self-image is due to his mother's rejection and her conviction that he is physically ugly (like her) and morally no good (like his father). The mother's narcissistic injury and rage are projected onto the son and perpetuated by him. Mathieu blames his mother for their impoverished circumstances (10) and for his low expectations; she is fond of repeating the cliché, popular in Quebec, that 'quand on est né pour un petit pain ... on doit s'en contenter' (12). Her resentment actually arises from the belief that she was *not* 'née pour un petit pain': on the contrary, she is 'faite pour commander' (95), and suffers from frustrated entitlement. Mathieu, however, has only ever known the humiliation of being a poor relation, in a social milieu where snobbery is the norm, as illustrated by the treatment accorded to an ex-maid who becomes a successful actress.

Lucienne Normand is not the only powerful female depicted in this text. Her friend, Eugénie Beaulieu, Etienne's wife, is an autocratic *reine du foyer*. Their daughter, Nicole, succeeds in fulfilling her own desires by any means available to her and excels in giving orders (159). Michelle, the former maid, is also ambitious and ruthless. Only Danielle, who is intrigued by Mathieu, represents a positive image of femininity, and even she turns a sexual encounter resembling rape into an incident in which she appears to have exploited a naïve man for her own ends (180–2). Apart from Danielle's brother, Bruno, who leads the actors and finally leaves for New York, the male characters – Etienne, his son Bernard – are dominated by the women around them. Etienne is reduced to renting a secret apartment in order to find his own space (the source of the blackmail attempt by Mathieu).

Mathieu, similarly, finds refuge only in his own room (60), a substitute womb/mother where he can be alone to read and write. Green (1983) describes this type of narcissistic withdrawal: 'Arrêtés dans leur capacité d'aimer, les sujets qui sont sous l'emprise d'une mère morte ne peuvent plus aspirer qu'à l'autonomie ... la solitude, qui était une situation angoissante et à éviter ... devient positive ... Le sujet se nide. Il devient sa propre mère ...' (237). Mathieu's mother is not dead (he is tempted to kill her, but not capable of it [140]), but it is as if she were dead, as a mother, that is, as a lost state of wholeness, of being accepted as part of an entity. At the mirror stage, it is the mother's gaze that enables the subject to form a self-representation.[4] In the case of Mathieu, the image conveyed by the mother, and internalized, is negative. This affects his facial expression (30) and his bodily stance (30, 231): he is 'voûté,' bent in submission. His body is the sign of his inferiorization and lack of freedom. In one sense, he has no mother; in another, he has never escaped from maternal containment, he is a fearful prisoner (95, 113) who has never been born/emerged. He perceives himself, like his sentences (61), as an aborted embryo fit only to be discarded: ab-ject (140, 175, 255). As his first poem eloquently proclaims: 'rien de bon ne pouvait sortir d'elle ... foetus, je m'accrochais à ce ventre qui ne me voulait pas ... Elle m'a rejeté, elle m'a vomi avec férocité ...' (63). Yet he adds: 'Je voulais vivre! Je vis.'

For the mother, this son is inadequate to function as a phallus. 'Le beau Jules' also, when found and brought back, is paralysed as a result of alcoholism and syphilis (114, 200), reduced to an abject state of infantile dependence and entirely in her hands. Ironically, he is now even uglier that the ugly son she wished to use to punish him (201). The forced return of the prodigal father, who usurps Mathieu's last refuge, his room, is the event that finally causes Mathieu to leave, and to attempt to commit suicide.

## The symbolic father's intervention

According to Kristeva (1980), 'la pulsion dite narcissique ne domine que si une instabilité de la métaphore paternelle empêche le sujet de se situer dans une structure triadique donnant un objet à ses pulsions' (55), and 'seule l'instance paternelle, en tant qu'elle introduit la dimension symbolique entre le "sujet" (enfant) et "l'objet" (la mère) peut

générer une telle relation objectale ...' (56). Absence of the 'instance paternelle' impedes identity formation and may lead to psychosis. In Mathieu, the actual return of the abject, failed father is what triggers a crisis. The real father's disappearance and destruction are connected to the failure of the symbolic in the Quebec context by the parallel disappearance or failure of God (61) – replaced by a matriarchal Church, against which Mathieu rebels (67, 69). His dilemma is 'par quoi remplacer ce Dieu si bon qui n'existe pas?' (135). In his imaginary dialogues Mathieu makes his interlocutor Christ, the suffering Son, with whom he identifies, although no one could mistake *him* for the 'son of God,' as he points out (133). He shares Christ's sense of being abandoned or forsaken by his father (70). Like Hertel's Anatole Laplante, Mathieu sees himself as 'crucifié sur place.' Like him, he creates 'l'illusion d'un ami qui m'écoute' (68): 'Je n'ai pas d'ami que toi, et encore faut-il que je t'improvise' (136). Christ becomes his 'double narcissique, comme représentation du Moi Idéal ... un camarade imaginaire' (Rosolato 1975, 23).

Although God and the real father are encoded as absent/failed, two other figures in the novel serve as fathers and intervene in God-like fashion to save Mathieu. The first of these is Etienne, his godfather, who has always helped him financially by finding him work, and who becomes an actual ideal listener and reader of the notebooks. Paradoxically, Etienne shows little interest in his own family, including his son, Bernard. His concern for Mathieu stems from a perception of the unknown diarist as a younger version of himself; he was also misunderstood and an acute observer of others (58, 124). Lucienne perceives him also as 'un mou' (116). Yet according to Danielle, her uncle Etienne sees and understands everything (101), he always finds a solution: 'Là où il est il ne peut y avoir de désordre' (168), and 'tout devient simple quand il est là' (312). Miraculously, he finds Mathieu the right job and intervenes to stop the appearance of a potentially disastrous review; it is he who finally removes Jules to the hospital and Lucienne to an old people's home, and provides Mathieu with a roof over his head ( his own secret abode) as well as a girlfriend (Danielle). He functions, in effect, as a fairy godfather.

The second God-like father-figure is Rochat, the Swiss octogenarian ex-wrestler who runs the Camp des Athlètes where Mathieu takes refuge after narrowly escaping death. Thanks to Rochat, Mathieu is transformed from a 'vaincu' into a 'vainqueur' (232), through physical

renewal. Paradoxically, this triumph is achieved because 'Mathieu, subjugué, retrouve la docilité de l'enfance pour remettre son sort entre les mains de ce maître qui accepte de le diriger' (233). In the stories told about Rochat he appears as a 'figure de dieu invulnérable' (269), possessing both superhuman strength and supernatural wisdom. Rochat is from another world (Europe) and Mathieu is transported into another world (a natural wilderness setting) for his re-incubation and rebirth. There he also moves beyond masturbation (276) to his first experience of voluntary sex with a woman who finds him 'beau' (274, 281, 283). He emerges 'l'égal des autres, sinon leur supérieur' (248).

## Salvation through the feminine and/or through language

The masculine intervention of Etienne and Rochat paves the way for a salvation that is achieved through access to the feminine, dissociated from the mother (who like the father is abandoned as abject). The feminine reappears in the symbolic register first, as nature and an emphasis on physical fitness and beauty – the body. There were numerous allusions to 'abêtissement' and 'abrutissement' in Mathieu's abject phase, but it is no longer construed as abject to be (a) 'bête.' Mathieu learns to accept and enhance his animal side, including his sexuality. Whereas he previously refused the advances of Nicole – who made him feel like a male prostitute (155) – he welcomes those of another unfaithful wife, Annette. The (feminine) narcissistic pleasure he experiences from being admired as an object and physically desired, is, however, short-lived. It is subsequently represented as de-generation, conveyed by a relapse into abjectness (alcohol and theft from his mother). The feminine is effective only in association with the paternal (Etienne), and initially friendship with Danielle is opposed to sexual desire.

Danielle also undergoes a 'cure' at the Camp des Athlètes: the image of 'Beauty and the Beast' evoked earlier by Mathieu to describe them together (173) is no longer dichotomous, since Mathieu is now good-looking and Danielle accepts her sexuality, moving beyond what Mathieu saw as overattachment to her brother (175). Although she is not encoded as a female sexual predator like Nicole, Michelle or Annette, Danielle nevertheless plays the active role in her relationship with Mathieu, who says 'son image est entrée en moi ...' (133) and asks himself 'pourquoi avait-il laissé cet amour pénétrer en lui?' (160). Mathieu

finally accepts her 'friendship' when it is offered for the third time, in a reversal of Peter's denial of Christ. He is 'saved' by Danielle as much as by Etienne and Rochat. She also, ironically, decides to 'liberate' him whether he likes it or not (316). Danielle is an actress and like her brother, Bruno, she acts rather than analyses: 'On ne peut pas vivre et se regarder vivre! Je veux vivre!' (178). She is distinguished mainly by her 'feminine intuition' (31, 101, 313) or instinct, which enables her to interpret others and play dramatic roles convincingly. For her, speaking, implying 'la chaleur d'une réaction humaine, le contact même de la vie' – as in the theatre – is preferable to writing: 'C'est tellement froid une feuille de papier!' (342). Salvation, in *Mathieu*, is related not only to 'finding one's self' and accepting one's sexuality, but to self-expression as essential for communication with others.

Mathieu moves from the belief that he cannot love or be loved because he was not loved by his mother to the conviction that one must first love oneself, in order to love an other (321). The monologue of the notebooks is replaced at the end of the novel by letters that establish a dialogue between him and Danielle. Mathieu continues to write, but for someone else – and eventually for a public. He admonishes himself at the end of his diary: 'Ferme ce cahier; cesse de te regarder vivre. N'écris pas ta vie. Vis-la!' (256). Nevertheless his goal remains to write (334, 341), and Danielle's advice is: 'Maintenant que vous vous êtes découvert, il ne vous reste plus qu'à trouver votre mode d'expression' (341). Yet the impersonal narrator tells us that 'en voulant former le Mathieu idéal, c'est à Danielle qu'il tendait inconsciemment à ressembler ...' (333). There remains a tension between the concept of self-discovery, implying a pre-existing essential self (cf. 121), self-construction through both living and writing, and self as imitation/emulation of a model.

A tension also continues between Mathieu's desire to 'vaincre' (137, 139, 208), and yet to interact in a situation where the other 'se donne' (62). Paradoxically, he must 'se dominer' and find a solution 'in himself,' yet his salvation depends on others (and on an unintegrated allusion to a piece of music, echoing *La Nausée* [217]). His mother had predicted that, unlike his father, he would never find a woman to 'keep' him – and yet he does: Danielle is going to provide his meals (344)! Mathieu remains dependent on a woman, and on a father-figure. He will never be a 'real man,' as represented by the world of capitalist finance (Etienne) but an 'artiste,' and marginal. One memorable scene

in the novel shows Mathieu, working as a cashier at the bank, where (like Gabrielle Roy's Alexandre Chênevert) he has made an error. His revolt takes the form of squashing a blueberry tart onto the account sheets – simultaneously showing contempt for symbols of the paternal and the maternal, and demonstrating his own revolt/ingness.

Mathieu is depicted as 'too conscious' (19). Introspection is condemned as leading to madness and suicide, the diary as a means to seduce oneself with one's own words (137). Alcohol and sleep provide ways to be less conscious, but are not a solution. The latter lies in physical action and interaction with others. A similar dialectic is developed in Robert Elie's *La Fin des songes* (1950).

### Elie, *La Fin des Songes* (1950/1968): 'Je suis vaincu d'avance' (166)

Elie's novel is also divided into three parts, each progressively shorter (104, 64, and 22 pages respectively). The first is a third-person account with a dual focus, on Marcel Larocque, the author of the diary that forms part 2, and on Bernard, Marcel's childhood friend, whose wife, Nicole, is the sister of Marcel's wife, Jeanne. The second sentence states: 'Marcel pense à Bernard' (17), and the novel ends with Bernard's reaction to Marcel's diary, which he reads after his suicide: 'Bernard cherche à combler un vide et à rejoindre Marcel en lui-même' (209). Throughout, a link and an opposition are established between the two. For Marcel, Bernard is 'l'ami de toujours' (17), his interlocutor in imaginary debates (18). Bernard is strong, athletic, good-looking (32), well-off financially, and outgoing. He becomes involved in the war, in business, and in politics. His marriage is not solid; he has a mistress and no children. His wife is not totally submissive (70) and actually prefers the company of Bernard's father (116). Marcel, on the other hand, is overweight, sedentary, introspective, and not good-looking. Like Claude Perrin, he works as a translator for a newspaper. He must, presumably, be less repulsive than he thinks (like Mathieu), since Jeanne's youngest sister, Louise, finds him attractive. Marcel has two children and a model wife: a pious, devoted mother whose only passion is Chopin (20). Unfortunately, they have no piano in their modest, depressing apartment in a dilapidated district of Montreal (131).

As in *Mathieu*, the opposition between two social milieux, one affluent and one deprived, is reflected by two male characters, one suc-

cessful, one a failure. The main difference is that Bernard is younger than Etienne, and Marcel already has a family, which should be a source of self-esteem. It is the wife, in this case, who plays the mother role. She is encoded as a source of dissatisfaction and of the diarist's negative self-image. Jeanne comes to represent everything from which Marcel wishes to escape, if only by his own death.

Marcel's journal is divided into eight chapters, following the pattern of the novel, but also into dated entries, conforming to the diary model. It covers the period from 5 January to 19 February, and provides the information that Marcel has already been absent from work for two months, owing to illness (129).[5] The diary reveals that the illness is mental, rather than physical. Marcel exhibits symptoms of narcissistic withdrawal, related to severe depression. He is unable to function either at work or at home and has cut himself off from communication with others, including Bernard (186). He spends most of his time sleeping (125, 137). While Mathieu sought refuge in alcohol, Marcel escapes into his *songes*, a lethargic, day-dreaming state that privileges the imaginary over the real and is characterized by silence rather than speech. The diary becomes an in-between vehicle to express his borderline state. Representing both withdrawal and an attempt to exteriorize his inner thoughts or dreams, his exercise book, black like Mathieu's, provides an intermediate stage between dialogue with an other and non-communication.

The book actually becomes a posthumous intermediary between Marcel and his male doubles, Bernard (202) and the shadowy Louis (210), but not, significantly, a means to communicate with the women in his life, Jeanne and Louise. Nicole is the first to see the diary, when it is found and returned after Marcel throws himself in front of a tram (199). She refuses to read it and gives it to Bernard, who has no such qualms. Although Jeanne and Louise are addressed in the journal (130–1, 136–7), they never become its actual readers, remaining 'characters' in Marcel's narrative: the mother and the whore, who are confused in this case. While Jeanne, like Mathieu's mother, represents what is to be escaped *from*, Louise, like Danielle, is a potential means of escape.

### Escape from – and through – the feminine

Marcel's mother is mentioned once in part 1, when we are told that as an adolescent Marcel confided to Bernard that he suspected her of an

extramarital affair: '... sa mère qu'il aimait, mais qui était restée une étrangère, jolie femme au charme particulier dont la vie n'était pas tout à fait ordinaire. Marcel avait soupçonné une liaison que rien n'avait pleinement confirmé, mais ... il en était venu à détester sa mère ... il était encore plus honteux de la pitié que son père lui inspirait. Rien d'autre que ce malheur ne le liait à cet homme timide qui ne se serait même pas cru justifié de se plaindre' (54). In marrying Jeanne, Marcel provides himself with a 'better' mother than the one he had. The two are merged, when he recalls his past in his journal: 'C'est le décor même des jours les plus heureux de ma vie, quand cette femme que j'aimais encore comme ma mère me retenait à la maison à cause d'un soupçon de fièvre' (134). The deictic *cette* femme' and comparative *comme* ma mère,' make this statement ambivalent, as it could refer to either his mother or Jeanne. From the beginning, Jeanne's attitude to Marcel is maternal: 'C'est vraiment un autre enfant qu'elle accueille avec toutes ses faiblesses' (21). Listening to her breathe in her sleep (she is 'l'éternelle endormie,' [132]), Marcel knows that he could also sleep in her comforting presence like a child (124). Their lives and their dreams have become merged: 'Je ne suis plus seul ... mon passé se mêle à celui de ma femme ... Comment se reconnaître dans cet entremêlement des souvenirs, cette confusion des personnalités? Je prends nettement conscience pour la première fois de ce qui m'arrive' (124). Marcel finds himself in a reconstruction of a state of primary narcissism, of symbiotic fusion, which is no longer reassuring but invasive, assimilatory, a threat to his survival as a separate entity. In reaction he seeks solitude, attempting to shut himself up in the bedroom, which is not even completely separated from the living room.

Jeanne is passive in bed (42, 130); she only really cares for the children: 'on la sent vraiment mère, avec tout ce que ce mot suppose d'expérience vitale' (26). She has thought of leaving Marcel, in order to protect the children (116), but does not dare to (43). Marcel, although no longer a practicing Catholic, believes divorce is impossible, that they are united for 'eternity' (130, 173). Yet he is ready to leave her, to attempt a new beginning with her younger sister, Louise: 'Certains regards de Louise m'ont entraîné plus loin que je n'aurais eu le courage d'aller moi-même' (127). Louise, at twenty-six, is still awaiting the sexual awakening that will make her fully 'alive' (30). She does not wish to become an embittered old maid, like Henriette (100). Unlike Jeanne, she is not resigned, but rebellious (134). In Marcel's dreams she becomes the means to 'se retrouver' (137), his only hope of happiness (142), and a way of escape (158). She listens admiringly when Marcel speaks (180) and shares his interest in art. An exhibition provides a pretext for a clandestine meeting that brings them together in a sordid hotel room. The liberating sexual act of Marcel's imagination is in reality more like a rape. For the first time, Marcel is 'autoritaire' (181–2); he recognizes that his aim is to *punish* Louise (for being like his mother?), that he could kill her (184). Louise's disappointment and disgust (184) leave him in despair. The failure of this last attempt at 'living' leads to his death. Marcel's journal, with its echoes of *La Nausée* (on 'l'existence,' [148]) becomes a counter-argument to the Sartrean contention that life begins on the far side of despair (148). Marcel's life ends. It is Bernard's that may benefit from his self-destruction.

**Negative narcissism: Why shave?**

Marcel's revolt against Jeanne and all she represents takes the form of a withdrawal into lethargy and sleep – an exaggeration of his previously passive and resigned attitude to life, which Jeanne shares. He declines into physical abjectness, conveyed by his unkempt, unwashed, and unshaved appearance. Jeanne, by contrast, is always neat and clean (99). Initially, she imposes her standard on Marcel by shaving him (133). He has a 'désagréable impression en passant ma main sur mes joues nues. Je n'ai pas insisté de crainte de reconnaître certains traits' (133). Marcel's madness takes the specific form of a phobia of shaving, related to seeing himself in the mirror (125–6, 132). The self that he sees when shaving is castrated. At sixteen, he had been embarrassed by his 'joues aussi lisses que celles d'une jeune fille' (18). Now, the clean-shaved self that he sees in the mirror is the image of his conformity, of his submission to a feminine/feminized code of behaviour. The self that he wishes to 'retrouver' is his manhood (cf. the 'beast' in Mathieu), as his first, exhilarating experience of unbridled passion with Louise (184) demonstrates. The fact that Louise does not share his enthusiasm may be interpreted as a comment on the feebleness of her own revolt against femininity, or as a negative assessment of Marcel's prowess as a lover. It may also be seen as an illustration (or criticism?) of the construction of masculine pleasure as violent (rape) and feminine pleasure as passive/ masochistic (Louise is unconscious). Either way, physical contact between bodies, as a source of communication and understanding, proves to be a false 'songe': the imaginary ideal woman does not exist.

Louis (the possible confusion of Louis and Louise is mentioned by Marcel [127–8, 160, 186]) also represents an illusion associated with femininity: religious faith (155–6). A desexualized bachelor at the service of others, he is also addressed in Marcel's journal (153). Marcel no longer believes that God *must* exist, because he needs to pray (160). Louis advances arguments in favour of 'life': '... la bêtise, les faiblesses, la laideur ... si on insiste un peu ces mauvaises apparences se lèvent et c'est la vie qui apparaît' (157). Marcel, however, sees this persistent optimism in the face of 'reality' as an illusion (158). How can he love his neighbour when he hates himself? (153) He is convinced that only he himself can save himself (174), and his attempts fail. Religion, male friends, and female love objects all prove unable to provide reasons for living. Unlike Mathieu, Marcel does not find solace in either art or his journal.

The diary reflects his 'crise de dédoublement' (126–7). Prompted by the moment of lucidity when he recognizes himself in the mirror, it is part of an attempt to 'me dégager, m'affirmer' (132). The motivations he attributes to himself read like a catalogue of clichés from previous *journaux intimes*: 'fixer mes impressions ... me retrouver ... trouver un sens à ma vie ... en faire le triste inventaire ... bien voir ceux qui m'entourent pour savoir ce que je suis devenu' (125); 'marquer les points (128) ... fixer (nos rapports) une fois pour toutes et m'enfuir' (141) ...'essayer une dernière fois d'y voir clair' (177). He is aware that the diary may lead him into 'des voies sans issue' (132) and that illusion/dreams intrude in his attempts at self-awareness: 'je suis tenté d'écrire ce journal comme un roman, d'imaginer tout ce qu'il me faudra vivre pour me sauver' (128); 'Je dois ... vivre attentivement chaque moment de l'aventure et me refuser au rêve qui ne ferait qu'épaissir l'ombre' (128). The shadow referred to is the third of his 'personnages': 'Entre le personnage qui faisait appel à la pitié des autres et celui qui leur criait son mépris, il devait y en avoir un troisième. Je ne vis encore qu'une ombre' (127). He adds, 'Cette ombre m'intéresse ... c'est mon âme, si ce mot a vraiment un sens' (128). Like Mathieu, he is seeking his 'real' self. He finds none – or rather, no one, but at least three – and these are not exhaustive: 'Je sais que je puis donner de moi-même une tout autre image' (127). He recognizes himself in the mirror, as a *representation*.

## Postscript/post-mortem: The diary's repercussions

The image Marcel projects depends on his potential reader: himself (130–1), Jeanne (130–1), Louise (136–7), Louis (153). He does not envisage Bernard as a narratee, as he believes their friendship is over. Yet it is Bernard, followed by Louis, who actually reads the journal. That it is meant to be read is indicated by the name and address on the notebook. That it is not meant for Jeanne may be deduced from the fact that Marcel took it with him. How would she react? Speaking of another resigned and neat woman, Marcel remarks, 'Que c'est lourd la souffrance des muets!' (140).

In any case, Jeanne has the children: six-year-old Jacqueline, who is already like her mother (19), two-year-old Claude, already 'pas destiné aux conquêtes' (19). Like his father, Claude is 'vaincu d'avance' (166). Marcel does not believe that one can 'se retrouver dans ses enfants' (124). When he plays with them, it is as another child – at their level, on the floor (134) – not as a father. He claims, regarding parents, that 'notre chair ... désire leur mort, comme si elle ne pouvait s'épanouir autrement' (142). By his own death, he avoids being a parent. As Simoneau puts it, Marcel 'rejoint son désir de ne pas s'engager, de ne rien assumer et de n'accepter aucune responsabilité' (1979, 28). In doing so, he leaves the future (the children), like the past, in the hands of the mother – with his pen/phallus: 'Tu attends que je laisse là mon stylo et que je m'en aille?' (185).

Can Bernard and Nicole form a new type of couple? Perhaps, but they are unlikely to write about it, being focused on action. Belleau remarked, with reference to this novel, '... il semble que le discours québécois ne puisse représenter le destin de l'écrivain autrement que dans la déchirure' (1980, 83). Marcel's journal is a cry for help: 'on me croira fou si j'appelle au secours et n'ai-je pas tort de troubler le sommeil des autres?' (167). Part 3 of the novel, a brief account of the reactions to the diary and to Marcel's death, implies that the others are woken up, that Marcel has successfully fulfilled the poet's function of being a 'réflecteur,' in the sense of a spotlight. With 'la fin des songes' they may become less like Marcel, that is, impotent (167).

Marcel is mad, and commits suicide. Yet his attempt at lucidity, as represented in the diary, shows madness as a 'normal' result of lucidity, in a situation of enforced impotence. The latter is represented as a man's subjection to a woman, in spite of her apparent submissiveness. One more novel from this period depicts the drama of the relationship to the phallic mother, in horrific terms; Jean Filiatrault's *Chaînes* (1955) also entails madness and suicide for the male protagonist.

### Filiatrault, *Chaînes* (1955): Attachment and constraint: 'Sa mère ... à qui il était enchaîné' (135)

The volume entitled *Chaînes* is composed of two texts, 'La Chaîne de feu' (176 pages) and 'La Chaîne de sang' (70 pages). It is the second that takes the form of the diary of a young man who has killed his mother and is interned in a mental hospital. The first, narrated in the third person, focuses on a mother-son relationship, mainly from the mother's point of view. The author refers elsewhere to these texts as two separate 'nouvelles,'[6] but the reader assumes at first that the diary is written by the son of the first story. This impression is confirmed by cross-references to common elements, such as the death of a cat. When the names (of the cat, of the son) are given as different in the second text, this might be attributed to the narrator's madness. Robert Melançon (1987, 169) is justified in claiming that Filiatrault failed to exploit the possibilities of the juxtaposition of the two texts as complementary. My reading will be based on the assumption that they are connected. This ambivalence regarding connection/separation (identification/difference) in fact reflects the theme central to both texts.

In the first part the mother, Eugénie, like Lucienne in *Mathieu*, has been left by her husband to raise her son alone (14). It is not clear whether the father is dead or alive (15, 71). Her previous love for her husband has been transferred to the son, Serge, who resembles him (14). Eugénie sees herself as a victim (71) and her love for her son as positive. It becomes apparent, however, that Serge is a prisoner of his mother's excessive and possessive passion: she is compared to a ball-and-chain restraining him from autonomy: he is the victim, enslaved to a despot (12, 19, 120). Even his achievement as a pianist is a fulfilment of her ambition, rather than his (119). When Serge is attracted to a young woman, Véronique, the mother's jealousy knows no bounds. Becoming an 'ogresse de conte de fée' (33), she frightens her rival away by telling her that Serge cannot marry. The reason given is that his father was a suicidal maniac, now interned, and the son shows symptoms of the same illness (100). The impersonal narrator calls this a lie (106), but Véronique has reason to believe it when Serge threatens to kill if she no longer loves him (163). Eugénie appears to have succeeded in keeping Serge for herself ('le posséder, le garder éternellement' [13]). She has prevented him from becoming a man, he will remain 'mon petit,' dependent on her.

The situation changes because of the intervention of Véronique's brother, Alban, who is attracted to Eugénie. In an incestuous generation confusion reminiscent of *Angéline de Montbrun* (with genders reversed), Eugénie succumbs to the advances of Alban, seeing him as a double of Serge (157, 160). Alban, unlike Serge, adopts a masterful attitude to her. He is glad to be a man (28), and the concept of masculine pleasure as rape (as in *Mathieu* and *La Fin des songes*) recurs (159). Véronique, unlike the mother, is submissive towards Serge (57), although she believes herself to be a liberated woman (94). Conventional heterosexual interaction is depicted as a reversal of the underlying, archaic relation of son to mother, in which the phallic mother is omnipotent.

When Serge surprises Eugénie with Alban, having lost Véronique (and blaming his mother), he is tempted to kill her (133, 135). He does not, however, and leaves with his mother's photograph, rather than Véronique's. Her loss is the greater one.[7] The picture shows the cat, Musta, with Eugénie (172). The cat represents the barely hidden sensuality between mother and son (cf. 16, 73, 145–6). Once the son has left, the mother kills the cat. We are told that Eugénie 's'était reprise à penser avec logique' (173). In 'La Chaîne de sang,' 'la logique' is the term used by the narrator to designate his madness. The implication at the end of 'La Chaîne de feu' is that it is not the father who is mad and has tainted the son, but the mother.

## Primary narcissism and madness

The name of the diarist in the second text, Bastien, is revealed only at the end. He has killed his mother, because he loved her. Now that she is dead, no one can condemn the love between them and she can appear to him at night, in his dreams (188, 201, 227) (cf. *La Fin des songes*). He recalls that previously he killed their cat, Noireau (189, 219, 237). He was (and is) also in the habit of catching flies and tearing off their wings

(217, 220). He has been interned by his father (193), 'Maxime Patry' (power + lineage). Although Bastien recollects his father being cruel to his mother when he was a child (221), he had lost touch with him. The journal is addressed to the father initially (231, 233), but the diarist recognizes that he writes primarily for himself (236). His mother's voice tells him that writing about her will reinforce his 'faith in her' (236), rather than provide a paternal condemnation (or legitimation) for his act of murder. The mother encourages him to close his eyes, to sleep, to dream (236); yet writing the journal is a means to lucidity, to see 'la vérité' (184) and 'sortir de moi' (187) – to reach the father. It is prescribed as therapy (183) by the psychiatrist, Isabelle, onto whom Bastien predictably tranfers his love (212, 214).

His treatment by electric shock in the psychiatric hospital (206, 209) requires and induces a passivity and submission associated with infantilization. Bastien is bathed and massaged by a 'maternal' male nurse, whose attentions appear to be sexually motivated (197, 199). He becomes obsessed with Isabelle (who is merged with his mother) and disoriented when she leaves to get married. His writing is disrupted by the activities of other patients: 'J'ai perdu le fil de ma pensée ...' (189). Yet he has no real distractions: 'J'ai tellement d'heures à ma disposition pour réfléchir' (189). He has already been in hospital for eight months, and at the end of the diary, which covers six months (3 July 1954–12 January 1955) he expects to be released in a few weeks' time. The hospital stay represents an incubation period, intended to result in a rebirth into paternal logic (the symbolic order) through writing (language) in the journal. His release would finally break the umbilical cord attaching him to his mother and the realm of the imaginary.

A letter appended to the journal, from Bastien, informs us (and his father) that this will not happen, since he is about to hang himself, with a rope that resembles an umbilical cord. He chooses madness and connection to the dead mother over the 'real' world of the father: 'Il était préférable que je garde ma folie. J'étais heureux alors et maman me visitait de temps à autre. Maintenant je suis vaincu et seul ...' (245). He adds, 'Avec moi se brisera la chaîne de sang. Il n'y aura plus de folie dans ta famille' (246), implying that madness is irremediably associated with the mother, and sanity (logic) with the father. According to patriarchal logic, murder is a crime punishable by death, and only Bastien's death can make him pardonable (246). Yet the maternal, imaginary logic prevails, since the son will rejoin his mother. His *dédoublement* between child and man (197, 205, 229) is resolved by the refusal to live, that is, to grow up and grow old. He can remain the ideal self of primary narcissism, 'tel que je suis, tel que je veux être' (235).

## The 'diary of a madman'

In 'La Chaîne de sang' Bastien mentions another family member who burned her house down 'en souvenir de son père': 'l'image de son père s'installa dans son propre coeur. Elle brûla donc avec sa maison' (216–17). This apparently marginal reference underlines the central premiss shared by this fictional journal and those of Loranger's Mathieu and Elie's Marcel: self-destructive madness is associated with narcissistic identity confusion between the diarist and a parent of the opposite sex, that is, with an inability to separate, implying incest. *Angéline de Montbrun* illustrated the father-daughter link, but that situation was seen to be ambivalent, since Charles de Montbrun functioned as both father and mother – in fact, more as a phallic mother than as a symbolic father intruding into the mother-child dyad. In the three novels discussed in this chapter, a son struggles to escape from an all-powerful phallic mother (Marcel's wife is the equivalent), to be 'born' through language in the journal (the birth metaphor will be examined more closely in chapter 9). Bastien states: 'Je suis né avec ma maladie, à vingt-trois ans' (183), before strangling on his umbilical cord. His mother will not let him go, and in killing her he kills himself. The concept of 'possession' by an other who is the self echoes another famous example of diary fiction – Maupassant's 'Le Horla,' a prototype of the 'diary of a madman,' a subgenre popular in the nineteenth century.[8] The intimate diary was considered an appropriate means to convey the state of mind of a woman, or of a mad (superfluous/underground) man.

According to the patriarchal paradigm, identification with the mother, for a male, implies feminization and the inability to become a 'real man' by dominating an other/a woman. All three narrators perceive themselves as emasculated. In a discussion of the correlation between madness and femininity, Shoshana Felman (1975) agreed with the following claim made by Phyllis Chessler (1973): 'What we consider "madness," whether it appears in women or in men, is either the acting out of the devalued female role or the total or partial rejection of one's sex-role stereotype' (Felman, 2; Chessler, 56). In the Quebec examples discussed so far, it is women who reject their 'sex-role stereotype,' men who find themselves 'acting out the devalued female role.' Madness in women (frequently designated hysteria from the Greek for uterus) is shown by Chessler and Elaine Showalter (1985) to be the logical conclusion of their position as women, that is, defined as other and condemned to alterity/alienation. Felman quotes Chessler: 'It is clear that for a woman to be healthy she must "adjust" to and accept the behavioral norms for her sex even though these kinds of behavior are generally regarded as undesirable ... The ethic of mental health is masculine in our culture' (68–9). Chessler makes the connection with incest: 'The *sine qua non* of "feminine" identity in patriarchal society is the violation of the incest taboo, ie. the initial and continued "preference" for Daddy, followed by the approved falling in love with and/or marrying of powerful father figures' (138). In the 'colonized' society of Quebec as depicted in diary fiction of this period, powerful father-figures are not there to be preferred: the 'instance paternelle' is missing. Consequently, the mother-figure remains phallic, and sons identify with their mothers rather than their fathers. The potential implications for a homosexual orientation will be explored in the next chapter.

Like women, madmen are defined as outside the symbolic order. They speak from an 'other' place, and their discourse does not 'make sense.' Rather, it questions the foundation of patriarchal meaning, and language as an adequate means of expression. This dimension – the play of the signifier in 'le langage des déments' – is not exploited in these novels written in the 1950s.[9] It is developed later, for example, in Pierre Châtillon's *Le Journal d'automne de Placide Mortel* (1970), which bears the subtitle 'récit poétique.' Filiatrault's Bastien has his own 'logic,' at odds with the father's. His recovery of sanity leads him, like Marcel Larocque, to the rational decision that death is preferable to integration into the paternal order. Mathieu survives only by making a conscious effort to be *less* conscious, less analytical. In the final instance, his model is not so much Rochat or Etienne, but Danielle, who urges him to live (act, observe others), rather than indulge in introspection.

These marginalized young men strive to become like the strong women around them, while recognizing, like women, that they are ultimately powerless. They reflect Felman's observation on madness in women: 'Depressed, terrified women are not about to seize the means of production and reproduction: quite the opposite of rebellion, madness is the impasse confronting those whom cultural conditioning has deprived of the very means of protest or self-affirmation. Far from being a form of contestation, "mental illness" is a request for help, a manifestation both of cultural impotence and of political castration. This socially defined help-needing and help-seeking behaviour is itself part of female conditioning' (2). The narcissism experienced by women and by colonized men is necessary for survival when the self is defined in relation to a dominant subject (the one). Yet paradoxically, the self-as-other can only become a subject by contesting the existing relation of dominance – for these men, by 'killing the mother,' the only way to assert their own virility. Jane Gallop's comments on the phallic mother have particular relevance in the Quebec context: 'Perhaps it is the seemingly paradoxical term "phallic mother" which can most work to undo the supposedly natural logic of the ideological solidarity between phallus, father, power and men ... If the phallus were understood as the veiled attribute of the Mother ... this logical scandal could expose the joint imposture of both Phallus and Mother ...' (1982, 117).

In the Quiet Revolution period of the 1960s, the colonized Quebec male diarist is depicted as attempting to emerge from narcissistic dependency or assimilation into decolonized 'autonomy,' related to self-affirmation and a 'rebirth' through language. Eclipse into (or by) a dominant other – whether the paternalistic colonizer or matriarchal refuge values – is construed as madness, in terms of survival. Revolt takes the form of political contestation and the end of the sexual repression (impotence) imposed by the mother. Yet narcissism resurfaces, in the form of masculine homosexuality: a rejection of the feminine as object, in favour of its appropriation as part of the self. This element is central in the texts to be discussed in the next chapter.

# PART IV

# GENDER CONFUSION AND SELF-GENERATION (1960–1990)

CHAPTER EIGHT

# Homosexuality, Androgyny, and Bi-Section: *Pinsonneault, Blais, Richard, Tremblay, Monette*

'Ayant fréquemment constaté la présence d'une mère dangereuse et toute-puissante chez les homosexuels efféminés, on n'est guère surpris que ces hommes soient terrifiés par le corps féminin.'

ROBERT J. STOLLER IN PONTALIS (1973), 144

'It is impossible, in practice, to test the hypothesis that physical or emotional removal of the father causes homosexuality.'

K. FREUND AND R. BLANCHARD IN ROSS (1985), 8

'Quand les hommes critiquent les femmes, cela vient souvent de leur dépit de n'avoir pas la possibilité d'être eux-mêmes une femme.'

FELIX BOEHM IN PONTALIS (1973), 283

'L'assignation d'*un* sexe prive des organes et des pouvoirs de l'autre sexe, de celui qu'on n'a pas; le bisexuel apparaît comme complet.'

J.-B. PONTALIS (1973), 15

## Phallic mothers and homosexual sons

The novels discussed in chapter 7 illustrate the ways in which phallic mother-figures were blamed, in Quebec, for the impotence and effeminacy of the colonized male. The latent homosexuality of these misogynist men is suggested, but not depicted as such. In the first example of diary fiction by Hertel, *Le Beau Risque* (1939), the priest identified with a male double representing narcissistic attachment to his younger self. Such identification illustrates the spiritual fatherhood associated by Plato, in the *Symposium*, with the Greek model of male homosexuality.[1] This image corroborates Freud's claim that homosexual paedophilia is based on a narcissistic desire for the former self (see Green 1983, 34). In *Le Journal d'Anatole Laplante* Hertel showed another version of homosexual male bonding, between Laplante and Lepic, albeit at the sublimated level of the cerebral exchange of idea(l)s. Women were excluded and condemned, as also by Baillargeon's Claude Perrin and Simard's Fabrice Navarin. Both of these, in their recollections of their time spent in the Catholic *collèges*, mentioned the emphasis placed on masturbation, a narcissistic pursuit associated with the taboo on male homosexuality (see Baillargeon 1945, 95–6; Simard 1956, 106). Masturbation entails the simultaneous playing of both active and passive roles. If active is equated with masculine and passive with feminine, as is usually the case in Freudian theory, masturbation connotes a self-sufficient bisexuality.[2] Male homosexuality, however, is assumed to involve the assumption of a passive, feminine role on the part of at least one of the partners. While this may not reflect the actual activities or attitudes of male homosexuals, it does influence the dominant stereotype of the gay man as effeminate, which developed in the eighteenth century and is still prevalent in both Europe and North America (see Ross 1985, 1–2; Stoller in Pontalis 1973, 135–53).

Male 'inversion' was attributed by Freud to over-identification with the mother, and later theorists added aversion to the father (Lewes 1988, 196; Green 1983, 34–5). The absence or weakness of the father has been considered a motivating factor in the homosexual orientation of boys. This has been questioned by more recent studies that, while confirming the distant relationship between many gay men and their fathers, interpret this as an effect rather than a cause: it may be due to the father's disapproval of the son's effeminacy, or to the son's fear of a too close (homosexual + incestuous) attachment to the parent of the same sex (Freund and Blanchard in Ross 1985, 7–25). Simard's fictional journal, like those of Loranger, Elie, and Filiatrault (see chapter 7), illustrated the connection between identification with the mother/the feminine, the incapacity to become a 'real man,' distance from the father, and madness. Madness is often (some say always) associated with the repression of homosexual tendencies (see Lewes 1988, 42). Loranger's Mathieu finally embarks on a relationship with a woman in whom he admires masculine qualities that he lacks – autonomy, forcefulness, directness, sexual freedom. He is 'mothered' by a godfather who resembles Gide's Edouard in his fascination with a younger version of himself. Yet the suggestion of latent homosexuality remains implicit, as in the other works of that period. What is explicit is the attribution of his problems to his domineering mother, who does not love him and gives him the impression that no one ever could. He identifies with her in perceiving himself as abject and detestable.

Male homosexuality may arise from a refusal to separate from the mother, a desire to remain a part/extension of her, as in the case of Filiatrault's Serge/Bastien (*Chaînes*). In this situation, the mother becomes dangerous because of her excessive love for her son (a narcissistic self-object), who enables her to be the phallic mother. For Freud, the child – especially a son – functions as a phallus for women who become mothers. The son is in effect placed in a feminine, passive relationship to the mother. He is defined as the object of her desire and narcissistically identifies with her in desiring himself, or a double of himself.

## Gender ambivalence

The male who defines himself psychically as feminine may perceive himself as bisexual, androgynous, combining the qualities of both sexes and narcissistically self-sufficient. He in fact becomes (like) the phallic mother, a woman with a penis (Lewes 1988, 44, 78, 198). The ultimate dream of the narcissistic bisexual is self-engenderment and self-perpetuation: reproduction or resurrection of the self, phoenixlike, without the contribution of an other. This aspect is present in the myth of Hermaphrodite, as discussed in a special issue of the *Nouvelle Revue de Psychanalyse* devoted to bisexuality (Pontalis 1973). The story of the youth Hermaphrodite and the nymph Salmacis (5–8) has similarities to that of Narcissus and Echo, also told by Ovid. Both Hermaphrodite and Narcissus perceive themselves as sexually ambivalent: Hermaphrodite combines the qualities of his father, Hermes, and his mother, Aphrodite; Narcissus is attracted to the image he sees in the pool (in one version) because it recalls his dead twin sister (see Green 1983, 76–7). Both refuse the advances of an attractive female and are punished by losing their strength, that is, by becoming impotent and no longer fully men. However, Hermaphrodite is a self-sufficient bisexual and wants no other, whereas Narcissus is in search of an imaginary, ideal mirror image of himself. He illustrates a homosexual desire for completion of the self by union with a double–the same.

The sense of the self as incomplete, as seeking its other half or alter ego, is 'explained' in Plato's *Symposium* by Aristophanes' story of the androgyne. Lacan invokes this myth to relate the birth of desire to the recognition of 'lack.'[3] In Aristophanes' story the original, spherical 'whole' beings were of three types: male, female, and bisexual (androgynous). Bisected by Zeus, who was afraid of their rivalry with the gods, they became 'sexed' (divided) beings, all seeking their other part, in an attempt to retrieve their lost integrity. Those originally part of a male or a female unit became male or female homosexuals, while those who were originally bisexual sought their opposite complement. Heterosexual union is the means whereby the latter re-converge, while homosexuals seek to establish a psychic androgyny related to the desire for non-sexual self-production. The real lack, according to Lacan, is death, which is entailed in all reproduction dependent on heterosexual intercourse (see Silverman 1983, 152). The nostalgia for a perfect state of oneness has obvious associations with the pre-Oedipal (pre-desire) stage of primary narcissism, of symbiotic union with the phallic (non-sexed) mother. As Green (1983, 208ff) has shown in his work on the 'neuter' (*ne uter*: neither), actual regression to that stage of pre-sexualization/non-individuation is synonymous with death. Bisexuality may ultimately be connected to asexuality and the disappearance of desire, whereas homosexuality expresses desire, but for an other who is the same, dissociating it from the will (or necessity) to procreate.

## The Quiet Revolution and sexual liberation

In chapter 5 we saw that moral narcissism was inseparable in Laure Conan's fictional journals from the messianism prevalent in late nineteenth-century Quebec. Moral narcissism is associated with desexualization (see chapter 2). The aim was to become an 'angel,' just as Hertel's, fifty years later, was still to become a 'pure spirit.' The soul or the mind were dissociated from the body, which was encoded as 'bestial' – a necessary evil. Loranger's *Mathieu* (1949) provided a major departure, in depicting a rehabilitation through the body and in presenting extramarital sexual relations without moral condemnation. This was exceptional for Quebec at the time, and coincided with the first efforts, by artists (*Refus global*, 1948) to break away from the repression of the period known as 'la grande noirceur.' Previous attempts in literature to deal with sexuality in any form were censored or censured – for example, Jovette Bernier's *La Chair décevante* (1931) and Jean-Charles Harvey's *Les demi-civilisés* (1934). Sex was admissible only within marriage and with the avowed purpose of contributing to the revenge of the cradle. Contraception was severely condemned – and largely unknown.[4] This Puritan/Jansenist attitude was widespread in North America and by no means confined to Catholic Quebec. It was opposed to the liberal attitudes associated with France and attributed in Quebec to the 'free-thinking' that produced the French Revolution. Many (most?) of the great texts of French literature were included in the Catholic Index of forbidden books (see *Le Libraire*). The French models available to novelists raised in Quebec were Mauriac, Bernanos, Julien Green – the Catholic writers – not Proust or Gide. Quebec was cut off from the tradition of homosexual writing that emerged in France (see Stambolian and Marks 1979).

The increased exposure of Quebec intellectuals to French culture after the Second World War, through visits to Europe and the influence of those who returned from there, contributed as much to the secularization of Quebec society as did the emergence of an educated middle class (Postgate and McRoberts 1976). During this period writers such as Hertel, Baillargeon, and Anne Hébert opted for exile in France. After 1960, when the death of Duplessis allowed a change of political regime, writers in Quebec, beginning with the poets of *Parti pris*, undertook a new role of contestation of refuge values. Following the precepts of Memmi and Fanon (see chapter 3) and putting into practice existentialist concepts of *engagement*, they contributed to the awareness necessary for a movement towards decolonization.

Their revolt encompassed the open discussion of sexuality, including homosexuality. Claude Jasmin's *Délivrez-nous du mal!* (1961) was the first novel to address the issue, followed by Pinsonneault's *Les Abîmes de l'aube* (1962), one of the first full-length fictions in Quebec to be written entirely in diary form. During the 1960s, various types of first-person narration became widespread in Quebec fiction, as discussed by several critics – for example, Bourneuf (1970), Whitfield (1987), Kwaterko (1989). This phenomenon is sometimes attributed to the influence of French models (the *nouveau roman*), but is also related to the fact that these narrative forms, particularly the *journal intime*, are appropriate to convey the 'collective identity crisis' experienced in Quebec during this period. This *prise de conscience* takes on three dimensions: individual sexuality (related to self-definition, self-representation, and desire), the political self-determination of Quebec (related to the passage of time and the construction of history), and the survival of French culture in Quebec (related to the use of language and literary institutions). These three elements correspond to the self-time-writing pyramid developed in my model for the functioning of the fictional journal (see chapter 1 and Raoul 1980).

Three diary fictions published in the 1960s focus on the first dimension, sexual identity, and introduce homosexuality or bisexuality. The first, already mentioned, is Jean-Paul Pinsonneault's *Les Abîmes de l'aube*, written in 1959 and published in 1962. It depicts an adolescent who confides in his diary in order to come to terms with his homosexual inclinations, which are closely connected to his identification with his dead mother. In the second, Marie-Claire Blais's *L'Insoumise* (1966), the diary of a mother is interspersed with that of her son (who dies), who may be homosexual – or seeking union with his mother. The third, Jean-Jules Richard's *Journal d'un hobo* (1965), is innovative in both its form and its depiction of a literally bisexual (hermaphrodite) narrator. Sexual ambivalence may be condemned, repressed, or lived out, as illustrated in these three texts.

### Pinsonneault, *Les Abîmes de l'aube* (1962): Adolescent narcissism and homosexuality

*'Ce qu'il faudrait, c'est haïr en moi le mal' (35)*

*'Il faudrait me refaire. Mais comment y arriverai-je jamais?' (68)*

According to André Green, narcissism is typical of adolescence: 'Le narcissisme est une maladie de jeunesse' (1983, 78). It is a symptom of resistance to final separation from the mother: 'La différence instaurée par la séparation entre la mère et l'enfant est compensée par l'investiture narcissique' (127), as at the first stage of individuation in infancy. Adolescent narcissism may be accompanied by homosexual attachment to an object of the same age and sex, as is the case for Jean, the seventeen-year-old whose diary forms the text of *Les Abîmes de l'aube*. The narrative has no dates, but otherwise it conforms to the diary model in its divisions, in the closeness of the events related to the time of narration, and in the narrator's self-analysis and metacommentary on diary writing. Whether narcissism, homosexuality, and diary writing are acceptable only as a stage from which the subject must emerge as different is the central issue in this text.[5]

Jean starts his diary after being expelled from a Catholic school for an incident involving another student, Laurent, for which he has taken the blame (10). His parents do not know that his relationship with Laurent was 'too close,' although his (step)mother suspects that Jean is 'vicieux' and 'indésirable' (51–2). He himself recognizes his attraction as 'the love that dares not speak its name,' and confides his secret to the diary, although he also avoids naming it. His fantasies of physical contact with Laurent are associated with masturbation, which leaves him feeling 'souillé' and aware that he has found only himself, a narcissistic object (33–5). His reaction is one of both guilt and shame, as he shares his parents' condemnation of such an orientation and their perception of it as evil: 'Je suis écoeuré du mal qui est en moi' (104). His only self-defence is that he did not choose to have this tendency (167) and that he is sincere in his attempts to be honest, at least with himself (139).

This honesty alternates with efforts to deny the 'truth' and to prove to himself that he is 'normal.' However, his liaison with a girl, Sylvie, proves unsatisfactory, as he finds physical contact with her repulsive (58, 65–6, 100). A visit to a prostitute is primarily an attempt to take revenge on Laurent for having abandoned him for a girl, and leaves him feeling abject (163–5). Cries of distress directed to God ('Apprenez-moi un amour qui n'est point le mal' [74]), and confession to a priest (75), also fail to bring him any relief. It is only after a failed suicide attempt (169) that he believes he may see an end to his suffering, a 'dawn' (echoes of the title occur throughout the diary) associated with faith in a greater Love, that is, of God, who alone can enable him to 'extirpate' the evil in him (173). Yet his love for Laurent is confused with the search for God (141), for an ideal all-comprehending listener (74) superior to the members of his immediate circle.

## The false (imaginary?) mother and the true (symbolic?) father

This circle is complicated by the fact that Jean was adopted at the age of two. His (false) mother makes no secret of her hostility towards him.

His father, however, defends him. The discovery of a photo of the father at his age reveals that he is his real father: 'Ce visage au regard mélancolique et aux traits presque féminins ... un visage qui est le mien' (97). The father loves him because he is the trace of the woman he loved, whereas the stepmother resents him for the same reason (149). The novel has been criticized for introducing a situation that may appear superfluous to the central theme,[6] yet in the context of the theory of narcissism these elements are significant. They provide an explanation for Jean's inversion, as he identifies (like Henriette Dessaulles) with his dead, real mother, in opposition to the wicked stepmother. He believes that the former is the only person who would have understood him and loved him unconditionally (54). The diary becomes a projection of her, as well as of Laurent, and of God as the ideal father. We are informed that Laurent also (incidentally?) became involved in the relationship with Jean shortly after the death of his mother (13).

The real father, as in the earlier examples, is mostly absent (14), and when he is there he is unable to stand up to the stepmother, who always 'has the last word' (18, 19, 23). He drowns his sorrows in drink, and Jean (like Loranger's Mathieu) shows signs of following in his footsteps in this respect (104–5). When his father lends him the keys to the car, saying that he is no longer a child, the mother confiscates them, symbolically castrating them both. Jean does not dare to draw too close to his father, who is affectionate (95), for fear of discovering that the attraction his father exerts on him may be similar to what he feels for Laurent: 'Mon amour pour mon père s'alarmerait-il de la sorte s'il n'avait pas quelque chose d'excessif et de monstrueux lui aussi? Ce sentiment ne ferait-il qu'un avec celui qui m'attache à Laurent? Y grouillerait-il à mon insu la même inquiétante pourriture? Je rougis en écrivant ces lignes, mais mon désarroi est si profond que je ne saurais m'en abstenir' (120). Similarly, he holds back from greater intimacy with another male friend, Pierre, in whom he is reluctant to confide in case his overtures are misinterpreted (71, 73).

The journal once more represents a narcissistic withdrawal: condemned to solitude, the diarist tries to prefer it. He shuts himself up in his room, creating walls between himself and others (131). His attempts to leave are abortive, because he is still dependent on his parents His final decision to 'quitter à jamais ces murs qui m'étouffent' (119) relates to the psychological barriers he has established. He plans to forget the past, to begin over again in the light of day: yet the lucidity acquired through the journal warns him that his 'inclination' may not be so easily erased: 'J'imposerais silence à mon coeur, que ma chair, malgré cela, continuerait de réclamer Laurent' (68). The diary ends, as he decides to abandon this 'désir stérile' (168), to conform, even at the expense of (self) deception. The epigram from Saint Augustine's *Confessions* asks: 'Où donc, en effet, pour mon coeur, s'enfuir de mon coeur?' Jean's attempt to confess, to a priest who is his stepmother's ally, led him to conclude that this was a 'tentative de fuite. Je voulais m'enfuir de mon coeur, de moi-même, mais je n'y ai pas réussi' (77). His apparent success in changing himself, at the end of the diary, remains questionable.

No one reads Jean's diary, except himself (44–5, 82–3). Within the fiction, it remains a private document of self-appraisal. Yet as a novel it serves as a means to expose a forbidden topic, giving the reader the impression of eavesdropping. The final message is ambivalent: Is this a defence or a condemnation of homosexuality? Similar questions are raised in Marie-Claire Blais's *L'Insoumise*, with the added perspective within the fiction of a secret diary read furtively, through the eyes of the diarist's mother. For the first time, the mother is not presented as on the side of repression and censorship.

### Blais, *L'Insoumise* (1966): Gide with a difference

*L'Insoumise* was published shortly after *Une Saison dans la vie d'Emmanuel* (1966), the novel that established Blais's reputation as a writer with a unique, horrific vision of Quebec and a powerful, surrealistic style to convey it. Blais included the journal of Jean-le-Maigre as an element in that novel (like Evans' diary in *Tête Blanche*), but *L'Insoumise* was seen by critics as a disappointing follow-up, in its 'classic' imitation of the Gidean *récit*.[7] The use of the diary form was associated by Marcotte (1989, 139) with a 'sage écriture de roman psychologique,' surprising in a text by Blais, and for the Quebec of 1966, when others were experimenting with *joual*. The juxtaposition of three first-person narrations – by the mother (Madeleine), the father (Rodolphe), and their dead son's friend (Frédérik) – is certainly reminiscent of Gide's tripartite *L'Ecole des femmes:* even more so since part 1 is the diary of a disillusioned middle-class wife, while the other two accounts are retrospective, situated after the main event, which is the death of the son, Paul, in a skiing accident. Jacques Pelletier referred at the time to 'des procédés littéraires originaux' (*Le Campus estrien*, 19 Oct. 1966), but this does not apply to the combination of diary and *récit*. Françoise Laurent considered the juxtaposition 'une des faiblesses essentielles de la technique romanesque de Marie-Claire Blais' (1986, 55–6), finding the three parts insufficiently linked: 'Les trois tranches de désespoir tendent à rester éparses au lieu de se joindre sans effort en un tout organique. Le lecteur bute sur ces béances du texte alors qu'il aspire à une totalité sans faille' (56). While one critic finds the text too 'classical' (Marcotte), the other (Laurent) judges it incoherent in relation to that paradigm. These divergent views provide some indication of the interest of this particular novel (otherwise not one of Blais's most successful works) in the perspective of reader response to a fictional journal.

The innovation here is not in the juxtaposition of three narratives reflecting three solitudes (the surname *Robinson* is significant); rather, it lies in the inclusion, in the mother's diary, of extracts from Paul's private notebook that she is secretly reading. Paul's diary could have been presented separately, with greater *vraisemblance*, since it is difficult to imagine Madeleine copying out selected pages (in italics in the text) into her own notebook. The effect, however, would have been quite different. As it is, the first part of the novel becomes an imaginary dialogue between Paul and his mother, who otherwise do not communicate. This oblique exchange may be provoked by Paul. Otherwise, why would he leave his diary on his bed (10), knowing that she makes it for him (44)? Has he not noticed that she has torn out a page, at one point (25)? The references to a mysterious Anna in Paul's notes provide an enigma, which the reader is invited to solve, along with Madeleine. The suspicion that Anna is a fiction (16) is encouraged by the references that equate her with Madeleine (11, 16, 17). She is a married woman, old enough to be Paul's mother (53, 115), with a young son who is like Paul (114). She mothers Paul, buying his clothes (39), paying his tuition (33), and organizing his life (42). Madeleine's jealousy of this double of herself reveals her 'too close' attachment to Paul, just as Paul's choice (or dream) of Anna confirms his desire to remain connected to his mother.

Paul's diary is a mixture of concrete, everyday detail (about his athletic activities, his failed exams, his banal outings with friends of both sexes) and the evocation of what appear to be dreams. These alternate between fantasies of fulfilment involving Anna, and nightmares of destruction that include a male double, Frédérik. Paul perceives both himself and Frédérik as destined for early death, associated with a war (see Marcotte 1989, 150). His 'accident' may not be premeditated, but his failure to live is certainly anticipated, and prefigured in his lack of motivation to study – an attitude that incurs his father's wrath.

## A question of (in)subordination

Paul's vision of himself (or Frédérik) being shot remains blurred: it may be in battle, or for refusing to fight. Although the novel is entitled *L'Insoumise*, inferring a focus on the mother's secret revolt, it is Paul who appears as the rebel (see Marcotte 1989, 151). He is the one who refuses to sign a declaration of Catholic orthodoxy for the university. Madeleine, while inwardly admiring this gesture, appears to share the disapproval of her husband, and her tears are ambivalent (29–30). Rodolphe assumes that she agrees with him, that he can speak for them both ('ta mère et moi ...'). He calls her, paternalistically, 'ma petite fille' (10, 55). Dedicated as she is to domesticity and her three sons, Madeleine's discreet insubordination may be seen as representative of the suppressed revolt of the *reine du foyer* on realizing that she has no control, even over her own house and children. Her dissatisfaction is associated with narcissism: 'Les tables sont polies et fraîches, on peut y mirer son visage comme dans une source ...' She admits that her jealousy of Anna is because of a narcissistic injury: 'j'avais pitié de mon image offensée' (55). Her self-representation as a conventional bourgeois wife and mother is damaged by the idea that her son has a married mistress, while her unconscious desire for continued connection to her son, through whom she may vicariously rebel, is threatened by his choice of a substitute. She is no longer the phallic mother, but castrated by his betrayal.

Marcotte commented in 1966, 'A quelle femme n'arrive-t-il pas, vers le milieu de sa vie, de se sentir démunie, inutile, étrangère à son mari aussi bien qu'à ses enfants' (*La Presse*, 7 mai). Like Gide's Eveline, who is also disillusioned by her conventional husband, Madeleine is ripe for liberation. She begins her journal by declaring: 'Mon histoire ... ne mérite peut-être pas d'être racontée; aussi je pense me faire à moi-même ce récit d'une solitude qui ne servirait à personne d'autre' (9).

Rodolphe does not really know her and his son, who share a strong imagination, a desire to write, and the urge to subvert what he stands for. He spends all his time 'helping' others, as a dedicated doctor in the psychiatric hospital next to their house. His attitude to knowledge and to life is cerebral, scientific, and pragmatic. Although he calls Madeleine his 'insoumise' (54), he does not believe her capable of being unfaithful (which she has been). Madeleine is afraid of going mad, of crossing the line that separates her from Rodolphe's patients. Rodolphe has been considered the only normal character in the book: 'Le personnage le plus complexe et le plus humain' (Laurent 1986, 59). Yet he is the one who refuses to be lucid, who in fact remains submissive to convention. The refusal of the son and the mother to conform, at the risk of death or madness (as in Filiatrault's *Chaînes*), exposes the father as subordinate (law-abiding) rather than dominant (law-making) or subversive (law-breaking).

Rodolphe's reading of Paul's journal, after his death, produces a different interpretation of the enigma. The text he has access to (expurgated by Madeleine?) appears to contain no mention of Anna, only of a mysterious A (71), whom Rodolphe assumes to be male. Conscious of Paul's narcissistic self-engrossment – he was constantly looking at himself in the mirror (43, 50, 75) – he concludes that Paul could only be attracted to someone of the same sex (75). Like Madeleine he projects his own desire, since it is only after Paul's death that he is able to recognize his love for him. This love is transferred onto Paul's friend, Frédérick, who has no parents (94).[8]

Frédérik's account, which completes the trilogy, reveals that both Madeleine and Rodolphe are right in their suspicions. Paul did have a relationship with Anna – but also, potentially, with Frédérik. Frédérik admits his own homosexuality to himself and to Paul, and appears to make no attempt to repress it, although he has not yet had an opportunity to put it into practice (105). Paul's reaction is ambivalent: on the one hand, he formally rejects Frédérik's advances (at least for the time being); on the other, his behaviour is seductive and provocative, as he flings himself onto Frédérik's bed (113), and caresses his hand (104) and face (110). Frédérik is described as slim, blond, unmasculine (89), and has 'feminine' handwriting (87, 91). Both he and Paul are athletes, competing in a male rivalry/bonding reminiscent of Greek homosexuality. Although Paul chooses to have an affair with Anna, the women in his

life fall into two categories: mother-figures, or insignificant marginalia for whom he has no time (16, 75). In Paul's dreams, both he and Frédérik are executed – victims of (homophobic?) violence. Frédérik is actually attacked, and rescued by Rodolphe (94–5). Paul's death remains designated an accident, but one wonders whether his unexpected failure to perform, as a skier, is related to his inability to come to terms with his own sexual ambivalence.

Rodolphe cannot accept that his son may have been homosexual (94), yet he recognizes that probability and consequently fears for his younger son, Marc, who replaces Paul in Madeleine's affections (73). The implication is that Paul's too close relationship with his mother may be the cause of sexual perversion, and the reason for his death. Yet Rodolphe accepts Frédérik as a substitute son (118), having admitted that it is easier for him to love someone else's son than his own (72). After Paul's death he lives through a brief spell of erotic pleasure with his wife (we do not know her version of this episode), but he has 'l'impression de tromper son fils avec sa femme' (Cloutier 1966, in *Blais: Dossier* 66–8). In spite of his horror of homosexuality as a perversion, Rodolphe is very much a part of the 'hommo-sexual' economy described by Irigaray (1979). His wife remains, for him, an object of (degrading) sexual satisfaction, the mother of her (rather than his) children, and a mystery: she must be made to submit, or be 'lost' (60), since his concept of love is one of possession, involving subordination of the feminine other.

### Gender definition and the *journal intime*

In an interview when *L'Insoumise* was published, Blais admitted that her focus shifted as she wrote the book: 'Je voulais écrire une histoire des difficultés du mariage ... mais j'ai préféré le personnage du fils. Car la mère se révoltait contre cette vie qu'elle menait et elle avait besoin de quelqu'un pour refléter cette révolte. En général, je préfère décrire des personnages masculins. Les garçons, c'est plus franc, plus solide, plus facile à comprendre que les filles qui sont si sensibles et si vulnérables' (*Châtelaine*, 5 août 1966). Blais returned to the 'difficulties of marriage' in 'Fièvre,' a radio play published in 1974, and to diary writing in another play in the same collection, 'Disparu.'[9] The diary in this case belongs to a seventeen-year-old boy (like Pinsonneault's Jean), who has committed suicide. The boy's mother describes to her other son a

dream that recalls the situation in *L'Insoumise*: 'J'ouvre la porte de sa chambre et je cherche à m'approcher de lui. Mais il s'éloigne de moi, il va à la cheminée et il brûle le petit cahier que tu lui avais donné ... pour écrire son journal ... je sens soudain que j'ai perdu de lui un aveu important' (*Fièvre*, 55). The 'aveu' contained in Paul Robinson's journal is ambivalent: it may be either that he has loved Anna, an incestuous mother substitute, or that (because of his over-identification with his mother?) he has homosexual tendencies – or both. In 'Disparu' the father condemns those who keep diaries: 'J'ai ... dit que je n'aimais pas les écrivains de journaux intimes. Et c'est vrai (63) ... Ce penchant qu'il avait pour l'analyse de ses petites misères me déplaisait fort ... C'était surtout une perte de temps pour un garçon déjà distrait dans ses études (64) ... Un être solitaire qui se penche sur ses problèmes ne peut pas être quelqu'un de fort (66) ... J'éprouve de l'hostilité à l'endroit de semblables idées, ce sont des idées de femme ... J'ai essayé de l'aider à faire face à la vie comme un homme' (*Fièvre*, 66). The dead son, Gérard, was 'délicat comme une fille' (68). His brother, Robert, admits: 'C'était menaçant pour nous, ce cahier, ce symbole' (69). By means of his diary Gérard, like Paul Robinson, disobeyed his father and betrayed his manhood, choosing to escape from life (action) by writing (like a woman). Once more introspective writing is associated with femininity and with suicide.

The diary mode adopted by Madeleine in *L'Insoumise* was described as follows by Jacques Pelletier (1966): 'Le style effacé, délicat, d'une souplesse surprenante, tisse cette frêle toile où les fils sont à peine liés entre eux, où les pensées de Madeleine s'écoulent sans ordre évident, pour se rejoindre toutefois au terme d'une démarche dont la logique si peu rigoureuse charme, étonne et inquiète à la fois: on est reconnaissant à l'auteur d'être capable d'une telle sensibilité, d'une touche si conforme à l'esprit proprement féminin.' Here again, the *journal intime* is considered suitable for a woman. Any man who indulges in it is suspect, prone to identification with the feminine, to nostalgia for a state of non-separation from the mother, and 'at risk' of homosexuality.

Why did Marie-Claire Blais, whose lesbian orientation is well-known and central in her later works, at that time prefer writing about young men? Why, like Marguerite Yourcenar, did she depict homosexuality in male terms? Evidently she identified more with the ambivalent (bisexual?) son, than with the domesticated and frustrated, but definitely feminine, mother. In *L'Insoumise*, as in *Les Abîmes de l'aube*, homosexuality remains a possibility, rather than a praxis. Frédérik, who has never experienced sex with anyone of either sex, may never do so, as he appears to be turning, like Pinsonneault's narrator, to religion as a refuge (113). There is an enormous difference between the repressed homosexuality of *L'Insoumise* and the sexual polyvalence central to Jean-Jules Richard's *Journal d'un hobo* (1965), published in the previous year.

## Richard, *Journal d'un hobo* (1965)

*'Les homosexuels, mâles ou femelles, sont-ils des ébauches ou des chefs d'oeuvre?' ai-je demandé. 'Et toi?' 'Moi, je ne suis ni l'un ni l'autre. Je suis un être parfait.' (149)*

In an interview entitled 'Sexuality: A Fact of Discourse' (Stambolian and Marks 1979), Serge Leclaire comments on the difference in psychoanalytic theory between man's 'discourse' and woman's 'speech' (*parole*): 'Man's discourse is typically the discourse of repression ... Man's position in relation to castration is different from woman's, and a different position in relation to castration results in a different discourse' (44). In *L'Insoumise* it is significant that the repressed woman, Madeleine, uses the diary form, which although written is defined by informality, openness, incoherence, and non-sense. Rodolphe, however, writes a retrospective account implying control of the events and their interpretation (Benveniste's *récit*). His narration veers towards the diary when events prove unexpected, and this coincides with his consideration of homosexuality. The fact that Paul also adopts the diary form and refuses to accept his father's repressive discourse places him on the side of the feminine. Frédérik, however, in spite of his admitted homosexuality, writes a retrospective account that ultimately joins the father and his discourse, renouncing sexual deviance and social defiance. Jean-Jules Richard, in *Journal d'un hobo*, conveys a different message concerning potential castration and uses an original combination of diary form and retrospection to do so.

This text functions on the basis of two fundamental suspensions of disbelief. The first is that the narrator is a hermaphrodite, a being equipped with the organs of both sexes. The second is that the narration is almost contemporaneous with the action (the diary convention), when it must in fact be retrospective: the child at the beginning could not be responsible for the account, and the end explains that the narrator 'transcribed' this story of his life as an adult, at the point where the narrative ends. The diary, which has no dates but is composed of 'entries,' is therefore fictional to an extra degree, since the fictional narrator is imitating a diary. The diarist also is encoded as a fantastic realization of the bisexuality of which the *intimiste* dreams. This novel is a metacommentary on gender indeterminacy, and on living life as a fiction in the context of a repressive society whose discourse of control has become ineffective.

. The narrator is a nameless Acadian hobo who crosses Canada during the Depression, joining thousands of anonymous others who belong nowhere. For them the Depression, with all its economic hardships, actually represents a respite from the boredom of repression, that is, meaningless work. Surviving at subsistence level (the subtitle is 'l'air est bon à manger'), these marginal men – and a few women – live according to the pleasure principle rather than that of reality. They choose the independent world of the imaginary (fantastic/horrific/dangerous/exciting) over the security provided by submission and dependency.

L'Acadien, as he is known, is both male and female. His picaresque adventures are based on this ambivalence, and the final outcome represents a choice: the refusal to choose. Léandre Bergeron commented on the hero's 'healthy' attitude to sex, on the complete absence of guilt associated with it, which was new in Quebec: 'Cet être est un, unifié, non-divisé contre lui-même comme le sont les civilisés ... [Ce roman] se renie lui-même comme livre. La vie qui y vibre refuse le cadre et la vie artificiée du roman. Un roman qui ne se renie pas est l'instauration de la littérature comme mode de vie et donc négation de vie' (1965, 32–3). In contrast with many other diary fictions, this novel does not preach the message of salvation through writing. Rather, writing is a vehicle to spread a doctrine of salvation through androgyny, which is equated with the liberation of the senses (32, 72, 160). As Leclaire puts it, if a man 'wants to free himself from a power discourse in which of necessity he participates, he ... is compelled to call upon something of the woman in him' (45).

## Marginality as central

The diary begins with an account of the narrator's childhood on the Atlantic coast. The fact that he is Acadian marginalizes him in relation to both the anglophone majority in his province and the francophones of Quebec, where he finds himself as an adolescent. His first years, as the youngest in a family of sixteen children, are lived between his mother, who protects him and is concerned for his education (15), and his father, who is frequently away (14). The mother represents order and constraint as well as a refuge: she is 'dominatrice ou n'en pouvant plus de dominer' (22). The father is associated with freedom, adventure, and virile strength, but he eventually disappears at sea. In this case he is not weak, but nevertheless absent, and overwhelmed by a feminine element. When the local witch doctor declares the 'boy' a true 'bardache' (hermaphrodite) (24), the father is prepared to drown the monster and to die with him (19-20). The mother, however, arranges for him to enter a Catholic boarding school for boys, once he has decided to develop in the male direction. He declares this choice to be 'pour plaire aux femmes' (29), which pleases his mother, whereas it is really in order to be able to accompany his father as much as possible. His sexual orientation is construed as homosexual (that is, directed towards his father), because of the female in him, who is jealous of the mother, identifying with her in her desire to be desired by a man: 'J'aurais voulu être la fille aînée d'Eve pour lui enlever mon père' (15). Later, in his relationship with a woman, he sees himself as imitating 'l'homme-père ... de tous les amours' (136). For most of the novel, this hermaphrodite is perceived by others as male, even when naked. He has a small penis and a 'muscular' chest. His vagina and internal female organs remain hidden. In this he conforms to the most common type of hermaphrodite, as clinically described by Kreisler (in Pontalis 1973, 117-33). This type is, in fact, usually genetically female, with female chromosomes and hormones, and a relatively minor operation can make such a person a 'normal' woman.

The hobo enjoys sexual relations with women, but we do not learn whether he actually ejaculates: though he does worry at one point that his girlfriend may be pregnant, he does not necessarily assume that he would be the father. He leaves the Catholic school, however, at the age of thirteen, when he begins to menstruate. As he puts it, he must 'accoucher d'ELLE' (40). The woman in him must 'come out' (another echo of Adam and Eve?). He wonders whether he would be able to give birth without being castrated. As Kreisler (130) points out, this type of anatomical anomaly presents, in disconcertingly concrete terms, the characteristics of the phallic mother. When he finally is pregnant, the hobo refuses to be mutilated, either by castration or a caesarian section:

'Mon sexe mâle n'est pas un obstacle à la naissance des enfants. Ce sexe est le prolongement d'un attribut femelle et son perfectionnement' (290). He gives birth as a man, as well as a woman (in both senses). He is not, however, the father of his own child: he is a phallic mother.

The presence of duality within a single physical unit is conveyed grammatically by the hobo's use of an Acadian regionalism, 'j'étions' for 'je suis.' The phrase 'j'étions double' (21) combines the single and the plural, the present and the past, in a neat, paradoxical formula that sums up his unique situation. Unique, but also representative of every man with a feminine identification, trapped in a male body, that is, the stereotypical homosexual. For although the Acadian has relationships with women, he is attracted above all to a red-haired homosexual of his age, called the Fauve. This designation as wild or untamed is belied by the Fauve's passive devotion to the Acadian, whom he is willing to follow to the end of the world (72, 145), or at least to Vancouver, the railroad's last stop. The Fauve's submission and fidelity are feminine, whereas the Acadian's attitude to him is one of masculine dominance. At one point the Acadian is prepared to rape him (62). With more virile male characters, such as the Moustachu, he adopts a more submissive role himself. It is the Moustachu who, on discovering his female aperture, arranges for him to be raped by a succession of hobos and left to suffocate in a closed boxcar (182-3). This experience is related with ambivalence. It leaves him almost dead, but simultaneously 'empli de vie' (185), as he subsequently proves to be pregnant, 'de plusieurs pères' (287).

The hobo's world is peopled with marginal characters, particularly prostitutes (Pastel, Bijou) and homosexuals. These include an adolescent who hangs himself on being called 'Tapette' (69), a young doctor who recognizes the Acadian's anatomical peculiarities (148, 281), and a group of transvestites (80). The hobo feels an affinity with those who are 'des pas pareils, des autrement' (82). He himself is 'pas pareil' (asymmetrical) in his own body, having one hip (the left) 'gonflée,' round like a woman's. He imagines being bisected by a train, lying on the rails (177). But it is finally the Moustachu, who ties up women 'pour leur bien' (244) who is destroyed by this classic phallic symbol.

The Acadian's experience of being treated as a woman, when he is obliged by circumstances to dress like one (224), makes him aware of the disadvantages entailed: 'tout me semble interdit, à moi, femelle'

(225). His final maternity and withdrawal, with the Fauve, to produce more red-haired children somewhere in the British Columbia wilderness, implies an acceptance of the femininity within himself, combined with a refusal to be treated as if castrated, that is, like a woman. By implication, the Fauve's homosexuality is exonerated, since he loves a 'woman' and becomes a father. The only type of sexuality that is not accepted is female homosexuality: Bijou does not want her hobo to choose to become a woman, because she hates the idea of having unknowingly been a lesbian (285). This reticence may, however, be the last trace of her Englishness, associated with hypocrisy and repression.

**Bisexuality and bilingualism**

The hobo's travels take him across Canada, from Toronto to Winnipeg, Calgary, and Vancouver. He is told to 'speak white' (128) and has to learn enough English to get by (139). Bijou, the English girl he seduces, is interested in learning French, although it is not necessary. It gives her an extra attraction later, when she has become a prostitute. They both discover that it is 'irritant de penser en deux langues à la fois' (132). The Acadian is particularly frustrated, since words are part of his powers of seduction, and he sees them as 'des buées de sauvetage' (68, 90). The witch doctor, on telling him that he was an 'être complet,' 'infirme en mieux' (25) also promised that he would have unusual powers of persuasion. The bisexual being is chosen, he has a mission (138); Christ himself may well have been a 'bardache' (214). Like Christ, he also runs the risk of being destroyed because he is different (287). The hobo's message is one of sexual liberation and the acceptance of difference: 'On devrait faire l'amour avec tout le monde. Ensuite, il y a le calme et le droit de vivre' (168). Salvation lies in making love, not war, in sensuality (160). His message belongs to the 'on the road' generation of Jack Kérouac; sexual freedom is associated with physical displacement, the choice of rootlessness.

The opposite of narcissistic withdrawal, this attitude is dependent on openness to the other, and to otherness within the self. As Léandre Bergeron remarked (1965, 32–3), in this novel the English are not simply the enemy/the oppressor. There is room for difference among them, and some are as marginal, as different, as the Acadian himself. The family of the Moustachu are Native people, with whom the Acadian is as at home as with his local witch doctor. The hermaphrodite's role is to interpret one side to the other – sexually and linguistically. The danger here is not of merging into a homogeneous 'one' (the herd/horde mentality of refuge values), but of becoming a strictly anonymous, rootless and aimless fragment of a scattered diaspora. Salvation lies in the contact of bodies, whose 'identity' changes according to the fiction of the moment, defined only by a shifting, kaleidoscopic context.

Yet language remains a barrier between strangers, and a bond between those who speak 'the same.' Speaking, here, has priority over writing, and the writing attempts to convey its flavour. Speech – the voice and its tone – is inseparable from the body, the senses. The hobo claims that what Quebec French lacks in vocabulary, it makes up for in a wide range of intonation (133). He is sceptical regarding the 'purity' of any language, and the possibility of a universal one. Translation is the source of confusion, as the Fauve seeks the meaning of 'pregnant' (275–6): 'ça pète autant que tapette.' The presence of the referent is more significant than the word in the dictionary.

One of the first ludic texts of this period in Quebec, *Journal d'un hobo* makes self-conscious reference to its picaresque model. *Vraisemblance* is of no importance (136, 165), and the characters are adjectives, written with a capital letter (235). Writing is only for those who are not living through the senses, and the Acadian produces his one book while he is immobilized by pregnancy. The fiction of the diary as life writing is underlined as a fiction. At the end, the narrator has become one of the 'giants' of British Columbia Indian legend, a god who leaves a sacred text, his 'testament' proclaiming the gospel of fertile promiscuity. Found in a cave, the 'livret couvert d'une écriture serrée' requires analysis: 'Les autorités de l'université étudieront le document et feront des commentaires ...' (292). Not (in my case) without feeling some shame at having become cerebral, as does the hobo, who at one point laments: 'Mon activité est devenue mentale, comme chez un grand nombre de gens déçus ...' (259).

L'Acadien, like Hertel's Lepic, is an *être lunaire*, a fantastic globe-trotter who revels in his marginality and bisexuality. Another more recent diary novel, published in 1984, also imitates (and parodies) the picaresque model and depicts a sexually ambivalent diarist who chooses the imaginary over the real: Michel Tremblay's *Des Nouvelles d'Edouard*.

## Tremblay, *Des Nouvelles d'Edouard* (1984)

*'Je vais ... me réfugier dans un scénario dont j'aurai le total contrôle ... on a envie de se cacher derrière une histoire imaginaire pour se protéger de notre complexe d'infériorité.' (93)*

In *Journal d'un hobo* Richard depicted his picaresque hero as eventually marginalized even further, to a mythical place in the Far West, a mountain cave (both up, or masculine, and in, or feminine). There self-other relations (within the self and between selves) become fertile and (re)productive. Tremblay's homosexual transvestite hero(ine), Edouard (Duchesse de Langeais), undertakes a journey in the opposite direction, east to France, in 1947, that is, as part of the Hertel-Baillargeon generation to which Richard, surprisingly, belongs while Tremblay does not. Whereas Richard's Acadian travels as a hobo, joining a community of misfits and outcasts, Edouard, from the working-class Plateau district of Montreal, goes first-class in a transatlantic liner, thanks to an inheritance from his mother, Victoire. He is no longer young and already obese. His account of an epic quest to discover his roots and to experience 'Paris' takes the form of a diary (without dates) destined to be read by his closest friend and ally, the 'fat woman' of *La Grosse Femme d'à coté est enceinte* (the first novel in the four-part series *Les Chroniques du Plateau*, of which this is the last). For the Acadian hobo, Paris represented an imaginary place of sexual freedom (Richard, 261), as it does also for Edouard, who is well aware that the French are supposed to be 'les meilleurs baiseurs du monde' (257). But for him it is above all a fictional world, belonging to Zola's Gervaise and Simenon's Maigret, that he expects to enter. Richard's novel ended by conferring immortality on the hero, who has become a god. Tremblay's story of Edouard's 'fugue' begins with a Prelude recounting the death of the duchess in 1976, the culmination of her 'myth.'

Edouard's diary is read posthumously, in bed, by another homosexual, Hosanna, to his lover, Cuirette, in three instalments. These are interrupted by amorous interludes (171) and commentary on Edouard as storyteller, as Schéhérazade. Edouard's account reveals that all his tales of months spent in France in the company of the famous were fictitious: he really spent ten days at sea and thirty-six hours in France. Yet the confirmation of his readers' doubts regarding his veracity serves to establish the duchess as a master myth maker, the creator of her own character and life by means of the imaginary. That the imaginary is preferable to the real is the conclusion reached by all Edouard's admirers. His diary is divided into 'La traversée de l'Atlantique,' 'La traversée de la France,' and 'La traversée de Paris.' The voyage represents an unsuccessful attempt to return to the mythical womb/origin (France), which is dis-closed as patriarchal and exclusive. It is followed by a reverse journey, into the arms of the waiting double/mother-substitute ('la grosse femme') and a conscious choice of the ludic/imaginary (acceptance) over the symbolic/cultural (rejection) represented by French 'superiority.'[10] That the whole event is provoked by Edouard's mother (89, 238) is significant: 'du fond de sa tombe, elle me poussait à réaliser cette absurdité de rêve qui, sans elle, serait resté inaccessible' (238).

Edouard, a modest shoe salesman, is an unlikely candidate to be an *intimiste*. First, he is not a solitary type. On the contrary, he says, 'J'ai toujours vécu en troupeau' (71) and 'chus venu au monde en gang' (300). It is not only lack of education that causes him to hesitate between 'je' and 'nous' and to avoid the choice by using 'on.' He has not read a great deal, and notes that 'chez les riches aussi, c'est les femmes qui lisent' (77). He is very much aware of belonging to two 'families,' both of which have an identity problem. The first is Québécois, and specifically from the east side of Montreal. It recognizes its members by the way they talk. Snobs from Outremont, like Antoinette, who disguises her accent, are denying their membership in it. Edouard himself is horrified to hear his own voice change, as he converses with French people (175). This family is characterized by an inferiority complex (93), a 'manque de courage chronique' (234), by 'notre insignifiance congénitale' (239). It destines Edouard to be 'un raté, un sans allure' (310) and leaves him with a 'sentiment d'impuissance' (267). Its members, like Edouard and his sister-in-law, the fat woman, prefer to dream, rather than attempt to change their life (299). Edouard is a potential intellectual, yet 'Kulture' appears to him as a substitute for sex – le Kul (105) – just as physical activity is perceived by him as a therapy for masturbation (187).

This is only one side of Edouard's double life. At night, he has found a sexual and social activity that enables him to disguise his corpulence and lack of virility (103) by a physical performance that underlines them: he has already become an embryonic Duchesse de Langeais. His other 'family' is composed of fellow homosexuals, and he can immediately recognize its members (73, 248). Being homosexual is a source of guilt for a Catholic Québécois: 'la culpabilité est imprimée dans mon âme au fer rouge' (292). Although Edouard makes no secret of being gay and delights in his skills as a transvestite, homosexual acts are still condemned to furtive secrecy: 'c'est presque toujours ça qui se passe entre nous: dans le noir, à la sauvette, avec la culpabilité qui te saute dessus aussitôt que c'est fini' (74). When he broaches the topic of sexual arousal in his journal – he claims to be avoiding self-censorship (58) – he warns his imaginary reader, the fat woman, to skip that part (97, 281). Edouard's attitude to himself is not apparently narcissistic. The only time he 'likes' himself is when he manages to respond to humiliation by embarrassing someone else (129, 182), breaking a social taboo. One suspects that these are incidents that he is making up. Otherwise, he is ashamed of his own efforts to conform. His one triumph on board ship is his appearance at the *bal masqué* magnificently costumed (and 'made up'), to find that everyone else is literally wearing a mask. He, in contrast, is revealing his hidden self. This hidden (imaginary/ideal) self, whom he does love, is a woman: a double of 'la grosse femme.'

## 'C'est la femme en moi que j'aime et l'homme en eux qui m'excite' (101)

The previous volume of the *Chroniques*, *La Duchesse et le roturier*, ended with Edouard about to board a ship, *La Liberté*, in New York, having said farewell to the fat woman in Montreal.[11] She instructed him to look at everything as if she was with (in?) him: 'Je te prête mes yeux, Edouard! R'garde toute comme si on était deux!' (*La Duchesse* [21]). Referring to his 'poor mother,' Edouard recalls that, like the fat woman, she put everything in the feminine (for example, 'toute' in the quotation above). He adds 'même moi' (140), implying that he holds her responsible for his feminine identification. The fat woman, who is an 'impossible' object choice (she is his sister-in-law, and he is an avowed homosexual) is nevertheless the one person he really loves, as he confesses to her on his return (309–10). His homosexual relationship with Samarcette is not love: 'Il n'a toujours été qu'une commodité pour moi. Pour l'hygiène de l'esprit comme pour l'hygiène du corps'(278); 'l'amour, c'est pas juste deux corps qui se frottent ensemble' (310). The fat woman is his narcissistic object choice, representing what he would like to be. The only other character in his diary with whom he identifies in this way is (unknown to him) Simone de Beauvoir, whom he sees in a café in Paris: 'C'est peut-être à elle que j'aimerais ressembler, en fin de compte' (289), 'j'aurais eu envie de tout lui conter. Comme à vous' (292). Only a woman could understand him, because he identifies himself, to himself, as a woman. He imagines being the leading lady in a film (92, 121) and sees himself as a 'damsel in distress' (113). In his transvestite performances, his aim is to appear to be a woman, and his reaction when someone claims that Mae West may have been a man, is 'Si Mae West était un homme, elle s'en vanterait!' (100). Although Edouard is a homosexual, he hates masculine men (101) and prefers women (119). His aim, in going to Paris, is to come back 'une femme du monde jusqu'au trognon' (238), to deserve his title of *duchesse*.

Apart from Simone de Beauvoir, the only women he sees during his brief stay in Paris are prostitutes (267), who provoke in him a 'sentiment d'impuissance': not because he does not find them sexually attractive, but because he can do nothing for them. He himself feels like 'une vieille guidoune qui vient de perdre sa dernière illusion' (234), recognizing that in order to seduce a French public he would have either to change not only his accent but his whole self (237), or play the ridiculous 'Canadien' of French folklore (286). His departure from Paris is precipitated by the realization that in that context he does not have 'le droit de vivre' (291) as himself. Communication is impossible because of the insurmountable gap between his own self-representation and the perception others have of him.

Gabrielle Poulin summed up Edouard's experience of France and the French as a metaphor for the situation of Quebec: 'L'univers d'Edouard, si fortement enraciné dans la vie et dans la culture du Québec, traduit, dans son désarroi, sa solitude et sa marginalité, le drame de la minorité québécoise dans un monde qui, après lui avoir fourni, au long des siècles, non seulement sa langue et sa culture, mais même jusqu'à la substance de ses rêves, la considère comme étrangère, la bafoue et la confine aux nuits étriquées de son folklore' (1985, 19). For Edouard, Paris is 'une défaite de plus' (239). His rejection of (and by) France (the symbolic order) and his return to the refuge of the maternal imaginary is nevertheless presented ultimately as a triumph. His success, through acting the role of a woman, is an artistic achievement transcending that role – an escape not available to the fat woman, who really is one, and who remains 'pognée ici,' while Edouard can 'courir la galipote à l'année longue' (22).

## 'Moi qui ne suis rien mais qui sais parler' (112)

Edouard's relegation to the margins by speakers of standard French is based on his non-conforming speech patterns. He invests in a dictionary and wants to buy a French grammar, as he becomes aware of linguistic disparities and of the problematic relation of speech to writing. The diary is written, but he plans to write in the same way that he speaks (59), 'au fil de la plume, sans me censurer' (301). The result is disappointing, for him: 'Je trouve ce que j'écris tellement confus ... c'est pas ça qui va m'aider à me comprendre' (94). Yet the diary does make him aware of two significant issues. The first is the relationship of language to experience: 'j'ai pas les mots pour exprimer tout ce que je ressens et, en plus, je me dis que si je les avais ça voudrait dire que j'aurais plus d'éducation que je n'en ai, que je ferais partie d'une autre caste et que je n'aurais absolument pas les mêmes problèmes! Ou bien t'es ignorant et t'arrives pas à exprimer tes malaises ou bien t'es éduqué et tes malaises ne sont pas les mêmes! Est-ce que ça veut dire que nos malaises, à nous, ne sont pas exprimables? Pourtant, il me semble que ce que j'ai écrit jusqu' ici est relativement clair ...' (163). This passage sums up a central problem concerning the dual authorship of the diary novel. Edouard manages to convey his message, because it is Tremblay who is writing, and who has more education than Edouard. Edouard's text is not an authentic transcript of an individual experience, but a conscious representation of a deliberately representative one.

Edouard's second realization through his diary is that 'ce n'est pas l'expérience qui compte, c'est le mensonge bien organisé' (302). He chooses performance over real life and the imaginary over the everyday. In this sense, his diary is less a record than a performative act, one that enables him to become fully the *duchesse* of his dreams by abandoning the prosaic self-analysis that the diary represents in favour of the flight ('fugue') of fancy. His decision to return home is necessary for his rebirth as the immortal *duchesse*, whose gestation is recounted in these 'nouvelles' (fictions, rather than 'news'). Although Edouard realizes that 'un écrivain lutte en moi pour faire surface,' he remains 'd'abord et avant tout acteur' (108).

The diary-writing model proposed by Julien Green is rejected; 'Me voyez-vous, moi, publier ce que je vous écris là?' (81). Edouard prefers to revert to oral improvisation, because 'la duchesse de Langeais est en moi, dans mon imagination, et elle ne sera efficace que si je l'invente de toutes pièces ... Fini, l'écriture' (302). Here, Edouard equates writing with the real, speech with the imaginary, echoing the masculine (discourse)/feminine (*parole*) dichotomy. Yet his diary, which is written, illustrates the role and final domination of the imaginary in writing, and his return to the speech of Montreal is for him a reintegration of his reality.

## Bisexuality, bitextuality, and female homosexuality

Both Richard and Tremblay consciously exploit the journal form to produce a commentary on the relation of life to fiction and on masculine and feminine modes of living and writing as constructs rather than the result of biological destiny. Both equate the ludic, subversive, receptive, open, and oral aspects of the journal with the feminine (or male homosexual) and the closed, logical, controlled aspects of a complete and publishable text with the masculine. The hobo, who refuses to be castrated, exhibits his phallic side before becoming a mother by bequeathing his testament, making his journal a definitive statement. Edouard, by giving his journal to the fat woman (who gives it back to him before she dies), keeps his *nouvelles* in the realm of the private (identifying with the mother) and chooses feminine speech/acting over masculine writing-as-action (that is, publication). His text is read (within the fiction) only by his female double and by other male homosexuals. Both novels represent the appropriation of the feminine by men. Women are excluded, except as mother-figures, or prostitutes whose marginalization is analogous to the gay male's. A female reader is left wondering if there is any place in this schema for her own desire and possible narcissistic preference for the same rather than the opposite sex.

The psychoanalytic theory of male homosexuality has been extensively reviewed and discussed (Lewes 1988). Female homosexuality, however, has been less systematically analysed. For Freud, the lesbian refuses to accept that she is castrated. She identifies with the father, wishing to be (like) him (active, desiring a female, that is, the mother or her self) rather than to become (like the mother) the passive object of his desire. The female homosexual, like the male homosexual, retains her attachment to the mother, refusing to separate from her and regard her as a rival for the father's love. Rather, the father is a rival for the mother's attention. Some psychoanalysts have claimed that the male child's sexual development is more difficult and complex than the female's, since the boy has to break his connection to the (castrated) mother, in order to identify with the father, and suffers from castration anxiety because of rivalry with the father over the mother as object (Stoller in Pontalis, 151; Lewes, 197) Female/feminist psychoanalysts, such as Kristeva, tend to adopt the opposite position, that the girl's development at the Oedipal stage is more complex and difficult than the boy's, as she is expected to transfer her desire from an object of the same sex (the mother) to one of the unfamiliar opposite sex, and to become passive rather than active (that is, to live out her own castration). Freud saw women as 'already castrated' and therefore less threatened by the father and consequently developing a less strong superego. This view neglects the girl's fear of penetration/rape/paternal incest, which may be considered analogous to the boy's castration anxiety (and more realistic). A significant difference occurs, however, since the threat is posed by the parent/sex to whom her desire is supposed to become directed (entailing the theory of female masochism). Similarly, the Freudian concept of penis envy on the part of girls ignores the equally important envy experienced by males of the female capacity to give birth (the subject of the next chapter).

According to the Freudian schema, the individual's relationship to the mother or father may be one of 'identification with' (being the same, on the vertical axis of substitution), or of 'desire for' (having the other as object, or being the other's object, on the horizontal axis of combination). This dichotomy rules out desire for the same sex, or being like the opposite one. Homosexuality is therefore classified as deviant (inversion/perversion) and frequently, by implication, as deficient: infantile-regressive, a refusal or incapacity to go beyond the pre-Oedipal narcissistic, oral, and anal stages of development. Yet Freud himself recognized the primitive bisexuality of all, and feminist analysts have emphasized the ongoing latent bisexuality of women, because of their initial recognition of both sameness and connection to the mother.

Female homosexuality was rarely broached by Quebec authors until second-wave feminism made it a central aspect of contemporary writing by women. One notable exception was Louise Maheux-Forcier, whose novels published in the 1960s dealt with attraction between women.[12]

She did not, however, use the diary form to explore the relationship between masculine and feminine modes of discourse and the construction/representation of a lesbian identity. One novel written by Madeleine Monette in 1980 does, and its title already indicates the convergence of form and theme in this innovative version of the diary novel.

### Monette, *Le Double Suspect* (1980)

'*Quand une femme séduit une autre femme ... on s'imagine que le désir n'y est pour rien ... même s'il y était pour quelque chose, on aurait trop peur de l'admettre.*' (28)

The novel begins with the diary of a nameless narrator, a Québécoise who is on holiday in Rome. She begins her notes with a retrospective account of the last evening she spent with her friend, Manon, also from Montreal, who has just been killed in a car accident. Manon had changed her plans to spend some time with the narrator in Rome, ostensibly because she wished to meet a man, Hans, in Germany. Before leaving she had urged the narrator to move into her vacant, prepaid hotel room. The suspicion that Manon's death was not accidental is aroused by the fact that she did not take her clothes. It is confirmed by a series of black notebooks that the narrator also inherits – Manon's diary. She reads them only after much hesitation, torn between *pudeur* and curiosity. The act of reading them is construed as an invasion of Manon's private parts, a violation or rape (39). Yet the fact that Manon leaves the journal indicates an invitation to intimacy that she was unable to express directly, and a self-exposure/confession (an *aveu*, which is also a declaration of love) that she could perform only posthumously.

The narrator's account of their last evening together is fraught with the tension of repressed desire. Manon had raised questions about the possible dynamic of desire between women, but both avoided discussing their own relationship in those terms – although the narrator compares them to two lovers about to part (20). Manon had turned her camera on the narrator, in what the latter saw as an act of phallic aggression, making her an object to be possessed (30–1). Her farewell embrace was intense (22), but the narrator did not respond. Her subsequent obsession with Manon is based on the fear that this lack of response was the reason for her suicide (32). According to Manon, a

## Homosexuality, Androgyny, and Bi-Section 163

woman needs to feel desired, an attitude that conforms to Freud's concept of feminine narcissism. At the time, the narrator resented being abandoned for a man, but also felt that Manon 'n'avait pas le droit de vivre *à ma place* ce que j'aurais moi-même voulu vivre' (25). Her relationship to Manon is one of both identification and cathexis. She wishes both to be her and to be desired by her, but does not want to admit her own desire for her. Both aspects are narcissistic projections, underlined by her increasing resemblance to Manon. She not only wears her clothes, but also buys high-heeled shoes and red nail polish, eliminating the differences that previously distinguished them. This identification with a dead double is one of the classic types of *Doppelgänger* described by Delozel in his classification of the varieties of double found in literature.[13] As the narrator reads Manon's journal, Manon takes possession of her and becomes an obsession. The narrator's strategy to gain control (to possess Manon) is textual, rather than sexual, but it represents a shift to masculinity as part of an 'aventure amoureuse' (135).

**Textual intercourse between diary and novel: 'Moi seule pourrai faire la différence entre fiction et réalité.' (53)**

The reader of Monette's novel never has access directly to Manon's diary, not even over the narrator's shoulder. The originality of the diary/novel relationship here is that the narrator decides to rewrite her friend's *in medias res* account as a *fictional* journal, that is, as one in which the end is actually at the beginning, the order is re-established to ensure coherence, and the gaps are filled in (48). The diary is to become a diary novel in which the 'I' attributed to Manon actually emanates from the narrator (52, 126), who in turn appears as a character, Anne, in Manon's text. We know that Anne is not her real name (*An*/onym:M*anon*), for she explains that Anne was the name her mother wished to give her, but her father's choice (after a dead sister) prevailed (235). Anne's rewriting is accompanied by a Gidean 'diary of the novel': two series of black exercise books written in by her join the original ones by Manon. Her aim is no longer to discover and comprehend Manon (Ma/*non*), but to 'refaire le trajet d'une écriture en m'efforçant d'y retrouver cette part de moi-même qui semble y être enfermée' (49): M(an)on.

In her 'novel' the narrator has Manon quote Anne, who is quoting Gide: 'Je ne vis que par autrui: par procuration' (215). This is not the only literary reference. Sartre's *La Nausée* is also evoked (130–1) to underline the tension between diary and novel and the framing that turns the ongoing *discours* of the journal into a finished *récit* or *aventure*. The first epigraph from Barthes (to Monette's novel) underlines 'la désinvolture qui fait venir le texte antérieur du texte ultérieur,' the ingenuity with which Manon's original journal is evoked through a transformation of it. The second epigraph from Barthes (to Anne's novel) states: 'Savoir qu'on n'écrit pas pour l'autre, savoir que ces choses que je vais écrire ne me feront jamais aimer de qui j'aime, savoir que l'écriture ne compense rien, ne sublime rien, qu'elle est précisément *là où tu n'es pas* – c'est le commencement de l'écriture' (57).

This claim is particularly relevant to the keeping of a private diary, which is not for 'l'autre.' It is relevant also to the reading of Manon's diary, which is possible only when she no longer exists, just as Anne's rewriting, which is an attempt to dialogue with Manon, to force her to speak (48–9), is dependent on her not being there. Writing, in either form, is a process of self-projection and self-representation through language, Lacan's 'Autre,' which functions in the absence of, or in spite of, the 'speaking subject.' Within Manon's diary, the same schema is played out, as a *mise en abyme* of the situation in which Anne begins a diary because of Manon's death. Manon is also depicted as starting her diary on the death of her husband, Paul, who has, she discovers, committed suicide because he cannot come to terms with his own homosexuality. The man who initiated Paul into homosexuality (*Lemire*, another double or mirror image) is in his turn 'doubled' in Manon's own life by a woman, *Andrée* (*andr*ogyne?), who would have initiated her into lesbianism, had she been willing. Andrée sees no reason to condemn sexual 'deviance' (202), which she associates with 'l'invention.' With her, Manon feels self-castrated: 'j'ai enfin compris que j'étais, vis-à-vis de moi-même ... le plus impitoyable de tous les castrateurs. Victime de la règle, je me privais du plaisir de la *déviance* ... et de l'invention' (156). Yet Manon flees Andrée, unable to surmount her fear, and Andrée is in turn replaced by Anne. Manon is attracted only by feminine, homosexual/bisexual men: her husband, Paul; the ambivalent Michel; and a young piano student, Daniel. They all have names that can be feminized; 'H*ans*' also includes 'Anne.' She is repulsed by the advances of masculine men, yet she does not wish to be perceived as a lesbian (177–8), and finally kills herself rather than relive the same dilemma and danger with Anne that she experienced with Andrée.

This is not the only reason for Manon's suicide. In fact, she has recognized her own insurmountable narcissism. Recalling the 'tu me tues, tu me fais du bien' of Duras's *Hiroshima mon amour* (229), Manon perceives suicide as the ultimate spiritual orgasm, the final, masturbatory, narcissistic act of homo/self-arousal and extinction. She accepts her narcissistic orientation as a death wish, a desire to return to union with the mother, *la mer/la mère* (230), to be part of a cosmic whole in which the self is eclipsed (cf. Green on the 'neuter'): 'j'imagine que la marée monte, que les vagues me lèchent ... l'eau monte ... je sens l'eau qui me pénètre et qui se glisse au-dedans de moi par ma bouche, mes yeux et mon sexe' (230).

To follow the pattern of mirror images and substitutions established in *Le Double Suspect*, Anne should also commit suicide, on recognizing her own repressed homosexuality. She does not do so, because of her *roman* (written from a distance, in *Rome*). A literary critic by profession, she recognizes fiction as a means to live out her own potential 'perversion,' by the 'invention' that Manon feared (43). Yet she denies that what she has written is a product of 'l'invention romanesque,' using Manon's diary as proof that her *récit* is not 'une pure construction imaginaire, mais le résultat d'une lecture attentive' (127). Monette's novel, in its turn, could make the same claim, as it echoes the author's reading of Barthes, Gide, Sartre, and Lacan (162). Writing and reading are interrelated, two aspects of the same activity, each both active and passive rather than polarized. Both are narcissistic pursuits, based on identification with the text. Manon admits that her notebooks are 'un autre moi' (209). Anne reads professionally, and is delighted to 'vivre, par procuration, les *perversions* des autres' (213). Manon adds that 'elle devait certainement y trouver un pâle reflet de ses propres désirs inquiets ...' Since it is Anne herself who depicts Manon as writing this in her diary, this is an oblique confession. Neither Manon nor Anne will openly admit to being lesbian. The attraction of their texts lies in what is not said, the silences that force the reader to become part of the process of substitution and combination essential to textual erotics.

Homosexuals of both sexes are depicted in these diary fictions as fixated on the phallic mother, the ultimate bisexual being. The image of the diarist as androgynous writer/reader, creator of her own self (image), is central in *Le Double Suspect*. Both Manon and Anne go into a period of narcissistic withdrawal after the death of their 'significant other.' Manon is saved from madness by the diary, but fears to re-emerge from the womb/tomb that her journal represents: 'j'ai peur ... que la nuit accouche avant-terme, que ce soit de moi qu'elle accouche et qu'elle me laisse aussi démunie et dépaysée qu'un nouveau-né' (122). Speaking of her relationship with Andrée, who mothers her, she expresses the fear that 'notre amitié ne donne naissance à un monstre' (181). In Freudian theory, homosexual love does not produce children, but artistic/literary reproductions of the self. By transforming the transitory text, Manon's journal, into a work of art, Anne confers immortality on both Manon and herself. Her diary novel may be construed as their offspring. This image is central in the novels to be discussed next.

CHAPTER NINE

# Self-Part(ur)ition or Giving Birth to the Book: *Bessette, Godbout, Garneau, Amyot*

> 'Men may congratulate themselves upon the productivity of their own mental wombs, but they are displeased to come upon women with mental penises.'
> MARY ELLMANN (1968), 21

> 'The context of the childbirth metaphor is the institution of motherhood in the culture at large.'
> SUSAN STANFORD FRIEDMAN (1989), 75

## The childbirth metaphor and the Quiet Revolution

Réjean Beaudoin entitled his study of the emergence of literature in Quebec in the nineteenth century *Naissance d'une littérature* (1989), but the 'birth of a culture' image is more frequently associated with the Quiet Revolution period of the 1960s. At that time Quebec intellectuals identified with the colonized countries of Africa (see chapter 3), seeing themselves as catalysts in a movement towards separation/independence closely related to a *prise de parole* (literally 'taking the word') to express their collective *prise/crise de conscience*. The images of movement (after a long paralysis) and enlightenment (after *la grande noirceur* of the Duplessis era) are all-pervasive in writings of the period, which convey the urgency of emergency. A new autonomy and self-esteem appeared attainable, whose success depended on the rejection of the maternal refuge values of the Church, the family (the revenge of the cradle), and the land (*la terre*/nature). Whereas nineteenth-century expressions of nationalist fervour were conservative and nostalgic, appealing to *la fidélité* and *l'appartenance*, those of the sixties were forward-looking, socialist/revolutionary, and motivated by a sense of being part of a worldwide phenomenon, as theorized by Memmi, Berque, and Fanon. In psychoanalytic terms, the construction of an 'identity' in the nineteenth century and the first half of the twentieth was comparable to physical birth and the pre-Oedipal imaginary stage based on identification with the phallic mother; whereas the political and cultural upheaval of the 1960s and 1970s was an attempt to gain access to the symbolic order, associated with language, law, and identification with the rule(s) of the (dead) father.[1] The concept of political independence is thought of in terms of becoming a male adult, that is, fully weaned and able to speak for/as oneself, as a subject rather than as 'other.'

Novels of the period have often been categorized as both representing (mimesis) and performing (diegesis) the act of speaking – and later, self-consciously, of writing. The popularity of first-person narration in fiction is seen as relevant to this dual function.[2] It is certainly true that many major Quebec authors during the 1960s chose the fictional journal as a narrative technique. The diary form, as already discussed in the 1984 example of Tremblay's *Des Nouvelles d'Edouard* in chapter 8, constitutes a type of written text that may imitate the patterns of everyday speech. During this period, the debate over the use of *joual* in literature was a significant part of the shift to language as the main focus of a national identity distinct not only from the surrounding anglophone majority, but also from its French origins. The desire to 'write as one speaks' is an in-between stage, privileging the (feminine) *parole*, a contextualized speech act marked by the presence of those engaged in dialogue (Benveniste's *discours*), over the apparently impersonal absence or trace of (masculine) writing, characterized by the distance of the third-person and the preterite (Benveniste's *récit*).[3] The 1960s are also a pivotal period in that the *ébullition*[4] of literary production was accompanied – indeed delivered and nursed – by the development of literary institutions (publishing companies, university courses dealing with Quebec literature) to recognize, legitimize, and sustain it.

Two of the best known and most read novels of the period, Bessette's *Le Libraire* and Godbout's *Salut Galarneau!*, use the fictional journal to convey a mimetic and instrumental message of awakening. Both represent a narcissistic withdrawal to the 'womb' and a period of gestation culminating in an escape/delivery associated with the end of the diary. This image was already present in several earlier diary fictions, as has been seen, but not developed to the same extent. The birth metaphor serves a dual purpose, designating the creativity associated with writing (the birth of the book as narcissistic self-extension) and the self-production of the diarist, who emerges phoenixlike[5] as a writer/author, that is, capable of auto/nomy (self-naming) and of author/ity, implying access to the symbolic order. The maternal image of parturition is in both aspects inextricably entwined with phallic imagery suggesting masculine potency.

The childbirth metaphor is by no means new in literature, particularly for male writers. In a 1989 article, Susan Stanford Friedman discusses numerous examples of its use and analyses some differences involved when the writer is a woman. Building on Mary Ellmann's insights into male appropriation of female body imagery (1968, 16–18), she points out that when a man speaks of giving birth, he is referring to something he *cannot* do.[6] He is using a physical image associated with the feminine to designate a mental activity with masculine connotations. This is a reversal of the cerebral misogyny discussed in chapter 4 with reference to Hertel and Baillargeon, which derides the physicality of women in favour of phallic abstract thought. It conveys a primitive male envy of the female power of procreation, for which artistic production is seen as a substitute.[7] Yet the birth of the book does not imply the death or eclipse of the author-parent, who is also reborn, ultimately identifying with the foetus (the product), rather than with the mother-as-womb, or container to be discarded.

When women writers use the same metaphor, its meaning is construed differently. It becomes a challenge to the 'fundamental binary oppositions of patriarchal ideology between word and flesh, creativity and procreativity, mind and body' (Stanford Friedman, 74). In the case of Quebec women, whose duty was previously considered to be primarily the (re)production of offspring to assure the survival of the species, choosing the pen over the cradle as a means to contribute to the national cause is problematic. As Stanford Friedman claims, 'male paternity of texts has not precluded their paternity of children. But for both material and ideological reasons, maternity and creativity have appeared to be mutually exclusive to women writers' (75). Whereas men's use of the metaphor 'begins in distance from and attraction to the Other,' women's use of it 'originates in conflict with themselves as Other' (84, 85).

This schema needs some modification in the particular context of Quebec. As has been established in analysing earlier diary fiction, the identity of the Québécois male is marked by the dominance of the phallic mother and identification with her. The concept of a man who gives birth (as literally represented in Richard's *Journal d'un hobo*, discussed in chapter 8) is a means to enable the male author to become the phallic mother. The book, as fetish, serves as a substitute for the phallus, disguising the colonized male's emasculation. On the other hand, when a woman chooses to write rather than to become a mother (as Laure Conan did), the mental/spiritual parenthood of the book and of the self brings her closer to the father's position (as in *Angéline de Montbrun*). In choosing the subject position in the symbolic order, she may appear to renounce her femininity.

The different effect of the use of the same image by male or female writers or narrators depends to some extent on the reader's knowledge of their sex, and also on the sex of the reader. It may also be influenced by whether the author or reader has actually given birth (Stanford Friedman, 37, n97). The same modifications apply when the birth image is adapted to that of an abortion or miscarriage. The fictional diary may function as representative of an unfinished or unsuccessful work, or of an identity 'étouffé dans l'oeuf.' These aspects will be developed in a comparison of two less well-known Quebec diary fictions published more recently, in 1978 and 1979, one by a man (Jacques Garneau's *Les Difficiles Lettres d'amour*), and one by a woman (Geneviève Amyot's *Journal de l'année passée*). Ten years after the Quiet Revolution, two years after the election of the Parti Québécois, the born-again Québécois identity was still embryonic. The image propagated in 1960 by Bessette, in his 'seminal' *Le Libraire*, may be more appropriately re-interpreted as the scattering of seed.

### Bessette, *Le Libraire* (1968)

'*Le mal québécois se ramène essentiellement à une difficulté d'être.*' (*Cotnam 1971, 293*)

'*... les romanciers se détachent maintenant de cette forme de complaisance qui consiste à vouloir se définir avant d'être.*' (*Bourneuf 1970, 266*)

'*Nous souffrons ... d'avoir perdu la faculté de dire, aux autres et à nous-mêmes, ce que nous sommes.*' (*F. Dumont 1961, quoted by Arguin 1985, 136*)

Hervé Jodoin, the diarist-narrator of *Le Libraire*, has been labelled 'l'homme de la Révolution tranquille' (Marcotte 1976/1989, 48), and this novel's publication hailed as heralding the start of the latter. Bessette's manuscript, completed in 1958, was actually initially refused publication in Quebec and considered unsuitable for a subsidy (Robidoux 1987, 138–9). It was published in France in 1960, the year of the Liberals' election in Quebec, following the death of Duplessis. Yet Jodoin is not, in fact, very different from the characters in diary fiction produced in the late 1940s, the period in which the story is set.[8] The Saint-Joachin that he discovers has not changed much since 1936, the year Duplessis came to power and the date on the only map that he can find. Jodoin is a stranger to the town, yet everything is familiar and predictable. The Church is as powerful as ever, and 'thought' is as dangerous as it was for Hertel or Baillargeon, who went into exile to indulge in it. Jodoin shares the cerebrality, the apparent cynicism, and the sarcasm of Anatole Laplante and Claude Perrin, and holds similar views on both women and the primacy of French culture. He also has a great deal in common with the heroes of the psychological novel of the fifties, as described by Arguin: 'Le héros du roman psychologique est celui qui, devant l'échec, prend conscience de son aliénation et revendique le droit d'exercer sa liberté individuelle dans l'accomplissement de sa destinée' (1985, 107). Jodoin defends the rights of the individual against the collective authority of the Church, as represented by the Index of censored books. However, as Françoise Maccabée Iqbal (1976) has pointed out, his lack of any sense of individual or collective destiny makes him still a part and product of *la grande noirceur*. He is determined to forget the past (13, 34) but has no idea what the future might be, hence his retreat into a state of limbo – of cocooning, or suspended animation – in which his main desire is to 'tuer le temps' (11). Like Loranger's Mathieu or Elie's Marcel, he is prepared to 'se vautrer dans la médiocrité' (*La Fin des songes*, quoted by Arguin, 90). Time stands still for Jodoin, as it does for Saint-Joachin, where it does not matter if the newspaper is several days old (7), since nothing ever happens anyway. Keeping a diary, in these circumstances, is not expected to produce an account of any memorable events.

**Regression: Reluctance to become a man**

Like many earlier fictional male diarists, Jodoin perceives himself as 'un homme fini' (136), unlikely ever to marry and become a father, or even hold down a respectable job. He is more or less impotent, and sterile. Although he manages to make love to his landlady, Rose, and proves that he is still '(si l'on peut dire) viril' (88), he has no desire to repeat the experience (88), and chooses to sit alone at the railway station rather than be forced to perform regularly (92). This lack of sexual capacity is not restricted to Jodoin alone; Rose's son-in-law is impotent (58), and all the other women mentioned are frustrated 'old maids.' The only sexually potent men are Rose's other, *American* son-in-law and her seventy-year-old boss (58, 73). A depressed, unmarried customer called Anasthasie Lessort (whose fate is indeed anaesthetic) also has an impotent father (33). By working at the bookstore, Jodoin places himself in the same category as the other employees – two disappointed spinsters. On arriving in Saint-Joachin, he hesitates over whether to look at rooms available for men only, or for 'les deux sexes' (9). The doubt seems to be over which sex he belongs to, as much as a desire to avoid women.

Jodoin's reluctance to become further embroiled with Rose must be extreme to force him to leave his room, one of the three enclosed spaces where he finds refuge. He emerges only because he can no longer be alone there. His initial overtures to Rose are motivated less by sexual frustration than by the desire for a non-sexual, comforting, and nurturing human contact. Rose is a large-breasted, motherly woman, who feeds him (52, 86) and takes care of all his needs. What he really wants to do is hold her hand (83–4) and (literally) sleep with her (86). Any activity requiring exertion is anathema to him; his avowed and often reiterated aim is to move as little as possible (7, 12, 22, 24, 32, 78, 95) and to sleep whenever he can (11, 19, 28, 66, 83). He seems to be attempting to attain the pre-life state of inertia that Green terms *le neutre*: a return to the womb. Far from being 'un homme fini,' he has never become one.

Jodoin laments the infantilization of the Québécois (48), but he himself has regressed at least to the oral/anal stage. At his second refuge, the pub, he imbibes twenty beers a night, and when he is not drinking he is chewing/sucking on a cigar (7, 13, 135). His previous attitude to books was that of a 'dévoreur' (67). He is also preoccupied with elimination (13) and aids to digestion ('Safe-All,' 13, 89). One of his favourite derogatory terms for others is 'constipated' (22, 48). At his place of work, the bookstore, he has a third retreat behind the counter, where he hides beneath a visor (31, 35, 67) that serves as a barrier, rather than an aid, to vision – although he eventually makes peep-holes in it (98). Claiming to be usually oblivious to the visual (125) and unobservant, in spite of his 'good eyes' (90), Jodoin emphasizes in his diary the more 'primitive' senses: smell (12–13, 44), temperature (55, 125), and touch (84).

Rose is not the only person whose hand he likes to hold. In a rare moment of confidence and elation, he shakes hands at length with Chicoine, the owner of the bookstore (127) – and later ostentatiously refuses to do so (142). Before leaving the tavern for the last time, he shakes hands for the second time with 'le père Manseau' (145, cf.112). This silent and immobile old alcoholic attracts him as a narcissistic projection of what he is likely to become. The only other incident in which he experiences sympathy for another human being involves the adolescent schoolboy to whom he sells an illicit copy of Voltaire's *Essai sur les moeurs*, the event that changes his life.

Jodoin admits that he identifies with this boy, who reminds him of himself at that age (67). This attitude is similar to that of Father Berthier in Hertel's *Le Beau Risque*, and typical of a potential homosexual orientation (as discussed in chapter 8). The curé's suspicion that Jodoin is abnormal (106), and the rumour that he is a 'débaucheur de collégiens' (120) may not refer to his mental capacity alone, as he assumes. After all, he has lost his previous job in a boys' school for some unexplained and embarrassing reason (17, 34). He is also self-consciously precious in his use of language, a trait associated in Bessette's *La Bagarre* (1958) with homosexuality (see Maccabée Iqbal 1976, 340, 343). The echoes of Sartre's *La Nausée* scattered throughout *Le Libraire* – such as the reference to 'quatre dimanches d'ennui nauséeux' (54)[9] – may include a veiled suggestion that Jodoin has much in common with l'Autodidacte, as well as with Roquentin. However that may be, Jodoin's only good memories are associated with his own time at school and subsequent reunions with his 'confrères' (13, 20, 22, 80). This early male bonding is far more significant in his life than his relationship with Rose, whom he abandons with as little compunction as her 'no-good' husband (52, 58), who also disappeared.

Rose, who is a mother, shows more initiative and energy than Jodoin. It is she who 'penetrates' into his intimate private space. The fact that her elderly employer is sexually active, and M. Chicoine has a wife and six children (136), implies that only men in a position of power are potent. Jodoin believes that Chicoine is 'maître chez lui' (45), and Chicoine waves a 'mince index' to prove it (42). But his phallic finger proves no match for the Index of the priest. By the end, he is no longer 'maître chez lui' (100) and 'il ne lèvera pas le petit doigt' (152). In contrast, Jodoin congratulates the curé on his excellent eyesight 'à un âge où la plupart des gens sont impotents' (73). In fact, in *Le Libraire*, it is only the old, the priest, and the American who are 'potent.' The power of the priest, le père Galarneau, is sustained by the old maids: the one who sells 'les objets de piété' is called Mlle Galarneau. As Jacques Allard pointed out in an influential article subtitled 'Comment la parole vient au pays du silence' (1969), the curé's power resides in 'la Parole,' represented here by the Index, the final word/authority of the Church. Jodoin pits his own words against the Word (Allard, 59), with some success, 'une petite victoire' (74), but his language is 'châtié' (hypercorrect, literally castrated; see Allard, 57 and Maccabée Iqbal, 347). It is also not quite his own, as he self-consciously uses French terms, both literary and colloquial, and even grammatical, for example, '*un* job,' (23), rather than the Québécois ones familiar to his interlocutors – and to him, as he admits to Rose (57).

Much as Jodoin desired, earlier in his life, to benefit from books and acquire the power of language, he has now regressed to a non-reading mentality, almost on a par with the local consumers of the toys sold by Mlle Placide. These evoke the family, one of the refuge values of the colonized, like the naïve religion represented by the 'objets de piété.' However, the sale of the latter, like that of the forbidden books in the 'capharneum,' is an infraction of those values for crass commercial ends. When Jodoin finally acquires the stock of prohibited books, he also sells them unscrupulously, becoming himself 'le libraire' in an ambivalent ending that does not make it clear whether he has 'emerged' or not.

### (R)ejection: Delivery, abortion, or false alarm?

As several critics have pointed out, the censored books, like Jodoin, are buried, or dormant, imprisoned in Chicoine's padlocked 'capharneum,' which is tomblike in its gloom, silence, and smell of decay (44). It is also womblike: the books are waiting to be born(e), to be released in order to speak. Like Jodoin, who goes to the railway station only to remain in the waiting room, they must become mobile in order to be free. At the end of the book, an enclosed space (the truck) becomes a 'moving' vehicle. Ben Shek has commented on the possible connotations of the title, *Le Libraire*, including 'le libre-air' of freedom (and of the outside, 'la libre-aire') and 'la libre-ère.' One could add 'le libre/livre *erre*,' evoking both the immigration of these books from France, their subsequent clandestine wanderings, and their condemnation in Quebec as 'wrong' (that is, in error: Jodoin is also in this sense a 'Canadien errant,' like Hertel). If the books are seen as incubated or in gestation,[10] then the role of Jodoin is that of midwife, as he liberates and (literally) delivers them.

His own release to a new life (?) is inseparably bound up with the fate of the books. When asked by the truck driver, 'C'est vous, les livres?' he replies that 'en effet, les livres, c'était moi' (146). As Shek and others have pointed out, his identity as student, teacher, ex-reader, bookseller, and ultimately writer (of the diary) is defined by books. These in turn are part of his wider preoccupation with the questionable efficacy of speech as a medium of communication. His recourse in dialogue to metacommentary on words is part of his narcissistic self-image as capable of eloquence (10, 47). The preciosity and Frenchness of his level of language is typical of the narcissistic use of language to regulate self-esteem, rather than to communicate.

Jodoin 's'écoute parler,' and this is the main function of his journal – aside from filling in time. He listens critically to his own conversations and to his own narration, commenting on his progress and artfully structuring his story, in spite of his claims to the contrary (see Allard, Shek).

## The diary and the novel

Jodoin's diary is unusual, because it is written in instalments, which for some critics makes it not a diary at all: Robidoux calls it a 'hebdo' (1971, 17). Apart from the last entries, when the action catches up with the narration (rather than the reverse, as in Butor's *L'Emploi du temps*), Jodoin writes only on Sundays, when both the bookstore and the pub are closed. This periodic recording produces a compromise between retrospective narrative and the 'narration intercalaire' (Genette) typical of the *in medias res* diary situation. Although the narrator's avowed aim is to 'tuer le temps' by establishing a timeless routine, the unpredictable proves triumphant. While external events appear to be beyond his control, and the reader assumes that he will leave Saint-Joachin in disgrace, he himself finally, and unexpectedly, takes control of what happens when he diverts the books to Montreal. This *prise de pouvoir* (it is a 'coup') by someone who appeared impotent is parallel to the *prise de parole* by someone who appeared taciturn. It is the equivalent, at the level of the action, of Jodoin's successful transformation of his text from a diary to a novel: as he, the diarist and 'écrivain de dimanche,' becomes an author, so his 'personnage' (14) is metamorphosed from victim/observer to triumphant protagonist. The narration contributes to his transformation of a 'vulgaire combine' into an 'escapade,' an adventure (14, cf. 112).

The tone of his narrative is, like the railway station (94), both intimate and impersonal. The resemblances to Camus's *L'Etranger* were immediately remarked. Jodoin's account has two striking stylistic features that contribute to this effect. One is the frequent use of the *style indirect libre*, which several critics have commented on (for example, Belair 1974, 60; Kwaterko 1989, 87–116). Bessette has mentioned that the first version of *Le Libraire* contained much more dialogue, and that he eliminated most of it because it read too much like a novel, rather than a diary (Robidoux 1987, 142). In fact, what is retained mostly records the words of others, and the indirect style is used mainly to evoke Jodoin's own words. This distances himself as narrator from himself as actor – and, as Maccabée Iqbal has pointed out (1976, 344), he is an excellent actor. The indirect style underlines his awareness of himself as playing a role. A related feature, which seems to have passed unremarked, is his switching back and forth from the *passé composé* to the *passé simple*, that is, from the tense associated with *discours* to the one associated with *récit* (Benveniste).

These shifts are the symptom of Jodoin's dual function as diarist (*in medias res* and acted upon by others/events) and self-conscious storyteller, in control of the narrative. The abandonment of all chronological coherence, analysed in detail by Robidoux (1971, 17–18, 1987, 145), is not noticed by the casual reader, since the storyteller takes over from the diarist. The transformation from diary to novel, an essential element of the 'self-begetting text,' as in *La Nausée*,[11] is reflected in the text, as Allard and Shek have remarked. Marcotte also observed that the dimensions of Jodoin's room (11 x 8.5 feet) correspond to those of the page (1976/1989, 44). Jodoin's recreational pursuit of writing in fact re-creates him, as both actor and author. Unlike most diarists, he thinks initially that he knows himself ('Je me connais' [7]), and believes that his identity is stable, but the reflexive activity of writing produces a transformation. 'To write,' like 'to be born,' is, as Barthes (1970) claimed, a verb of 'middle voice': the subject engaged in either of these activities both effects the action and is affected by it – is its effect (see Raoul, 1980, 62, 73–6).

Jodoin becomes a writer, but his text remains private, that is, not read by anyone else. Within the fiction, the diary function dominates. Like the books in the capharneum, he is silenced/castrated, deprived of his potential subversiveness. His novel would not pass the censors (Bessette's did not). As a review of the reaction to *Le Libraire* in Eastern Europe has shown (Kwaterko in Hamm 1982, 135–46), the (secret) diary is the appropriate form for dissident writing in a repressive society. This *Essai sur les moeurs* (Maccabée Iqbal 1976, 345), like Voltaire's, is not 'à mettre entre toutes les mains' (40, 70). Those who would be sympathetic (whose hands Jodoin holds – Rose, le père Manseau) are marginal and would not be able to read and understand. Jodoin becomes a writer, but his writing, like his revolt, remains a 'vice solitaire,' a form of mental masturbation associated with the refusal to grow up – or to be born.[12]

Yet there is a glimmer of hope. Jodoin admits that, in a sense, 'je pense' (35), and is condemned by Chicoine as one of those who 'raisonnent trop' (101). Although he claims to have no imagination and to be incapable of 'invention' (34), he both lives and writes an 'adventure' (112). His fear of having nothing to say in his diary is groundless (53), and he manages to render both Chicoine and the curé powerless. By the end, he may even have acquired some virility: to defend himself against Chicoine he grabs a long pole (99), and when he leaves Saint-Joachin his beard has grown (150). His dream that he might still have 'un rôle utile' is not 'étouffé dans l'oeuf' (49). His belief that it is better *not* to be free, so that time will pass more quickly (35), is also abandoned. Emerging from his 'coquille' (125), he realizes that 'l'air du dehors m'a fait du bien' (49), and uses the key provided by Chicoine – the second, real one (61) – to liberate both himself and the books. His initial, cowardly agreement with Chicoine that 'le livre est un produit commercial comme les autres' (41) is refuted, 'autrement, à quoi bon?' (49).

The diversion of his precious cargo to Montreal, where the books may be dispersed, appears as a triumph for the freedom of thought. It also liberates Jodoin from the need to work, giving him the freedom to write on any day he chooses. Yet he decides to end his diary: his birth as a writer remains potential. The books also may continue to remain in storage (151), and Jodoin's next move is to find another room – another enclosed space in which to retreat. He does not decide to publish his diary: indeed, he could not do so under his own name without admitting to a crime.

Jodoin states that he has no progeniture, to his knowledge (136). Yet to Québécois readers of Bessette's novels, he became 'le père de l'écriture.'[13] As the parent image shifts from that of the flesh (the mother, the self) to that of the word (the father, *l'Autre*), the book becomes the seed, rather than the baby. The writer, rather than being the mother (womb) or the child (product), reverts to being the phallic source of life. Michel Belair (1974, 69) stated that 'un nouvel être' was about to be born, to 'percer une membrane de non-parole,' but it is not clear whether it is the foetus trying to get out, or the (finally erect) penis trying to get in. Jodoin's book, like the other 'livres différents' (109), is a 'livre qui cogne' (65). The image of returning to the womb in psychoanalysis is associated with the suppressed desire to have intercourse with the mother, replacing the father (see Lewes 1988, 44).

This interpretation of the image is central in Godbout's *Salut Galarneau!* In *Le Libraire*, the name Galarneau is associated with the Church. It is also a familiar expression in Quebec for the sun. Godbout's novel provides a different commentary on the relationship of the birth of the self/the son, in relation to the mother, the dead father, and a new dawn.

## Godbout, *Salut Galarneau!* (1967)

*'Je ne fais pas des phrases tous les jours. Je ne moisis pas des heures dans ce maudit cahier seulement pour vous amuser, stie!' (85)*

At first glance Hervé Jodoin and François Galarneau, the narrator of Godbout's third novel, appear to have little in common. Jodoin is middle-aged, Galarneau is only twenty-six (see Bellemare 1984, 126).

The *libraire* sells books (food for the mind/soul), François is 'le roi du hot-dog,' owner-operator of a fast-food stand near Montreal. Jodoin was a teacher, François left school at sixteen and is an 'autodidacte.' His extended reading, originally motivated by his mother's love of 'romans-photos' (his father did not read) and his own childhood passion for comics, is due to the guidance of his brother Jacques. Jacques is a professional writer of television scripts, a 'vendu' (86), exploiting his facility with words for pecuniary gain. François, unlike Jodoin or Jacques, has little time for French culture and stylistics, preferring the *américanité* of the popular idiom of Quebec, from which Jodoin distanced himself. Jodoin's diary was motivated by time to fill, solitude, and a fascination with language. Galarneau's notes are recorded in spite of his lack of time, in spite of the demands and availability of the woman he claims to love, and in spite of his anti-intellectual preference for spoken language. Jodoin began his journal with no avowed intention of producing a book and does not plan to publish the final product. Galarneau, on the other hand, starts his *cahier* with the desire to be read and to become famous as a writer; it is only gradually, and mainly in his second notebook, that his fragmented but undated autobiographical narrative becomes a *journal intime*, that is, written for his own benefit and addressed to himself. An unlikely *intimiste*, Galarneau does not see himself as in the same category as Gide ('une vieille fille peureuse' [81]) or Anne Frank (48). Yet he reaches the point where he accuses himself of becoming 'le bedeau niais d'une mélancolie d'adolescent' (60–1). He follows Jacques's advice: 'Pense pas à ceux qui vont te lire' (56), and the emphasis shifts from 'raconter' to 'dénoncer' (Lazaridès 1973, 76), from detached *récit* to engaged *discours*.

Both Jacques and François's common-law wife, Marise, have urged him to write, for several reasons. One is that he is not happy (14), and writing is perceived as therapeutic. He is not happy because his life does not correspond to his vision of an ideal self as poet. Unlike Jacques and his other brother, Arthur, who has a 'respectable' job as a fund-raiser for Catholic charities, he is marginal and barely surviving financially. Marise believes that he could write a profitable best-seller and 'être quelqu'un' (29). Like his estranged wife, Louise, she wants him to be more ambitious, 'que je me dépasse' (44). The challenge, for François, is to become a writer while remaining what he is, that is, defined by *le joual*, a form of French that is 'raped' by English, the language of the colonizer. Paradoxically, the 'French' French of Jodoin is perceived by François (the name is significant) as effeminate. The intrusion of English and of *le sacre* (the swear words associated with the Mass, unique to Quebec) gives vigour and virility to a 'dead' language associated in Quebec with the power of the Church (cf. Lazaridès, 74–5). François derides a local 'colonisé' who is unable to perform sexually unless his wife says 'I love you' in English (57), yet his own *prise de parole* is marked by his *américanité*, and defined in opposition to French literature. Ironically, this aspect of the text is the reason it *was* accepted for publication in France (see Godbout in *Le Devoir*, 31 October 1967, and *La Patrie*, 11 September 1967).

## Writing as compensation for impotence

The effect of writing, for François, is that it forces him to think about himself – especially about his situation as a francophone North American. His hostility to English Canadians is clear: he blames everything on 'les Anglais' and 'les Curés' (41, 72, 211), although he continues to frequent a pub called Le Canada. His attitude to the United States, however, is ambivalent. He feels that it is stupid to remain a French Canadian (25), that Marise would love him if he were an American (41); the (professional?) advice he receives from his father's friend, the fireman Beaupré, is to 'partir ... quitter la place' (47). Americans have money and therefore sexual potency and political power. Jacques is successful with women because he is Americanized. Arthur, however, has control of money, and 'la maison paternelle' (120), but is homosexual (119–120), having chosen to identify with the Church, which represents the feminized French-Canadian past. He has no faith in François's capacity to succeed in business. François, a Québécois in transition, is afraid that he cannot be a man and remain a Québécois. He identifies with the old horse, Martyr, who is confined, not going anywhere, waiting to die – when the Québécois travel, it is to 'nowhere' (35). Galarneau's hot-dog stand is a bus without wheels, an 'automobile immobile' (26), a 'refuge.' When, at the end, he fantasizes about departing in the bus with his brothers, it is to Lowell (Massachusetts) that he dreams of travelling. That is where their mother now is (like Rose's daughter in *Le Libraire*), having gone to join her sister. Apparently women have easier access to the masculinity of the States.

## Self-Part(ur)ition 181

François's job surrounds him with phallic symbols ('si je pouvais leur rentrer dans le corps aux Anglais, avec mes saucisses, ça me soulagerait d'autant' [119]), but places him in a feminine role. He is a cook – a servant comparable to Tremblay's waitresses – providing maternal (and American) nourishment – rather than a *chef* like Jacques, who succeeds in everything (15). Sometimes cooking seems an art, or at least a skill, of which he is proud; at others, it is simply a waste of time (76). Ostensibly the 'roi' of his 'château' (41), François is actually more like a *reine du foyer* in his apron (106). He perceives himself as emasculated, and not a good lover (14) like Jacques, who has lived in France. He imagines having power over women, but only by reducing them to the status of objects: prizes at a game of cards (42), or stuffed like his uncle Léo's animals. His inability to control either Louise or Marise results in sadistic fantasies of violent murder using sharp instruments, for example, a razor (105). On marrying Louise, he became part of her family (the Gagnons/gagnant) rather than the reverse, and was trapped by a false pregnancy (97, 100). Marise cannot bear his name, as he is not yet divorced (80, 106); in fact, she would like him to take hers and call his restaurant Chez Marise (33). She has not borne him a child, either (80), to his disappointment. In search of a submissive, supportive and fertile woman to reflect/confirm his manhood – like all Godbout's protagonists (see Plante 1974) – he finds articulate rivals who want to be Simone de Beauvoir to Sartre or George Sand to Musset (29). Both Louise and Marise show more initiative than he does.

Rather than increasing his stature in Marise's eyes, François in his preoccupation with his notebooks diverts his attention from her; feeling neglected, Marise is seduced by Jacques. François loses at one fell swoop both his love object ('Marise ... je t'aimerai toujours' [39]) and his father substitute. He no longer has anyone to talk to, either at home or in his notes: 'Je ne sais plus à qui parler' (75). Consequently, he 'shuts up,' literally enclosing himself in a fantastic acting-out of the narcissistic withdrawal to the womb/tomb typical of the intimate diary. Writing becomes his way of being silent (136), as he surrounds himself with a wall of paper (136) as well as a wall of concrete.

### Writing as sequestration/separation

Galarneau becomes a recluse in order to reclassify himself: 'je fais l'inventaire de mon âme' (57). The list of heteroclite elements he finds recalls Virginia Woolf's description of her diary as a 'capacious hold-all' (1973, 23). All distractions are now eliminated; he can suck his pen in peace (cf. 80) and dialogue with himself. This exchange becomes a correspondence with an imaginary female adviser, whose replies he concocts (130–1). In spite of his claim to be 'burying Marise' (136), it is obvious that he is attempting to rejoin the original Marise, his mother, who has the same name and a resemblance to the second one (38, 76). Marise's departure left him feeling that he was 'fini' (105), that he had lost an essential part of himself (117). He now seeks to restore the primary state of wholeness experienced before separation from the mother: 'restauration,' like digestion, is a recurring image. His enclosed place is simultaneously a refuge and a prison (75, 125, 130), and he is both prisoner and guard. As Lazaridès has shown, he attempts to create a timeless space, conveyed by the leaves stuck to the ceiling. He builds a survival shelter (139), which saves him from suicide, the only other means to achieve oneness and timelessness. The erection of a self-incarcerating wall is 'constructive' (117, 125) to the extent that it may provide him with a space from which to emerge separate from the mother in him. Like his father on his boat, he is 'heureux comme un homosexuel en prison' (21). His descent into the depths of despair is accompanied by the tools of resurrection – a ladder to the sky, and his notebooks.

Galarneau's mother never left the house, unlike his father, who spent his days on his boat in the company of prostitutes. Since she was awake only at night, when the (nameless) father was asleep, they were never seen together. Faced with the choice between night and day, mother or father (65, 102, 148), all three sons preferred to identify with their mother. She is still, for François, the phallic mother, who appeared all-powerful: 'elle avait toute notre admiration puisqu'elle ne dormait jamais, veillant sur les armes tel [sic] Sir Lancelot avant la bataille' (89). As she was from a 'grande famille,' she did not need her husband's name to know 'who she was.' She was also eminently desirable, half-nude in her flowing robes imbued with the sweet, pervasive smell of chocolate. André Smith's study of Godbout's first four novels (1976) shows how, in *Salut Galarneau!* as in the others, the narrator is unable to love another woman successfully, because of his continuing fixation on his mother (Smith, 17). Incestuous desire encounters no obstacle, thanks to the absence of the financially unreliable and sexually unfaithful father, who deserves to die – and does, a victim of the feminine element, water.

Immediately after his father's funeral, François discovers that he has a moustache: he has become a man (21). Yet this metamorphosis from child to adult male is also attributed, by his grandfather Aldéric, to an earlier initiation ritual involving a lengthy swim (135). Lazaridès, in his 1973 article, analysed the significance of this episode in depth. The water represents the feminine to be conquered, associated with time (mortality). François, who is conscious of his resemblance to his father – including his voice and his desire to have children (43, 63, 64, 67) – discovers that, unlike his father, he can swim. Yet later, when tempted to suicide after his father's death and his mother's departure, he thinks of jumping 'au bout du quai' (46). He actually does so, when the second Marise leaves with his father substitute, Jacques, but he survives because of his strong swimming (134). This is the incident that provokes his memory of the initiation, the only episode recounted in quotation marks, as if 'dictated' to Jacques (131). His survival is the proof that he is a man, and that therefore he should be capable of impregnating a woman. He refers to his first experience with Louise as 'mon premier bain,' adding: 'j'avais plongé les yeux fermés, mais j'avais avalé de l'eau: je ne savais donc pas nager. Stie' (99–100). Now, shrinking to a foetal state and position (128–9), François waits in the 'salle de bain,' his surrogate womb, to find out whether he can swim (out).

Before Marise's departure, François claimed that having lost faith in God is no reason to lose faith in women: Louise believed in her mother as God (100). In the final pages of his diary, Galarneau's apparent loss of faith in women seems to inspire a renewed faith in God, that is, in the paternal principle: the day, the sun, Galarneau (57). By choosing to identify with the castrated father over the phallic mother, he hopes to gain access to the symbolic order of the text, which supersedes the imaginary, maternal order of (real) sex.

## Sterility and self-engrossment

In *Partage des femmes* (1976), a psychoanalytic study of pregnant women, Eugénie Lemoine-Luccioni maintains that men desire to give birth, women desire to speak, each longing to enter the other's domain (1976, 8). Inconsolable for not being able to produce a child, François

Galarneau initially believes that he chose the wrong container (97): Louise was not the right 'enveloppe' (for his 'letter'?). Afterwards he is so disappointed with Marise that he imagines filling her (full = *pleine* = pregnant) with his poems, so that she would have 'la peau tendue' (137). His taxidermic equivalent for Louise involved stuffing her with her mouth open; Marise will have her mouth shut. In another fantasy she is decapitated with a razor, while François continues to 'tricoter' his notes, in a scene recalling the revolutionary guillotine. It is clear that in order to 'free' himself, François must get rid not only of the English and the Church, but of women. The dual project of the 'pays' and the 'femme' to be 'conquered' is central not only in Godbout's work, but in a great deal of the 'revolutionary' literature of the 1960s (see Plante, and Poulin 1976).

Woman cannot be conquered as long as she alone can give birth and as long as she will not be silenced. François's solution is to abandon the desire for children, leaving 'reality' to Jacques: 'Jacques peut bien garder ma femme ... lui faire des enfants blonds' (155: 'blond' = American?). Previously he dreamed of taking revenge on Louise: 'Un jour, Louise, je me vengerais, j'aurais autant d'enfants que de passants au coin de Peel' (101). Now he knows that to be in control of his own paternity, he will have to engage in the reverse parthenogenesis of writing (a sperm but no egg). He will 'dominate' and become 'maître de soi' by giving birth to more notebooks, the product of his own creativity: 'chaque mot, c'est une histoire qui surgit, comme un enfant masqué ...' (154). The book will emerge from and with him, a narcissistic self-extension and self-representation replacing the phallus, as a child does for a mother. For he still perceives himself as a colonized, impotent man, and as such he has the same difficulty as a woman in speaking as a subject. The paradox of his situation is that as long as he is colonized he cannot become a father; he has recourse to artistic creation as a substitute, entering the symbolic order not as a man, but as a fake phallic mother.

After proclaiming that 'faut naître un jour ou l'autre' (155) and wishing himself Happy Birthday (in English), François simultaneously salutes himself, the sun, and the book we are reading, in the greeting 'Salut Galarneau!' The three are conflated as a male trinity, excluding the repudiated feminine associated with birth: the Father, the Son and the Holy Word (see the end of chapter 5). Woman is recast in the role of 'ideal reader' (79, 108), and the projected visit to his mother will be to present her with a child – his book. In the book, he will become immortal: he lives and relives in the notebooks (105–6), becoming 'éternel' (63) by the process of 'vécrire' (154). He will also have immortalized Marise, finally controlling her (106). The book is his alone: 'C'est à moi' (113). He appears to have achieved his other reiterated desire: 'je veux dire,' and his 'sayings' may have contributed as much to the survival of Quebec as any potential children.

Many critics have interpreted the conclusion of this novel as optimistic (for example, Bellemare, 191; Pelletier 1991, 37, 76), and as a positive shift from a self-centred 'je' to a more collective 'nous' (Lazaridès, 84; Plante, 164). Yet Galarneau's emergence is still only potential, and he is 'not a separatist' (119; see Kwaterko 1989, 180, 243). In the perspective of the theory of narcissism, the end may be more accurately described as a move from the 'nous' of primary narcissism (oneness with the mother) to the 'je' of individuation (after ceding the mother-Marise to the father-Jacques), followed by the hope of integrating the self into the symbolic order. Refusal to enter the symbolic order, retaining identification with the mother, may be related to fascist nationalism, as André Smith points out (83, 90). As Godbout has intimated, however, full access to the symbolic order may only be possible if the Québécois become American (Boivin 1977, 30). Yet American civilization in general is seen to be narcissistic and mother-oriented, by Kristeva (1986) and Larose (1987). The fact that Galarneau's mother is in the United States, where he plans to join her, complicates the situation in *Salut Galarneau!* Godbout himself expressed the view that Kérouac was right to leave Quebec ('Entrevue,' 1977). He also gives his own name, Jacques, to François's brother (the Americanized and successful writer and lover), rather than to François, and entitled a more recent novel *Une Histoire américaine* (see Tétu 1971 on *l'américanité* in Godbout's works).

The narcissism of the self-begetting novel is inseparable from that of the author, who represents the genesis of his own creation (in both senses). As Yvon Bellemare has shown (1984, 191, 210), the recurring use of types of narration resembling the diary form in Godbout's novels (*L'Isle au dragon*, 1976, is another example) is directly related to this phenomenon, which Godbout himself has recognized (Bovin 1977).

The childbirth metaphor also appears in other less successful Quebec diary novels of the late 1960s. The male narrator of Jean-Marie Poupart's

*Angoisse Play* (1968, revised in 1980) claims to belong to both sexes (Leméac 1980, 14) and talks of his 'delirious mental menstruations' (25). He attributes his impotence to too frequent masturbation and calls his sterility a 'ménopause cosmique' (55). Both pregnant woman and foetus, he states: 'je suis rempli de moi. Je suis rempli des autres ... J'ai le volume et la taille de l'univers' (79). The words of the journal are his offspring: 'Les mots m'échappent, eux qui ont leur vie propre et leur autonomie' (84), but he concludes pessimistically: 'J'échoue grammaticalement comme j'ai échoué sexuellement' (85).

Any conclusion that can be drawn from Pierre Châtillon's *Le Journal d'automne de Placide Mortel* (1970) is equally negative. The diarist's reiterated affirmation that 'il faut faire un homme de soi' (38) is as vain as his claim to be helping 'le soleil à sortir d'entre les cuisses de la neige comme on dégage péniblement la tête d'un gros enfant rouge' (25). He belongs to 'cette multitude informe qui ne doit jamais naître' (87–8) and even his words disappear on the page as he writes them, lamenting that 'Il faut se mettre au monde sans arrêt' (88). This 'diary of a madman' ends with the chilling image of a foetus in an ice coffin (107). The hallucinatory effect of Châtillon's 'récit poétique' is rivalled by that of Jacques Garneau's barely comprehensible *Les Difficiles Lettres d'amour* (1979), which develops the birth image extensively (see Mélançon, *Le Devoir* and Paul 1979, 46–7). A comparison of Garneau's novel with Geneviève Amyot's *Journal de l'année passée* shows clearly the different implications of this metaphor for a female writer.

## Masculine birth and feminine writing: Garneau and Amyot

Geneviève Amyot published her *Journal de l'année passée* at the end of 1978, and *Les Difficiles Lettres d'amour* by Jacques Garneau appeared a few months later. Amyot's text is situated somewhere between autobiography and fiction, since the narrator-protagonist is called Geneviève Amyot, is the same age as the author, and has also written a book called *La Mort était extravagante*. In the preceding year she completed a text that resembles Amyot's *L'Absent aigu*. Garneau's narrator is nameless but claims that his account is not an invented story (1979, 134). Both narratives are composed of fragments of a story, told in the first person, which forms a puzzle. In both the narrator writes and focuses on his/her identity, especially gender definition.

Both texts refer self-consciously to the *journal intime* model and comment on the complex relationship of time to writing. In *Journal de l'année passée* the paradoxical title and almost complete absence of punctuation underline the problems of chronology and continuity (see Vanasse in *Lettres québécoises* 1979). The *Difficiles Lettres d'amour* are letters only because the narrator designates others (all women) as projected or hypothetical narratees in his dialogue with himself. His *dédoublement* is conveyed by various pronouns (je, tu, il) that serve to convey his desire to identify with the missing 'elle.' Garneau emphasizes diary precedents by a series of epigraphs, including quotations from Anaïs Nin and a (real?) *Journal d'une folle*. Both authors live in Quebec City, and Amyot mentions Garneau twice in her 'diary': the first time, she states that she has read his manuscript (54: *Les Difficiles Lettres?*). The two 'novels' have one striking similarity: their extensive development of the childbirth metaphor.

## Garneau, *Les Difficiles Lettres d'amour:* Letters from exile, to the lost origin

Garneau's enigmatic text begins with the first of a series of three letters distributed throughout the book addressed to 'la mère.' It is subtitled 'le ventre,' which may mean womb or stomach. As in *Salut Galarneau!* there is a risk of confusing gestation and digestion. Like Galarneau the narrator is shut-up in womblike solitary confinement: 'Je ne veux pas parler. Donc, je m'enferme dans ma chambre: un point, c'est tout' (13). The isolation of writing is a preferable alternative to the painful presence of speech. His bedroom becomes successively a womb, a coffin, a hall of distorting mirrors, and a stage bound by curtains of blood – the last in a section called '*Ma* Délire,' where the modification of the noun's gender is significant. The narrator's refusal to accept the outcome of his first birth is connected to a repudiation of the male sex assigned to him. Born a twin and thirteenth in the family, he perceives himself as superfluous (20, 29). The mother is imagined as laying a dozen eggs, that is, the children who 'la sacreraient mère et femme' (33-4): the thirteenth is an unnecessary supplement. Admitting to his desire for the mother and jealousy of the father (22, 30), the unwanted child nevertheless rejects Oedipal identification with the father in favour of a narcissistic desire to remain part of the all-powerful mother. The symptom of his refusal to become masculine is that he remains dumb, replacing speech (communication) by writing for himself (narcissistic regulation of self-esteem). No one is going to read his notebooks but him (37).

Since it is impossible to return into the mother, the diarist withdraws into himself. He wishes to be female in order to possess his own inner space equivalent to the mother's womb. For this reason he envies his sisters: 'Si au moins j'avais été une fille ... Je voulais une autre histoire que la mienne ... Une histoire de femme' (20). One of them mothers him, in place of the children she does not yet have (36). He himself dreams of giving birth. Hiding his penis, he fantasizes the delivery of a doll, in the bathtub: 'Je me perce le nombril. Je me déchire sous les cuisses et j'ouvre très grand en poussant ... Je m'éventre ... Je m'accouche tout seul dans un bain' (53). The reflexive 'je *m*'accouche' conveys the self-production of this horrific vision of parturition, involving the destruction of the origin.

Ultimately, he is the child, not the mother, and wishes to begin life over again with no debt to the (m)other's womb (see Lemoine-Luccioni, 59, 129, 130, 140ff). The procreation/literary creation analogy proceeds from this desire: 'Un jour, ma mère, je m'enfanterai ... J'écris pour venir au monde' (21); 'J'ai gonflé mon ventre ... et j'ai commencé à m'écrire' (70). He writes to himself, and in order to produce a new self (as text and as writer): he even sustains the image by mentioning 'les forceps appliquées en haut des pages' (35), and cites Aquin's Lacanian admission that 'Je n'écris pas, je suis écrit' (59).

## Creation and destruction

Writing, like birth, is associated with the painful expulsion of something within. Garneau attempts to introduce the fluidity associated with the feminine: 'Il avait essayé de s'imaginer dans la salive ... une source d'eau d'où part le reste des eaux. Il y avait du plasma aussi et du lait dans une enveloppe de cellophane. Un globe. Un ballon. Une terre ... une bombe' (62–3). His attempt at femininity fails, because the creative image of birth is transformed into the destructive one of explosion, the violence of a bomb that evokes the FLQ, rather than a 'Quiet Revolution.' One is reminded of Galarneau's declaration that his book will 'les éclabousser' (*Salut Galarneau!*, 146). The birth metaphor is converted to one based on masculine ejaculation; giving birth is construed as the ultimate orgasm, the baby as the (separated) phallus (see Lemoine-Luccioni, 42, 51). The narrator will 'accoucher d'une fleur dont la tige sortirait à la place du pénis' (62). Maternal, uterine elements are conflated with the paternal, phallic; he will 's'exploser dans un fusil de lait' (65). The doll will emerge broken, and the text will be fragmented, because 'mon ventre d'homme est aussi un détonateur' (63).

This diarist finally recognizes that the only way for a man to return to the womb is to impregnate a woman: 'cherchait celle qui l'enfanterait vraiment ... qui lui ferait éclater les eaux ... qui le ferait rentrer de nouveau dans les cuisses ... cette fois-là il arriverait entre les jambes d'une femme et que ce serait doux, tendre et beau' (27). The last 'letters' are addressed to 'la femme,' whom he represents as being reborn with him: 'on foulait la même terre, comme sortie de notre sève, de notre déchirure, de notre césarienne' (113). Heterosexual relations are interpreted as a mutual fecundation entailing a new life for both partners, in an idyllic vision similar to Irigaray's concept of 'la parousie' in *Ethique de la différence sexuelle* (1984). Yet allusions to Adam and Eve evoke the fantasy of woman emerging from the man, rather than the reverse. Furthermore, this mutually narcissistic self-generation of both potential parents actually eliminates the need – or the possibility – of a third person, the 'real' child. If the origin/parent is not to be destroyed, then the child must die (see Lemoine-Luccioni, 50, on 'generation conflict' as a 'fight to the death'). It appears that *Les Difficiles Lettres d'amour* are provoked by the guilt associated with an abortion: 'Ce ne fut pas facile de tuer notre enfant,' but 'nous étions encore trop fragiles' (121). The child was 'vomited' by the woman and had to 'explode,' to provide them with 'la clef qui devait nous ouvrir' (123). The 'opening' is not the vagina, or the stomach, but the *mouth*: 'Longtemps après, nous avons eu des remontées dans la gorge' (123). The parents will become their own child (127), by producing words, 'l'enfant qui s'écrit entre les lignes' (140). The last letter, called 'la plus belle,' is subtitled 'le livre.' One of the enigmatic pronouncements near the beginning of the book is explained: 'Il s'agit de l'autopsie d'une naissance et non d'un meutre' (35). The 'child' *is* the 'letters.'

The back cover of this book bears the following commentary: 'A l'occasion de l'Année internationale de l'enfant, ce roman apporte une illustration de la dépossession de l'enfant à qui on refuse *la parole*.' This observation is singularly inappropriate, since the choice seems to be between 'vivre' (for the child) or 'écrire' (for the author), and the two are presented as mutually exclusive. The same fundamental quandary is central in Amyot's text, but the problem is more 'real' than hallucinatory, for a female writer-narrator. As Stanford Friedman maintains, the childbirth metaphor produces a *collision* for a man, but evokes *collusion* for a woman (1989, 93).

### Amyot, *Journal de l'annee passée* (1978): The maternal synecdoche: Container and/or contained

According to Luce Irigaray in *Ethique de la différence sexuelle* (1984), the maternal represents for men the lost origin, a mythical/mystical place of wholeness, prior to the separation and subsequent 'lack' that provokes desire. Man is 'interiorized,' his self-definition depending on a concept of time as linear, based on subjective experience of change. Woman, however, is perceived by him primarily in terms of space, and as external to male self-consciousness. He also perceives his own body as external, including his penis, which is visible and can be treated as an object. The woman, however, is construed as inseparable from her body, and as having 'no sex' because hers is not visible. The male body is closed, whereas the female one is open. Irigaray claims that women have a different relationship to space and to their own bodies, because their *jouissance* is both external and internal. Their sense of body boundaries is less defined, more permeable. In giving birth, the mother experiences the separation of part of herself, and this is not an amputation, since the part becomes a whole and she remains whole (see Irigaray, *Le Corps à corps avec la mère* 1987, 19–33).

For a woman, the relation to the mother is not simply that of 'lost origin,' since she may herself become a mother. The relationship is one of resemblance and duplication, as well as separation and distanciation. She may experience birth from both sides, in a 'Russian doll' effect (see Lemoine-Luccioni, 48), as both container and thing contained, producer and product. The pregnant woman experiences interdependence with an other that is part of the same, yet different (see Irigaray, *Et l'une ne bouge pas sans l'autre* 1981). Although the child functions as a phallus, it does not correspond to the penis, because it is detachable and replaceable.[14]

Like Garneau, Amyot begins by invoking her mother as origin: 'Les commencements ô ma mère' (10). She claims to have considered 'la mère à boire' as a possible title (16). Garneau's narrator wanted to return into his mother's womb 'comme dans un restaurant' (19–20). Amyot's diarist, Geneviève, takes refuge in the 'chic restaurant Bernier,' which she calls 'cet utérus de pacotille cette matrice à rabais' (95). Like Garneau's character, she is the last in a large family (sixteenth) and has also been mothered mostly by a sister (40). We learn that her mother has been paralysed since her birth (124) and has had one leg amputated. The daughter sees her own parallel experience of bodily mutilation as a punishment for her mother's pain and loss.

The diary recalls the events since 1 April of the preceding year, when the narrator completed one book and had one ovary removed (20). Creative production (of a book) is perceived as achieved at the cost of self-mutilation entailing less likelihood of reproduction. Now she is afraid that if she writes another book – this book – she may lose the other ovary (48), just as her mother is about to lose her other leg: 'quand je suis allée à l'hopital j'ai pensé ... que je ne pourrais plus jamais me permettre d' entreprendre aucun livre et quel morceau y risquer ... quel organe à la poubelle ... je trouvais juste qu'ils me coupent quelque chose puisque j'étais coupable à propos de ma mère une jambe égale un ovaire mais il était tout à coup question de la deuxième'(136–7). Geneviève feels guilty towards her mother not only because of her amputations but because she herself has chosen to write rather than to be a mother. In fact, it appears that her gynecological problems may be attributable to an abortion that occurred also in the previous year.

At the end of the journal she challenges the reader to solve an enigma: 'Allez donc savoir si j'ai eu un enfant ou non' (166). Clues are scattered throughout the text. At the beginning she states that a year ago she had not had any children (20), implying that she had one since then (though she now has none). Later she adds that a year ago she was 'vide ainsi qu'à présent et nulle honte' (39). On meeting a priest she expresses her relief that he does not know 'ce que j'ai fait de la chair de ma chair' (53). She mentions that her lover of the year before did not want her to become pregnant (82). By October, he had agreed to have a child and at Christmas they sang 'il est né ...' in anticipation (127), but by Easter she was in mourning: 'le temps est un enfant qui ne se laisse pas étreindre ... et toujours toute splendeur me file entre les pattes' (124). There is also the mysterious episode of a man she drowned, on the way to Vancouver, wrapped in a scarf that she had knitted, who adopted a foetal position and resembled an 'avorton' (72). References to knitting (needles) evoke both preparation for a birth and an improvised abortion. She calls her narrative a 'chapitre d'aveux débridés,' adding 'peut-être serai-je absoute de mes fruits défendus' (71–2).

Her 'fruits défendus' may be unwanted children – or unwanted books. As in Garneau's text, the process of writing is compared to gestation. The narrator attributes to herself the physical symptoms of pregnancy: she does not have a period, she feels nauseated, and the colour of her nipples changes (10); she has cramps (16, 21) and is swelling up (35, 81). Writing, she claims, is 'le travail le plus exigeant que je connaisse je le dis pour en avoir essayé d'autres ... je parle proprement de travail exactement comme quand on dit une "femme en travail"' (79). On fainting, she wonders if she *is* pregnant (148). Since she is a woman, the reader asks the same question. The reply is negative, her 'travail' is to 'finir ce livre délivrer le suivant' (146). The pages are 'dures à pondre' (130), and she is afraid that this, too, may turn out to be an abortion or miscarriage. She is also afraid that by writing she will lose her feminine ability to procreate, indeed her femininity. Whereas Garneau's narrator wished to feminize his name, Geneviève says: 'je n'avais point peur pour mon e muet' (76).

For her, refusing to be a silent female incubator is associated with a change of sex. She may become a bearded lady, an androgyne able to 'renverser sur soi-même mon propre corps composer par mes seules forces contraires la splendeur totale du chaos d'origine' (83). But it is not by losing her female organs that she will become 'complete.' The neuter, 'la perfection catholique asexuée,' (100) is as useless as the man with a womb whom she claims to know (85; one is reminded of Richard's hobo). Geneviève wonders if Michelangelo would have painted if he had been castrated, and whether losing her ovaries would 'castrate' her or make her more creative artistically, since she would be masculinized. She wishes she had a 'ventre d'homme ... sans fente,' unlike her mother's, which is 'trop gras, l'orifice est trop grand' (149). Feminine openness is construed as insecurity, as vulnerability to both invasion and the unplanned loss of internal parts. Her comments illustrate remarkably the theory of Lemoine-Luccioni in *Partage des femmes* (1976), where she describes women as haunted by the fear of 'partition,' which must be reformulated as symbolic castration in order for them to accept their place in the symbolic order, their 'partage.' Emphasis on the capacity to reproduce constitutes woman as paradoxically more phallic than man, since the child functions as the phallus; but the birth of the child leaves a space or a gap that needs a 'bouchon.' The female body is redefined as lack, as 'troué,' and woman must turn to the male/paternal penis to (temporarily) fill it.

The daughter is also, like the son, the exposed particle that must be outside in order to 'ex-sister' (Lemoine-Luccioni, 125), and shares his nostalgia for a state of protective envelopment. Garneau's narrator refers several times to protective coverings, and to 'changing his skin.' Amyot uses an old fur coat as a comforter, since her lover left with her bedspread. Like Garneau's letter writer, she tries to be both the envelope and the letter, to carry herself to term in her book (147). The metaphorical relationship of mother and child as analogous to author and book poses problems of metonymy: the part for the whole, the container for the contained. Unlike Garneau, Amyot has difficulty in subordinating the role of producer/vehicle to that of end-product.

Her second reference to Garneau is juxtaposed with the remark that 'la littérature va me sauver de tout' (102), yet this claim lacks conviction. Moved by 'un certain sens de la solidarité féminine' (62) she reassures herself that 'par chance il y a au moins les enfants' and states 'les enfants c'est vraiment ce qu'il y a de plus grave' (120). She does not wish, by writing, to lose the opportunity to become a mother, and the flowering of her red geraniums at the end of the text represents menstrual flow as well as the product of planting cuttings. She sees writing, like menstruation or gestation, as cyclical rather than linear and teleogical, reflecting a feminine relation to time: 'je sais que je recommencerai demain dans un mois dans neuf autres et l'année suivante' (9). Her survival as a woman and as a writer depends on it. As a woman writer in Quebec, she also asks the fundamental question: 'Le pays a-t-il davantage besoin de mes enfants que de mes livres?' (87).

Amyot's novel illustrates the incorporation into the text of female body imagery in terms of feminine experience rather than male fantasy. Her next book, *Petites fins du monde* (1988), focuses on the child as part of the text, rather than as an alternative to it. Her anguish when confronted with the apparent dichotomy of *écrire/reproduire* is a feminine version of the *vivre/écrire* choice perceived by male diarists. For women, both *vivre* and *écrire* may be perceived as in opposition to childbirth: becoming the (m)other may exclude all possibility of being also the subject/the 'one,' of action or of speech.

Writing 'au féminin' – to use Nicole Brossard's expression – is a perilous pursuit. Yet even before Madeleine Gagnon and others spoke of 'writing the female body,' women used the diary form to attempt to convey a feminine experience and identity crisis in fiction. In Quebec, woman-as-mother was perceived as having a particular function as obstacle to the male diarist's 'liberation' both before and during the Quiet Revolution, as we have seen. How is this situation represented in diary fiction by women? The next section will begin by considering some novels that provide answers to this question.

PART V

WRITING AND
SELF-ESTEEM: FROM
MIRROR TO VOICE

CHAPTER TEN

# Separation and Survival: Women's Diary Fiction from Saint-Onge to Mailhot

'Aussi la femme se vit-elle consacrée reine du foyer. Elle est représentée comme y jouant un rôle déterminant pour la survivance de l'ethnie.'
MARIE COUILLARD (1981), 47

'Psychoanalysis ... while helping to account for the construction of the female subject and current manifestations of sexual difference, cannot offer any kind of theory of social transformation and is unable to account for the possibility of women acting on or changing aspects of the structures which shape them.'
RITA FELSKI (1989), 58

'What is striking in the work of virtually all women writing about themselves in the present and in the past, is the degree to which writing itself is a solution to their most pressing problems.'
PATRICIA MEYER SPACKS (1973), 34

## Being a woman writer in Quebec

Godbout's novels, as illustrated by *Salut Galarneau!*, demonstrate the close association in writing by men in the Quebec of the 1960s between two aspects of 'emancipation': independence from English Canada and the end of the Québécois male's impotence/feminization, by his 'conquest' of a woman. Both projects remain desired rather than fulfilled, as seen in the examples discussed in the last chapter. Meanwhile, women are still imprisoned in two categories: the mother, from whom the son must escape (whether he hates or loves her) in order to become separate/autonomous, and the woman-as-object whose submission would confirm his own subjecthood. Since the woman still represents the mother, the two are linked. The woman who resists becomes, like the mother, an obstacle to the man's emergence as a man. The 'birth of the self' as a separate individual is construed as a repudiation of the collective (feminine) refuge values of the past. Yet it is also depicted in fiction as representative of a collective phenomenon, since the narrator-protagonist's diary is part of a specifically Québécois attempt to 'speak.' Turcotte describes 'l'âpre conquête de la parole' (1969) and Allard, writing on Bessette, proclaims 'comment la parole vient au pays du silence' (1969). This *prise de parole* by male authors/narrators is part of their accession to masculinity and implies a silencing of women, whose discourse can only be that of the mother (to be repudiated) or that of the unsubmissive object (to be suppressed).

In this situation, how can a woman speak, let alone write? Marie Couillard, in a discussion of the position of women writers in Quebec in relation to dominant ideology (1981), emphasizes that the reproductive role of women had a particularly important mythical dimension in a society that genuinely perceived itself as being threatened with extinction. The 1960s saw the advent of widespread contraception and greater availability of abortion, and the concomitant sexual liberation and decline in the prestige of both motherhood and marriage. The revenge of the cradle became a thing of the past, as women who came from large families decided that they did not want to have several children, refusing (like Geneviève in Amyot's *Journal de l'année passée*) to duplicate their mothers. A study of women in Quebec who have chosen not to have children (Carmel 1990) reveals that the decision still meets with collective disapproval. The survival of the Québécois once again appears threatened, this time by the proliferation of non-francophone immmigrants who do not wish to integrate and whose birth rate is higher than that of the Québécois *pure laine*. Within the Canadian federation, the Québécois are also decreasing as a proportion of the total, and the provincial government has adopted pro-natalist policies (see Carmel 13, 28–30). When Amyot asks which the 'pays' needs more, her children or her books, this is not simply a rhetorical flourish, as Lise Payette's controversial documentary film *Disparaître* (1989) showed.

What tends to be forgotten is that there was also a long tradition in Quebec of celibate women who had careers as members of religious orders, avoiding both the burden of multiple motherhood and the stigma of being 'old maids' (see Carmel, 14–18 and Danylewycz, *Taking the*

*Veil* 1987). Laure Conan, however, was exceptional in refusing either option. Neither the family nor the convent gave women the opportunity to write. The number of men who could do so was also relatively small, as long as the majority were engaged in agriculture: 'faire de la terre' corresponds to 'faire des enfants' as a *natural* rather than a cultural pursuit. The move from the farm to perform unskilled labour in the city did little to improve the situation before 1960, and the articulate élite identified with the culture of France, as seen in chapter 5.

Women were seen as a civilizing influence, an aspect reflecting the American cultural context, but they were not expected to participate in institutionalized culture. In an overview of the history of women's writing in Quebec, M.-J. Green, P. Gilbert Lewis, and K. Gould (1985) single out only one novelist in the period before the Second World War: Jovette Bernier, who wrote *La Chair décevante* (1931). The authors of the article point out that at the beginning of the book she adopted a form resembling the journal, but that it became something closer to the 'monologue intérieur.' Both the form and the story met with disapproval at the time. Didi Lantagne, the narrator-protagonist, is, at the beginning, an unmarried mother abandoned by her fiancé for a richer woman. This plot, as Martens established (1985, 101–2), is a typical one in nineteenth-century women's diary fiction in Europe. More surprisingly, Didi is sleeping with another man, who wants to marry her. She does not dare to confess her 'fault' and leaves, missing the opportunity to marry a man who will love her forever (possibly because she is unattainable). When she finally does marry, for the sake of her son, it is to a father-figure who dies. The son's life will be ruined, because she does not tell him the name of his real father, and he unwittingly falls in love with his half-sister. The father commits suicide on discovering this, and Didi goes mad. One can deduce from this melodrama that the woman who does not conform to collective norms for feminine behaviour is a source of suffering to all the men in her life, and to herself. Her position is untenable, as evidenced by her madness.

Bernier's experiment with narrative technique was exceptional. Germaine Guèvremont and Gabrielle Roy, the successful women writers of her generation, adopted conventional third-person forms, which nevertheless enabled them to 'speak' of women's 'difference' (see Smart 1988). Anne Hébert succeeded by appropriating the stereotype of woman-as-other – mysterious, dreamlike, mad – opting for the imaginary over the rational/symbolic. She did not depict a character who wrote until *Les Fous de Bassan* (1982). Françoise Loranger, in *Mathieu* (1949), chose to depict a male identity crisis, as did Roy in *Alexandre Chênevert* (1954), where a diary is mentioned but not incorporated into the text. Marie-Claire Blais used the diary form in *L'Insoumise* (1966), but her initial project to write about a housewife's life is diverted to focus on male homosexuals (see my chapter 8). In the 1960s it was left to a minor author, Paule Saint-Onge, to write the story of a *reine du foyer* from the woman's perspective. She did so in two diary novels, *Ce qu'il faut de regrets* (1961) and *La Saison de l'inconfort* (1968). Another, stranger diary fiction is *Peur et amour* by Yolande Chéné (1965), which depicts the 'diary of a madwoman,' a victim of sexual abuse who is 'saved' by an American man. Claude Lamarche's *Je me veux* (1976) is the first diary novel in Quebec to ask directly how a woman can become a 'subject.' The situation she represents has been taken up and developed more recently in a more sophisticated version of the diary form by Michèle Mailhot (*Le Passé composé* 1990).

The female diarists in these novels perceive their dilemma primarily in terms of their relationships with men, rather than as Québécoises. Only Hélène Ouvrard, in *L'Herbe et le varech* (1978), chooses to identify with the male desire to be decolonized, and her appropriation of the *femme/pays* image illustrates its problematic nature from a woman's perspective. These diary fictions by women depicting women narrators demonstrate some important differences from those by men discussed so far, as well as significant similarities.

### Saint-Onge, *Ce qu'il faut de regrets* (1961): The diary of a wife and mother

The very fact of a woman writing (about) her life in a journal or autobiography 'transgresses patriarchal definitions of female nature by enacting the scenario of male selfhood' (Sidonie Smith 1987, 8). The author who projects a fictional narrator writing a private diary in a novel produced for publication goes one step further in transferring the private (feminine) sphere into the public (masculine) one. She no longer only mirrors herself as object for the man's desire/gaze, but for her own assessment and that of other women who are likely to be her readers. The diary form has proved a useful intermediary for women, between autobiography and fiction and between the openness of *discours* and the controlled closure of *récit* (see Raoul 1989; Lensink 1987; Juhasz in Jelinek 1980). The first diary novel by Saint-Onge, *Ce qu'il faut de regrets*, is conventional in form but unconventional (for Quebec in 1961) in its subject matter, which anticipates in some respects Simone de Beauvoir's *La Femme rompue* (1967). Saint-Onge dedicated it to 'Claude, mon premier et mon plus cher lecteur.' The epigraph, attributed to Brassens, quotes Aragon: 'Il n'y a pas d'amour heureux.' Since love, in the context of Saint-Onge, is resolutely heterosexual, the novel is ambivalent before it even begins and invites a comparison between autobiography and fiction: an unhappy relationship between a married couple is to be recounted for the benefit (or approval) of a beloved male narratee/spectator.

The diarist, Isabelle, begins her diary as she waits for her husband to return from a conference to which she was supposed to accompany him. She did not, ostensibly because of financial exigency – she chose to buy a vacuum cleaner! (13) – but actually because her husband, Marc, did not want her to go. She describes him as 'un grand enfant, en mal d'indépendance' (14). On his return he confesses that he is in love with another woman, Sylvia. The couple has four children already, and the narrator suspects that she is pregnant again. Her initial reaction is disbelief, as her self-representation excludes this happening to her (68). Her husband's infidelity is a narcissistic injury that forces her to rethink her self-definition. Her confirmed pregnancy is depicted throughout the journal, which lasts a year, as a further narcissistic injury. She refers to 'l'esclavage de cette nouvelle maternité' (14), 'l'atroce et humiliante déformation' (20), and 'les malaises d'une fin de grossesse' (83), illustrating Lemoine-Luccioni's analysis of the negative effects of pregnancy on a woman's self-representation.[1]

Motherhood is also demystified in other ways in this novel. Isabelle comments: 'le rôle de la mère, à propos duquel la littérature déverse tant de lyrisme, fait souvent surgir un aspect de mon caractère que je désavoue totalement' (24). This remark is provoked by her shame at being impatient with her children – at not being the ideal mother, 'une mère sereine' (46–7). She herself spent a miserable childhood with a morose aunt: her mother died giving birth to her, her grandmother was tyrannical, her grandfather 'taciturne et violent' (26), her father an 'étranger prestigieux' who died in an accident (28). She would like to kill herself, but is prevented by the child in her. At one point she regrets that she is unlikely to die in labour, like her mother (42, 57). Yet she considers her children the 'very essence' of her life (64-5) and cannot bear the thought of separation from them. The husband, incidentally, foresees no problems if she should leave, since he can call in his mother to mind the children.

Isabelle's attitude to her home is equally ambivalent. Lemoine-Luccioni has commented on the significance to a woman who is a housewife of her domestic 'interior' (1976, 154-6). This one, who says, 'Cette maison, c'est mon navire' (158), nevertheless complains bitterly about her chores, 'la vie quotidienne avec son misérable fardeau de travaux ultra-prosaïques' (71). Yet they also serve to occupy her (52), and she admits that 'à défaut d'être heureux, ou même nécessaire à quelqu'un ... on peut toujours être utile: pour cela, il suffit d'accomplir, au jour le jour, la montagne de besognes ... Ce rôle, si vous finissez par vous en contenter (j'y suis encore assez mal résignée), personne au monde ne peut vous l'arracher' (131). Obviously, no one lucid would choose this role.[2] As Isabelle loses faith in Marc, she becomes critical of her own subservience, noting in her journal with some irony that *he* is the one who demands comfort and consolation (44) and the one who takes time off to be alone (52, 56). When they do not sleep together, *she* is banished to the sofa, and she even apologizes for waking him when she is in labour. His reaction to the birth is to complain about the hospital bill.

Why does Isabelle want to stay with this self-centred, narcissistic man? Because her own narcissism is involved, and her physical survival. Having abandoned her studies in order to marry, if she leaves Marc she can only hope for a menial job, and wonders who will mind the baby while she works (69). She experiences the loss of Marc's love as destructive of her, rather than liberating. What she misses is his 'regard' (115), which confirmed her attractiveness as a woman/object. As soon as she has regained her figure (once more 'Isabelle' is 'belle'), she embarks on the seduction of an old flame, to reassure herself. Realizing that she is still desirable (108), she is 'reconciled' and less bitter towards her rival (157). As the importance of Marc's approval diminishes in her eyes, he predictably returns to the fold. The housewife's dream of independence is shelved indefinitely. Writing never becomes a source of self-esteem, only a substitute for the other's gaze, and thus a means of survival. The diary serves as a confidant (she refuses to confide in the woman next door), and no one will read it, not even Marc, who has no curiosity regarding her (124).

In spite of her pregnant state, Isabelle never thinks of the birth of the book or her own rebirth. Rather than a shift from 'life' to 'story,' this diary represents the reverse. The Cinderella myth (38) is exposed as a fantasy that women still believe(d?) in. The change in Isabelle at the end of her diary is that she can admit 'que ce qu'on avait pris pour des sentiments d'exception n'étaient, en fin de compte, que des amours ordinaires' (106). Diary writing itself is not dramatized. Although she contemplates suicide, the banality of everyday life triumphs over melodrama: 'le coeur étreint d'une indéfinissable mélancolie, je commence à grignoter une rôtie' (23). The distribution of roles between Marc and Isabelle is still the same as when they were adolescents; he was 'tourmenté de désirs et d'ambitions' and she was 'une petite fille trop sage' (37). In these conditions 'il n'y a pas d'amour heureux,' and the woman's revolt remains secret and repressed.

### Saint-Onge, *La Saison de l'inconfort* (**1968**): Mother + Writer = Phallic mother?

In her third novel and second diary fiction (the intervening novel in 1963 was called *La Maîtresse*) Saint-Onge returns to the unsatisfactory marital relationship. In *La Saison de l'inconfort* the wife, Odile, is a writer of *nouvelles* and the children are older. The husband, Fernand, a doctor, is not indifferent or unfaithful but jealous and possessive. Odile is a prisoner, and he is her cage (20, 104). The woman's revolt takes the form of an affair with a married man, Eric, who turns out to be impotent for medical reasons (56) and unwilling to leave his wife, who is anglophone. Odile's diary incorporates extracts from her journal of the preceding year, when this episode began (as in Amyot's *Journal de l'année passée*), as she attempts to turn her aborted love story into a novel (cf. Monette's *Le Double Suspect*). She believes that she already knows the outcome, but events overtake her narration (104). The relationship between life, life writing and fiction becomes a theme. Odile defines herself as a wife and mother – she would never leave her children (74) – *and* a writer.

The two roles are conflictual. The writer is equated with her true self (in terms reminiscent of Winnicott),[3] the one suppressed by Fernand (28, 34, 145), which nevertheless escapes him in the secret diary. Eric gains her love by complimenting her on her intelligence rather than her looks (11). Another man, Morin, remarks that she is attractive but makes no effort to 'please' (30). Her published writing is characterized by a combination of 'lucidity' and 'ingenuity' in the sense of naïveté or freshness. This juxtaposition sums up Odile's position as representative of a generation of women who 'se seront révoltées trop tard' (165). Married young, she now regrets her choice but is trapped. Writing is her salvation – and so are the children (74, 102). She refers to writing as an outlet for steam (20, 128) and a 'dérivatif' (137), a sublimation of her frustration. When Fernand strikes her in anger, she writes 'pour ne pas hurler' (167). She sees writing as a substitute for life (137): life, in her (feminine) terms, being love (34). From this point of view, Eric's impotence is significant (59). She claims that it is a disappointment, but it enables her to continue writing – while making love mechanically to her husband (24, 51). Yet she also feels guilty for taking time from her chores to write (22, 83) and is afraid that she has no talent (26, 83, 146).

Odile was born at the wrong time, before the availability of birth control (119) and women's liberation, and she lives in the wrong place: 'il est bien difficile de s'affranchir dans ce satané pays' (48). Eric's impotence may also have something to do with his anglophone wife who refuses to speak French. Yet Odile's oppression is attributed mainly to her husband, a narcissist who sees her as 'un robot créé pour répondre immuablement à toutes ses attentes' (53) and uses language as an 'entreprise de stratification' (161) rather than to communicate. He reproaches her for failing as a wife: 'tu ne me donnes plus ce dont un homme a besoin: ton admiration et ton estime' (123). Morin tells her that a marriage cannot be happy if the wife is more intelligent than the husband (157). Her opinion is that 'sans les abus de pouvoir que leur faiblesse encourage, les femmes de mon genre ne rêveraient jamais d'autonomie' (21–2).

Odile does dream of autonomy, and of making her story public, as an escape from Fernand's 'implacable censure domestique' (24). He is an obstacle in her attempt to discover 'who she is' (24). The truth is that she is a woman: her young son asks, 'Tu n'as pas de sexe, toi, Maman?' (34). Morin also asks her: 'Vous ne trouvez pas cela épuisant à la longue, d'être celle qui moralement est toujours obligée de soutenir l'autre?'

(31). The answer is 'yes,' but what else can she do? She can write. As Patricia Meyer Spacks commented, for many women writing is the solution to their most pressing problems (1973, 34). Odile states, 'On ne peut attendre le salut que de soi-même,' but adds, 'mais vaut-il la peine de se sauver?' (142). She continues to wonder if her writing is a worthwhile product, but the process is essential to her survival, allowing her to be separate at one level from her family; being reborn, as her true self, is for her an ongoing, iterative state.

## Chéné, *Peur et amour* (1965): Salvation through writing, or through a man?

Another novel from the same period poses the question of psychic survival in starker terms. The narrator of *Peur et amour*, Marianne, is also a novelist. She has isolated herself in a country house by the sea where she spent a childhood holiday, in order to relive her traumatic sexual experiences as a child. Her narrative is defined in opposition to her novels, although she is reluctant to admit, at first, that her text is a *journal intime*: 'je méprise ceux qui tiennent un journal intime! Mon but procède-t-il de la même faiblesse, de la même complaisance?' (10). Her recollections are interspersed with comments on the difficulty of writing about them, and on her current relationship with a mysterious man called Leonard, who is staying close by. Marianne's journal is interrupted in places by brief notes from Leonard's diary, a dual journal technique used more recently by Francine Noël in *Babel: Prise deux* (see chapter 12).

Marianne is unable to love herself or anyone else, because of something that happened when she was a young girl, which has left her with the sense that all physical love is 'impure' (52). Three incidents that she painfully recalls establish a frame for her self-understanding, and for the reader's (problematic) understanding of her. Although Marianne claims to have no faith in psychoanalysis (43), the book's epigraph is from Freud and the author writes with implied reference to psychoanalytic theory.

The first incident serves to explain the child Marianne's hostile relationship with her mother. When she was about six, a boy her age was showing her his penis, when her mother saw them and accused her of being 'vicieuse' (15). She herself has difficulty, even now, believing that she was 'innocent' (19). Distancing herself from her mother's pious moral narcissism – 'elle se vénérait' (73) – the daughter chose to identify with her father, despised by the mother because he was 'porté sur la chose' (21). Her fantasy of incest with the father (75) was not fulfilled, but after his death her mother remarried. Her hypocritical stepfather's behaviour, which is only alluded to – 'A moi-même, je n'arrive pas à tout raconter' (13) – was the reason that Marianne had to become a boarder at a convent school. Her earlier remarks, which appeared to throw suspicion of sexual misconduct on her father, apply in retrospect to her stepfather: 'Une bonne petite fille ne révèle pas les fautes de son père' (11) and 'ne pas induire le père en tentation' (51).

Attracted by one of the nuns – a 'good mother' – and loved by a mad girl at the school, she later hallucinates images of herself as a hermaphrodite, George Sand in men's clothes, and admits that she wanted to be a boy (59). She is unable to accept herself as a woman, or love a man, because her mother's rejection caused her to hate the idea of being a woman, and she has introjected her mother's distrust of all men. She admits to herself, 'Je désire cette sorte d'amour que seul le père donne' (68).

Using a combination of first- and third-person pronouns to refer to herself, Marianne accomplishes a cathartic, therapeutic exercise in writing: 'En écrivant, je sors de moi ce qui mène ma vie' (16). She is the last in her family to still bear the name of the father, Berger (86), as her mother and four sisters have all changed theirs by marriage. Marianne is attracted to Leonard, but also afraid of being judged by him, and of losing her independence, her name. The writing of her 'confession' reduces her to a state of delirium bordering on madness (Leonard calls her 'ma cinglée'); she has a high fever and hallucinates. At this point Leonard, who has sworn not to invade her privacy, steps in to 'save' her.

Part 1 of the book consists of this journal focused on Marianne's past. Part 2 begins in the third person and then reverts to 'je,' as she describes her subsequent idyllic union with Leonard, who reads the journal and accepts her as she is. In fact, he prefers it to her 'false' novels. Having initiated her into a joyful experience of sex (although he refuses to say 'je t'aime'), he takes her to his home in the United States and marries her in a civil ceremony. Marianne, who previously showed contempt for women who live to please their husbands, is tempted to fall into the role of 'une vraie femme,' passively allowing Leonard to organize her life, and living for him. Leonard is also a writer, but she has not read his books (because they are in English?). He is unsympathetic to the Quiet Revolution happening in Montreal, where they met, as he blames the Québécois for not revolting (129, 130), and in their place would simply leave the province (130). His life remains a mystery to Marianne. While they live together in New Jersey, his attitude is paradoxical, as he *orders* her to be 'free,' that is, not to assume the role of a traditional housewife. As he says, he did not want to marry his mother (122-3). Given the opportunity to become a woman unlike her own mother, who resisted her husband, she complies – in order to please him.

The third part of the book becomes melodramatic, as Leonard's house is burned down and he is finally killed in Korea – not by political opponents, as one suspects, but by the enraged brother of his first wife, whom he divorced because she wanted to be a traditional wife and mother. Marianne is still sufficiently Québécoise to feel that she was not really married to him, since he was divorced, but she decides to go on writing under his name, which is English – Wakefield – rather than her father's. She cannot admit that she would have liked a child, and must instead perpetuate Leonard in her books. She must become (like) him, that is, ready to 'be herself' – an oxymoron that renders the interpretation of this narrative enigmatic.[4] Chéné also dedicates the novel to her husband.

In some ways this work fits into the category of diary fiction described in chapter 7, in which male narrators blamed their sexual frustrations and impotence on a repressive Quebec mentality embodied in mother figures. Marianne asks: 'Pourquoi une famille organisée autour d'une femme mesquine, sentinelle des enfants, et d'un homme affairé, lointain, distant, inaccessible?' (29). Marianne's sexual ambivalence also aligns her with the cases of gender ambiguity analysed in chapter 8. Her failure to become a mother and her recourse to writing in order to deliver herself is related to the childbirth metaphor discussed in chapter 9. And her discussion of the position of women places her in this section. The combination of first- and third-person narration, apparently both attributable to the same narrator, contributes to the strangeness of this text. The introduction of an American male saviour may have political as well as anti-feminist implications. All these elements combine to leave the reader perplexed. The degree of self-consciousness in the discussion of women's situation in Quebec can be seen to increase, and becomes foregrounded in Claude Lamarche's *Je me veux* (1976). This novel specifically refers to the women's movement, but also depicts a woman who begins alone and ends up with a man.

### Lamarche, *Je me veux* (1976): 'Ai-je besoin d'un homme pour me sentir femme?'

The back cover of this book makes the following statement: 'Que peut bien penser une *femme silencieuse* face au féminisme et à l'engagement social? Est-il possible de *n'avoir rien à dire* et de tout de même trouver une voix pour faire entendre la femme, la citoyenne et l'être humain tout à la fois? C'est le parti-pris de l'auteur. Le parti-pris de Claude Lamarche, et, à travers elle, toutes celles qui veulent être, en toute autonomie.' One would assume from this description that the diary in question is autobiographical, and the book is not conspicuously designated *roman* anywhere. Yet the narrator's name is Chantal – 'Moi je suis la faible Chantal, l'indécise' (11) – not Claude. The relationship between author and narrator is underlined by the further identification of both with all 'celles qui veulent être' and the book's dedication 'aux femmes.' One is reminded of earlier references to 'tous les Québécois qui ont choisi de l'être' (D'Allemagne's epigraph, 1966). The question raised (as for the Québécois) concerns the relationship between being born one (a woman/a Québécois) and becoming one: of pre-definition in relation to self-naming, or auto-nomy. The author renames herself (?) as narrator, just as Chantal and her school friend Suzanne invented names for themselves (21). This renaming is relevant to the projection of a voice from a previously silent (listening) space. Writing in the diary provides a means to be simultaneously speaker, actor, and listener, and to invent a self: 'Je voudrais écrire. Ecrire ce que je ne vis pas. M'inventer une vie ... Etre une autre par le roman' (9). The representation of the (true) self is seen from the beginning as producing a fiction.

The narrator describes herself as 'indécise' and like a chameleon, changing according to her context: 'Je suis (du verbe suivre)' (40). The diary entries also follow one another, bearing numbers (1–132) rather than dates. Like Echo, Chantal has 'rien à dire' (71), that is, nothing that she perceives as being her own: 'Je suis moi mais aussi l'autre' (49); 'je suis relative' (88). Chantal identifies in particular with her friend Hélène, who has just married Marcel.

Chantal's introspection is motivated by a reassessment of her life as an unmarried thirty-year-old country schoolteacher. It has been two years since she and Hélène left life in a convent. Previously her most important relationships have been with women (and with God). Now she wonders if she can be a 'real woman,' without a man (17). She remembers that with Suzanne she was 'subjuguée, dominée, inférieure. J'étais ravie' (23). She is feminine in that she has no willpower, she is passive: 'Je ne sais pas vouloir' (39). Courted by a colleague, Michel, she discovers that a relationship with him does not make her feel whole, but 'coupée de moitié ...' She finds him 'inférieur, faible ... inutile ... un indécis, un tourmenté' (46). He is too much like her, too feminine, and she does not want a 'satellite' (65). She concludes, like Chéné's Marianne, that 'je ne m'aime pas encore assez pour pouvoir en aimer un autre' (64).

Her journal is a means to effect a shift from the position of Echo (the excluded other) to that of Narcissus. It serves as a mirror (51), which she hopes eventually to break. Preoccupied with her own search for an authentic self, she refuses to feel guilty for not participating in nationalist or feminist movements: 'Traitez-moi de Narcisse, d'a-politique, je m'en fous' (70); 'je suis sans doute ... une intimiste' (75). Refusing to accept that woman is necessarily man's 'other,' she begins her 'wishing' by deciding what she does not want to be: 'je ne veux pas être la négation de ce qui est' (77). She also refuses to 'lose' herself in a collective 'nous' (77–8) and proclaims a narcissistic preference for being over having (82), although her final position is ambivalent: 'Je suis Je; J'ai Je' (78). Her wish is to believe in an essential self (79), but she begins to wonder if this is a refuge value, like the religion that previously protected her (81). To become an adult (82) she must be able to 'vouloir les autres' (81).

Chantal embarks on a successful relationship with a man when Hélène dies and Marcel becomes available. Her preference for women is overcome, through identification with a double, by substitution. She previously maintained that she did not want to have to become famous or a mother in order to be considered 'une femme à part entière' (32) and that she did not want to have children (48). She also claims that her urge to write has its source in a desire to communicate with other women, not in her father (30), and that her identity is not limited to language – 'Je ne suis pas la langue qui ne veut qu'elle-même' (51). Like Chéné's Marianne she hopes to have found a form of reciprocity in a heterosexual relationship, in which 'nous' is not an agglomerate or a hierarchical takeover, but 'tous les deux' (98). She adds, 'Il me l'a dit,' becoming a man's echo, although she ends with 'Je suis (du verbe être').'

As in *Peur et amour*, the narrator's discovery of her self through a man, as well as through writing, remains ambivalent. Have these women achieved independence, or is their reconciliation with a dominant male other evidence that independence, like the concept of an authentic self, is an illusion? Are women imprisoned in relativity to a male one, as long as they wish to continue to define/find themselves as women? One other diary fiction suggests a different, though no happier, scenario: *Dans les ailes du vent* by Diane Giguère, first published in 1976 and reissued in a revised version in 1984. This novel shows what Chantal might have become if instead of communicating with Marcel she had remained fixated on her dead female double (cf. Monette's *Le Double Suspect*). Giguère's diarist, Amédée, is a thirty-year-old librarian who lives a solitary, monastic life. Her ill health is attributed to a hereditary problem with alcohol. She occupies herself by writing in her diary, knitting, and crocheting. These activities are connected, as life is a 'travail de constant raccommodage' (27) by manual work or words that preserve her precarious sanity. She is obsessed with the memory of her friend Rosalie, an American Jew of French origin who has died in New York. As she rereads letters from her and undertakes a pilgrimage to Rosalie's family in France, Amédée embarks on the project of rewriting Rosalie's life, imagining a 'journal à deux voix' (48), which does not, as in Monette's novel, form part of the text. This novel partly in diary form leaves an impression, as does Chéné's *Peur et amour*, of failure on the part of the author to knit the pieces together to form a satisfactory whole. The text is poetic rather than narrative, but remains enigmatic in a way that is frustrating rather than thought-provoking.

The plight of the woman who is alone and feels a social outcast is addressed more successfully in Michèle Mailhot's poignant and skilful commentary on the relationship between self, time, and writing in *Le Passé composé*.

## Mailhot, *Le passé composé* (1990)

*'Ma solitude n'est-elle pas le lieu de ma différence? ... Solitude = être = écriture. Voilà!' (95)*

*'N'écrit pas qui veut.' (106)*

Judith Turcot, Mailhot's narrator, is by no means naïve in her conception of literature and attitude to writing. Forced by the advent of computers to take early retirement after twenty years as an editor with a publishing company, she is very familiar with the workings of the literary institution. Authors are well-known to her as people whose manuscripts she has corrected. In the role of editor she has typified the feminine function of invisible support to the speaking subject. Her exactitude illustrates the concept of woman as speaking/writing hypercorrectly, because she *imitates* rather than creates, where discourse is concerned. Although Judith has not been a nun, she says, 'Je suis entrée en littérature comme ... on doit entrer au couvent' (155).[5] In the eyes of her family and friends she represents the stereotype of the single woman, the old maid (68, 122). She has a certain authority in her own domain, but it is circumscribed and defined essentially as subsidiary and subordinate to creative writing. Her imagination was 'castrated' by the nuns in elementary school, leaving her with the 'practical intelligence' (120) of an ideal employee (98).

Her new freedom provides her with the opportunity to find out whether she herself could be a writer. She begins by imitating models such as Balzac (writing in her dressing gown), but these do not suit her; she is an imposter. Her attempts to create a persona for her self-as-writer are parallel to her experiments with various forms and genres of text. She has already written short 'rimettes,' which she calls 'poèteries' rather than poems, because of their humour and down-to-earth quality. Judith ends up with an array of different coloured notebooks: one for the rhymes, one for the journal, and another for notes that are less personal and might become a novel.[6]

Those that she makes in the diary are confidential and destined to remain so (9). In them she aims at 'complete sincerity' (14). She has never had such a 'personal possession' (23). As she attempts to 'dire à mesure' (55) the trivial events of her daily life, she is depressed to discover that writing cannot convey the complexity of even such a simple existence. Keeping a journal makes her melancholic, and she tends to agree with her former employer's severe judgment of the *journal intime* and those who indulge in it (15). Who else but her could possibly be interested in what she has to relate (53, 134)? She despairs of finding material in her own life that would be suitable for publication. The only solution is to invent, to write a novel, or at least a *nouvelle*, in which she would 'revivre avec plus de conscience' the major events of her life (45).

There have been two such events, both precipitated by her relationships with men. The first was her sexual exploitation as a girl by her uncle, and the subsequent abortion decreed by her mother. She now claims not to regret that she is childless – or at least, not often (32, 109). Judith, like Amyot's narrator, considers that children and writing are incompatible (109). The other drama in her life has also remained secret. She was the mistress of a distinguished academic who also happened to be a priest, *'le père* Charles' (42–3), who managed to fit a regular visit to her into his Sunday schedule. After twenty years, and with no warning, he left for Europe to marry a much younger woman, the secretary from Judith's office.

This is the episode that she attempts to rewrite as a fiction, in which the Editions du Midi become the Editions du Soir (Mailhot worked for the Editions du Jour from 1972 to 1974), and Judith appears as Pauline, who works in a bookstore (70). *Le Passé composé* is dedicated to Marie-Claire Blais, and the narrator of *Les Manuscrits de Pauline Archange* and *Vivre, vivre!* is echoed in this Pauline's desire to choose life over writing (74). Judith, 'in reality,' lost her chance at 'life' when Charles disappeared, and is also afraid that she cannot write. In fact, Charles was a sadistic chauvinist, who used her and dumped her like a 'pair of old socks' (70). His treatment left her feeling worthless, confirming her father's opinion: 'toi, tu vaux pas cher' (190).

In both the diary and the projected fiction Judith attempts to rewrite the past. It was 'à l'imparfait' (10) and she wants to turn it into the 'passé indéfini' (151). The 'passé composé' is a compromise: past, but including the present of narration, the participation of the speaker. The intermingling of diary and novel mimes the inevitable shift from *discours* to *récit* in a diary and the reverse effect in a diary novel. The tension is evoked concisely in the following juxtaposition (59): 'bien choisir mes mots' (control, choice), followed by 'merde, on sonne à la porte' (the irruption of the unexpected, language as expressive rather than referential or stylistic in function). Judith recounts her past, because she appears to have no future, other than old age and death (36) and possibly Alzheimer's disease, like her mother (12). Writing gives her the sense that she exists (125: Lacan's *ex-sister?*), that she is doing something (37) and therefore not dead – 'Ecris ou meurs' (38). Yet she is sceptical about 'salvation through the book' (54, 123) and asks 'save what?' (192). One of her authors commits suicide, unsaved, and possibly condemned, by writing. Judith's notebooks become a commentary on 'Why write?' (128), with answers ranging from *jouissance* (18) to addiction (92) and harsh judgment of the writer's 'nombrilisme' (153).

She tries in vain to convince herself that she has a 'vision unique' (42, 133) that should leave a 'trace' (193) that others might want to read/follow – especially 'les gens d'ici' (69). Concluding that writing does not necessarily make one a writer (173), Judith finally accepts being simply a memorialist, recording the lives of other authors rather than her own: 'ma petite histoire des grands écrivains prise sur le vif, au jour le jour' (194). Her *oeuvre* will be parasitic, contributing to the fame of others. She may have the potential to write 'dans le ventre' (130), but what she will deliver will be someone else's child. Like Chantal in *Je me veux*, she plays with the two meanings of 'je suis' (16, 58), but Judith accepts her role as following the trace – the literary lives and works – of others.

The diary, for writers, is often a subsidiary activity to other (public) forms of writing, supplying 'practice,' conserving potential material, or recording critical comment on other types of text. Many of the fictional narrators discussed so far occupy jobs that cast them in the role of literary supporters rather than performers: translators, critics, booksellers, teachers of literature, editors, librarians. All these fulfil the role of midwife rather than mother to the prestigious literary work. The diary may also be perceived as an unfinished work, a first draft of narration, lacking the distance presumed necessary to aesthetic effect. In the case of female narrators, the diary-writing activity is analogous to their marginal lives and their inability to impose meaning and form on their existence. For narrators who are childless, the diary may represent an abortive attempt to substitute a creative text for a child. For those who are mothers, writing is in competition with their parental role, and perceived as either a threat to or an escape from their femininity/motherhood.

One novel that loosely approximates to the diary model makes a conscious comparison between the *pays à produire* and the *texte à écrire*, for a Québécoise who experiences herself as 'impuissante' in spite of her maternity: Hélène Ouvrard's *Entre l'Herbe et le varech* provides a feminine perspective on a situation that entailed, for the male writer, 'la triple conquête du pays, de la femme et de la parole' (Arguin 1985, 197).

## Ouvrard, *L'Herbe et le varech (1980)*

*'Je cherche un homme et je cherche un pays.' (114)*

*'Ouvrard does not ... identify herself as a feminist but confuses the two autonomies, that of women and that of Quebec.' (Verthuy 1986)*

As the title indicates, Ouvrard's fourth novel is based on an opposition between two elements: the land ('l'herbe') and the sea ('le varech'), both of which may be identified with woman. The anonymous female narrator begins writing her journal on a seashore in Gaspésie, where she has escaped from her usual life in Montreal. She has left behind a man, whom she still loves but does not want to live with, and her fifteen-year-old daughter. Alone, she returns to her origin, 'le ventre de la mer' (34). She is trying to write a novel, but produces a heteroclite collection of memories, descriptions, dreams, and poems. Like the narrator, the text hesitates between two definitions: fiction and journal. The 'Notes de voyage' (followed by 'Notes de séjour' and 'Notes de retour') begin with a 'lettre pour toi,' to an unnamed male narratee, stating, 'me dissous dans la mer. Ne suis plus que $H_2O$' (9). Although the text is labelled *roman*, the initials are those of the author, *H*élène *O*uvrard.

This woman is torn between two images of herself, and of femininity. One is associated with the earth: stable, solid, and there to be discovered, possessed, fertilized, and exploited by (a) man. The other is represented by the sea: fluid, moving, uncontrollable, and seductive but dangerous. Her identification with the land is expressed in nationalist terms: '*Moi*, seule, parcourant un *moi* plus grand: le pays' (10). But the land is external to her, and is defined by what it is not: the water, which is not only beyond the land, but in flux, external and internal. The 'origin,' usually associated with feminine fluidity, requires also a masculine element, 'les pierres.' Speaking to her hypothetical male narratee, she says: 'j'ai trop réfléchi à la nature des pierres pour ne pas comprendre toute la symbolique qui s'y rattache – la tienne' (19). The two elements become merged, where they meet – in her, and on the beach: 'Il y a en moi une plage [page?] blanche où ne peuvent sourdre les larmes' (28); 'je suis sous toi la plage que tu submerges par vagues successives. C'est toi, la mer qui monte en moi' (31). The ocean represents not only the source of life, but the scene of suffering (the salt water of tears) and death. The narrator imagines a woman in a 'fur coat' of seaweed, disappearing into the waves and calling her to join her and other women, to choose them rather than the man (58).[7]

She blames the man for failing to respond adequately to her love (39), and exclaims, 'O Homme québécois, ton éternelle absence! Fuite. Silence. Départs.' She did not choose him: 'Les femmes sont toujours choisies avant d'avoir eu le temps de se choisir elles-mêmes. A plus forte raison ne choisissent-elles jamais l'homme' (46). When she addresses him, he is never there: 'je parle toujours à quelqu'un qui n'est pas là' (60). She has not escaped 'la condition féminine' (65), which is 'un amour qui nous subjugue. Une maternité qu'on porte seule' (65). In her marriage she realized that women's task is to 'mettre la vie sur la planète et de l'y entretenir au jour le jour aux prix d'elles-mêmes' (71). They are destined to remain 'habitantes du quotidien dévalorisé, qui sans elles serait inhabitable' (71); 'volées d'elles-mêmes ... [elles] appellent en vain au fond des miroirs leur être perdu' (71).

Allusions to mirrors and reflections abound throughout the text (40, 42, 53), as the narrator-as-woman recognizes that a man cannot be her double, that she is his 'sosie dissemblable' (89). The mirror becomes a speculum, turned inward on herself: 'plonger en soi ... retrouver le regard intérieur ... la force d'attraction qui me tire sans cesse en moi-même' (44). Closed in by the walls of domesticity, she escapes to an inner world, confirming her castration: 'Je vivais une castration de tous les instants. Je n'existais que par personne interposée' (70). What replaces the 'personne interposée' is a narcissistic self-extension – writing: 'l'expérience libératrice, désopprimante, désaliénante, jouissante et solitaire de l'écriture' (70).

Nevertheless, writing is a masculine activity: 'L'homme se reconnaît à lui seul le droit de vivre pour lui-même. Et de créer' (73). As a woman, she was limited to procreation, and 'l'être libre ne peut être la mère' (82). While she does not regret having a child (83), and wishes she had more (83), she suffers the same anguish as Amyot's Geneviève: 'Si j'ai un autre enfant, je ne ferai jamais l'oeuvre que je porte' (81).

Once more, giving birth and producing books are seen by a female narrator as competing commitments that tear her apart: but writing in the journal can serve to 'coudre avec des mots des parties de moi-même' (45). She abandons story, characters, and 'le temps du roman' in favour of 'celui du poème, de la réflexion' (27). Her (self) reflection brings her face-to-face with another choice: between writing (about) the child/book dichotomy, and the 'pays à faire naître ici' (150). She adds, 'Il est resté dans mon ventre.' Who is to blame, if the country is stillborn – or still-to-be-born? Is it the Québécoise? Is 'Québécois woman writer' a triple impossibility?

## (One) Woman/Women: Singular and plural

The texts discussed in this chapter provide a wide range of variation in both style and focus. The narrators are of different ages and social milieux; some are married, some are not. Yet most are concerned with motherhood or its absence in their lives, and all except Giguère's Amédée discuss their relationships with men. They all perceive their individual attempts to write their experience and find a voice as inseparable from their femininity. In this respect, these novels conform to the autobiographical 'feminist confession' discussed by Rita Felski in *Beyond Feminist Aesthetics* (1989), although these narrators do not label themselves feminist. Several of the observations that Felski makes (see especially 92–120) apply to this body of texts by women with female narrators, although none of them is overtly autobiographical.

Felski mentions the parallel between texts by women that depict a subjective experience as significant for a collectivity and those by members of other oppressed groups, such as blacks or gays. My review of diary fiction by women in Quebec reveals many similarities to those by male authors who also attribute their *impuissance* to a collective situation. Yet there is an important distinction. The impotent male can increasingly envisage a change in the situation, in which he may become *maître chez lui*, by political or revolutionary means. When he demands the right to *la parole*, the symbolic order agrees that he has been unjustly deprived, since as a man he is expected to aim for independence and autonomy, to participate in the 'will-to-power.' These women, on the other hand, have been socially and psychologically conditioned to accept a situation of dependence and of subordination, and any attempt to escape from it is in conflict with their self-definition as women, whose value has been assessed in terms of appearance, motherhood, and usefulness to others. They need to separate, both from the dominant men in their lives and from their previous role and self-representation, if they are to construct themselves as (problematic) 'subjects' speaking from a place of difference. This logic is in contradiction to their perception of intimacy and closeness (connection and caring) as positive values and mutual reliance (for example, faithfulness) as desirable.[8]

As Felski points out, publishing a confession addressed primarily to other women is a means to indulge in the narcissistic withdrawal necessary for introspection, and to emerge from it by an intimate communication with readers who will identify with the narrator and approve of her (the narrator's or the author's) decision to go public. This may be as far as the writer goes, in terms of action or feminine solidarity. Keeping a diary functions as a therapy, as a means of achieving self-awareness and self-expression. As such, it is a popular technique in self-improvement courses.[9]

The presentation of a particular case as representative of all women (or at least of a sub-category such as housewives, elderly spinsters, or women novelists) may contribute to the indeterminacy of the author/narrator distinction, as in Amyot's *Journal de l'année passée* or Ouvrard's *L'Herbe et le varech*, where there is deliberate confusion at the level of names within the text, or Lamarche's *Je me veux*, where the same effect is produced by a comment on the cover. Epigraphs or dedications may effect a similar conflation of life (the author) and fiction (the narrator), as has been seen. In addition, the fictional journal inevitably incorporates a commentary on the relation between lived experience and its written representation; the latter is always ultimately perceived as a construct remote from the original and therefore fictional.

When the text is realistic in its imitation of a diary, it partakes of the 'familiarization' of which Felski speaks (97). Opposed to the 'defamiliarization' of modern or post-modern texts that flaunt their literariness, such as those discussed in the next chapter, the effect of naturalness in the evocation of a supposedly spontaneous and sincere narrative is to co-opt the sympathy of the (female) reader, who recognizes elements of her own experience. This effect contributes to the production and definition of a common identity for that group, and to the sense of participating in a collective protest and affirmation of a desire for change. That the change in a diary is usually at the level of a personal transformation rather than a social or political manifestation of revolt is central to the personal-political link established in feminist fiction. 'Woman' is a construct of the social-symbolic order, but each woman confirms that construct/contract in her individual, subjective experience in relation to others – men/children/her own mother/other women. Political involvement in militant campaigns for change at the level of social institutions is generally perceived as incompatible with the subjective, narcissistic self-indulgence of daily intimate autobiographical writing. In a fiction, the latter may be depicted as a stage to be left behind, as in *Je me veux*, where the narrator affirms her need to find herself before she can become involved as a citizen or feminist. Similarly, Godbout's Galarneau may be seen as emerging from his personal crisis ready to become a separatist.

The two notions of finding an authentic self and being separate/autonomous are linked for both women and male Québécois. These female diarists withdraw from their relations with others in order to see what they might be or become without them. The withdrawal may be voluntary (Ouvrard, Chéné) or imposed from without (Mailhot). All those discussed in this section end up returning to others with a modified sense of self-as-centre. Their marginalization or subordination is attributed to their own complicity. Self-pity frequently becomes self-castigation (see Felski, 105), as the narrator, adopting an independent subject position, shares the dominant, derogatory view of those who (like her) are dependent or defeated. As in the case of Quebec, links with the other are seen as positive only if they can be engaged in with the full awareness and consent of both sides. This implies a belief that non-hierarchical self-other relationships may be possible, even in situations involving non-equivalent pairs, such as male-female or majority-minority groups.

In terms of psychoanalytic theory, and particularly Lacan's version of it, this supposition remains problematic. Within Lacan's frame of reference, the subject is constructed by a split predicated on the corresponding dimension of otherness ('l'Autre' and 'l'autre' as 'objet petit a'). For Felski, writing, with its implication of absence and deferral/trace epitomizes the alienation of the self (100, 108). Women writers seek to prove that a feminine subject position may be possible, without the female speaking as a man, that is, without imitating/becoming a victim of echolalia. This project is based on the presumption of a true or authentic self that may emerge if the false one is destroyed (see Flax 1990, 89ff, on Winnicott.) The traditional feminine role (or female plot) is refused, but the alternative may resemble the masculine role (or plot?), which is condemned by women, and which for Lacan is equally false, since the penis is not the phallus and masculinity is also founded on lack.

In a Lacanian context, where all selves are constructs and the true/false distinction becomes meaningless, women cannot speak: or if they do, they 'do not know what they are saying' (Lacan, *Encore, Séminaire* 1972; see Gallop 1982, 38–44). That is the difference, according to Lacan, between them and him. But does he know what he is saying? Men, even Lacan, are also 'spoken' by language, according to his own theory. The 'outside' position of awareness and authority belongs to God/the 'dead father.' Felski and Flax maintain that this theorization of human relations neglects the possibility (which does exist) of modifying the structures of which we are a part, through 'agency': human beings speak as well as being spoken.

None of the novels discussed in this section is self-consciously situated in the category of post-modern 'écriture au féminin,' as described by Louise Dupré and France Théoret (in Neuman and Kamboureli 1986). Yet they all participate in an attempt to write women's experience. None plays self-consciously with signifiers to the extent that the texts of Ducharme, Aquin, and Brossard do (see chapter 11), although Mailhot develops an elaborately self-reflexive text, as do Amyot and Monette in works discussed in earlier chapters. These fictional journals by women depict the importance of writing, but not the aesthetic solution of textual control. Rather, the narrators are depicted as only tenuously able to write, and writing escapes from their control. In what is probably a related phenomenon, discussed in chapter 11, most of these women still acknowledge the relevance and supremacy of male opinion, as well as appealing to other women for support.

'Separation' for women may involve a divorce and the need for financial independence. It cannot entail living completely cut off from men – even for a radical lesbian like Monique Wittig. For these women the possible separation of Quebec from Canada is marginal to their concerns. It would not affect their position as women. Rather, they are specifically Québécoises in their ambivalence to the refuge values that gave power to mothers and the Church – two elements that have contributed to their oppression as women who want to be free. Daughters, like sons, seek emancipation from the world of the (phallic) mother; yet recognizing the mother's castration is also accepting their own, and like men they retain a nostalgia for the security of wholeness/oneness. This problematic is further complicated by the potential, for the woman-as-writer, to play the phallic-mother role: to want (and possibly have) the best of both worlds in a particular form of androgyny. This situation continues, as long as men in Quebec are defined as impotent or absent, leaving a vacuum to be filled, rather than positions to be shared.

Before returning to a discussion of 'difference' as potentially plural rather than dichotomous, and the implications for the role of the phallic mother, I shall examine two of the best-known post-modern texts written in Quebec by men. I shall attempt to situate the concept of formal experiment as emancipatory in relation to Brossard's theorizing of women's relation to language. The question raised by Felski (108), as to whether formal experiment is a type of radical politics or a self-indulgent form of narcissism, will become central.

CHAPTER ELEVEN

# Language and (R)evolution: *Ducharme, Aquin, Brossard*

'La suprématie du signifiant se traduit ... en une domination du sujet par le signifiant qui le prédétermine là même où il croit se soustraire à toute détermination d'un langage qu'il pense maîtriser. Il s'agit d'une des propriétés les plus fondamentales qui scelle le rapport du sujet à son discours et que nous pouvons ranger au fondement même de la notion de parlêtre chez Lacan.'
JOËL DOR (1985), 58

'Access to language implies something of castration – a renouncing of a primal narcissistic image.'
SERGE LECLAIRE IN STAMBOLIAN AND MARKS (1979), 45

'Le récit est le support du narcissisme.'
ANDRÉ GREEN (1983), 71

## The subject of language

The discussion so far has established that both male narrators who become aware of their state of impotence as victims of colonization and female narrators who become conscious of their definition as man's Other share one project that is inseparable from any concept of liberation: a *prise de parole*, a breaking of the silence. The fact that in diary fiction the attempt to speak/write is depicted as occurring in a private journal, addressed, initially at least, to the self, is an indication of how tenuous this effort is. The diary tends to represent an in-between stage, a trying out of the possibility of communication. As such, it may be 'gone beyond,' and the subject may 'emerge' ready to participate in dialogue with others. The diary may also serve, however, to prolong the illusion of self-sufficiency, providing an autistic refuge where a semblance of communication with narcissistic projections of the alienated self replaces and precludes an exchange involving alterity.

Language may serve primarily to regulate self-esteem, and the narrative may function as a re-imposition of coherence on a fragmented self-representation. When the diary in question is fictional, that is, when it forms part (or the whole) of a novel, the depiction of the journal as private is necessarily a deception or *trompe-l'oeil*, entailing the reader's willing suspension of disbelief (see Raoul, 1980). Even if the narrator is shown as choosing continued isolation, this decision must be interpreted in the light of the author's publication of the novel, which implies a different conclusion.

This choice or tension between communication and self-esteem as alternative emphases in language use plays an important part in determining the language used in a diary. In a genuine *journal intime*, the narrator does not need to be intelligible to anyone else. Benjamin Constant, for instance, kept a diary in code, in an effort to remain incomprehensible to anyone else. At the other end of the spectrum, a diary written with great care at the level of language and form tends to appear suspect, as the narrator is assumed to be secretly hoping for a reader. Yet a self-conscious emphasis on style or form may serve primarily to reassure the writer, to confirm a sense of self-esteem. Such a project assumes that the use of language is controlled by the speaker/writer, a position opposed to that of Lacan. It may also be based on a desire to exteriorize the self (that is, the language of the self) to such an extent that rereading will reveal the workings of the unconscious, as in psychoanalysis.[1]

Some narrators of fictional journals do not appear to be in control of their writing: Pierre Châtillon's *Le Journal d'automne de Placide Mortel* (1970), for example, depicts the ravings of a madman and parts of it are more or less incomprehensible. Amyot and Garneau were both accused by some critics of being insufficiently intelligible for their diary fictions to be considered successful novels. The dilemma faced by the novelist in such a case is to find a means to convey the discourse of someone whose language is incoherent, in a way that will enable the reader to continue reading. Any attempt to *faire parler* characters defined by their silence or inability to communicate – for example, women – involves a similar quandary. A first-person narrative implies that the narrator has access to speech *from the start*, rather than acquiring it at the end of the narration.

These reflections on the ambivalent communication situation in the diary novel illustrate some of the problems of Lacan's theory of the relationship between the subject and language, and the objections to it voiced by some feminist theorists (for example, Flax and Felski). For Lacan, access to language/the symbolic order occurs as a result of the split (*Spaltung*) in the subject arising at the mirror stage, and the subsequent oedipal situation involving the intervention of the 'instance paternelle,' which breaks up the mother-child dyad. Speech is only possible beyond the stage of primary narcissism. Kristeva, in *La Révolution du langage poétique* (1974), posited a semiotic mode of language use, related to the pre-Oedipal imaginary and the feminine, which continues to co-exist with the symbolic and plays an essential role in the production of avant-garde literary texts. She revises the usual association of the feminine/the imaginary with conservative/regressive values, claiming for the semiotic the power to subvert and disrupt the structures of the symbolic.

For many women writers, a similar opposition has been founded on the non-coincidence of (oral) speech and (written) text. Derrida decries the metaphysics of presence and origin associated with speech, in favour of the absence/trace of writing. Speech tends to be associated with the feminine (frivolous, personal, transitory, *bavardage*/gossip), and written documents with the 'serious' institutions of man (history, science, law, theology). Fiction lies somewhere between a personalized act of communication depending on its context for its effectiveness (speech) and the impersonal distance of collective, transhistorical (inter)-textualization. In Quebec fiction, the relation between speech and writing has had particular importance.

## From speech to writing: Experience/experiment

In *Le Romancier fictif* (1980) André Belleau showed a *progression* in the evolution of the Quebec novel from the 'roman de la parole' to the 'roman de l'écriture,' from a depiction of the attempt to speak to a self-conscious formal experiment in textuality. The diary fictions discussed by him appear to corroborate this claim. There is a tension, however, between two traditional concepts of the Québécois in relation to language. One sees them as taciturn, silent peasants, whose reluctance to enunciate anything may be attributed to various motives: nothing to say, no means (words) to say it, no reason for saying it, or no one to listen. Yet they are also depicted as sociable, excellent raconteurs of stories, with a vigorous, colourful popular idiom, 'gens de causerie,' in the words of a Vigneault song quoted by Larose in *La Petite Noirceur* – that is, as loquacious, if not garrulous. The two concepts are compatible, if one distinguishes between two types of contexts. The Québécois were silent and unheard as far as outsiders were concerned, and particularly in written communication involving distance (separation/absence). The epistolary novel is conspicuous by its absence in the history of fiction in Quebec, in spite of real feminine models such as Marie de L'Incarnation and Elisabeth Bégon. Yet they excelled in speech-related performance in private, among themselves.

This disjunction was perceived as having its source in the lack of self-esteem involved in speaking 'québécois,' if the assessor was presumed to be French, and in speaking French if the judgment was from an anglophone ('speak white'). The designation 'canadien-français,' necessary once 'Canadien' no longer implied French, provided no positive identification that is not an *écart*, a marginalized and inferiorized exception in relation to something else. The shift to self-designation as Québécois was inseparable from a revaluation of 'what we are' in relation to language, particularly since this movement coincided in the 1960s with the eclipse of the two other distinguishing features of Quebec: the Church and agriculture.

The result was a wave of literary texts, mainly between 1965 and 1969, attempting to transcribe in writing the spoken idiom of working-class Montreal, *le joual*. This pejorative term, introduced by 'le Frère Untel,'[2] became a rallying cry for writers like Claude Jasmin and Renaud and others associated with *Parti pris*. It sparked off an intense debate on whether speaking a *langue bâtarde*, assumed to be inadequate to convey meaning successfully, could possibly have a positive role in self-definition. The exaggerated imitation of the popular speech of the east end of Montreal by Michel Tremblay in his plays was initially condemned as caricature or imposture (middle-class writers do not really speak this way). Quebec critics were amazed when the phenomenon of *joual* was recognized in Europe as 'universal' and in colonized countries as typical of the infiltration of a dominant alien culture.

The *bataille du joual* did not last long, but it left its mark. Subsequent writing in Quebec, without having recourse to the exaggeration that risks being parodic, no longer attempts to appear to be French French. Rather, the *américanité* of Quebec in relation to France becomes a central theme, as does its *québécitude* (by analogy with *négritude*) in relation to the surrrounding anglophone majority. Writing no longer ostentatiously draws attention to itself by initially enigmatic transliterations of particular pronunciations (à la Queneau), but incorporates rhythms of speech and lexical features, not only into dialogue, the mimesis of speech, but into the narration, as in Tremblay's novels or Francine Noël's. The language of Quebec is no longer only represented, but becomes the vehicle for representation.

There are obvious similarities to the position of women in relation to writing. Many studies now show that there are quantifiable differences in women's use of speech and language, compared to men's.[3] These are not biologically innate but produced by women's situation in relation to men. Yet women do not speak a 'different language' or a dialect that is geographically or historically determined. The differences transcend linguistic boundaries, where similar social structures prevail. Nor do women have any difficulty in using the standard language; indeed, this is referred to as the mother tongue/*langue maternelle* and girls acquire it more easily than boys. In North America women usually speak more correctly than men of the same social class. In spite of this, women have experienced a lack of correspondence between standard written forms and the way that they think/speak as women. Like the Québécois, women have gone beyond the attempt to prove that they can speak as well as the dominant group, since success in those terms is achieved at the expense of speaking as/like the other, rather than to him (or to each other) from a position of difference; it implies a degree of imposture. Contemporary attempts by women writers to produce an *écriture féminine* in France or to write *au féminin* – the expression preferred by Nicole Brossard and others in Quebec – are analogous to the Quebec writers' determination to produce texts *au québécois* and *aux Québécois*. Yet the reaction to experimental texts by feminists has been mixed in Quebec, as some critics, usually male, (for example, Larose 1987, 168ff), see them as derivative, as imitating previous attempts by male avant-garde or post-modern writers to subvert the structures of logical discourse by ludic and iconoclastic texts.

Such texts illustrate a poetics of the marginal as opposition and resistance. This assumption also gives rise to accusations of false pretensions/pretences, since writing produced with conscious reference to Derrida and Lacan may be seen as related to an academic hegemony imbued with a narcissistic sense of superiority, rather than tenuously emerging from the fringe. Others would reverse the proposition that 'feminine' writing is a sub-category of subversive literature, maintaining that genuinely non-conforming texts are 'feminine,' even if produced by men. Yet this claim is difficult to reconcile with other statements to the effect that any 'parler femme' must give new expression to the female body.

The texts by Ducharme and Aquin that I shall discuss in this section contribute to this debate in their self-conscious depiction of the construction of masculinity and femininity in relation to writing. They may be seen as part of a wider category of decolonizing/post-colonial literature. They may also be perceived as specifically Québécois, identifiable by the particular physical experience of those living in a distinct geographical, historical, linguistic, and cultural context. The latter is related to the body as the source of speech, since the Québécois idiom is very dependent on intonation for its effect. Hearing it is a non-visual physical experience that which must be conveyed visually, through writing. Male sexuality is incorporated into these texts as problematic, since the narrators' manhood is affected by their status as Québécois, and access to full (masculine) subjecthood is perceived as related to the control of language/the text, which becomes analogous to Woman.

The problematic interplay between control of and control by language in relation to subject-ivity is central in post-modern texts. Those of Réjean Ducharme and Hubert Aquin illustrate in different ways two distinctly Québécois forms of self-conscious, narcissistic literature, and the individual/collective narcissism associated with them. The more recent writings of Nicole Brossard epitomize the parallel phenomenon in women's writing. Similarities and differences emerge more clearly from a closer analysis of sample texts by these three authors, who have all experimented with the diary form.

### Ducharme, *Le Nez qui voque* (1967)

*'Je ne suis pas un homme de lettres. Je suis un homme.'* (8)

*'Je ne suis pas moi: voilà en deux mots incompréhensibles ce que je veux dire.'* (196)

Who is the narrator of Ducharme's first novel (though not the first to be published), *Le Nez qui voque*?[4] At least one critic reads it as (almost) the diary of Ducharme himself (Dupriez, 1972). Yet the text is encoded from the beginning to convey one fundamental message about the writer: that he is a fiction, whose identity lies in the 'lettres' (words/text) attributed to him. He is not a (real) man: the whole drama of the *récit* depends on the reluctance of this adolescent to become an adult. And even if he is forced to see himself as a man by the end, he is still not an 'homme de l'être,' but an 'homme de lettres,' a product of language. This does not make him an intellectual ('homme de lettres') in spite of his prodigious and unexplained familiarity with the texts of the past. He not only does not want to be a man, he does not want to be identified with the symbolic order, as represented by institutionalized culture. His culture is that of 1960s counter-culture.

The narrator calls himself Mille Milles,[5] mentioning that this should be '*Dix* Mille Milles' (14); he is '*dit*' (known as) Mille Milles, but it is the '*dit*' that is declared redundant, rather than the echo of 'Mille(s).' Later he recounts a joke, a pun based on the discrepancy between speech and writing and between language as referential or as a system of signifiers (273). The punchline is the transformation of 'J'ai un nez' into 'j'ai dix nez/j'ai dîné' (which could also be 'j'ai dit nez/né'). The equivocal title, *Le Nez qui voque*, also provides clues as to Mille Milles's status as signifier/speaker. He is 'le nez' (qui voque), a metonymy/body part with phallic connotations (as pointed out by Desmond Morris in *Man Watching* and Gogol in 'The Nose'). Mille Milles claims not to possess what men have (257), but he has a big nose. Questa maintains that this means he must like women (148). The phallic nose is interchangeable with the phallic pen: she adds, 'Vas-tu sortir ta plume et m'écrire un poème?' Mille Milles admits, 'Je me suis engagé dans l'obscur et le honteux avec cette plume' (141). Once more, writing in a private diary is equated with masturbation ('se hortensesturber', see Marcotte 1989, 79), and the text is 'le beau nez' (7), analogous to an 'erection' (7), composed of a form of writing that is 'surrectionnelle' (133), and 's'étend, s'étire, s'allonge' (146).

'Le beau nez/le beau n'est (7)/le beau naît.' Mille Milles claims that 'on naît enfant ou on naît adulte' (154), quoting an oral remark that would be heard as 'on est enfant ou on est adulte.' Mille Milles has difficulty being born as an adult/man. At one point he claims to be 'rené' (193), but the whole text is a commentary on the questionable viability of what is left when the old self is dead: 'moi l'enfant' is a dead body at the beginning (9), as is Chateauguay at the end. 'Je ne suis pas pareil à ce que j'étais,' therefore 'Je ne suis pas moi' (196). The man he is becoming is a stranger to his former self, who still participates in the *dédoublement* facilitated by writing. Either self (past or present) is referred to by the other in the third person, when the 'other self' speaks.

Mille Milles has another name: Etin Celant (148). 'Les mots sont des mirages' (230), but mirrors are equally false. The 'tain' enables one to see an image, but this is not 'vous-même:' 'Vous voyez un miroir qui réfléchit votre image et l'image de ce qui vous entoure' (230). Mille Milles' dazzling (*étincelant*) mirror of words is not reliable. The 'tain' is worn (10) and the mirror may become transparent, no longer 'celant' (hiding) what lies behind it. This diarist relives the mirror stage, vacillating between rejection and recognition of the image he sees – 'Je suis indésirable' (247); 'je m'aime' (261).

Mille Milles's attempts at self-sufficiency – reclusion in his room, masturbation, and the diary – are accompanied by a dream of androgyny reminiscent of the works discussed in chapter 8. He is '*un* équivoque,' and the change of gender is echoed in that of 'hostie' (he describes himself as '*une* hostie de comique' at the end; see Leduc-Park 1982, 147ff). He also refers to himself as 'un lesbien' (214) and 'une écrevisse,' which he suggests as the feminine of 'écrivain' (146). Tate (69–70, 188) is the name given to the combined agglomerate of himself and his 'sister' Chateauguay. His nostalgia for childhood is associated with a desire to return to pre-Oedipal non-separation with the feminine, and a refusal to rejoin the feminine by 'having' a woman-as-object outside the self-mother dyad.

Chateauguay is described as an Eskimo, and Mille Milles also claims at one point to be one, although he then denies it (144). Eskimos are those who have no identity papers, who are seen as even more marginalized and threatened with extinction than the Québécois. They also belong to an imaginary world of snow-clad purity and splendid isolation, like the innocence of childhood that Mille Milles wants to make Chateauguay represent. But she has other functions that constitute her also as 'une équivoque.' 'Chat' can designate the female sex, the 'sexe faible' (21) to which she belongs, a 'porte déguisée' (264), the door that Chateauguay does not open – 'Ouvrez! Donnez-asile! Accueillez-moi dans vos mystères!' (256). She is also the 'eau' that accompanies him (as Narcissus), providing a (false) mirror image, and the 'gué' (ford) that would enable him to cross the water safely. Yet he refuses to perform the function of saviour and refuge for her, when she exclaims, 'Tu es mon château et j'entre ...' (214). The indifferentiation of Tate has to give way to the individuation of sexual identity and desire based on separation and lack.

Is Chateauguay 'real'? Even within the fiction, there are indications that she may be a figment/projection of Mille Milles's imagination.[6] She is, like words, a 'mirage' (135), a state or action rather than a person. Yet she is also constructed by the text as an element that escapes the narrator, even if he is her creator. He wonders if he can 'réussir' Chateauguay, that is, successfully make her what he wants her to be (83). But he is not sure what he wants her to be, since she represents the feminine, and his two male fantasies of it are in conflict. One is the pure, non-sexual, innocent double associated with childhood – the other half of the androgyne, part of the self and therefore not desired as other: Narcissus' twin sister, in one version of the myth (Green 1983, 77). As such she is identified with the utterly reliable phallic mother: whole and sexless, undivided/uncastrated. Even Questa ends up assigning her this role, when she entrusts her children to her (253). Yet Chateauguay is also, for Mille Milles, potentially 'impure' (140), an object of desire who torments him, an 'allumette/allumeuse' (see Leduc-Park, 265) and as such she fills him with the 'horror' (cf. Kristeva 1980) inspired by the 'castrated' mother.

Just as Mille Milles is depicted as having to become a man, Chateauguay (if she does not die) will have to become a woman (162). Mille Milles echoes Beauvoir's 'on ne naît pas femme, on le devient,' as he warns her that she cannot remain unmasked in the 'bal masqué' of feminine masquerade (206). Her suicide may demonstrate the triumph of the *chevaleresque* ideal of woman as chaste/pure/unattainable, and prove her moral superiority over Mille Milles, who has capitulated to reality/sexuality and agreed to become a man. But she triumphs only by killing herself, and it seems to be because Mille Milles will not regard her as a real woman, rather than because she does not want to be one. If she is his creation, he 'kills' her for her resemblance to him, in his 'impurity': 'Je veux la femme, l'impureté. Je veux l'impureté aussi sauvagement que je la repousse ... Je te veux, femme, pour te tuer' (140); 'quant à la femme ... je la martyriserais' (135).

The discourse of Mille Milles on femininity is an extension of the misogyny conveyed by earlier writers like Hertel and Baillargeon, although he has moments of sympathy for the plight of women. He cannot stand the feminine in himself – 'j'exècre son influence sur mes idées' (135) – and wants to eradicate it in order to become a 'man' with *his* house, *his* children and so on (233), able to be the 'maître chez lui' (219). Chateauguay's death happens at the point where he appears to have changed his mind and to want to return to her – but it is too late. He wishes to redeclare his loyalty to Nelligan (260, cf. 190) and all he represents in terms of the ideal, narcissism, and madness (the choice of the imaginary over the symbolic, identification with the mother rather than the father: on Nelligan, see Larose 1987, 63). He has lost touch with Questa, who represented Eve (147); she has gone from being the bad mother, 'Pas Bonne' (146), to being also a 'sister' (261). Mille Milles wants to return to the 'Virgin Mother' evoked by a statue at the beginning (11), and represented by Chateauguay (Questa says Chateauguay is also *her* mother), but she is dead.

Questa: 'questa cosa,' 'cette chose' in Italian (146): 'ça.' In the preface, the question is posed as to the difference between 'cela' and 'ça' (8). Questa, the bad mother, is abject in her drunkenness, although she provides food and money. The Freudian reference to the *id*, the unconscious, is underlined by Mille Milles's assertion that Freud would have been interested in his mother fixation (129): 'Je sens l'appel de la vocation psychanalytique et je frémis' (164). 'Vocation' harks back to the 'voque' of the title, the new verb 'voquer,' which evokes 'voguer' (movement) but also 'invoquer,' the vocative of naming/calling (see Dupriez, 185): 'qui voque'? and calling whom? The split that Mille Milles must accomplish involves a change of interlocutor, from the feminine/maternal to the masculine 'instance paternelle,' and this occurs through the diary.

This journal is private, to the extent that the narrator does not allow anyone to read it, and certainly does not want Chateauguay to write in it (136). The black notebook is his alone (133). He writes for himself, but also for 'les hommes' (as if to his 'fiancée'?), whom he wants to reach and join (10). He wants to provoke a response, an echo in others (254), even for posterity. But he cannot communicate with Chateauguay (who appears to be his fiancée, when they steal the wedding dress), although they have their own code (for example, 'se branle-basser' for 'se suicider'). He tells her, 'Tais-toi, si tu n'as rien à dire' (106). When she speaks, he does not listen, he only 'sees the words' (85), as if they did not emanate from her in a particular context. She is the one who first paints her lips with ink, as if to transfer the power of writing to words straight from the mouth. As Marcotte says, she speaks a different language (1989, 78). Mille Milles is confined in the written world of men of letters and can no longer function in the real world of women. But women are presented as incapable of autonomy, or of naming others: Questa calls all three of her daughters Anne; they remain *anonymous*. In Mille Milles's imaginary world there is no room for Chateauguay to experience or express her own desire. In order to wear the wedding dress she must become like the model, lifeless.

If Chateauguay is imaginary she is murdered, excluded by Mille Milles so that he can become a man. If she is real, she commits suicide, either because she does not want to become a woman, or because she cannot since Mille Milles will not behave like a man – although he thinks he has become one. She cannot become a man, even if she should want to. She can live only as excluded, and this is unbearable. She does not, apparently, have Mille Milles's option of becoming a writer. Questa's journal was a failure (165). Only in the mirror-play of writing can the subject be both 'amoureux' and 'amoureuse' (261), both 'action' and 'reaction' (198) Only in writing can the self claim 'je ne suis pas moi' (196) and not only not be mad (10), but make sense.

## Quebec: Context and intertext: 'Que je me méprise! Que je suis noir! ... victime de la noirceur' (37)

Marilyn Randall, in her study of *Le Nez qui voque* (1990), emphasizes the integration into the text of the sociopolitical context and the discourse of colonization as an important strand in the intertextuality that is so prominent in this novel. The extent of the reader's knowledge of the events and characters alluded to controls the degree of coherence attributed to the text and/or the narrator (Randall, 93). Marcotte asks, referring to a later diary novel by Ducharme, *L'Hiver de force* (1973), which he calls a 'remake' of this one: 'Pourra-t-on [le] lire dans vingt-cinq ans, sans un arsenal de notes explicatives?' (120). Anyone who did not know, for example, that Duplessis died in 1959, rather than 1954, would not immediately categorize Mille Milles as an unreliable narrator as a result of his erroneous or deliberately misleading comment (9). A Québécois reader, who *would* know, would assume that the discrepancy is deliberate rather than a mistake – unless the mistake is in the typesetting, as one critic suggests it might be. This aspect of *Le Nez qui voque* brings into question the aspects of diary writing associated with veracity, accuracy, and sincerity. A narrator who continually contradicts himself and claims that he does not mean what he says (see, for example, 124) is not simply equivocal: he is both infuriating and performing a commentary on the interpretation of his text. The inability to conclude imposed on the reader is analogous to the narrator's inability to decide if he is on the side of the men (cars and Americans: 'Go homme!'; cf. 56) or of the women (Chateauguay and bicycles).

Under Questa's influence, both Mille Milles and Chateauguay find jobs in a restaurant. Like Tremblay's waitresses and Godbout's Galarneau they are forced to adopt a servile role and to speak English. The Italian owner says only one word to them in French: 'Pédale' (241). This not only evokes the narrator's betrayal of the bicycle, but emphasizes his sexual ambivalence, since *pédale* is slang for 'homosexual.' Mille Milles comments near the beginning of his journal that Americans assume that all French Canadians are gay (16). Pavlovic and Leduc-Park have examined the various references in the text to Mille Milles's bisexuality. Asked what sex he is (it is not obvious), he replies that it does not matter (15). He also frequently says 'la plume m'a fourché,' a variation on the expression 'la langue m'a fourché,' a graphic image of bilingualism: *bilingue* is also slang in Quebec for 'bisexual.' He speaks two languages, constantly: they are not French and English, but one that functions as referential and another that 'sees' the signifiers. Yet he admits: 'Je ne parle, couramment, aucune langue' (123). He refuses to identify with either French or 'American.' Mille Milles would not like to be French, because 'il faut trop parler pour rien, il faut s'estimer trop meilleur que les autres' (123). This is not a judgment of any particular French people, but of the French language. 'Je ne fais que répéter ce que j'ai entendu dire' (124). His own idiom is the one he learned by hearing it. French French is familiar only through reading/writing. France is defined by its absence.

English, however, is omnipresent, in advertising and at the movies: 'Qui, au Canada, n'est pas de la race des hot-dogs ... du rock'n'roll ... de la Metro-Goldwyn-Mayer ... de Popeye ... du Coca-Cola ... ?' (122). In his subservience he is like Chateauguay when she tries to please him: he appears to be seeking a master, as he assumes women do. But in Canada – he does not use 'Québec' and says 'le Canada, c'est mon pays' (221) – there is apparently no master. He is an exile in his own country, since the Italian boss has more authority than he does. The image of exile is also evoked by the reference to Léandre Ducharme on page 7, his little-known 'ancestor,' who was the author of a 'Journal d'un exilé politique aux terres australes' (1845). Part of the difficulty Mille Milles experiences in being born – an echo of the texts discussed in chapter 8 – is attributed to the fact that 'on essaie toujours de naître dans son propre pays' (221), and he is not sure that he has one. The solution is the 'pays de papier' built by the 'Partipristes': 'Si tu veux un moi bien fidèle à une définition, forge-t-en un ... crois (surtout aux mots)' (197). The problem for Mille Milles is that he loses his faith in words, as he loses his faith in the imaginary/Chateauguay (197).

In *Le Nez qui voque* the opposition between child and adult serves as a metaphor for the state of the colonized population of Quebec, which is unable to attain independence and autonomy. Feminine refuge values, as represented by Chateauguay, must be renounced in order for him to become a mature man, to be 'auto-mobile.' The self-as-subject is constituted through the elimination/murder of the other (as) self, which must be abandoned. Self-definition as other can only be transcended by a metamorphosis into the one, either by 'assimilation to' or 'identification with,' that is, by becoming the same. The male subject can become potent, whereas the female can only recognize her castration and decide whether it is possible to continue to live as the other, *alone*. A similar scenario is played out in Aquin's *Trou de mémoire*, but the child-adult dichotomy is replaced by the black-and-white one, and the corresponding feminine-masculine opposition is problematized even further. As in Ducharme's text, language is the vehicle and self-conscious fiction the proof of a painful integration into the symbolic order, accompanied by an attempt to undermine it.

### Aquin, *Trou de mémoire* (1968)

Like Angéline de Montbrun, *Trou de mémoire* has provoked an exceptionally large number of lucid analyses, which attest to the power of the text to resist resolution. In spite of the numerous discussions of anamorphosis as the key to the enigma – including studies by Smart, Maccabée Iqbal, Martel, Söderlind, Paterson, Heidenreich, Randall – elements of this novel continue to disturb. Some are particularly distressing for the feminist reader, since the liberation (and/or suicide) of Magnant, the male narrator usually perceived as primarily responsible for the text(s), is associated with the murder and rape of a woman (see Saint-Martin 1984). The signification of these two events remains enigmatic, especially as Magnant's violence is explicitly related to his own feminization as a colonized man, and the subjection of the woman remains in doubt at the end. The *dédoublement* of the narrator by a black African revolutionary who also keeps a diary contributes to the muddying of what is nevertheless frequently read as a limpid allegory – as does the definition of both female doubles in the text as *English*-Canadian.

### Race and sex – not simply black and white

*'Je viens d'expérimenter moi-même, rat blanc dûment mandaté par une sous-race de colonisés ... la glu noirâtre qui me monte à la gorge ... Je m'endors ... Je l'ai tuée ... dans une nuit blanche interminable ...' (32)*

Throughout *Trou de mémoire* numerous allusions to black and white echo the colonized/colonizer dichotomy, while also forming a network of references to writing. Pierre-Xavier Magnant is not sure whether he is a 'sale blanc' (9) or a 'sale nègre' (163): in either case, he is *sale*, marked by the guilt of self-assertion at the expense of the (feminine) other. This is central to his 'roman autobiographique' that becomes a diary, as well as to his 'cahier noir,' a diary that becomes a fiction; it dominates both his telling of events and his commentary on them (and on the telling) as 'editor.' It is called into question at the end by the second intervention of R.R., Rachel Ruskin, the surviving victim of the rape and sister of the murdered woman, Joan. Yet this conclusion is also dubious, and perpetuates the ambivalence towards racial and sexual difference that prevails from the beginning, whatever name the writer claims to bear. Naming and racial/sexual identity are two poles of a dialectic that can only be modified through language, but that language serves to perpetuate.

As mentioned in chapter 3, Aquin had contact with Albert Memmi,

Language and (R)evolution 235

author of *Portrait du colonisé*, and Patricia Smart reminds us that he was also personally acquainted with another theorist of colonization, Berque. *Trou de mémoire* is a product of the period of *nègres blancs d'Amérique*, when Quebec revolutionaries and *indépendantistes* identified with the struggle of black Africans to liberate themselves from European domination. Yet the Québécois are the descendants of French colonizers and share the (relative) economic prosperity as well as the culture of Europe/North America. The letter from an African revolutionary, Olympe Ghezzum-Quénum, with which the novel begins, brings out the ambivalence of Magnant's status as both white and colonized.

Olympe adopts an obsequious tone to address Magnant (as a white) and assumes that he shares pejorative judgments of African behaviour and beliefs, as he does himself, being Europeanized (see Heidenreich 1990). At the same time, he claims that they have much in common, as revolutionaries and as pharmacists. However, when Olympe is in Europe with R.R., a white, English-Canadian woman, his treatment by the police underlines the difference of skin colour, rather than the resemblance between Canadians and Africans as colonized. The white English Canadian, however, experiences herself as non-European, as much the product of European colonization as a French Canadian, and the black African has the advantage of speaking the language – French, in Lausanne and Paris – better than she does; indeed he claims it as his own (188). Olympe is paradoxically more at home in European culture than he is in Africa, and than the white woman from Canada is. Yet his inner identification with Europe is not recognized by the symbolic order (the police), because his body marks him as different. R.R. is not suspect, because she is white, though she is equally at a loss as to her place of belonging (the hotel) and her identity (we never learn her 'real' name). She is supposed to have been working as a nurse in Lagos – that is, voluntarily 'serving' to improve the health of Africans – and is living with a black man, elements that contribute to a representation of the English Canadian (woman) as attempting to identify with the colonized rather than with the colonizer. Similarly, her sister Joan, who works with monkeys, a parodic, speechless African 'race,' has a relationship with a revolutionary Québécois and wishes to become a French Canadian (91), although her father is mentioned as a typical anglophone financier. R.R. is decoded as 'erre, erre,' as non-fixed and erroneous, a female anglophone *Canadienne errante*. The surname given her and her sister, Ruskin, includes the word *skin*, and they both want to 'changer de peau' by becoming either African or francophone. Magnant himself claims to be partly a 'Redskin,' with Cree blood – 'le sang cri/crie' (87).

The representation of an African or French-Canadian man who dominates or is loved by a woman belonging to the dominant culture appears to be a wish-fulfilment fantasy of revenge on the white male conqueror, who is usually presumed to gain access to the women of the conquered race. The image of the conquered male as feminized and raped by the conqueror is explicit in *Trou de mémoire*. Quebec 'se fait enculer' by 'le fédéralisme copulateur' (39) and is 'archi-fourré' (70). Although Olympe and Magnant perceive themselves as terrorists, they both absorb drugs that produce only imaginary and linguistic revolutions, and a physical incapacity that precludes effective political or sexual action. Magnant admits that 'avaler n'a rien de révolutionnaire ...' but claims that 'geste féminoïde entre tous, avaler ne me féminise pourtant pas; au contraire, dirais-je, l'homme prouve sa supériorité par la pharmacopée' (23). He goes on to admit, however, that if he were not a pharmacist, he would be sexually active; as it is, we learn that he is actually frequently unable to perform (109). It is his impotence, the mark of the colonized male, that leads him to seek other proofs of male supremacy over women – his 'supériorité naturelle' (41) – that is, rape or murder: 'mon comportement sexuel est à l'image d'un comportement national frappé d'impuissance: plus ça va, plus je sens bien que je veux violer' (112).

The sexual exploits attributed to Magnant are primarily exhibitionistic and involve public masturbation of Joan, in front of the monkeys, in London, at the Neptune restaurant. His own pleasure in this 'caresse tyrannique ... unilatérale' (61, 63) is in his control and humiliation of Joan. The euphoric state of prolonged *jouissance* that he experiences as a result of narcotics (and of writing as a drug) does not culminate in orgasm. On the contrary, his whole body becomes a phallus (as for the narcissistic woman), and his state is continually that of 'attente,' of expectation and excitement – a tension compared to 'l'image du Québec secoué par ses propres efforts pour obtenir un spasme révolutionnaire qui ne vient jamais' (120).

Olympe also feels 'violé' (170) and 'impuissant' (161). He is able to make love to R.R. only when she believes he is someone else (Magnant, that is, white) or when she is unconscious (174)[7]. She is transformed, no longer herself, since she was raped by Magnant. Even if this act never occurred (she cannot remember), she believes it did. Olympe, who has none of Magnant's fantasies of violence and aggression, also perceives his penetration of her unconscious body as a rape. Yet he shares the male assumption that a woman must enjoy being raped (171), and the attitude that a woman who has been raped is defiled, 'gâchée' (174)[8]. Magnant, in this instance, plays the part of the white intruder who 'spoils' the black man's woman. R.R. is supposed to have reached the heights of erotic pleasure during the rape, and therefore to be reliving it constantly at the unconscious level, veiled by her amnesia and aphasia concerning the event. Her temporary disappearance causes Olympe's own 'trou de mémoire,' when he forgets what hotel he is staying at. His loss of identity can be blamed on Magnant, more logically than it can be compared with the Québécois absence of identity.

R.R., in a drugged state induced by Olympe, desires to die like Joan at the hands of her 'conqueror' (recalling Duras's 'tu me tues, tu me fais du bien,' quoted in Monette's *Le Double Suspect*); the victim of rape appears as a willing masochist, legitimizing the rapist's sadism. What is disturbing here is that any parallel with passive acceptance on the part of the colonized (of Quebec) as complicitous with colonial rape is rendered problematic by the identification of the rapist with Quebec's liberation. The transformation of Joan's role from that of anglophone enemy to be punished to that of the 'body' of the dead country is similarly contradictory. A concentration on the narrative pragmatics of the text or on its characteristics as post-modern does not account for the ethical dilemma of the reader forced to accept murder and rape as appropriate, even necessary, metaphors for the metamorphosis from 'acted upon' to 'actor' (see Saint-Martin 1984).

A misogynist ethic is also elaborated in the 'apocryphal' passage in which R.R. claims to have been Joan's lesbian lover. She is depicted as unable to be a 'real woman,' 'comme les autres' (124-5), the 'femme frigide' of the book Magnant decides to buy – rather than a book about impotence or masturbation, his own 'problems' (116). Rape is necessary for her to accept her femininity, to discover her *jouissance* and become fertile, if she is indeed pregnant, as she claims at the end. Her attempt to write, to control the text, appears to fail: yet she is the survivor, the container that will permit the reincarnation or resurrection of Magnant, whose narcissistic fantasies of immortality may be fulfilled. Once more, woman finds her place as the mother. Joan's dead body is also described as 'lactating' (28). Robert Richard has discussed the phallic function as central to the narration in Aquin's novels, based on 'la généalogie comme axe de la transmission des noms et donc des fictions' (1987, 12). He relates the function of the phallus as lack to the 'fantôme phallique' that Lacan discerns in the same anamorphotic painting by Holbein mentioned in this novel (1972/1978, 11: 82). The emergence of a child called Magnant at the end is essential, in this perspective, to establish his proof of paternity. His paternity has previously been *lost*, as indicated by an obscure reference to a daughter buried in Toronto (85). Magnant's own father was condemned to be an 'esclave' (96), belonging to the 'Côte des Esclaves' that is in Montreal, and was the generator of Magnant's own *noirceur* that justifies his identification with Olympe.

Magnant's potential paternity remains questionable. R.R. appears to attribute her pregnancy to the rape, and assuming Magnant to be the father, expresses her intention to hide this dubious conception from the child (196). This is only possible if the dates in Olympe's journal should refer to 1967 (201), rather than 1966 (147); the change would also allow a rational chronology for Magnant's whereabouts. Is this another *trou de mémoire*? And whose – Olympe's or Aquin's? The numerous mistakes throughout the text (spelling, and so on) and Aquin's admission that he lost his plan for the book[9] suggest that this possibility should not be ruled out. But even if the chronology made sense, there remains Olympe's contention that she could not be pregnant as a consequence of the rape, because of her 'time of the month.' He, however, made love with her when she was presumably fertile, and there is no mention of the contraceptive jelly and other devices that are inscribed elsewhere in the text. It is possible – and may be more probable – that if she is pregnant, it is by Olympe: that is, ironically, Magnant would emerge from *la noirceur* of colonized Quebec as a black child (a girl?), bearing the name under which Olympe dies. Olympe himself is not welcome in Quebec: although Mullahy-Magnant resists the temptation to kill him (199), their meeting results in his suicide. Olympe may be only an imaginary dark 'shadow' of Magnant, his father's double, whose death enables Magnant to continue to live, 'underground' or invisible like the 'zombies,' which are frequently mentioned. In that case, Olympe is easily disposed of, like Chateauguay, when his usefulness is over. His disappearance is necessary for Magnant's survival.

Some critics have seen Magnant – or the nameless 'author': whoever can really say 'personne n'écrit sauf moi' (57), that is, Aquin? – as undergoing a change of sex, becoming R.R. In that case, Magnant survives as another projection: the female alter ego who refuses to commit suicide, unlike the partners of his models, Kleist and Zweig, or Chateauguay. This may represent an unusual recognition of the power of women in Quebec as responsible for *la survivance*: indeed, if R.R. is also responsible for the text (as Aquin claims she may well be[10]), she becomes a phallic mother, capable of both reproduction and production, procreation and creation. The fact that she is of English-Canadian origin but wants to become a 'Québécoise pure laine' and speak only French remains ambivalent: is this a sign of identification of the woman with the colonized/black man, against white phallogocentrism, or identification with Magnant because he is no longer colonized/black? Has Magnant won or lost the 'guerre de succession' (59–60)? And is it against the English or against women? The ending could be interpreted as conciliatory rather than revolutionary. As Aquin admitted, the subversion/terrorism of Magnant (or Aquin) is textual and sexual, rather than directly political.

## Logic and/or 'semiotic': Colonized/feminine discourse

'*Ecrire en spirale comme un colonisé.*' (120)

'*Joan ... a réussi à me voler les antiques privilèges de mon peuple sur l'incohérence et la déraison raisonnante.*' (87)

In the opening letter Olympe mentions that Africans tend to 'substituer à la raison un système séméiologique de remplacement' (8). This opposition corresponds surprisingly with Kristeva's concept of the semiotic as a means of communication that precedes the symbolic and continues alongside it in literary works of the avant-garde. The blackness of Africans is associated in the novel with woman as the unknown, Freud's 'dark continent': 'J'ai tué ... Joan et tous les continents noirs qu'elle contenait ...' (86). *Noirceur* is also associated by Magnant with menstruation (191) and the feminine world of childhood (108), and by

Olympe with a return to the womb of Africa (200). Both Magnant and Olympe are depicted as expressing their *noirceur* through writing ('l'épaisse nuit d'encre' [139]) in a drug-induced state of exultation or despair that defies the 'logic' of colonized/regulated society (10) and language (58). Writing becomes a 'logorrhée' (14), a 'verbalence fonale' (15), a 'verbigération' (22), a means to 'forniquer ... avec ma langue maternelle' (95). Opposed to a 'langue châtiée' and dead (94, 95), 'l'action matricielle de la parole' (57) enables the narcissistic *intimiste* – Magnant or Olympe – to be reborn: 'le roman *d'ailleurs* c'est moi' (19, my emphasis; cf. the editor's 'ce roman est plus moi que moi-même' [63]).

Once more the tension between control of language and control by language is central. Words have 'des vertus pigmentaires pour âmes blafardes' and can lead the writer in unexpected directions (108). Joan is 'liberated' by her *jouissance* into a delirium, recognized by Magnant as like his own (87), culminating in the desire for death/nirvana. Magnant sees his 'graphisme' (50) as a 'propédeutique de l'existence,' an 'acte privatif,' but also an 'apprentissage ... de la révolution' (55). He begins by writing in order not to speak – for fear of 'confessing' his crime to someone else (24), but the 'roman autobiographique' and the 'cahier noir' replace his revolutionary speech to the crowd. His desire to 'violer la foule' is converted into the seduction and rape of the reader-voyeur, who risks being 'drugged,' like the monkey that dies. The novel becomes the substitute for another murder (21): the reader is forced into the role of the (female) victim – Joan, R.R. – while adopting the point of view of the male perpetrator. Like the editor and Olympe, the reader attempts to 'voir clair' (138), to understand, in vain. Vacillating like the narrator(s) between the roles of author, actor, and reader (murderer, victim and detective, as in Butor's *L'Emploi du temps*), the reader lives the split between self and other and between the real (unknowable truth) and the fiction proposed and produced by writing.

Writing is powerful, as powerful as revolution; but it is construed in this novel as a perverse power to legitimize rape and murder as acceptable signifiers for narcissistic/dionysiac *jouissance* (see Maccabée Iqbal 1978, 97ff) – the means to emerge from the shadows of 'la noirceur' as 'le soleil' (24), as in *Salut Galarneau!* Magnant passes from abjection to megalomania and apparent self-extinction in an evolution that reads like a case-study in narcissism. Even if R.R. is the lone survivor and compiler of the polytext that constitutes *Trou de mémoire*, it is because she also has ruthlessly eliminated all the 'others' except the text/child (phallus/narcissistic self-object).

Aquin himself claimed in an interview with Anne Gagnon[11] that the end represents 'une harmonie finale et très positive' (12). Yet he was unable to reply to Gagnon's objections that no relationship appears possible for a couple, since the survival of one seems to depend on the subjection/elimination of the other. He also readily agreed with her suggestion that his treatment of the reader is sadistic: 'Je me venge du lecteur, je l'admets. Le lecteur pose sans doute le problème de l'altérité dans toute son amplitude' (8). He adds, 'L'autre, c'est d'abord un être dépourvu d'individuation, de différentiation sexuelle ou autre. C'est indifférencié' (8). This last remark applies, however, not to the other-as-reader-to-be-raped (*autre* with a small *a*, feminine or feminized) but to '*l'Autre*', Lacan's Other constituted by language. As he states in the same interview, 'la dialectique est à l'intérieur de la reflexivité, de l'écrivain avec son écriture ou son langage. C'est un rapport entre lui et son propre langage, qu'il manipule parce qu'il l'a hérité culturellement' (5). Language constitutes the presence of alterity within the subject (see Harel 1989), and it can be wielded in fiction as a weapon for survival, a means to overcome the impotence experienced in other dimensions: 'on peut vivre différemment les mots et donc habiter différemment le langage et lui infliger des distorsions importantes, lui ajouter des acceptations nouvelles (Aquin 1969, 17). As for Ducharme, the dialectic of control between subject and language becomes the perspective that makes sense of the conflict between self and other experienced in both political and sexual relations. The anamorphosis described in *Trou de mémoire* presents the same enigma as the concept of anastomosis mentioned in *Le Nez qui voque* (11): how can two different elements – the one and the other – interact and be double, without entailing the exclusion of one of them? Anastomosis is a medical term for the converging of two organs, of which neither can be separated without retaining the trace of the other. In *Trou de mémoire*, as in *Le Nez qui voque*, this phenomenon is illustrated by the merging of diary and novel, of feminine and masculine, of reading and writing.

This solution – or post-modern ludic delight in insolubility – may be seen as a betrayal of the ideal of revolution as political tranformation (see Dorsinville 1972). Aesthetic formalism may appear as a narcissistic substitute for other types of (messianic?) engagement (see Randall on Aquin 1990). Similar choices face feminist writers, who also vacillate between the two sides of the subject-language dialectic: language as the vehicle for a tranformation of perception, and language as the source of self-definition. The image used by Aquin, 'écrire en spirale'(120), is central in the work of Nicole Brossard, but as a positive aspect of *l'écriture au féminin* rather than a negative feature of *le colonisé*.

## 'Ecrire: *Je suis une femme* est plein de conséquences' (Brossard 1977, 43)

Magnant in *Trou de mémoire* perceives his writing as a means to 'forniquer incestueusement avec ma langue maternelle' (95). Brossard also connects writing with a relationship to the mother (and to being a mother), but what Irigaray terms 'le corps à corps avec la mère' (1987, 19–33) takes on a new perspective for a woman writer who sets out to define herself in relation to the maternal, rather than as 'other' in the patriarchal symbolic order. She raises the same question, indirectly, that Lewes (1988, 180–2, 217) and Gallop (1982, 117) ask directly: could there be an alternative symbolic order founded on an 'instance maternelle' rather than the 'instance paternelle'? Like French proponents of *l'écriture du corps* Brossard attempts to bridge the gap between sensuality and abstract formalism, denying the binary conception that subjugates nature in order to attain culture. Yet her work, like Aquin's, is situated in the intertextuality of the post-modern, and dismays some feminists by its uncompromising cerebrality. Words, for Brossard as for Ducharme and Aquin, are powerful primarily as signifiers, and like them she plays with the forms of language in order to evoke new meanings.

One of her works that by its title immediately conveys this approach is *L'Amèr ou le chapitre effrité* (1977). Two epigaphs to the first part ('L'A Mèr') attest to the symbolic disjunction between mother and child, and its recuperation by the concept of 'théorie fiction' – an oxymoron that is an anamorphosis/anastomosis similar to the journal-novel conjunction in *Le Nez qui voque* or *Trou de mémoire*.

> C'est le combat. Le livre. La fiction commence suspendue mobile entre les mots et la vraisemblance du corps à mère dévorante et dévorée.

Théorie fictive: les mots n'auront servi que dans la dernière étreinte ... La théorie commence là quand s'éloigne le sein ou l'enfant ...

Like Magnant or Mille Milles, the narrator confesses: 'J'ai tué le ventre et je l'écris' (19). The difference is that this narrator *is* a mother, but refuses to be 'la mère symbolique' (19); her *ventre* is no longer accessible to men (12): 'S'il n'était lesbien, ce texte n'aurait pas de sens. Tout à la fois matrice, matière et production ... ne plus être illégitime' (14). Brossard rehabilitates the 'vision' of R.R. in *Trou de mémoire* (from her 'loge supérieure'); the editor's assessment in *Trou de mémoire* of female homosexuality as worse (more subversive?) than male homosexuality (125) appears here as a triumph, since the aim is dislocation of the symbolic order.

This first part of *L'Amèr* is composed of fragments that contain elements of poetry, of theory (reflection), and of the 'everyday' that belongs to the *journal intime* and to mothers: 'Nous nous quittons pour la journée. Parce qu'il faut que j'écrive ce livre ... Je fais cuire les aliments. Mon temps est fragmenté par ces mêmes objets' (18). Her body, too, is fragmented, by 'tout le champs symbolique' appropriated by man (19). In *L'Amèr* the physical reality of the mother's life intrudes into the discourse of the poet or theoretician and transforms it. In 1983 Brossard composed a text entitled *Journal intime ou Voilà donc un manuscrit* (1984), which was broadcast on radio. In this 'real' diary (the narrator is Brossard, and is writing *in medias res*) poetry/language as a system of signifiers intrudes into, and prevents, the discourse of the everyday that is expected and even required. This non-fictional and non-theoretical text deals with the same issues as *L'Amèr* in a very different way, because of the *journal intime* model that is both adopted and denied; it demonstrates the impossibility of 'innocent' self-recording in a postmodern and post-colonial context.

### Brossard, *Journal Intime* (1984)

'Qu'est-ce que vous me voulez au juste? De la littérature qui n'en aurait pas l'air? De l'écriture qui n'en serait pas?' (54–5)

'Le journal ne me suffit pas. Ne me convient pas. C'est une forme d'écriture qui exige trop de moi et pas assez de ce que je suis.' (74)

This diary is defined by the *journal intime* model. It is written regularly, in short entries covering a two-month period (26 January – 28 March, 1983, according to the preface) and it is to be 'personal,' 'intimate.' Yet it is written in response to an external order – a request from Radio Canada to participate in a series of programs aimed at providing listeners with an inside look at a writer's life. It will be public, although the subject is private, and it will be read aloud by someone (Pol Pelletier) who is not the author, that is, in 'another voice.' Its initial reception will be aural, rather than a visual reading of the text, although publication was obviously envisaged from the outset. The listeners are assumed to expect to gain an impression of 'une journée dans la vie de Nicole Brossard' (26), to learn something about the life of a 'person' rather than the 'author' who is known/constructed through her published writings.

This concept is problematic for Brossard. She does, apparently, have at least two series of *cahiers* in which she makes notes; but she is not the kind of person who keeps what is usually meant by a *journal intime*. 'Que peut-on dire dans un journal qu'on ne le pourrait ailleurs? ... Qu'y a-t-il de si intime dans un journal qui ne saurait être partagé, entamé par la lecture de quelqu'un d'autre?' (17). This comment is paradoxical, in the context of a journal conceived to be shared, that is, false, an imposture or imitation from the beginning. Rather than being a *journal intime*, this text becomes a reflection and commentary on diary writing – as does a fictional journal. It becomes, in effect, another, more accessible version of theory fiction. Brossard's commentary on the diary form begins by questioning the status of the 'subject' concerned in relation to the other/others, time/space and language/writing, reformulating the problematic of auto-bio-graphy from a feminist postmodern perspective.

**The narcissistic subject: 'Le journal ... me semble être un lieu où le sujet tourne en rond jusqu'à l'épuisement de lui-même.' (9)**

According to Louise Dupré in *Stratégies du vertige* (1989),'Chez Nicole Brossard la vision du sujet est marquée par un certain classicisme' (85); the treatment of subjectivity in her texts 'cache la nostalgie d'une unité perdue, d'une intégralité à retrouver' (88). Larose (1987, 141–71) reproaches Brossard for her 'narcissistic' desire for oneness, which is pre-

Oedipal and in his perspective conveys a regressive attachment to the maternal imaginary over the paternal symbolic (see chapter 2 on primary narcissism). Brossard's homosexuality can be seen as an extension of the same (narcissistic) values to secondary object choices: the other-as-woman (double) echoes the other-as-same represented by the mother. Brossard contests this notion of sameness as excluding the other by emphasizing the difference(s) between women, as well as their affinities. She attributes the derogatory assessment of female homosexuality to the fact that it poses a threat to the patriarchal order of compulsory heterosexuality, which assigns women to the role of other in relation to men, objects in the 'hommo-sexual' economy of exchange. The only escape from the binary opposition of sexual difference, for women, is seen to lie in refusing to accept this designation: Brossard and her friends symbolically throw their wedding rings into the sea, in a gesture that conveys their determination no longer to be defined by and in relation to men. Brossard confirms Lacan's assertion that 'entre les sexes chez l'être parlant le rapport ne se fait pas' (*Séminaire* xx, *Encore*, 63). For her, the solution is to refuse to reject the mother (substitute), to establish a system of difference and desire within the category of woman.

In *Journal intime* this system functions between generations: Brossard's relationship with her own mother is evoked, when she records that her mother regrets not being mentioned in her books (72–3). To the reader of *L'Amèr* aware of the 'mère imaginaire' (*Journal*, 27), this perception is ironic. Brossard's own role as mother to her daughter, Julie, also functions on two levels: as part of the 'quotidien' (17) and as symbolic of female continuity and contiguity (40). She and Julie share a privileged, private domestic space, an 'interior.'

The 'other woman' is constantly present in two other contexts. One is the unnamed 'amante,' the 'tu' to whom her thoughts and her desire are addressed (21–2), who is construed primarily as a body and as the experience of absence/separation when they are apart. The second category is a circle of female friends, especially other writers, who provide a community to which she belongs. This is evoked mainly by the non-competitive, non-hierarchical exchange of feminine conversation. They meet at familiar cafés, a space that is in between the private (home) and the public (travel) spheres.

This private version of Nicole Brossard is inseparable from her own city. Yet the public persona/author travels extensively, and her perception of where she is (Montreal) is coloured by her experience of having been elsewhere. Being Québécoise, for her, is an identity acquired by the experience of strangeness/foreignness. Intercalated into the diary of a two-month period in 1983, which includes a journey to British Columbia, are passages (quoted/reconstructed/imagined?) of diaries of other years and other places: Rome (1981), Tokyo (1982), Paris (1980), Martinique (1981), Paris (1975), Athens (1973), Budapest (1978), Greece (1973), New York (1975). One journey is anticipated, recounted in advance (Paris, April 1983), underlining the imaginary dimension of all actual or potential life writing. By incorporating memory and exotic displacement into the 'everyday' of a certain period in time, Brossard escapes from the constraints of the diary form and brings into relief the discontinuity of subjective consciousness. The 'I, here, now' of Henriette Dessaulles's diary becomes 'who, where, when?,' as in a fiction.

### The real and the imaginary: Time and space

*'A quelle mémoire nous adressons-nous lorsque nous prétendons faire revivre un passé, aussi rapproché soit-il?' (17)*

Memory is inseparable from the individual/subjectivity: the moments recalled by Brossard are associated with the senses, and with the (in)capacity of language to describe or convey a fleeting impression. The moments worth remembering – that is, recording in writing – are those that stand out from *le quotidien*. The banal daily round of domestic chores and dentist appointments has no charm for this author whose work is far removed from social realism: 'Je cherche à éviter le quotidien, ce continu durable qui n'a de cesse qu'au moment où l'on ne parvient plus adéquatement à le nommer réalité' (15). Keeping a journal, like housekeeping (19), is a chore, a habit that holds no appeal for someone who seeks the unexpected. The anecdotes that she feels obliged to tell are an 'encombrement' (10) to the expression of what Brossard considers her real life: 'Ma vie qui n'est qu'un tissu de mots ...' (15). Rather than enabling her to 'voir clair,' the diary blinds her (17) to what is 'l'essentiel': 'on invente la réalité sur du papier en intervenant dans la langue ... on n'a qu'une vie et tant d'autres' (10).

The intimacy of memory is also problematic. As Brossard crosses her city in the bus – or Vancouver by taxi – she is constantly aware of collective memory. She is part of the generation of Québécois that engaged in the independence movement, only to see their hopes dashed by the 1980 referendum. Thinking of 24 June, the *fête nationale* (a date evoked by 'note 24,' at the point where she gives up providing dates), she makes a bitter prediction: 'Il n'y aura pas de pays, il n'y aura que des chansons pour les anciens du Collège Brébeuf et du Sainte-Marie' (88). When the Vancouver taxi-driver berates women poets who 'pensent à leur carrière au lieu de penser à leur devoir de mère' (35), her reaction is one of solidarity with all the mothers who 'disent ne pas avoir le temps de tenir leur journal. Et alors on n'entend que leur voix et leurs voix ne sont jamais tout à fait leur voix' (40).

A third collective identity is also constantly evoked throughout this atypical diary: that of a commonwealth of poets, writers who are not *intimistes*, but whose faith in words leads them to reinvent the world, rather than to keep an inventory of their life. It is evident that the diary is a form defined, in Brossard's terms, in opposition to poetry. *Tout dire* is not only impossible, but undesirable, since 'l'essentiel' (89) is a poem characterized by condensation. To each of the five parts of the journal Brossard adds what she calls a 'posture': 'Tous les jours, il me faut risquer de nouvelles postures mentales sinon je sombre dans l'anecdote de la pensée ...' (64). The *posture* eliminates the *imposture* of narrative, reproducing selected elements of the preceding text with a very different effect based on the juxtaposition of disparate items without punctuation. It is followed by a five-line poem that condenses even further, sifting out 'l'essentiel' in a process that involves the reader in the act of tranformation from the 'aujourd'hui' of the diary (87) to the literary text.

This diary brings out the major transformations in theories of narration and of the subject since the days of Henriette Dessaulles. First, the female self is no longer defined in relation to a man, but to other women. Secondly, diary writing is not seen as a substitute for sexual contact or verbal exchange with an other, nor as therapeutic. The choice is not perceived as between writing and living, as in so many diary novels, but between 'écrire et écrire' (37). Brossard's notebooks are divided into 'ceux oú j'existe et ceux dans lesquels j'écris. Ceux où il y a de l'héroisme et ceux dans lesquels les héroines refont le texte' (52–3). Her voice is merged into 'la spirale des voix qui nous entourent' (73) and 'toutes les courbes sont lesbiennes au moment d'inventer le retour à soi' (48).

## Life and letters / the life of letters

Ducharme's Mille Milles says, 'Je ne suis pas un homme de lettres. Je suis un homme' (8). Brossard is both a 'femme de lettres' and 'une femme' (8): the two are inseparable, as are 'le provisoire qui est moi dans ce journal, dans la vie et l'absolu qui est je suis' (74). This 'absolu' is an effect of language. Reading the translation of *L'Amèr* into English, the author comments: 'Etre traduite, c'est être enquêtée non pas seulement dans ce que l'on croit être mais dans sa façon même de penser dans une langue, de même que dans la façon dont nous sommes pensées par une langue' (22–3). This text illustrates the tension between what Brossard sees as the common experience of women in different countries and in different languages, and the specific, distinct experience of a lesbian intellectual Québécoise in 1983; the latter can be translated, but necessarily loses something because for Brossard the 'essence' is *formal*. For Larose, her formalism is a sign of being blocked in the mirror stage, of identifying with the text. He claims that in the writing of Brossard and other Quebec feminists such as Théoret 'le sujet s'évade des contraintes du code vers l'arbitraire d'un imaginaire singulier' (1987, 163). He specifically relates this to identification with the phallic mother: 'le fétiche tient la place du pénis qui, pour le fétichiste, ne manque pas à la mère' (164). What he does not seem to recognize is that the 'imaginaire' of these women writers is not 'singulier,' since it is shared by them and by their female readers. It may be the exclusion of men from their 'miroir' that is disturbing from the male point of view, and the radical feminist assumption that identification with the feminine imaginary/semiotic can be subversive of the 'code,' rather than regressive.

In the summer of 1988 *La Parole métèque*, a Montreal feminist magazine, produced a special issue on the *journal intime*, with contributions from a large number of contemporary Québécoises including Brossard, Madeleine Gagnon, Louky Bersianik, France Théoret, and Yolande Villemaire, all authors of texts written *au féminin*. Like Brossard, Villemaire admits that an experiment in keeping a detailed diary led her to the conclusion that another kind of writing and another kind of life are preferable: 'Cette cartographie insensée de l'insignifiant m'a permis de deviner la possibilité d'un véritable art de vivre dont je n'ai, pour l'instant, qu'une vague intuition' (21). Her post-modern novel, *La Vie en prose* (see Paterson 1990, 83–93) can be read as a logical extension to the evolution of the fictional journal, beyond its development in *Le Nez qui voque* or *Trou de mémoire*. The reader no longer knows who the narrator/narrators is/are, or what is real/imaginary within the fiction. The narrators are aware that they are fictions, created by language. But Brossard's *Journal intime* raises the same questions in relation to a narrator who claims to be the author. The distinctions between autobiography and fiction, diary and novel, self and other all break down, as such binary oppositions become meaningless. Difference itself no longer has the same meaning in Quebec. One diary novel published in 1990, by Francine Noël, conveys the multiplicity of differences in contemporary, multicultural Quebec. It raises questions regarding the viability of any concept of identity based on either gender or ethnicity, in a post-colonial and post-feminist setting. This dual diary fiction will serve to illustrate the danger and the necessity of narcissistic identification(s) for both women and Québécois in the contemporary Quebec context.

# CONCLUSION
# COLLECTIVE (CON)TEXTS AND (IN)DIFFERENCE

CHAPTER TWELVE

# Autism, Assimilation, or Babel: *Noël*

'Toute culture est par essence paranoïa. Elle n'assure son identité narcissique que par négation des autres ...' (75)
'Si le concept d'identité a un sens en théorie analytique, ce ne peut être que par rapport à la vulnérabilité narcissique. Son seul rôle est de permettre la venue de la différence, une fois l'illusion unitaire créée.' (170)

ANDRÉ GREEN (1983)

'Nous sommes tous en train de devenir étrangers dans un univers plus que jamais élargi, plus que jamais hétéroclite sous son apparente unité scientifique et médiatique.(152)
La psychanalyse s'éprouve alors comme un voyage dans l'étrangeté de l'autre et de soi-même, vers une éthique du respect pour l'inconciliable.' (269)

JULIA KRISTEVA (1988)

## Language, aestheticism, and accessibility

The works of Ducharme, Aquin, and Brossard have in common an emphasis on the dimension of language in the elaboration of the subject, and on literary form as innovative and disconcerting. Their texts illustrate these aspects in their material composition, as well as treating them as themes. All three authors have been accused of being narcissistic in their formalism. Their post-modernism illustrates another remark made by Kristeva in relation to narcissism: 'S'il nous reste aujourd'hui une religion, elle est esthétique, car le narcissisme s'abrite le plus intensément dans les déploiements fugaces du sens fictionnel' (1983, 170). Their fictions are difficult to read, not only because of their play with words, but because the fictional world as illusion of the real is constantly called into question. They require a commitment and effort on the part of the reader, who becomes an accomplice, sharing in the narcissistic pleasure of belonging to an élite capable of reading such authors, of being part of the 'happy few.' The novels of Francine Noël, however, while echoing the theories associated with the post-modern and with psychoanalysis, take the form of more traditional fictions. The world she evokes is presented as a mirror of reality and is constructed in order to be recognized by those who live in the one that it resembles. Yet she transforms the everyday, producing something else that we nevertheless believe in, and exposing the real also as fantasy. The fact that her books are best-sellers is an indication of her success in bridging one gap involving difference where the novel is concerned: that between academic theory and the general public's desire for entertainment. This is a different type of fiction theory, closer to the tradition of the novel of ideas. Her third novel, *Babel: Prise deux*, deals with Montreal as it is now, that is, no longer a homogeneous or even bicultural milieu, but a microcosm of the world. It is one of the first novels to focus on this to be written by a Québécois 'de souche.' Her choice of narrative form allows her to convey a feminine/feminist perception of this new situation. This work consequently serves as a meeting point for many issues related to narcissism and survival, for women and for the Québécois.

### Noël, *Babel: Prise deux ou Nous avons tous découvert L'Amérique* (1990)[1]

*'La question la plus importante de cette fin de siècle ... est celle de la migration des masses humaines ... Ces remous nous forcent à redéfinir des notions comme celles de territoire, nation, culture, légitimité, propriété.'* (402)

Francine Noël's novel ends on this note, emphasizing the post-colonial aspect of her depiction of Montreal as 'Babel, prise deux,' a city in which different ethnic groups live side by side separated by language and culture, and where the Québécois themselves feel that their identity is threatened from within: 'face à l'immigration, que j'ai toujours souhaitée, je sens de plus en plus la fragilité de l'identité québécoise' (195). The narrator of the diary that constitutes most of the text, Fatima

Gagné, is a Québécoise *pure laine*, named Fatima by her grandmother, who was devoted to the 'Vierge de Fatima' (69). Her identity incorporates an evocation of exotic otherness (the 'hand of Fatima' being a Muslim charm), along with a declaration of loyalty to the Roman Catholic faith/origin that means nothing to her. Fatima is part of a generation of women liberated by contraception, one of those described by Marlène Carmel (1990) who, coming from a large family, have decided not to have children (19) and to avoid the constraints of marriage. Fatima's relationship to her mother is one of denial: she refers to her always as Ginette, and disparagingly. She has chosen as a substitute her aunt and godmother, Aline, who levitates in a literal attempt to rise above the banality of everyday domesticity. At the beginning of the diary, Fatima's most important identification is with a female friend, Amélia, an immigrant from France of mixed French and Spanish origin, whom she perceives as an older double or model. The importance Fatima gives to friendship between women marks her as a feminist – albeit a 'passive' one (187) – although she is heterosexual (375) and promiscuous in her relationships with men.

At the beginning of her diary, which covers the period from 26 February 1988 to 6 February 1989, she is seeing a man called Germain, whom she abandons because he is boring. Fatima is not looking for security or reassurance from a man like her ('Germain'), but for dialogue with someone different. The ethnic and linguistic differences constantly alluded to throughout the text are parallel to a commentary on the nature of sexual difference as the fundamental paradigm for all others. Fatima does not believe in feminine faithfulness, in the sense of possessive exclusivity. She decides to share her life with two men, Louis and Guillaume, who must both be satisfied with 'le partage,' which is 'le secret de Fatima' (265; cf. Lemoine-Luccioni 1976). She also reiterates her belief that her connection to Amélia is stronger than her ties to any man: 'on me voit toujours avec des hommes et mon attachement le plus profond était pour une femme' (333). As far as men are concerned, she declares: 'Je ne veux plus m'attacher' (38). Her resistance to involvement may be attributable to a 'peine d'amour' experienced the previous year, recorded in a diary that she has no desire to reread. Her defensive attitude is expressed through her reluctance to allow her apartment – her own narcissistic space dominated by a large mirror (150) – to be invaded by her male partners (55). This desire to keep her own borders intact goes back to the occasion in her childhood when her mother read the secret diary she already kept, an intrusion into her privacy perceived as a 'viol' (168).

Fatima has been keeping a journal for years (245) and reflections on diary writing are scattered throughout her text. Like Brossard, she perceives it as an activity opposed to 'être écrivain', since its purpose is to record 'des choses vraies' rather than to 'inventer' (246). This diarist considers herself lacking in the imagination necessary to 'recomposer la vie' (246) as fiction. Yet Louis, Amélia's married ex-lover, who has rented a room across from Fatima's apartment, comments that Fatima has the ability – shared by Noël – to make a banal incident interesting, to turn ordinary people into characters (352). For Fatima, as for most *intimistes*, the journal is a means to 'voir clair,' to 'mettre de l'ordre,' a therapy (32) and an aid to memory, which is perceived (with language) as the main component in a sense of identity (374). She writes for herself alone, recording even fantasies that would be otherwise 'inavouables' (21), as well as her suspicions that she may be suffering from premenstrual syndrome (28). The diary enables her to come to terms with her most painful experiences, including Amélia's death in a plane crash. She is finally able to put away her souvenirs of Amélia, with her last letter, which she had copied into her journal, then cut out (351) She stores them in her 'placard de la mémoire,' a physical space analogous to the (verbal) journal, where the past can be relegated to the background, but not forgotten.

Louis becomes an important part of Fatima's journal. He, in turn, is writing his own, less extensive diary, in which Fatima and Amélia appear from a different perspective. The narrative technique of two intercalated journals, as in Chéné's *Peur et amour*, serves to illustrate the axiom that there is no reality, only 'des visions subjectives' (182) and that every life is limited by the individual's 'vision parcellaire' (226). Louis's vision is that of a man whose perception is primarily based on specularity and a relationship to the material world. He is an architect by profession and a sculptor in the hours he spends away from his wife and family at his secret studio. Fatima, in contrast, is a speech therapist working with aphasic patients (137). Her attention is focused primarily on language, in its oral/aural and structural aspects, and on people.

## Words and space: 'Construire et se construire. C'est cela, Babel, le Verbe et la Pierre.' (403)

The relationship between space and language was demonstrated by Jakobson in his study of aphasia, which enabled him to elaborate a theory of the relative importance of metonymy/contiguity (relationships of connecting, on the horizontal syntagmatic axis), and the metaphorical substitution of alternates from the vertical paradigm. Difference or other-ness can be constituted on either axis. In Fatima's journal, it is analysed in three dimensions: sexual, linguistic, and spatial in the sense of geographical. The last two are illustrated by two components: Amélia, her exiled and multilingual friend; and Montreal, as it appears from her street, which separates the bourgeois francophone and Jewish district of Outrement from the multi-ethnic, working-class area of the Plateau. She and Louis live on opposite sides of a partition that is 'au confluent de plusieurs petites sociétés distinctes' (38).

Although Fatima regards Amélia as her 'âme soeur,' she also represents what Fatima is *not*. First, she is an immigrant, one of those who find it impossible to forget their roots in Europe, where 'real life' goes on (233). She is also not entirely French, since her father was Spanish; although she grew up in France, her close emotional ties to him emerge in her attachment to the Spanish language. This fascination is reflected in her interest in the work of Latin-American women writers. Like Fatima she sees language as primordial in the construction of identity, and is a feminist. She is translating the journal of a writer called Délia Febrero (176). Unlike Fatima, Amélia is a mother and defines herself in relation to her two children, as well as to Fatima and to her new lover, Bernard, and her work involving language.

Amélia leaves for Europe in an attempt (parallel to that of Fatima in her journal) to 'recoller les morceaux épars de son histoire personnelle' (233). After returning to France and Spain, she declares her allegiance to Quebec as her 'pays' (314) and her intention to settle there for good. Yet her disappearance in mid-Atlantic on the way back is interpreted by Fatima as symptomatic of her 'incapacité radicale d'atteindre l'Amérique et de revendiquer cette terre comme la sienne' (375). Amélia's attempt to 'être à la fois ici et là-bas, abolir les différences et les distances' (145) is compared to the flight of Icarus, a noble effort to deny gravity, destined like the tower of Babel to fail (344, 389). Fatima, Amélia's double who inherits all her clothes (like the narrator of Monette's *Le Double Suspect*), as well as occupying her place in Louis's life, is overwhelmed with vertigo as she attempts to continue Amélia's efforts at fostering communication between continents and languages.

Amélia's life is constructed on the model of nomadism: of mixed origin and living in exile in any country, unable to feel at home in any house, she identifies with Febrero's treatment of such 'réalités universelles' as 'amour et déchirements, exil, fragilité des liens, métissage culturel' (59). Her surname is Malaise and she is not at ease anywhere. Fatima still lives in her home town, close to her family, but she nevertheless experiences a comparable sense of alienation because of the 'foreigners' who are her neighbours, especially the closed community of Hasidic Jews established on her doorstep. She discusses them with a Jewish Québécois friend, Allan, but is unable to break the barriers to actual contact, until a grandmother out alone finally returns her smile (369). Another neighbour, 'la grosse femme d'à côté' – an allusion to Tremblay's Plateau novels – perpetuates the image of the Québécois as xenophobic and racist. Fatima is not only aware of the potential for ethnic conflict in her own backyard, but of such conflicts all over the world, as she is a compulsive viewer of television news. The unrest of Native people at Oka is juxtaposed with Palestinian riots and Armenian uprisings. Foreign and domestic problems merge in the case of illegal Turkish immigrants, about to be expelled, whose desire to become Québécois and eagerness to speak French won wide support for their acceptance: 'On a le goût de leur dire: Lâchez-pas! Vous êtes d'ici, vous aussi!' (40).[2]

The Québécois community itself is not homogeneous. Fatima's parents are horrified at the prospect of their family business being taken over by a lower-class employee with an Irish surname, O'Sullivan – like Maryse in Noël's first novel. The anglophones of Montreal remain a source of frustration. Their protests against legislation to protect the French language provoke Fatima to exclaim: 'Ils me font suer! Majoritaires en Amérique du Nord, ils trouvent le tour de se sentir lésés! A leurs yeux nous sommes intolérants parce que nous sommes. C'est notre existence qui les dérange!' (34). She attends a rally in support of Bill 101, but another part of her life tends to make her less categorical over the language issue: her experience with a teenage patient, Linda, through whom she meets her other lover, Guillaume Lebel.

## Aphasia and bilingualism

Amélia claims that she is a different person depending on what language she speaks (76). Linda, who lost the ability to speak after an accident in a car driven by Guillaume, is from a francophone, *péquiste* family living in Longueuil, a district with many Italians. Surprisingly, she does not respond to therapy in French, but is able to compose sentences in English. This transfer is attributed to her emotional involvement with a young anglophone Italian, Sandro. The situation is compared to that of Romeo and Juliet, since her family are adamantly opposed to the relationship. Her bond to Sandro proves stronger than the one to her family, and she wants to learn Italian and become a translator, like Amélia. This desire to identify with the other is analogous to Fatima's closeness to Amélia, rather than to her own parents; she calls Amélia her 'vraie famille'(45), and dreams of having a black baby (156).

Linda's verbal incapacity is compensated for by her talent in painting. Louis claims that visual means of communication are as important as linguistic ones (304, 380). He explores his feelings about the three women in his life – Fatima, Amélia, and his wife, Hélène – in reproductions of the sculpture of three Amerindian women that appears on the book's cover. He is horrified by Fatima's 'touching up' of works of art. His sense of being in two places at once, like Amélia, is related to occupying two locations in the same city, rather than to speaking two languages. Difference, for him, is a function of spatial rather than linguistic separation. Similarly, Guillaume, who lives in Longueuil and is a geographer, finally moves into Montreal to be nearer to Fatima, after Amélia's death. He joins her to spend Christmas with her family, something she has not done for years, as Louis becomes closer once more to his family. The renewal of family connections that occurs for the main characters at the end of the book, confirming the value of sameness/identity, is counterbalanced by Linda's determination to defy her family and remain loyal to Sandro. Yet this is because she considers him her 'family,' by choice rather than by birth/blood. This option, like Fatima's attachment to Amélia, attests to the attraction of the other, of what is different, or the same in a different way. It calls into question the concept of origin as race-and-place in relation to identity. Allan, the Jew, and the Turks, are Québécois, whereas the English who have been there for generations are still intruders. Immigrants pose a threat only if they become anglophone. Linguistic/cultural identity is finally more powerful than blood or ownership of land (see Kristeva 1988, 287). Fatima recognizes that 'tout rapport a la langue est un rapport de pouvoir' (33), and the diary represents her own 'prise de pouvoir par la parole' (266).

Montreal is compared to Babel several times throughout the novel, and the myth itself is discussed at length (195–6, 402–3). The city is 'bigarrée' (37) and 'bâtarde' (175), a 'chantier' under transformation, occupied by mutants (49) who no longer resemble their origins (50). The Québécois must provide a 'lieu commun' for the allophones, if they are to survive (363). Like Jean Larose, whom she quotes (399), Fatima is doubtful about the capacity of the Québécois to succeed. She reproaches them for having changed so little since the 1950s (204), for being 'beige,' neutral (354), and 'Canadian' rather than American (399), echoing older diary novels in her remarks on the weakness of Quebec men (345). She concludes that the desire for self-determination is legitimate, but utopic (403), and wonders whether women will ever be as able to call Quebec their *pays* as men (180), and what language they would use to do so.[3]

Fatima is faced with a difficult personal choice. Guillaume provides a sense of (false?) security, in which she can almost believe (403); talking with him is an exchange, rather than a combat (199). But he does not want to share her (339), and he wants a legitimate child, 'signed' by him (236). With him, Fatima 'aime être aimée' (215). She satisfies her narcissistic desire for approval (180). With Louis she has no security and must accept being only part of his life. Like her, he protects his privacy. She is 'subjuguée' by him (220), because he inspires passion – 'le blanc de la passion' (161). Louis, although he has children, is more interested in survival through art (383). Like Fatima, he needs a mirror (217). He is Amélia's 'twin' (254), and like her he represents the attraction of otherness: 'avec Louis, il y a toujours cet effet d'éloignement et rien n'est jamais acquis, il est l'Autre' (389). He loves her, but not as much as she loves him. Her choice is between freedom accompanied by solitude (397, 398) or family ties – serial reproduction (25), the 'fondue' (55), and tribal coercion to conform (110).

The final message of Noël's novel is ambivalent, since sharing and identifying with the difference of others is set up as a model or a goal, yet it also appears as fraught with danger. The attempt to 'être à la place des autres' (14) may lead to an 'éclatement,' as for Amélia (328), or psychological and linguistic fragmentation resulting in aphasia, as for Linda. However, Fatima sees that refusal to accept diversity within the borders of Quebec is no longer an option, although the increase in allophones who choose to speak English threatens the survival of francophone culture.[4] The influx of immigrants is non-threatening only if they can be persuaded to become francophone, and the 'néo-Québécois/pure laine' distinction can be rendered obsolete. Survival depends on the Québécois accepting a modified version of their own culture, enriched by the integration (but not assimilation) of diversity, and on the others also accepting it, as it makes room for them and produces a new 'us.' The distinctness of Quebec – its Frenchness – is also threatened by indifference, as in the title of Arcand's film on the 1980 referendum, *Le Confort et l'indifférence*, since vigilance is necessary to protect the use of French. It is more subtly threatened by increasing non-differentiation from American culture and values. In face of these threats of assimilation or eclipse by the other, continuity depends on a new narcissism capable of accepting the other as part of the self, of maintaining a cohesion divorced from homogeneity. Paradoxically, the same can continue only by becoming different from what it once was.

## *Etrangers à nous-mêmes* (Kristeva) / *Je, tu, nous* (Irigaray): The post-colonial and post-feminist dilemma

Recent studies of Quebec fiction also reach the conclusion that self-other oppositions are now modified by a new recognition of otherness in the self and of sameness in the other (Harel 1989, 32; Kwaterko 1989, 69–71). The shift from an identity founded in the imaginary origin to one established through the alienation of language, according to the Lacanian paradigm, nevertheless poses problems in the Quebec context. On the one hand, evolution from a collective identity based on non-individuation within the group is seen to evolve into individual rather than collective narcissism (Kwaterko 1989, 16). This development appears to be parallel to a desire on the part of the group to attain political autonomy, an assurance of survival no longer based on refuge values. Both individuals and the collectivity are perceived as emerging into a state of mature independence. The new predominance of individual narcissism, however, corresponding to the American materialism and self-preoccupation described by Christopher Lasch (1979, 1984), would appear to work against the collective solidarity necessary for the goal of political autonomy to outweigh the risk of individual economic insecurity. For the individual, a sense of identity apart from the group of origin may paradoxically imply a closer affinity to the external, dominant group and therefore work against a collective move to separate from it (see Pelletier 1991, 12).

The ideal espoused by Noël, of increased permeability between individuals and between groups based on a potential for reciprocity, applies both within Quebec and to Quebec's association with English Canada. It is also, according to Irigaray (1990), the only potential solution to otherwise confrontational relations between the sexes. This may be possible in all three cases, but only under certain conditions: in Quebec, only if its minorities no longer appear a threat; for Canada, only if English Canada recognizes the distinctness of Quebec and the legitimacy of a narcissistic desire to remain different; between the sexes, only if the one does not continue to define itself in terms of the other.

In this respect, the self-conscious writings of Québécois or of women who perceive themselves as both the one and the other, epitomize the post-modern condition. Simon During has defined post-modern thought as 'that which refuses to turn the Other into the Same' (1987, 33). He also adds that 'the Other can never speak for itself as the Other' (33).[5] By speaking, the other becomes the subject: one of many 'new' subjects who must be capable of mutuality in order to survive. As Kristeva puts it, 'La société multinationale serait ainsi le résultat d'un individualisme extrême, mais conscient de ses malaises et de ses limites, ne connaissant que d'irréductibles prêts-à-s'aider dans leur faiblesse, une faiblesse dont l'autre nom est notre étrangeté radicale' (1988, 290).

If Quebec and Canada prove 'prêts-à-s'aider,' perhaps they can both survive, whether married, separated or living together in an *union libre* involving a relationship that would be both narcissistic and reciprocal: not what Freud termed *anlehnend* (anaclitic, dependent), but what the Québécois call *accotés* – mutually supportive. Since English-Canadian writing is increasingly conveying a self-reflective preoccupation with sameness and distinctness, similar to the one illustrated in Quebec diary fiction over the last hundred years, the outlook may be less pessimistic than many of us believed in 1992.

APPENDIX

# Diary Fiction in Quebec:
# *Chronology and Classification*

Novels or stories wholly/mainly (1) or partly (2) in diary form, or containing extracts from a journal (3) or references to one (4), in chronological order of publication:

| | | | |
|---|---|---|---|
| (1) | Laure Conan | 'Un Amour vrai' | 1878 |
| (2) | Laure Conan | Angéline de Montbrun | 1882 |
| (1) | Laure Conan | 'A travers les ronces' | 1883 |
| (1) | Henriette Dessaulles | 'L'Amour passa' | 1908 |
| (1) | Laure Conan | 'L'Obscure Souffrance' | 1919 |
| (1) | Laure Conan | 'La Vaine Foi' | 1919 |
| (1) | Joseph Carre | Journal d'un étudiant | 1925 |
| (1) | Joseph Raiche | Journal d'un vicaire de campagne | 1927 |
| (3) | Claude Robillard | Dilettante | 1931 |
| (1) | Adolphe Brassard | Mémoires d'un soldat inconnu | 1939 |
| (3) | François Hertel | Le Beau Risque | 1939 |
| (3) | François Hertel | Anatole Laplante, curieux homme | 1944 |
| (2) | Pierre Baillargeon | Les Médisances de Claude Perrin | 1945 |
| (2) | François Hertel | Journal d'Anatole Laplante | 1947 |
| (3) | Paul de Martigny | Mémoires d'un garnement | 1947 |
| (2) | Paul de Martigny | Mémoires d'un reporter | 1947 |
| (4) | Ringuet | Fausse Monnaie | 1947 |
| (4) | Pierre Baillargeon | La Neige et le feu | 1948 |
| (2) | Françoise Loranger | Mathieu | 1949 |
| (2) | Robert Elie | La Fin des songes | 1950 |
| (4) | Gabrielle Roy | Alexandre Chênevert | 1954 |
| (2) | Jean Filiatrault | Chaînes | 1955 |
| (2) | Jean Simard | Mon Fils pourtant heureux | 1956 |
| (1) | Emile Castonguay | Le Journal d'un bourgeois de Québec | 1960 |

| | | | |
|---|---|---|---|
| (1) Paule Saint-Onge | | Ce qu'il faut de regrets | 1961 |
| (1) Jean-Paul Pinsonneault | | Les Abîmes de l'aube | 1962 |
| (1) Adrien Thério | | Le Journal d'un chien | 1962 |
| (1) J.-Alphonse Deveau | | Le Journal de Cécile Murat | 1963 |
| (3) Laurent Girouard | | La Ville inhumaine | 1964 |
| (1) Jean-Jules Richard | | Journal d'un hobo | 1965 |
| (1) Yolande Chéné | | Peur et amour | 1965 |
| (3) Marie-Claire Blais | | Une Saison dans la vie d'Emmanuel | 1965 |
| (2) Marie-Claire Blais | | L'Insoumise | 1966 |
| (1) Roger Fournier | | Journal d'un jeune marié | 1967 |
| (1) Réjean Ducharme | | Le Nez qui voque | 1967 |
| (1) Jacques Godbout | | Salut Galarneau! | 1967 |
| (1) Jean-Marie Poupart | | Angoisse Play | 1968 |
| (2) Hubert Aquin | | Trou de mémoire | 1968 |
| (1) Gérard Bessette | | Le Libraire | 1968 |
| (1) Paule Saint-Onge | | La Saison de l'inconfort | 1968 |
| (3) Hubert Aquin | | L'Antiphonaire | 1969 |
| (1) Pierre Châtillon | | Le Journal d'automne de Placide Mortel | 1970 |
| (3) Jacques Ferron | | L'Amélanchier | 1970 |
| (1) Réjean Ducharme | | L'Hiver de force | 1973 |
| (3) Gilbert La Rocque | | Les Corridors | 1973 |
| (1) Diane Giguère | | Dans les ailes du vent | 1976 |
| (1) Claude Lamarche | | Je me veux | 1976 |
| (1) Geneviève Amyot | | Journal de l'année passée | 1978 |
| (2) Jacques Garneau | | Les Difficiles Lettres d'amour | 1979 |
| (3) Jean-Marie Poupart | | Terminus | 1979 |
| (3) Madeleine Monette | | Le Double Suspect | 1980 |
| (1) Hélène Ouvrard | | L'Herbe et le varech | 1980 |
| (3) Yolande Villemaire | | La Vie en prose | 1980 |
| (3) Anne Hébert | | Les Fous de Bassan | 1982 |
| (2) Michel Tremblay | | Des Nouvelles d'Edouard | 1984 |
| (3) Noël Audet | | L'Ombre de l'épervier | 1988 |
| (1) Robert Baillie | | La Nuit de la Saint-Basile | 1990 |
| (1) Michèle Mailhot | | Le Passé composé | 1990 |
| (1) Francine Noël | | Babel: Prise deux | 1990 |

# Notes

### Chapter One

1 See Raoul (1985) 'Les Femmes intimistes dans le roman français.'
2 See Preamble to this volume.
3 Agnès Whitfield uses *L'Avalée des avalés* to illustrate modification of the *journal intime* model, in *Le Je(u) illocutoire* (1987), 61–116. Thériault's novel is unusual, since it depicts a sort of diary, produced for someone other than the narrator, on tape.
4 See Raoul (1989), 'Women and Diaries: Gender and Genre.'
5 For example, Robidoux (1966), Bessette (1968), Cotnam (1971), Falardeau (1967, 1974), Marcotte (1976), Hébert (1982), Arguin (1985), Kwaterko (1989)
6 See Raoul (1983), 'Documents of Non-Identity.'
7 See, for example, Allard (1969) and Whitfield (1987).
8 See Kwaterko (1989) and Pelletier (1991).
9 Bridging the two is seen as desirable by many feminist critics, such as Elizabeth Abel in 'Race, Class and Psychoanalysis? Opening Questions.'

### Chapter Three

1 Beaudoin (1989) quotes Rameau (1859) on 'L'Amérique française': 'Tandis qu'aux Etats-Unis les esprits s'absorbent avec une préoccupation épuisante dans le commerce, dans l'industrie, dans l'adoration du veau d'or, il appartient au Canada de s'approprier avec désintéressement et une noble fierté le côté intellectuel, scientifique et artistique du mouvement américain, en s'adonnant avec préférence au culte du sentiment, de la pensée et du beau ...' (27–8).
2 Roch Carrier, 'Le Secret perdu dans l'eau,' in *Les Enfants du bonhomme dans la lune* (1983)

3 Beaudoin: 'Les premières visions de la nation, telles que proposées dans l'image de la ville mère, Ville-Marie, puis chez les écrivains français et canadiens qui contribuent à l'historiographie naissante, se distinguent par leur caractère féminin' (55)
4 See also Susan Mann Trokimenkoff (1983), 329–31.
5 See also Lori Saint-Martin, 'Mise à mort de la femme et "libération" de l'homme: Godbout, Aquin, Beaulieu.' It was also tragically confirmed by the Lépine massacre at the Ecole Polytechnique in December 1989, and the wave of domestic violence in the following year.
6 In France women could not vote until 1945, and during the French Revolution Olympe de Gouges, author of a text on the rights of women, was guillotined.
7 For example, New Brunswick Premier Frank McKenna was quoted in the *Vancouver Sun* (14 September 1990) as saying: '... it has become abundantly clear a status quo position in the relationship between Quebec and the rest of the country cannot be maintained. Marriage under the existing terms and conditions is not acceptable in Quebec and is probably no longer acceptable in other parts of the country either. So will it be reconciliation on new terms? Trial separation? Uncontested divorce? Will we all find new partners?' (A12). Also in the *Vancouver Sun*, 25 May 1990, Nicole Parton expressed frustration at Quebec's 'narrow self-interest and narcissism,' maintaining that 'the blackened eyes, bruised psyches and bickering just aren't worth it' (B1). In the *Globe and Mail*'s *Report on Business Magazine* (June 1990), the use of economic arguments against the separation of Quebec was compared to 'a husband telling an angry spouse that she can't walk out because she'd starve' (21). The divorce metaphor was also used by Peter Newman in a series of articles in *Maclean's* (9 July, 13 August, 17 September 1990). In the last, he quotes Pierre Laurin's statement on 'sovereignty-association' as being 'like getting a divorce and telling your spouse "After we're divorced I will become your associate"' (36).

## Chapter Four

1 Studies of diaries in Quebec by Lamonde, Van Roey-Roux, and Hébert all mention this type of diary. In fiction, *Journal d'un étudiant* (Des Bois 1925) and *Journal d'un vicaire de campagne* (Raiche 1927) imitate this model, which also existed in France. Thinking perhaps of Bernanos' *Journal d'un curé de campagne*, Sartre has Roquentin in *La Nausée* say that he is not 'vierge ou prêtre' and therefore should not be keeping a diary.
2 Other examples in French are the journals of Marie Bashkirtseff, Caroline B., and Geneviève Bréton. See Raoul (1989) and Begos (in Spender 1987, 69–74) on the diaries of adolescent girls. Dessaulles's diary is available in a translation by Liedewy Hawke entitled *Hopes and Dreams: The Diary of Henriette Dessaulles 1874–1881*. (Willowdale ON, Hounslow Press 1986).

3 The extract, entitled 'L'Amour passa,' is reprinted in Major's edition of Dessaulles's diary (627–44). It was published under the name of 'Françoise' in the *Journal de Françoise* (7e année, no. 3, samedi 2 mai 1908, 34–40) and corresponds to pages 252–79 in the diary (see Major, 92).
4 See Raoul (1980, 7–9) for a discussion of Lejeune's 'pacte autobiographique,' and Lejeune (1986) for his more recent revisions of it.
5 Parts of this analysis previously appeared in French in *The French Review* (Raoul, 1986) and are translated here with the editor's permission.
6 According to Girard (112–13) and Didier (74), even in France keeping an intimate diary was usually incompatible with a happy marriage for people of either sex. All the women whose diaries were published were unmarried, except Leseur, who could not communicate with her husband.
7 'Les Femmes et les lettres françaises au Canada,' *Bulletin du parler français au Canada*, 11, no. 9 (mai 1913): 341–8
8 Actually a play, entitled 'Si les Canadiennes le voulaient' (1886), reprinted by Leméac, 1974

## Chapter Five

1 Le Moine (1974) recounts that Conan visited the Dessaulles and frightened the children (20). She lived in a convent in Saint-Hyacinthe from 1893–8 (25). See the section of the bibliography on Dessaulles and Conan.
2 See Dumont 1960, 6 and Le Moine, 19. There are also many references, going back to Casgrain (1884, 9), to her 'virile' pen.
3 Poulin's article of 1983 summarizes most of the criticism preceding it. For autobiographical aspects, see especially Soeur J. de l'Immaculée (Suzanne Paradis), Le Moine, and Godin. Cotnam also claims that *Angéline* is 'dans une large mesure un roman autobiographique. D'où ... la supériorité de la troisième partie du roman, celle qui constitue le journal, sur les deux précédents' (152).
4 On the incorporation of real diaries into fiction, see Raoul 1980, 100 and Didier, 34–5, 149.
5 'Un Amour vrai' (1878), in Laure Conan, *Œuvres romanesques I*, with an introduction by R. Le Moine; also published in 1897 (without authorization) by Leprohon, under the title 'Larmes d'amour.' Dessaulles's extract is reproduced in Major's critical edition of her diary (627–44).
6 Patrick Imbert pointed to the comparison in '*Fadette, Journal d'Henriette Dessaulles (1874–1880)* ou l'ambivalence vécue.' Daphni Baudouin (Université du Québec à Trois Rivières has also done research on Dessaulles and Conan.
7 Le Moine (24) records that in 1863 Conan read and copied out pages from Eugénie de Guérin's journal. Girard cites Amiel's amazement that de Guérin's diary went through twelve editions in thirty months (1864; Girard, 476).

References to this model occur in *Angéline* (50, 66, 117), and both Casgrain and Henri D'Arles compare Conan to de Guérin. See Didier (155) on the relationship between Eugénie and her brother.

8 Brochu (1965, 127) was mistaken in assuming that the journal begins nine months after the father's death. Although the entry for 20 May, beginning 'c'est le 20 septembre que j'ai perdu mon père ...' (94) may give this impression, the one for 19 September (159) says clearly: 'Demain ... le troisième anniversaire de sa mort.'

9 See Paul C. Rosenblatt, *Bitter, Bitter Tears: Nineteenth-Century Diaries and Twentieth-Century Grief Theories* (1983). Many of the characteristics he points out apply to Angéline's diary, including the following: importance of place, objects, and anniversary dates in provoking renewed grief; the physical symptoms of extreme grief and psychosomatic illness; importance of the deceased's last words and wishes; the search for and rejection of substitutes, including the diary; need for unconditional love and acceptance; naming a child after the deceased (cf. naming the convert after Angéline, who has, so to speak, died with her father); religious doubts.

10 Brochu (1963) sees Mina and Maurice as serving to express, vicariously, the desire of Charles and Angéline for each other (117).

11 These elements were pointed out by Dawn Thompson (PHD program, Comparative Literature, UBC) in an unpublished paper (1990).

12 It may not be too far-fetched to interpret this literally, since P.-A. Tremblay, Conan's former suitor, is reported as having a 'mariage blanc'; his wife, Miss Connolly, was actually still addressed by her maiden name (Le Moine, 18–19).

13 Blodgett warns of the danger of too easily equating the gun and the phallus (19). Smart suggests the hypothesis that the tree may represent a revenge of nature (67). Trees appear throughout the text as signs of strength; Charles is 'robuste comme un chêne' (25); the tree planted by Maurice and the one he carved on are destroyed (98, 151); Angéline loses her 'feuilles détachées,' but 'l'arbre dépouillé tient toujours à la terre,' as she says in her final letter (185).

14 Conan herself defended Maurice, in a letter quoted by Dumont (1960, 9): '... on me blesse en disant du mal de Maurice, et on m'en a tant dit ... Je le trouve malgré cela digne d'être aimé.'

15 In the first version, Angéline developed a facial tumour. The passage is included in the Fides 1974 edition (155).

16 Anne Simpson (PHD programme, Department of French, UBC) pointed out the relevance of *Soleil Noir* in an unpublished paper (1990).

17 See J. Van Herik, *Freud on Femininity and Faith* (1982), to which I shall return in the next chapter.

18 Brochu (1965), Gagnon, Blodgett, and M.J. Green in particular

19 See Ann Douglas, *The Feminization of American Culture* (1977), part 2 ('The Sentimentalization of Creed and Culture'), chapter 6 ('The Domestication of Death'), especially 220ff, 'Heaven is our Home: The Colonization of the Afterlife.' The rhetoric is the same, whether the setting is Catholic Quebec, Puritan New England, or the Baptist South.

20 They include the following: despair at the monotony and boredom of daily life and menial tasks (*TR* 352, 353, 359; *OS* 3, 27–8); the desire for a great love and the recognition that this is rare, and probably impossible, in this life, particularly in marriage (*TR* 352, 357; *OS* 7, 18, 30, 32); nostalgia for the past and fear for the future (*TR* 344, 360; *OS* 43); reading of the *Imitation of Christ* (*TR* 359; *OS* 37, 53); consultation of a priest, after the feast of All Hallows (*TR* 359; *OS* 37, 53); a sense of useless aspiration and of 'refoulement' (*TR* 349, 353, 354; *OS* 17) and a need to live intensely (*TR* 353; *OS* 41); an awareness of being 'peu sincère avec soi-même' (*TR* 345; *OS* 7); appeal to God as a father and/or mother substitute (*TR* 350; *OS* 15–16); transfer of the desire to be loved to him; religious sublimation as a response to the horror that one might 'souffrir inutilement' (*TR* 349) and a way to transform suffering into a meaningful ordeal leading to a 'better' life more real than 'this one' (*TR* 343; *OS* 29, 59: 'la douleur est nécessaire pour féconder la vie'); reference to novels as pernicious (*TR* 361; *OS* 25), provoking false expectations: 'la réalité n'est pas le roman.'

## Chapter Six

1 On La Laurentie and the ideology of La Relève see Vincenthier, *L'Histoire des idées au Québec*, chapter 9.
2 Richard Giguère, in an article on Hertel for the *Dictionary of Literary Biography* (vol. 68, 175–9), explains that Hertel was the name of a French-Canadian soldier-hero (1642–1722). See also Robert Major, 'François Hertel: bilan provisoire d'un destin d'écrivain.'
3 See chapter 8 for a discussion of homosexuality in relation to narcissism.
4 *Anatole Laplante, curieux homme* also contains journal extracts, under the heading 'Fou' (see Kenneth Landry, *Dictionnaire des œuvres littéraires québécoises*, 46–8). Another novel by Hertel, *Six femmes, un homme* (1949), contains the journal of the protagonist, Gombauld, 'où la cruauté à l'égard du sexe faible le dispute au ridicule' (Robert Charbonneau, on Hertel, in *Romanciers canadiens*, 56–61; 61).
5 *Six femmes, un homme* confirms Hertel's misogyny and distrust of heterosexuality.
6 See Larose (1987, 69–70). Kristeva expressed a similar view of American

culture, albeit with a more positive interpretation, in the introduction to a special issue of *Tel Quel* on the United States (no. 71/3, 1977), translated in Moi (1986).
7  *Un Canadien errant* was the title of another autobiographical novel by Hertel; the reference is to the poem by Gérin-Lajoie, which became a popular song, in which the 'Canadien errant' is in exile as a result of the 1837-8 rebellion of the Patriotes.
8  Jacques Michon also comments on some similarities, in 'Esthétique et réception du roman conforme, 1940–57,' in Michon, *Structure, idéologie et réception du roman québécois de 1940 à 1960* (1979), 4–20.
9  See the preface by A. Gaulin, and the same critic in the *Dictionnaire des œuvres littéraires du Québec*, 215–16: 'l'affabulation ne tient guère ... sous l'artifice, c'est Baillargeon qui parle de lui-même.' Robert Charbonneau came to the same conclusion (in *Romanciers canadiens*, 4–9).
10 See G. Genette, *Figures III* (1972), 146 and Raoul (1980, 46–59) on the 'chronograph.'

**Chapter Seven**

1  See 'Why the United States?' in Moi (1986), 272–91. Kristeva's description of North American culture as 'non-verbal' relates to the role of the imaginary (associated with the feminine), as discussed by Jean Larose (1987).
2  See Jean Larose on Nelligan (1987, 63). The attribution of Nelligan's madness to his mother's oppression is central in Michel Tremblay's opera *Nelligan*.
3  On *Mathieu*, see Jean Filiatrault (1964); Soeur Sainte-Marie-Eleuthère (1964), 146–9; A. Gaulin in *Le Dictionnaire des Œuvres littéraires québécoises* (1987).
4  See D.W. Winnicott on Lacan's 'mirror stage,' 'Mirror Role of Mother and Family in Child Development' in *Playing and Reality* (Penguin, 1971) and the discussion by Elizabeth Abel in 'Race, Class and Psychoanalysis? Opening Questions.'
5  Pierre Simoneau, in 'Structures discursives de *La Fin des songes* de Robert Elie' in Michon (1979), 21–30, asks how Marcel can afford not to work for three months (28). In fact, his journal provides the explanation that he inherited some rental properties from his father (138).
6  Jean Filiatrault, 'Quelques manifestations de la révolte dans notre littérature romanesque récente' (1964), 185
7  See ibid, 186: 'Comme dans le cas de Mathieu, la révolte est une victoire, mais la victoire n'est pas complète ... même après avoir coupé les liens, (la soumission) reste marquée ... par l'étouffement. Cette soumission libérée représente un grand nombre de nos affranchis qui ... manifestent par ... leurs révoltes trop souvent ... infantiles jusqu'à quel point ils sont encore soumis et

comme la liberté leur est difficile. Voilà ce que le jeu des photographies voulait laisser entendre.'
8 See Martens (1985, 126–33) on this type of fictional diary and its relationship to the emergence of the stream-of-consciousness narrative technique.
9 See Irigaray, *Le Langage des déments* (1973) and *Parler n'est jamais neutre* (1986). In 'La Chaîne de sang,' Bastien does occasionally 'play' with words – eg, 'je console le saule,' (185) – and Mathieu's notebooks contain poems with surrealistic elements.

## Chapter Eight

1 See J. Brenkman, 'The Other and the One: Psychoanalysis, Reading, the *Symposium*' (1977). Godbout, on meeting Baillargeon, immediately classified him as a 'pédéraste athée de droite' ('Entrevue,'*Québec français*, mai 1977, 31).
2 See J. McDougall, 'L'Homme et sa masturbation' in 'L'Idéal hermaphrodite et ses avatars,' in Pontalis (1973), 268–75.
3 Lacan in *Quatre concepts fondamentaux de la psychanalyse (Séminaire, 11)*. See Silverman (1983), 151ff; also Brenkman (1977) and Brisson and Kreisler in Pontalis (1973), 27–48, 117–33.
4 Henriette Dessaulles ended her diary, on the eve of her wedding (1881) wondering how some people managed not to have children. In Gabrielle Roy's *Bonheur d'occasion* (1945), contraception is still unknown, or unacceptable. Condoms are mentioned in *Le Libraire* (1960), 'capote anglaise' in *Salut Galarneau!* (1967), jellies in *Trou de mémoire* (1968). Saint-Onge discusses the issue in *La Saison de l'inconfort* (1968).
5 On homosexuality as a developmental stage between narcissism and 'alloeroticism,' see Lewes, 71.
6 Normand Leroux, '*Les Abîmes de l'aube* de J.-P. Pinsonneault,' *Livres et auteurs canadiens*, 1962, 27–8. Aurélien Boivin, in the *Dictionnaire des oeuvres littéraires du Québec*, mentions that other novels by Pinsonneault also depict austere and hostile mothers.
7 Reactions to *L'Insoumise* are available in *Marie-Claire Blais: Dossier de Presse, 1959–1980*.
8 See Marcotte, (1989, 132, 138) on the orphan in Quebec literature and the relevance of Marthe Robert's *Roman des origines et origine du roman*.
9 See V. Tremblay, 'La Révolte contre le patriarcat dans l'oeuvre de Marie-Claire Blais' (MA thesis, UBC, 1980). In 'Fièvre,' as in *L'Insoumise*, le décor is of dazzling whiteness, although there it is white heat (the setting is North Africa) rather than snow. The husband, designated 'Homme,' is, like Rodolphe, 'un homme qui sait tout' (*Fièvre*, 149). The wife is indicated only as 'Voix.' Rodolphe mentions that he does not like Madeleine's voice (66). The

'Homme' of 'Fièvre,' like Rodolphe, tells his wife that she is 'avant tout une femme, une mère' (171) and that she is going mad (161). Like Rodolphe, he can threaten to have her interned, if her insubordination goes too far. Here the woman's refusal to accept her feminine subordinate role is not related to homosexuality in a feminine-identified son.
10 A comparison could be made with Claude Jasmin's *Maman-Paris, Maman-la France!* (1982).
11 See Gabrielle Poulin, 'Des Menteries si bien organisées.'
12 For example, *Une Forêt pour Zoë* (1969). See Raoul on Maheux-Forcier, *Dictionary of Literary Biography*, vol. 60, 188–92.
13 Lubomir Delozel, 'Le Triangle du double'

**Chapter Nine**

1 On the 'dead father,' see J.-J.Hamm's Derridean reading of the 'capharneum' in *Le Libraire* as Homais's store of poison, and the 'pharmakos' as scapegoat: 'Le dehors et le dedans,' in Hamm (1982), 67–79, especially 71–2.
2 For example, Bourneuf in 'Formes et réalités sociales dans le roman québécois' (1970), on 'un parallélisme entre, d'une part, la recherche d'une identité nationale et d'un destin collectif au Québec, et d'autre part le changement dans la conception du récit romanesque ... l'autoanalyse et l'autoportrait semblent devenus la substance même du roman québécois des dernières années' (265). Whitfield also discusses the relationship in *Le Je(u) illocutoire* (1987), and Kwaterko in *Le Roman québécois de 1960 à 1975*, (1989).
3 See Serge Leclaire, in Stambolian and Marks (1979), 42ff on feminine 'speech' and masculine 'discourse.' France Théoret's 1982 title *Nous parlerons comme on écrit* evokes a feminine reversal of the masculine attempt to 'write as one speaks,' raising questions that will be addressed in the next section.
4 Bessette entitled a collection of critical essays *Une Littérature en ébullition*, and Marcotte chose the expression *Une Littérature qui se fait* for one of his.
5 See chapter 7 on the bisexual and the narcissist as desiring a 'phoenix' type of immortality: Green (1983), 26 and Pontalis (1973), 14 ('autogénèse et immortalité').
6 New reproductive technologies make it technically possible for a man to have an embryo implanted in his abdominal cavity: what would motivate candidates?
7 See Stoller, in Pontalis, 144; also Adrienne Rich, *Of Woman Born: Motherhood as Experience and Institution* (New York: Norton 1976) and the work of Mary O'Brien in the social sciences.
8 Robidoux (1987, 140) deduces that the year is probably 1946. I was wrong, in my 1983 article in *Yale French Studies*, to assume that the story took place in the mid- or late 1950s.

9 Field (1989, 88) mentions the widespread comments by fictional diarists on the particular effect of Sundays: reference supplied by Anthony Sorrenti (MA program, UBC).
10 Bessette's later works include *L'Incubation* and *La Grossesse*.
11 See Steven G. Kellman, *The Self-Begetting Novel* (New York: Columbia University Press, 1980), mentioned by Shek (in Hamm 1982), 119–20.
12 Maccabée Iqbal (1976, 343), makes this judgment on the language of Sillery, the 'precious' character in *La Bagarre*. Didier discusses this aspect of diary-writing in *Le Journal intime* (1976).
13 Bessette, in an interview with *Voix et images* (I, 3, avril 1976, 320)
14 Jane Gallop, in *The Daughter's Seduction: Feminism and Psychoanalysis* (1982), discusses the 'quarrel' between Lemoine-Luccioni and Irigaray (92–112), and her 'Fraudian' analysis of the phallic mother is also relevant (113–31).

**Chapter Ten**

1 See Anne Brown on women's writing in Quebec in the 1960s: 'Unhiding the Hidden: Writing during the Quiet Revolution,' in *Anatomy of Gender: Women's Struggle for the Body*, ed. D. Currie and V. Raoul (Ottawa: Carleton University Press 1991), 234–45. She points out that pregnancy and all other female body functions are negatively depicted, even by female narrators. In a sexist diary novel with a male narrator, Roger Fournier's *Journal d'un jeune marié* (1967), the diarist is so disgusted with his pregnant wife that he has sex with her sister while she is in hospital giving birth. Marcel, in Elie's *La Fin des songes*, also preferred his virgin sister-in-law to his multipara wife.
2 The role is associated with madness, as depicted in two films based on diary novels: *Diary of a Mad Housewife* and *Dancing in the Dark*.
3 See Jane Flax (1990), *Thinking Fragments: Psychoanalysis, Feminism, and Postmodernism in the Contemporary West*, 89–132, for a lucid comparison of the concept of narcissism in Lacan and Winnicott.
4 Mathieu, in Loranger's novel, is in a similar predicament in his relation to Danielle; see my chapter 5.
5 An earlier novel by Mailhot, *Le Portique*, tells the story of a young novice who leaves the convent.
6 Doris Lessing used a similar technique in *The Golden Notebook* (1962); see Martens (1985), 233–45. Jean-Marie Poupart also introduces a series of different-coloured notebooks in *Terminus*.
7 Ouvrard's next novel was called *La Noyante* and has a picture of Ophelia on the cover. The image of the beach (the in-between) is comparable to the one in Audrey Thomas' *Intertidal Life* (1984), which also contains a journal. See Linda Hutcheon on that novel, 'Shape Shifters: Canadian Women Novelists

and the Challenge to Tradition' in *A Mazing Space* (ed., S. Neuman and S. Kamboureli, 1986), 219–27.

8 This concept of a feminine ethic is usually associated with Carol Gilligan's study, *In a Different Voice: Psychological Theory and Women's Development* (Cambridge MA: Harvard Univ. Press 1982). For a critical appraisal of it, see Grimshaw (1986),190–4.

9 Examples are Tristine Rainer, *The New Diary. How to Use a Journal for Self-Guidance and Expanded Creativity* (Los Angeles: Tarcher/St. Martin's, 1978) and Kay Leigh Hagan, *Internal Affairs: A Journalkeeping Workbook for Self-Intimacy* (San Francisco: Harper and Row 1988/1990).

**Chapter Eleven**

1 G. Poulin (in 'Romans québécois féminins des années '70,' [1976]) describes the narration in Andrée Maillet's *Lettres au Surhomme* (1976), where the letters function like a journal, as comparable to an analysis.

2 For a summary and bibliography of the debate over *joual*, see Lise Gauvin, 'Littérature et langue parlée au Québec,' 88–119.

3 For example, those by Marina Yaguello and Verena Aebischer for French, and Dale Spender and Robin Lakoff for English. See also Luce Irigaray, *Je, tu, nous* (1990), 35–44, 83–91.

4 See Yves Taschereau, 'Le Vrai Nez qui voque,' 312.

5 On the proper names in this novel, see Diane Pavlovic, 'Ducharme et l'autre versant du réel: Onomastique d'une équivoque' (1983). I have concentrated on aspects that she does not develop.

6 Pavlovic claims that Chateauguay 'est créée par Mille Milles' (82), and Taschereau that 'Chateauguay n'existerait pas' (323).

7 Scenes of women who are unconscious during sexual intercourse also occur in Elie's *La Fin des songes* and Mailhot's *Le Passé composé*.

8 Fanon, in *Les Damnés de la terre* (1968/1976), discusses the case of a colonized man whose wife was raped by the colonizer; the man experienced an inability to accept her, resulting in his impotence.

9 Interview with Anne Gagnon (1975) 'Hubert Aquin et le jeu de l'écriture' 5–18

10 Ibid.

11 Ibid.

**Chapter Twelve**

1 Another novel published in Quebec in 1981 had a similar title: Renaud Longchamp's *Babelle 1: Aprés le déluge* (Montreal: VLB).

2 Another diary novel published in the same year, Robert Baillie's *La Nuit de la*

*Saint-Basile*, similarly uses television (including the incident of the Turks) to draw parallels between the situations in Quebec and abroad. This novel also deals with the juxtaposition and overlap of racial and sexual differences, but adds a focus on environmental pollution. It is self-consciously situated in the tradition of Quebec diary fiction by references to previous examples such as *Salut Galarneau!*
3 For several accounts of this situation from the point of view of minority groups, see R. Vachon and J. Langlois, ed. *Who Is a Québécois?* An extensive discussion of the issues raised by images of foreigners in Quebec literature is provided by Simon Harel in *Le Voleur de parcours* (1989). Kristeva addresses similar problems arising in Europe in *Etrangers à nous-mêmes* (1988).
4 See also J. Brenkman, *Culture and Domination* (1987).
5 In his 1987 article, 'Postmodernism or post-colonialism today,' During makes a lucid analysis of the apparently irreconcilable differences between post-modernism (as pluralistic and opposed to all identity) and the post-colonial concern for 'becoming a subject.' His arguments would apply equally well to the tension between post-modernist thought and feminism.

# Bibliography

## I Novels, short stories, and diaries

Amyot, Geneviève. 1978. *Journal de l'année passée*. Montreal: VLB
Aquin, Hubert. 1968. *Trou de mémoire*. Montreal: Le Cercle du livre de France
– 1969. *L'Antiphonaire*. Montreal: Le Cercle du livre de France
Audet, Noël. 1988. *L'Ombre de l'épervier*. Montreal: Québec/Amérique
Baillargeon, Pierre. 1945/1973. *Les Médisances de Claude Perrin*. Montreal: L. Parizeau
– 1948. *La Neige et le feu*. Montreal: Editions Variétés
Baillie, Robert. 1990. *La Nuit de la Saint-Basile*. Montreal: L'Hexagone
Bernier, Jovette. 1931. *La Chair décevante*. Montreal: Albert Lévesque (and Fides 1982)
Bessette, Gérard. 1968. *Le Libraire*. Montreal: Le Cercle du livre de France
Blais, Marie-Claire. 1965. *Une Saison dans la vie d'Emmanuel*. Montreal: Editions du jour
– 1966. *L'Insoumise*. Montreal: Editions du jour
Brossard, Nicole. 1977. *L'Amèr ou le chapitre effrité*. Montreal: Quinze
– 1984. *Journal intime ou Voilà donc un manuscrit*. Montreal: Les Herbes Rouges
Castonguay, Emile. 1960. *Le Journal d'un bourgeois de Québec*. Quebec: n.p.
Châtillon, Pierre. 1970. *Le Journal d'automne de Placide Mortel*. Montreal: Editions du jour
Chéné, Yolande. 1965. *Peur et amour*. Montreal: Parti Pris
Conan, Laure (Félicité Angers). 1878. 'Un Amour vrai' in *Œuvres romanesques I*. Montreal: Fides 1974, 37–75
– 1882. *Angéline de Montbrun*. Montreal: Fides 1967
– 1883. 'A travers les ronces,' *Nouvelles Archives Canadiennes*, 340–61
– 1919. 'L'Obscure Souffrance' in *L'Obscure Souffrance*. Quebec: n.p., 3–59
– 1919. 'La Vaine Foi' in *L'Obscure Souffrance*. Quebec: n.p., 61–101

Des Bois, Jean (Joseph Carre). 1925. *Journal d'un étudiant*. Montreal: Edouard Garand
Dessaulles, Henriette. 1908. 'L'Amour passa' in *Journal* (1989), 627–44
– 1989. *Journal*. Edition critique, ed. Jean-Louis Major. Montreal: Les Presses de l'Université de Montréal
Ducharme, Réjean. 1967. *Le Nez qui voque*. Paris: Gallimard
– 1973. *L'Hiver de force*. Paris: Gallimard
Elie, Robert (1950). *La Fin des songes*. Montreal: Fides, 1968
Ferron, Jacques. 1970. *L'Amélanchier*. Montreal: Editions du jour
Filiatrault, Jean. 1955. *Chaînes*. Montreal: Le Cercle du livre de France
Fournier, Roger. 1967. *Journal d'un jeune marié*. Montreal: Le Cercle du livre de France
Garneau, Jacques. 1979. *Les Difficiles Lettres d'amour*. Montreal: Quinze
Giguère, Diane. 1976/1984. *Dans les ailes du vent*. Montreal: Pierre Tisseyre
Godbout, Jacques. 1967. *Salut Galarneau!* Paris: Seuil
– 1976. *L'Isle au dragon*. Paris: Seuil
– 1981. *Les Têtes à Papineau*. Paris: Seuil
Hébert, Anne. 1982. *Les Fous de Bassan*. Paris: Seuil
Hertel, François (Rodolphe Dubé). 1939. *Le Beau Risque*. Montreal: Bernard Valiquette
– 1944. *Anatole Laplante, curieux homme*. Montreal: Serge Brousseau
– 1947. *Journal d'Anatole Laplante*. Montreal: Serge Brousseau
– 1949. *Six femmes, un homme*. Paris: Editions de l'Ermite
– 1961. *Journal philosophique et littéraire*. Paris: Editions de la Diaspora française
Lamarche, Claude. 1976. *Je me veux*. Montreal: Quinze
La Rocque, Gilbert. 1973. *Les Corridors*. Montreal: Le Cercle du livre de France
Loranger, Françoise. 1949. *Mathieu*. Montreal: Le Cercle du livre de France
Mailhot, Michèle. 1990. *Le Passé composé*. Montreal: Boréal
Martigny, Paul de. 1947. *Mémoires d'un reporter*. Montreal: L'Imprimerie modèle
– 1947. *Mémoires d'un garnement*. Montreal: Editions du lévrier
Monette, Madeleine. 1980. *Le Double Suspect*. Montreal: Quinze
Noël, Francine. 1990. *Babel: Prise deux*. Montreal: VLB
Ouvrard, Hélène. 1980. *L'Herbe et le varech*. Montreal: Québec/Amérique
Pinsonneault, Jean-Paul. 1962. *Les Abîmes de l'aube*. Montreal: Beauchemin
Poupart, Jean-Marie. 1968. *Angoisse Play*. Montreal: Leméac, 1980
– 1979. *Terminus*. Montreal: Leméac
Raiche, Joseph. 1927. *Journal d'un vicaire de campagne*. Montreal: Edouard Garand
Richard, Jean-Jules. 1965. *Journal d'un hobo*. Montreal: Parti Pris
Ringuet (P. Panneton). 1947. *Fausse Monnaie*. Montreal: Editions Variétés
Roy, Gabrielle. 1954. *Alexandre Chênevert*. Montreal: Beauchemin

Saint-Onge, Paule. 1961. *Ce qu'il faut de regrets*. Montreal: Le Cercle du livre de France
– 1968. *La Saison de l'inconfort*. Montreal: Le Cercle du livre de France
Simard, Jean. 1956. *Mon Fils pourtant heureux*. Montreal: Le Cercle du livre de France
Thériault, Yves. 1969. *Le Grand Roman d'un petit homme*. Montreal: Editions du jour
Tremblay, Michel. 1984. *Des Nouvelles d'Edouard*. Montreal: Leméac
Villemaire, Yolande. 1980. *La Vie en prose*. Montreal: Les Herbes Rouges

## II On narcissism, psychoanalysis, and subjectivity

Abel, Elizabeth. 1990. 'Race, Class and Psychoanalysis? Opening Questions.' In *Conflicts in Feminism*, ed. M. Hirsch and E. Fox Keller. London: Routledge, 184–204
Alford, C.F. 1988. *Narcissism: Socrates, the Frankfurt School, and Psychoanalytic Theory*. New Haven and London: Yale University Press
Andréas-Salomé, Lou. 1921. 'The Dual Orientation of Narcissism.' Reprinted in *Psychoanalytic Quarterly*, 1962, 31: 1–30.
Appeau, Antoine. 1990. *Développement du concept d'organisation narcissique*. Lyon: Césura
Beauvoir, Simone de. 1949. *Le Deuxième Sexe*. 2 vols. Paris: Gallimard. I, 12–35 and II, 353–428
Bellemin-Noël, Jean. 1978. *Psychanalyse et littérature*. Paris: P.U.F.
Bergeret, Jean and Wilfrid Reid, eds. 1986. *Narcissisme et états-limites*. Montreal: Presses de l'Université de Montréal/Paris: Dunod
Bernstein, I. 1957. 'The Role of Narcissism in Moral Masochism.' *Psychoanalytic Quarterly*, 26: 358–77
Brenkman, John. 1977. 'The Other and the One: Psychoanalysis, Reading, the *Symposium*.' *Yale French Studies*, 55–6, 396–456
Brennan, Teresa, ed. 1989. *Between Feminism and Psychoanalysis*. London: Routledge
Butler, Judith. 1990. *Gender Trouble: Feminism and the Subversion of Identity*. New York: Routledge
Chasseguet-Smirgel, Janine. 1986. *Sexuality and Mind: The Role of the Father and the Mother in the Psyche*. New York: New York University Press
Chodorow, Nancy. 1978. *The Reproduction of Mothering: Psychoanalysis and the Sociology of Gender*. Berkeley: University of California Press
Davis, Robert Con, ed. 1983. *Lacan and Narration: The Psychoanalytic Difference in Narrative Theory*. Baltimore and London: Johns Hopkins University Press

Dessuant, Pierre. 1983. *Le Narcissisme*. Paris: P.U.F.
Dor, Joël. 1985. *Introduction à la lecture de Lacan*, 1. Paris: Denoël
Engel, Stephanie. 1980. 'Femininity as Tragedy: Re-examining the New Narcissism.' *Socialist Review*, 53: 77–104
Felman, Shoshana. 1975. 'Women and Madness: The Critical Phallacy.' *Diacritics* Winter, 2–10
Flax, Jane. 1990. *Thinking Fragments: Psychoanalysis, Feminism and Postmodernism in the Contemporary West*. Berkeley: University of California Press
Freud, Sigmund. 1905. 'Three Essays on the Theory of Sexuality.' In *Standard Edition of the Complete Psychological Works*, vol. 7 (London: Hogarth Press 1953), 135–243
- 1911. 'Psycho-analytic Notes on an Autobiographical Account of a Case of Paranoia.' In *Standard Edition*, vol. 12 (London: Hogarth Press 1958), 9–82
- 1914. 'On Narcissism: An Introduction.' In *Standard Edition*, vol. 14 (London: Hogarth Press 1957), 73–102. Reprinted in *Essential Papers on Narcissism*, ed. Andrew Morrison (1986), 17–43
- 1917. 'Mourning and Melancholia.' In *Standard Edition*, vol. 14 (London: Hogarth Press 1957), 243–58
- 1921. 'Group Psychology and the Analysis of the Ego.' In *Standard Edition*, vol. 18 (London: Hogarth Press 1955) 69–143
- 1925. 'Some Psychical Consequences of the Anatomical Distinction between the Sexes.' In *Collected Papers*, vol. 5 (London: Hogarth Press 1950), 186–97. Reprinted in *Women and Analysis*, ed. Jean Strouse (1985), 17–26
Gallop, Jane. 1982. *The Daughter's Seduction: Feminism and Psychoanalysis*. London: Macmillan
Gallop, Jane, and C. Burke. 1985. *Reading Lacan*. Ithaca NY: Cornell University Press
Gear, Maria C. et al, eds. 1981. *Working through Narcissism*. New York: Aronson
Goldberg, Carl. 1980. *In Defense of Narcissism: The Creative Self in Search of Meaning*. New York: Gardner Press
Granoff, Wladimir. 1976. *La Pensée et le féminin*. Paris: Minuit
Green, André. 1983. *Narcissisme de vie, narcissisme de mort*. Paris: Minuit
Grimshaw, Jean. 1988. 'Anatomy and Identity in Feminist Thinking.' In *Feminist Perspectives in Philosophy*, ed. M. Griffiths and M. Whitford. Bloomington: Indiana University Press
Grosz, Elisabeth. 1989. *Sexual Subversion: Three French Feminists*. Sydney: Allen and Unwin
- 1990. *Jacques Lacan: A Feminist Introduction*. London: Routledge
Grunberger, Béla. 1971. *Le Narcissisme*. Paris: Payot; in English, *Narcissism: Psychonanalytic Essays*. Trans J.S. Diamanti. New York: International Universities Press 1971

Henriques, Julian, ed. 1984. *Changing the Subject: Psychology, Social Regulation and Subjectivity*. London: Methuen
Hudot, Pierre. 1976. 'Le Mythe de Narcisse et son interprétation par Plotin.' In *Narcisses, Nouvelle Revue de Psychanalyse*, 13 (Spring): 81–108
Irigaray, Luce. 1977. *Spéculum de l'autre femme*. Paris: Minuit
- 1979. *Ce Sexe qui n'en est pas un*. Paris: Minuit
- (1981). *Et l'une ne bouge pas sans l'autre*. Paris: Minuit
- 1984. *Ethique de la différence sexuelle*. Paris: Minuit
- 1985. *Parler n'est jamais neutre*. Paris: Minuit
- 1987. 'Le Corps-à-corps avec la mère.' In *Sexes et parentés*. Paris: Minuit, 19–33
- 1990. *Je, tu, nous*. Paris: Grasset et Fasquelle
Jameson, Fredric. 1977. 'Imaginary and Symbolic in Lacan: Marxism, Psychoanalytic Criticism, and the Problem of the Subject.' *Yale French Studies*, 55–6, 338–95
Kegan Gardiner, Judith. 1987. 'Self Psychology as Feminist Theory.' *Signs*, 12: 4 (Summer), 761–80
Kernberg, Otto F. 1986. 'Factors in the Psychoanalytic Treatment of Narcissistic Personalities.' In *Essential Papers on Narcissism*, ed. Andrew Morrison, 213–92
Kofman, Sarah. 1980. 'The Narcissistic Woman: Freud and Girard.' *Diacritics*, September, 36–45. From *L'Enigme de la femme*. Paris: Galilée 1980
Kohut, Heinz. 1986. 'Forms and Transformations of Narcissism.' In *Essential Papers on Narcissism*, ed. Andrew Morrison, 61–87
Kristeva, Julia. 1980. *Pouvoirs de l'horreur. Essai sur l'abjection*. Paris: Seuil
- 1983. 'Narcisse: La nouvelle démence' and 'Notre religion: Le semblant.' In *Histoires d'amour*. Paris: Denoël, 131–70
- 1987. *Soleil noir. Dépression et mélancolie*. Paris: Gallimard
Lacan, Jacques. 1966. *Ecrits I*. Paris: Seuil
- 1972/1978. *Le Seminaire*, vols. 2 and 11. Paris: Seuil
Lasch, Christopher. 1979/1984. *The Culture of Narcissism: American Life in an Age of Diminishing Expectations*. New York: Norton
- 1984. *The Minimal Self: Survival in Troubled Times*. New York: Norton
Layton, Lynne. 1985. 'From Oedipus to Narcissus: Literature and the Psychology of Self.' *Mosaic*, 18, no. 1 (Winter), 97–105
Layton, Lynne and B.A. Shapiro, eds. 1986. *Narcissism and the Text: Studies in Literature and the Psychology of Self*. New York: New York University Press
Lemoine-Luccioni, Eugénie. 1976. *Partage des femmes*. Paris: Seuil
Le Poulichet, Sylvie. 1988. 'Le Concept de narcissisme.' In *Enseignements de sept concepts cruciaux de la psychanalyse*, ed. J.-D. Nasio, 75–114
Lewes, Kenneth. 1988. *The Psychoanalytic Theory of Male Homosexuality*. Markham, ON: Meridian

Meissner, W.W. 1986. 'Narcissistic Personalities and Borderline Conditions: A Different Diagnosis.' In Morrison, *Essential Papers on Narcissism*, ed. Andrew Morrison, 403–37

Miller, Alice. 1986. 'Depression and Grandiosity as Related Forms of Narcissistic Disturbances.' In *Essential Papers on Narcissism*, ed. Andrew Morrison, 323–47

Mitchell, Juliet. 1974. *Psychoanalysis and Feminism*. Harmondsworth: Penguin

Mitchell, Juliet and J. Rose. 1982. *Feminine Sexuality: Jacques Lacan and the Ecole Freudienne*. London: Macmillan

Morrison, Andrew, ed. 1986. *Essential Papers on Narcissism*. New York: New York University Press

Nasio, J.-D., ed. 1988. *Enseignement de sept concepts cruciaux de la psychanalyse*. Paris: Rivages

Ogilvie, Bertrand. 1987. *Lacan: La Formation du concept du sujet (1932–1949)*. Paris: P.U.F.

Pateman, Carole. 1983. 'Feminist Critiques of the Public/Private Dichotomy.' In *Public and Private in Social Life*, ed. S.I. Benn and G.F. Gans. London: Croom Helm

Pontalis, J.-B. ed. 1973. *Bisexualité et différence des sexes*. Paris: Gallimard; *Nouvelle Revue de Psychanalyse*, no. 7 (printemps)

Reich, Annie. 1953. 'Narcissistic Object Choice in Women.' *Journal of the American Psychoanalytic Association*, 1: 22–44

Rosolato, Guy. 1975. 'L'Axe narcissique des dépressions.' In *Figures du vide: Nouvelle Revue de Psychanalyse*, 11 (printemps), 5–33

Rothstein, Arnold. 1980. *The Narcissistic Pursuit of Perfection*. New York: International University Press

*Salmagundi*. 1979. Special issue on narcissism, no. 46

Schur, Edwin. 1976. *The Awareness Trap: Self-Absorption instead of Social Change*. New York: McGraw Hill

Segal, Naomi. 1988. *Narcissus and Echo: Women in the French 'récit.'* Manchester: Manchester University Press

Sennett, Richard. 1977. *The Fall of Public Man*. New York: Knopf

Silverman, Kaja. 1983. *The Subject of Semiotics*. New York: Oxford University Press

Smith, Paul. 1988. *Discerning the Subject*. Minneapolis: University of Minnesota Press

Stolorow, Robert D. 1975. 'The Narcissistic Function of Masochism (and Sadism).' *International Journal of Psycho-Analysis*, 56: 441–7

– 1986. 'Towards a Functional Definition of Narcissism.' In *Essential Papers on Narcissism*, ed. Andrew Morrison, 197–209

Strouse, Jean, ed. 1985. *Women and Analysis*. Boston: G.K. Hall

Taylor, Donald and F. Moghaddam. 1987. *Theories of Intergroup Relations:*

*International Social Psychological Perspectives*. New York: Praeger
Telos. 1980. Special issue on narcissism, no. 44
Van Herik, Judith. 1982. *Freud on Femininity and Faith*. Berkeley: University of California Press
Zweig, Paul. 1980. *The Heresy of Self-Love: A Story of Subversive Individualism*. Princeton NJ: Princeton University Press

## III On diaries, real and fictional, and autobiographies

(For a more extensive bibliography, see Raoul 1980.)

Abbott, H. Porter. 1984. *Diary Fiction: Writing as Action*. Ithaca NY: Cornell University Press
Beaujour, Michel. 1980. *Miroirs d'encre: Rhétorique de l'autoportrait*. Paris: Seuil
Campeau, Francine. 1988. 'Le Journal intime: Une multiforme.' *La Parole métèque*, 6 (été), 6–7
Didier, Béatrice. 1976. *Le Journal intime*. Paris: P.U.F.
Field, Trevor. 1989. *Form and Function in the Diary Novel*. Totowa NJ: Barnes and Noble
Girard, Alain. 1963. *Le Journal intime*. Paris: P.U.F.
Hébert, Pierre. 1985. 'Pour une évolution de la littérature personnelle au Québec: L'exemple du journal intime.' *Revue d'histoire littéraire du Québec et du Canada français*, 9 (hiver-printemps), 13–37
Hébert, Pierre, with M. Baszcynski. 1988. *Le Journal intime au Québec*. Montreal: Fides
Homans, Margaret. 1986. *Bearing the Word: Language and Female Experience in Nineteenth-Century Women's Writing*. Chicago: University of Chicago Press
Juhasz, Suzanne. 1980. 'Towards a Theory of Form in Feminist Autobiography.' In *Women's Autobiography*, ed. E. Jelinek. Bloomington: Indiana University Press, 221–37
Lamonde, Yvan. 1983. *Je me souviens: La littérature intime au Québec (1860–1980)*. Quebec: Institut québécois de recherche sur la culture
Lejeune, Philippe. 1980. *Je est un autre*. Paris: Seuil
– 1986. *Moi aussi*. Paris: Seuil
– 1989. *On Autobiography*. Minneapolis: University of Minnesota Press
Lensink, Judy Nolte. 1987. 'Expanding the Boundaries of Criticism: The Diary as Female Autobiography.' *Women's Studies*, 14: 39–53
Martens, Lorna. 1985. *The Diary Novel*. New York: Cambridge University Press
Meyer Spacks, Patricia. 1973. 'Reflecting Women.' *Yale Review*, 63 (Fall): 26–42
Miller, Nancy K. 1980. 'Women's Autobiography in France: For a Dialectics of Identification,' In *Women and Language in Literature and Society*. ed. S. McConnell-Ginet et al. New York: Praeger, 258–73

- 1986. 'Changing the Subject: Authorship, Writing and the Reader.' In *Feminist Studies/Critical Studies*, ed. T. de Lauretis. Bloomington: Indiana University Press
Raoul, Valerie. 1980. *The French Fictional Journal*. Toronto: University of Toronto Press
- 1985. 'Les Femmes intimistes dans le roman français.' *Atlantis*, 10, no. 2 (Spring), 66–73
- 1989. 'Women and Diaries: Gender and Genre.' *Mosaic*, 22–3 (Summer), 57–65
Rousset, Jean. 1983. 'Le Journal intime: Texte sans destinataire?' *Poétique* 56: 435–43
- 1986. *Le Lecteur intime*. Paris: Corti
Smith, Sidonie. 1987. *A Poetics of Women's Autobiography: Marginality and the Fictions of Self-Representation*. Bloomington: Indiana University Press
Spender, Dale, ed. 1987. *Personal Chronicles: Women's Autobiographical Writings. Women's Studies International Forum*, 10, no. 1
Stanton, Domna, ed. 1984. *The Female Autograph*. New York: New York Literary Forum
Van Roey-Roux, Françoise. 1983. *La Littérature intime du Québec*. Montreal: Boréal
Yardley, Krysia and T. Honess. 1987. *Self and Identity: Psychosocial Perspectives*. Chichester and New York: Wiley

## IV On Quebec (background) and colonialism

Balthazar, Louis. 1986. *Bilan du nationalisme au Québec*. Montreal: L'Hexagone
Barbeau, Raymond. 1962. *Le Québec est-il une colonie?* Montreal: Les Editions de l'homme
Bergeron, Gérard. 1986. *A Nous Autres: Aide-mémoire politique par le temps qui court*. Montreal:
Bernard, André. 1978. *What Does Quebec Want?* Toronto: James Lorimer
Bhabha, Homi. 1986. 'Foreward: Remembering Fanon: Self, Psyche and the Colonial Condition.' In F. Fanon. *Black Skin, White Masks*. London: Pluto Press, vii–xxvi
Brunet, Michel. 1968. *Quebec–Canada anglais: Deux itinéraires, un affrontement*. Montreal: HMH
Bureau, Luc. 1984. *Entre l'Eden et l'Utopie: Les Fondements imaginaires de l'espace québécois*. Montreal: Québec-Atlantique
Cambron, Micheline. 1989. *Une Société, un récit: Discours culturel au Québec (1967–1976)*. Montreal: L'Hexagone
Cameron, David. 1974. *Nationalism, Self-Determination and the Quebec Question*. Toronto: Macmillan

Carmel, Marlène. 1990. *Ces Femmes qui n'en veulent pas: Enquête sur la non-maternité volontaire au Québec*. Montreal: Editions Saint-Martin
D'Allemagne, André. 1966. *Le Colonialisme au Québec*. Montreal: Editions R-B
Danylewycz, Marta. 1987. *Taking the Veil: An Alternative to Marriage, Motherhood and Spinsterhood in Quebec, 1840–1920*. Toronto: McClelland and Stewart
Dion, Léon. 1987. *Québec 1945–2000, 1: A la recherche du Québec*. Quebec: Presses de l'Université Laval
Dorsinville, Max. 1972. 'Pays, parole, négritude.' *Canadian Literature* (Winter), 51: 55–64
Dupré, Louise. 1986. 'From Experimentation to Experience: Québécois Modernity in the Feminine.' In *A Mazing Space*, ed. S. Neuman and S. Kamboureli. Edmonton: Longspoon/NeWest, 355–60
Fanon, Frantz. 1968/1976. *Les Damnés de la terre*. Paris: François Maspero
Herripin, Jacques. 1989. *Naître ou ne pas être*. Quebec: Institut québécois de recherche sur la culture
Hertel, François. 1967. *Cent ans d'injustice? Un beau rêve: le Canada*. Montreal: Editions du jour
Larose, Jean. 1987. *La Petite Noirceur*. Montreal: Boréal
Légaré, Anne, and N. Morf. 1989. *La Société distincte de l'Etat: Québec-Canada 1930–1980*. Montreal: Hurtubise HMH
Memmi, Albert. 1972. *Portrait du colonisé suivi de Les Canadiens français sont ils des colonisés?* Montreal: L'Etincelle
Minh-ha, Trinh T. 1989. *Woman, Native, Other: Writing Postcolonialism and Feminism*. Bloomington: Indiana University Press
Monière, Denis. 1977. *Développement des idéologies au Québec*. Montreal: Québec/Amérique
Neuman, Shirley, and Smaro Kamboureli, eds. 1986. *A Mazing Space: Writing Canadian Women Writing*. Edmonton: Longspoon/NeWest
Ouellette-Michalska, Madeleine. 1987. *L'Amour de la carte postale: Impérialisme culturel et différence*. Montreal: Québec-Amérique
Pelletier, J., ed. 1984. *Le Social et le littéraire*. Montreal: U.Q.A.M.
Postgate, Dale and K. Roberts. 1976. *Quebec: Social Change and Political Crisis*. Toronto: McClelland and Stewart
Proulx, Serge and P. Vallierès, eds. 1982. *Changer de société: Déclin du nationalisme culturel et alternatives sociales au Québec*. Montreal: Québec/Amérique
Richler, Mordecai. 1992. *Oh Canada! Oh Quebec! Requiem for a Divided Country*. Toronto: Penguin
Rioux, Marcel. 1987. *La Question du Québec*. Montreal: L'Hexagone
Rogel, Jean-Pierre. 1989. *Le Défi de l'immigration*. Quebec: Institut québécois de recherche sur la culture

Séguin, Maurice. 1977. *L'Idée d'indépendance au Québec: Genèse et historique.* Montreal: Boréal

Stock, eds. 1979. *Dossier Québec.* Montreal: Stock

Teboul, Victor. 1975. 'Antisémitisme: Mythe et images du juif au Québec.' *Voix et images du pays,* 9: 87–112

Trokimenkoff, Susan Mann. 1983. *The Dream of Nation: A Social and Intellectual History of Quebec.* Toronto: Gage

Vachon, R. and J. Langlois, eds. 1983. *Who Is a Québécois?* Montreal: Tecumseh Press

Vallières, Pierre. 1968. *Nègres blancs d'Amérique.* Montreal: Parti Pris

Vincenthier, Georges. 1983. *Histoire des idées au Québec: Des troubles de 1837 au référendum de 1980.* Montreal: VLB

## V On the Quebec novel

Allard, Jacques. 1969. 'Le Roman québécois des années 1960 à 1968.' *Europe,* nos. 478–9 (février-mars), 41–50

Arguin, Maurice. 1985. *Le Roman québécois de 1944 à 1965: Symptômes de colonialisme et signes de libération.* Quebec: Presses de l'Université Laval

Beaudoin, Réjean. 1989. *Naissance d'une littérature: Essai sur le messianisme et les débuts de la littérature canadienne-française (1850–1890).* Montreal: Boréal

Belleau, André. 1980. *Le Romancier fictif: Essai sur la représentation de l'écrivain dans le roman québécois.* Sillery: Presses de l'Université du Quebec

Bourneuf, Roland, 1970. 'Formes littéraires et réalités sociales dans le roman québécois.' *Livres et auteurs québécois,* 265–9

Boynard-Frot, Janine. 1982. *Un Matriarcat en procès: Analyse sémiotique de romans canadiens-français, 1860-1960.* Montreal: Presses de l'Université de Montréal

Brault, Jacques. 1965. 'Notes sur le littéraire et le politique.' *Etudes françaises,* 2, no. 5 (janvier), 43–51

Cotnam, Jacques. 1971. 'Le Roman à l'heure de la Révolution tranquille.' *Archives des lettres canadiennes* 3: 265–97

Couillard, Marie. 1981. 'La Femme-écrivain canadienne-française et québécoise face aux idéologies de son temps.' *Canadian Ethnic Studies,* 13, no. 1, 43–51

Dorsinville, Max. 1974. *Caliban without Prospero: Essay on Quebec and Black Literature.* Erin, ON: Porcépic

Falardeau, J.-C. 1967/1972. *Notre société et son roman.* Montreal: Hurtubise HMH

Filiatrault, Jean. 1964. 'Quelques manifestations de la révolte dans notre littérature romanesque récente.' *Recherches sociographiques,* 5: no. 1–2 (août), 177–90

Gagnon, Claude-Marie. 1983. 'Autobiographie religieuse et roman sentimental québécois.' *Etudes littéraires,* 16: no. 3 (déc.), 441–62

Gauvin, Lise. 1974. 'Littérature et langue parlée au Québec.' *Etudes françaises*, 10: no. 1, 88–119

Green, Mary Jean, P. Gilbert Lewis, and K. Gould. 1985. 'Inscriptions of the Feminine: A Century of Women Writing in Quebec.' *American Review of Canadian Studies*, 15: no. 4, 363–88

Harel, Simon. 1989. *Le Voleur de parcours: Identité et cosmopolitisme dans la littérature québécoise contemporaine*. Montreal: Le Préambule

Hébert, Pierre. 1982. 'Un Problème de sémiotique diachronique: Norme coloniale et évolution des formes romanesques québécoises.' *Recherches sémiotiques*, 2: no. 3, 211–39

Heidenreich, Rosmarin. 1990. *The Postwar Novel in Canada: Narrative Patterns and Reader Response*. Waterloo: Wilfrid Laurier University Press

Hodgson, Richard and R. Sarkonak. 1989. *Le Roman québécois contemporain (1960–1986) devant la critique. Oeuvres et critiques*, 14: 1. Paris: Sedes

Imbert, Patrick. 1983. *Roman québécois contemporain et clichés*. Ottawa: Editions de l'Université d'Ottawa

– 1986. 'Parodie et parodie au second degré dans le roman québécois moderne.' *Etudes littéraires*, 19: no. 1, 337–47

Kwaterko, Joseph. 1989. *Le Roman québécois de 1960 à 1975: Idéologie et représentation littéraire*. Montreal: Le Préambule

Laflèche, Guy. 1977. *Histoire des formes du roman québécois*. Montreal: Presses de l'Université de Montréal

Lafortune, Monique. 1985. *Le Roman québécois, reflet d'une société*. Laval: Mondia

Lemieux, Danielle. 1984. *Une Culture de la nostalgie: L'Enfant dans le roman québécois de ses origines à nos jours*. Montreal: Boréal

Lemire, Maurice, ed. 1982. *Dictionnaire des oeuvres littéraires du Québec III. 1940 à 1959*. Montreal: Fides

Lewis, Paula Gilbert, ed. 1985. *Traditionalism, Nationalism and Feminism: Women Writers of Quebec*. Westport, CN: Greenwood Press

Mailhot, Laurent. 1981. 'Romans de la parole (et du mythe).' *Canadian Literature*, 88: 84–90

Marcotte, Gilles. 1976/1989. *Le Roman à l'imparfait: La Révolution tranquille du roman québécois. Essais*. Montreal: L'Hexagone

– 1979. 'La Problématique du récit dans le roman québécois aujourd'hui.' *Revue des sciences humaines*, 45: no. 173 (janvier–mars), 59–69

Michon, Jacques, ed. 1979. *Structure, idéologie et réception du roman québecois de 1940 à 1960*. Sherbrooke: Université de Sherbrooke

– 1981. 'Le discours du récit romanesque au Québec depuis 1940.' *Revue d'histoire littéraire du Québec et du Canada français*, 2: 67–73

– 1984. 'Figures du roman québécois.' *Voix et images*, 9: 165–8

Nepveu, Pierre. 1988. *L'Ecologie du réel: Mort et naissance de la littérature québécoise contemporaine*. Montreal: Boréal

Paradis, Suzanne. 1976. *Femme fictive, femme réelle: Le personnage féminin dans le roman canadien-français 1884–1966*. Quebec: Garneau

Paterson, Janet M. 1990. *Moments postmodernes dans le roman québécois*. Ottawa: Presses de l'Université d'Ottawa

Pelletier, Jacques. 1984. *Lecture politique du roman québécois contemporain*. Montreal: U.Q.A.M.

– 1991. *Le Roman national: Essais*. Montreal: VLB

Poulin, Gabrielle. 1976. 'Romans québécois féminins des.années '70: La Femme et les pays toujours futurs.' *Relations*, 36 (déc.),: no. 421, 347–50

Raoul, Valerie. 1983. 'Documents of Non-Identity: The Diary Novel in Quebec.' *Yale French Studies*, 65: 187–200

Robidoux, Réjean. 1968. 'L'Autonomie d'une petite littérature.' *Mosaic*, April, 97–109

Robidoux, Réjean, and A. Renaud. 1962. *Le Roman canadien-français du vingtième siècle*. Ottawa: Presses de l'Université d'Ottawa

Sainte-Marie-Eleuthère, Soeur. 1964. *La Mère dans le roman canadien-français*. Quebec: Presses de l'Université Laval

Smart, Patricia. 1988. *Ecrire dans la maison du père: L'Emergence du féminin dans la tradition littéraire du Québec*. Montreal: Québec/Amérique

Turcotte, Raymond. 1969. 'L'Apre conquête de la parole.' *Voix et images du pays*, 2: 11–30

Vachon, G.-André. 1974. 'Le Colonisé parle.' *Etudes françaises*, 10, no. 1, 61–77

Whitfield, Agnès. 1987. *Le Je(u) illocutoire: Forme et contestation dans le nouveau roman québécois*. Quebec: Presses de l'Université Laval

## VI On Henriette Dessaulles and Laure Conan

Amprimoz, Alexandre. 1986. 'Les Larmes d'Angéline de Montbrun.' In *Solitude rompue*, ed. C. Cloutier-Wojciechowski and R. Robidoux. Ottawa: Editions de l'Université d'Ottawa, 14–22

– 1976. 'Polarisation spatiale d'une critique romanesque: Une lecture d'*Angéline de Montbrun* de Laure Conan.' *Présence francophone*, no. 13 (automne), 79–101

Belle-Isle, Francine. 1978. 'La Voix séduction: A propos de Laure Conan.' *Etudes littéraires*, 11: 459–72

Blodgett, E.D. 1988. 'The Father's Seduction: The Example of Laure Conan's *Angéline de Montbrun*.' In *A Mazing Space*, ed. S. Neuman and S. Kamboureli, Edmonton: Longspoon/NeWest 17–30

Brochu, André. 1963. 'La Technique romanesque dans *Angéline de Montbrun*' and (1965) 'Le Cercle et l'évasion verticale dans *Angéline de Montbrun*.' In

L'Instance critique (Ottawa: Leméac, 1974), 112–120, 121–132
Casgrain, L'Abbé H.-R. 1884. 'Etude sur *Angéline de Montbrun*.' Preface to *Angéline de Montbrun*. Quebec: Léger Brousseau, 5–24
Cotnam, Jacques. 1973. '*Angéline de Montbrun*: Un cas patent de masochisme moral.' *Journal of Canadian Fiction*, 2, no. 3 (Summer), 152–60
Couture, Jeannine. 1966. 'Fadette: Vie et oeuvre de Madame H.-D. Saint-Jacques (1860–1946).' MA thesis, University of Ottawa
D'Arles, Henri. 1914. *Une Romancière canadienne: Laure Conan*. Paris: Librairie Duval, Editions de la Pensée de France
Dionne, René. 1976. 'Entre Ciel et terre: Pour une lecture littéraire de l'oeuvre de Laure Conan.' *Lettres québécoises*. 1, no. 1, 19–21
Dumont, Micheline. 1960. 'Introduction.' In *Laure Conan: Textes choisis*. Montréal and Paris: Fides, 5–20
Gagnon-Mahony, Madeleine. 1972. '*Angéline de Montbrun*: Le Mensonge historique et la subversion de la métaphore blanche.' *Voix et images du pays*, 5: 57–68
Gallays, François. 1985. 'Reflections in the Pool: The Subtext of Laure Conan's *Angéline de Montbrun*.' In *Traditionalism, Nationalism and Feminism: Women Writers of Québec*, ed. Paula Gilbert Lewis. Westport, CN: Greenwood Press, 11–26
Gautier-Cano, Mona. 1987. 'La Métamorphose du sujet dans le Journal d'Henriette Dessaulles.' MA thesis, University of Ottawa
Godin, Jean-Cléo. 1964. 'L'Amour de la fiancée dans *Angéline de Montbrun*.' *Lettres et écritures* (mars), 14–19
Green, Mary Jean. 1987. 'Laure Conan and Madame de Lafayette: Rewriting the Female Plot.' *Essays on Canadian Writing*, 34 (Spring): 50–63
Hébert, Pierre. 1987. 'Jalons pour une narratologie du journal intime: Le statut du récit dans le Journal d'Henriette Dessaulles.' *Voix et images*, 37 (automne), 140–56
Heidenreich, Rosmarin. 1979. 'Narrative Structures in Laure Conan's *Angéline de Montbrun*.' *Canadian Literature*, 81 (Summer): 37–46
Imbert, Patrick. 1981. '*Fadette, Journal d'Henriette Dessaulles* ou l'ambivalence vécue,' *Lettres québécoises*, 23 (décembre), 70–2
Le Moine, Roger. 1974. 'De Félicité Angers à Laure Conan.' In *Laure Conan: Oeuvres romanesques 1*, Montreal: Fides, 9–28
Marcotte, Gilles, 1962. *Une Littérature qui se fait*. Montreal: HMH
Ouellet, Lise. 1988. 'Le Journal d'Henriette Dessaulles ou le roman du "je" spéculaire au "je" social.' *Francofonia*, 7, no. 14 (printemps), 53–61
Paradis, Suzanne (Soeur J. de l'Immaculée). 1974. '*Angéline de Montbrun*.' In *Le Roman canadien-français*, ed. P. Wyczynski et al. *Archives des lettres canadiennes*, 3, Montreal: Fides, 105–31

Poulin, Gabrielle. 1983. '*Angéline de Montbrun* ou les abîmes de la critique.' *Revue d'histoire littéraire du Québec et du Canada français*, 5: 125–32
Raoul, Valerie. 1986. 'Moi (Henriette Dessaulles), ici (au Quebec), maintenant (1874–1880): Articulation du journal intime féminin.' *French Review*, 59, no. 6 (May), 841–8
Smart, Patricia. 1988. '*Angéline de Montbrun* ou la chute dans l'écriture.' In *Ecrire dans la maison du père: L'Emergence du féminin dans la tradition littéraire du Québec*. Montreal: Québec/Amérique, 41–82
Tremblay, Victor. 1989. 'Les Structures narratives et mythiques d'*Angéline de Montbrun*,' *Canadian Literature*, 121 (Summer), 198–204
Verduyn, Chrystl. 1983. 'La Religion dans le Journal d'Henriette Fadette.' *Atlantis*, 8, no. 2 (Spring), 45–50
Verthuy, Maïr. 1986. '*Femmes et patrie dans l'oeuvre romanesque de Laure Conan.*' In *Solitude rompue*, ed. C. Cloutier-Wojciechowski and R. Robidoux. Ottawa: Editions de l'Université d'Ottawa, 396–404
Wittenberg, Marie-Louise. 1972. '*La Porte étroite et Angéline de Montbrun*: Une comparaison.' *Présence francophone*, 4 (Spring), 123–38

## VII On other authors

Allard, Jacques. 1969. '*Le Libraire* de Gérard Bessette ou comment la parole vient au pays du silence.' *Voix et images du pays*, 1: 51–62
Belair, Michel. 1974. 'Du Silence à la non-parole' (*Le Libraire*). *Le Québec littéraire*, 1: 57–72
Bellemare, Yvon. 1984. *Jacques Godbout, romancier*. Montreal: Parti Pris
Bessette, Gérard. 1979. *Mes Romans et moi*. Montreal: Hurtubise
Boivin, Aurélien. 1977. 'Jacques Godbout: Entrevue.' *Québec français*, mai, 29–36
– 1982. '*Les Abîmes de l'aube*, roman de Jean-Paul Pinsonneault.' In *Dictionnaire des oeuvres littéraires du Québec*, 1–2
Bond. D.J. 1976. 'The Search for Identity in the Novels of Réjean Ducharme.' *Mosaic*, 9 (Winter), 31–44
Chanady, Amaryll. 1987. 'Autoreprésentation, autoréférence et spécularité – le narcissisme libérateur de *Trou de mémoire*.' *Revue de l'Université d'Ottawa*, 57, no. 2 (avril-juin), 55–67
Charbonneau, Robert. 1972. 'François Hertel' and 'Pierre Baillargeon' in *Romanciers canadiens*. Quebec: Presses de l'Université Laval, 4–9 and 56–61
Drapeau, Renée. 1986. *Féminins singuliers. Pratiques d'écriture: Brossard, Théoret*. Montreal: Triptyque
Dupré, Louise. 1989. *Stratégies du vertige. Trois poètes: Nicole Brossard, Madeleine Gagnon, France Théoret*. Montreal: Editions du remue ménage
Dupriez, Bernard. (1972). 'Ducharme et des ficelles.' *Voix et images du pays*, 5: 165–85

Filteau, Claude. 1976. '*L'Hiver de force* de Réjean Ducharme et la politique du désir.' *Voix et images*, 1: 365–73

Gagnon, Anne. 1975. 'Hubert Aquin et le jeu de l'écriture' (interview). *Voix et images*, 1: 5–18

Gaulin, André. 1982. '*Commerce*, essai de Pierre Baillargeon.' In *Dictionnaire des oeuvres littéraires du Québec* III, 215–17

– 1982. '*Les Médisances de Claude Perrin* de Pierre Baillargeon.' In *Dictionnaire des oeuvres littéraires du Québec* III, 627–9

– 1982. '*Mon Fils pourtant heureux*, roman de Jean Simard.' In *Dictionnaire des oeuvres littéraires du Québec* III, 649–50

Genuist, Monique. 1977. 'Mille Milles et la femme dans *Le Nez qui voque*.' *Atlantis*, 2: no. 2 (Spring), 56–73

Giguère, Richard. 1988. 'François Hertel (Rodolphe Dubé).' In *Dictionary of Literary Biography*, vol. 68, Canadian Writers, 1920–1959, 1 (Detroit: Bruccoli Clark Layman), 175–9

Hamm, Jean-Jacques, ed. 1982. *Lectures de Bessette*. Montreal: Québec/Amérique

Houde, Christiane. 1977. 'La Problématique de l'écriture dans l'oeuvre romanesque de Jacques Godbout.' *Québec français*, mai, 33–5

Imbert, Patrick. 1979. 'Révolution culturelle et clichés chez Réjean Ducharme.' *Journal of Canadian Fiction*, no. 25–6, 227–36

Juéry, René. 1979. 'Le Discours de Galarneau.' *Voix et images*, 5, no. 1, 33–49

Landry, Kenneth. 1982. '*Anatole Laplante, curieux homme*, roman, et *Journal d'Anatole Laplante* de François Hertel.' In *Dictionnaire des oeuvres littéraires du Québec* III, 46–9

Laurent, Françoise. 1985. *L'Oeuvre romanesque de Marie-Claire Blais*. Montreal: Fides

Lazaridès, Alexandre. 1973. 'Du roman au mythe: Essai sur l'imaginaire dans *Salut Galarneau!*' *Voix et images du pays*, 6: 65–85

Leduc-Park, Renée. 1982. *Réjean Ducharme: Nietzsche et Dionysos*. Quebec: Presses de l'Université Laval

Maccabée Iqbal, Françoise. 1976. 'Précieux et préciosité chez Bessette: Demi-mesure et démesure.' *Voix et images*, 3 (avril), 338–64

[Maccabée] Iqbal, Françoise. 1978. *Hubert Aquin, romancier*. Quebec: Presses de l'Université Laval

Maillet, Marguerite. 1972. '*Le Nez qui voque*.' *Co-Incidences*, 2, no. 1 (février), 3–24

Major, Robert. 1986. 'François Hertel: bilan provisoire d'un destin d'écrivain.' In *Solitude rompue*, ed. C. Cloutier-Wojciechowski and R. Robidoux. Ottawa: Editions de l'Université d'Ottawa, 267–78

(1981) *Marie-Claire Blais: Dossier de Presse, 1959–1980*. Sherbrooke: Bibliothèque du séminaire de Sherbrooke

Martel, Jean-Pierre. 1974. '*Trou de mémoire*: Oeuvre baroque.' *Voix et images du pays*, 8: 163–72

- 1976. '*Trou de mémoire*, un jeu formel mortel.' *Le Québec littéraire*, 2: 55–65
Mélancon, Robert. 1979. 'Les Décevantes Lettres d'amour.' *Le Devoir*, 19 mai, 21
- 1982. '*Chaînes*, nouvelles de Jean Filiatrault.' In *Dictionnaire des oeuvres littéraires du Québec III*, 169–71
Mocquais, Pierre-Yves. 1985. *Hubert Aquin ou la quête interrompue.* Montreal: Pierre Tisseyre
Pascal, Gabrielle. 1978. 'Geneviève Amyot, *Journal de l'année passée.*' *Livres et auteurs québécois*, 22–3
Paul, Raymond. 1979. 'Jacques Garneau, *Les Difficiles Lettres d'amour.*' *Livres et auteurs québécois*, 46–7
Pavlovic, Diane. 1983. 'Ducharme et l'autre versant du réel: Onomastique d'une équivoque.' *L'Esprit créateur*, 23, no. 3, 77–85
Pelletier, Jacques. 1966. 'Marie-Claire Blais: *L'Insoumise.*' *Le Campus estrien*, 19 octobre (See *Marie-Claire Blais: Dossier de Presse*, Sherbrooke, 1981).
Plante, Raymond. 1974. 'La Marche aux amours heureuses: Notes sur l'oeuvre romanesque de Jacques Godbout.' *Voix et images du pays*, 8: 163–72
Poulin, Gabrielle. 1985. 'Des Menteries si bien organisées: *Des Nouvelles d'Edouard* de Michel Tremblay.' *Lettres québécoises*, 37 (printemps), 17–19
Randall, Marilyn. 1990. *Le Contexte littéraire: Lecture pragmatique de Hubert Aquin et de Réjean Ducharme.* Montreal: Le Préambule
Raoul, Yvon. 1971. 'La Recherche d'une identité québécoise à travers la femme dans l'oeuvre romanesque de Jacques Godbout.' MA thesis, McMaster University
Richard, Robert. 1987. 'La Transmission du roman.' *Revue de l'Université d'Ottawa*, 57, no. 2 (avril–juin), 9–28
Robidoux, Réjean. 1971. 'Le Cycle créateur de Gérard Bessette ou le fond c'est la forme.' *Livres et auteurs québécois*, 11–28
- 1987. *La Création de Gérard Bessette.* Montreal: Québec/Amérique
Robitaille, Claude. 1982. '*Journal d'un hobo*, récit de Jean-Jules Richard.' In *Dictionnaire des oeuvres littéraires du Québec IV*, 482–3
Saint-Martin, Lori. 1984. 'Mise à mort de la femme et "libération" de l'homme: Godbout, Aquin, Beaulieu.' *Voix et images*, 10, no. 1 (automne), 107–17
Simoneau, Pierre. 1979. 'Structures discursives de *La Fin des songes* de Robert Elie.' In *Structure, idéologie réception du roman québécois de 1940 à 1960*, ed. Jacques Michon, 21–30
Smart, Patricia. 1973. *Hubert Aquin: agent double.* Montreal: Presses de l'Université de Montréal
Smith, André. 1976. *L'Univers romanesque de Jacques Godbout.* Montreal: Aquila
Smith, Donald. 1971. 'L'Invention verbale dans le roman québécois contemporain: Bessette, Godbout.' *Co-Incidences*, 1, no. 1 (mars), 4–19
Söderlind, Sylvia. 1984. 'Hubert Aquin ou le mystère de l'anamorphose.' *Voix et images*, 9, no. 3 (printemps), 103–11

Taschereau, Yves. 1975. 'Le Vrai Nez qui voque.' *Etudes françaises*, 11, no. 3-4 (octobre), 311-24
Tétu, Michel. 1970. 'Jacques Godbout ou l'expérience québécoise de l'américanité.' *Livres et auteurs québécois*, 270-9
Tremblay, Victor. 1980. 'La Révolte contre le patriarcat dans l'oeuvre de Marie-Claire Blais.' MA thesis, University of British Columbia
Vanasse, André. 1979. 'Un Bestiaire, quelques bananes et un journal qui s'écrit à l'envers.' *Lettres québécoises*, 14 (avril-mai), 16-17
- 1979. 'Jacques Garneau: *Les Difficiles Lettres d'amour*.' *Lettres québécoises*, 15 (août-septembre), 16-17
- 1980. 'Madeleine Monette: *Le Double Suspect*.' *Livres et auteurs québécois*, 52-3
Verthuy, Maïr. 1986. 'Flirting with Female Be-ing: The Uneasy Search of Hélène Ouvrard.' In *A Mazing Space*, ed. S. Neuman and S. Kamboureli. Edmonton: Longspoon/NeWest, 108-44
Wagg, Heather. 1985. 'Subject and Text in Réjean Ducharme's *L'Avalée des avalés* and *Le Nez qui voque*.' PHD thesis, University of British Columbia

## VIII Miscellaneous

Abel, Elizabeth, M. Hirsch, and E. Langland, eds. 1983. *The Voyage In: Fictions of Female Development*. Hanover: University Press of New England
Aebischer, Verena. 1985. *Les Femmes et le langage: Représentations sociales d'une différence*. Paris: P.U.F.
Badinter, Elisabeth. 1986. *L'Un est l'autre*. Paris: Odile Jacob
Barthes, Roland. 1970. 'To Write: An Intransitive Verb?' In *The Languages of Criticism and the Sciences of Man: The Structuralist Controversy*, ed. R. Macksey and E. Donato. Baltimore MD: Johns Hopkins Press, 134-44
Brenkman, John. 1987. *Culture and Domination*. Ithaca NY and London: Cornell University Press
Dällenbach, Lucien. 1977. *Le Récit spéculaire: Essai sur la mise en abyme*. Paris: Seuil
Delozel, Lubomir. 1984. 'Le Triangle du double: Un champ thématique.' *Poétique*, 64: 463-72
Derrida, Jacques. 1987. *Psyché: Inventions de l'autre*. Paris: Galilée
Douglas, Ann. 1977. *The Feminization of American Culture*. New York: Knopf
Dowling, Colette. 1981. *The Cinderella Complex*. New York: Pocket Books
Duplessis, Rachel Blau. 1985. *Writing beyond the Ending: Narrative Strategies of Twentieth-Century Women Writers*. Bloomington: Indiana University Press
During, Simon. 1987. 'Postmodernism or Post-colonialism today.' *Textual Practice*, 1, no. 1, 32-47

Ellmann, Mary. 1968. *Thinking about Women*. New York: Harcourt, Brace, Jovanovich
Felski, Rita. 1989. *Beyond Feminist Aesthetics: Feminist Literature and Social Change*. Cambridge, MA: Harvard University Press
Forman, Frieda Johles. 1989. *Taking our Time: Feminist Perspectives on Temporality*. New York: Pergamon
Gasché, Rodolphe. 1986. *The Tain of the Mirror: Derrida and the Philosophy of Reflection*. Cambridge MA: Harvard University Press
Grimshaw, Jean. 1986. *Philosophy and Feminist Thinking*. Minneapolis: University of Minnesota Press
Hutcheon, Linda. 1980. *Narcissistic Narrative: The Metafictional Paradox*. Waterloo, ON: Wilfrid Laurier University Press
Jameson, Fredric. 1981. *The Political Unconscious: Narrative as a Socially Symbolic Act*. Ithaca NY and New York: Cornell University Press
Kristeva, Julia. 1974. *La Révolution du langage poétique*. Paris: Seuil
– 1986. 'Why the United States?' In *The Kristeva Reader*, ed. T. Moi, 272–91
– 1988. *Etrangers à nous-mêmes*. Paris: Gallimard (Folio)
Moi, Toril. 1985. *Sexual/Textual Politics: Feminist Literary Theory*. London: Methuen
– ed. 1986. *The Kristeva Reader*. New York: Columbia University Press
Nye, Andrea. 1988. *Feminist Theory and the Philosophies of Man*. New York: Routledge
– 1990. *Words of Power: A Feminist Reading of the History of Logic*. New York: Routledge
Oksenberg Rorty, Amélie. 1973. 'Dependents: The Trials of Success.' *Yale Review*, 63 (Fall), 43–59
Rosenblatt, Paul C. 1983. *Bitter, Bitter Tears: Nineteenth-Century Diarists and Twentieth-Century Grief Theories*. Minneapolis: University of Minnesota Press
Ross, Michael J., ed. 1985. *Homosexuality, Masculinity and Femininity*. New York: Harrington Park Press
Sarde, Michèle. 1983. *Regard sur les Françaises*. Paris: Stock
Spender, Dale. 1980. *Man-Made Language*. London: Routledge
Stambolian, George and E. Marks, eds. 1979. *Homosexualities and French Literature*. Ithaca NY and New York: Cornell University Press
Stanford Friedman, Susan. 1989. 'Creativity and the Childbirth Metaphor: Gender Difference in Literary Discourse.' In *Speaking of Gender*, ed. E. Showalter. New York: Routledge, 73–100
Weedon, Chris. 1987. *Feminist Practice and Postmodernist Theory*. London: Basil Blackwell
Woolf, Virginia. 1967. *A Room of One's Own* (1928). Harmondsworth: Penguin
– 1973. *A Writer's Diary*, ed. Leonard Woolf. Granada: St Albans

- 1979. 'Professions for Women.' In *Virginia Woolf: Women and Writing*, ed. Michèle Barrett. London: Women's Press, 57–63
Zavalloni, Marisa, ed. 1987. *L'Emergence d'une culture au féminin*. Montreal: Editions Saint-Martin

# Index of Names

Abbott, H. Porter 3
Abel, Elizabeth ch1n9, ch6n4
Alford, C.F. 16
Allard, Jacques 174, 198, ch1n7
Amyot, Geneviève: *Journal de l'année passée* 186–7, 190–4
Andréas-Salomé, Lou 20
Aquin, Hubert 10, 13; *Trou de mémoire* 6, 233–42
Arguin, Maurice 170, 214, ch1n5

Badinter, Elisabeth 30
Baillargeon, Pierre 12; *Les Médisances de Claude Perrin* 8, 95–100
Baillie, Robert: *La Nuit de la Saint-Basile* ch12n2
Balthazar, Louis 31,
Beaudoin, Réjean 21, 32, 167, ch1n1, ch2n3
Belair, Michel 176, 178
Belleau, André 9, 101, 107, 223
Belle-Isle, Francine 80–1
Bellemare, Yvon 178, 185, 191
Bergeron, Gérard 33
Bernard, André 33, 35
Bernier, Jovette: *La Chair décevante* 139, 199

Bessette, Gérard 10; *Le Libraire* 12, 168–9, 170–8, ch8n4
Blais, Marie-Claire: *Une Saison dans la vie d'Emmanuel* 143; *L'Insoumise* 10, 143–9, 200
Blodgett, E.D. 68, 69, ch5nn13, 18
Boivin, Aurélien 185, ch8n6
Bourneuf, Roland 139, 170, ch9n2
Boynard-Frot, Janine 36
Brenkman, John ch8n1, ch12n4
Brochu, André 59, 72, 81, ch5nn8, 10, 18
Brossard, Nicole 225, 226, 256; *L'Amèr* 242–3; *Journal intime* 6, 13, 243–9
Brown, Anne ch10n1
Bureau, Luc 17

Cameron, David 31
Carmel, Marlène 198
Casgrain, L'Abbé H.-R. 76, ch5n7
Châtillon, Pierre: *Le Journal d'automne de Placide Mortel* 186, 222
Chéné, Yolande: *Peur et amour* 11, 200, 205–8, 210, 256
Chessler, Phyllis 130–1

Chodorow, Nancy 24
Conan, Laure 11, 56, 58–9; 'Un Amour vrai' 6, 59–60; *Angéline de Montbrun* 6, 7, 20, 60–77, 104, 130, 170; 'L'Obscure Souffrance' 60, 77–9; 'A travers les ronces' 77–8; 'La Vaine Foi' 60, 79–80
Cotnam, Jacques 73, 170, ch1n5, ch4n3
Couillard, Marie 197, 198

D'Allemagne, André 28, 30, 31, 32, 34, 38
De Beauvoir, Simone 23, 26–7, 30, 229
Delozel, Lubomir 163
Derrida, Jacques 21, 108–9, 223, 225
Des Bois, Jean: *Journal d'un étudiant* 8
Dessaulles, Henriette 6, 7, 11, 12, 47; *Journal* 47–57, 60–2, 246, 247, ch8n4; 'L'Amour passa' 59, ch4n3
Didier, Béatrice 21, 45, 46, 54, 88, ch4n6, ch5nn4, 7
Dionne, René 60
Dor, Joël 221
Dorsinville, Max 40, 242
Douglas, Ann 86, 110, ch5n19
Dowling, Colette 55
Ducharme, Réjean 10, 13; *Le Nez qui voque* 226–33, 241, 242
Dumont, Micheline 170, ch5nn2, 14
Dupré, Louise 219, 244
During, Simon 262, ch12n5

Elie, Robert 12; *La Fin des songes* 9, 112, 121–7, ch11n7
Ellmann, Mary 167, 169

Falardeau, J.-C. ch1n5
Fanon, Frantz 28, 33, 40, ch11n8
Felman, Shoshana 130, 131–2
Felski, Rita 197, 216–20
Field, Trevor 3, 4, 6, 8, ch9n9

Filiatrault, Jean 12, 34, 37, ch7nn3, 6; *Chaînes* 6, 9, 10, 112, 127–32
Flax, Jane 219, ch10n3
Fournier, Roger: *Journal d'un jeune marié* ch10n1
Freud, Sigmund 15, 17–18, 20, 22, 24, 230, 239

Gagnon, Anne 241
Gagnon, Madeleine 69, 248, ch11n9
Gallays, François 66, 73
Gallop, Jane 132, 219, 242, ch9n14
Garneau, Jacques: *Les Difficiles Lettres d'amour* 186–90, 193
Gaulin, André ch7n3
Gautier-Cano, Mona 54
Gauvin, Lise ch11n2
Giguère, Diane: *Dans les ailes du vent* 210, 216
Giguère, Richard ch6n2
Gilligan, Carol ch10n8
Girard, Alain 45, 75, ch4n6, ch5n7
Godbout, Jacques 10, 97 ch8n1; *Salut Galarneau!* 12, 168–9, 178–86, 188, ch8n4, ch12n2
Godin, Jean-Cléo 70, ch5n3
Goldberg, Carl 15, 19
Gould, K. 199, ch5n18
Granoff, Wladimir 109
Green, André 13–21, 72, 73, 74, 76, 90, 136, 137, 138, 140, 172, 221, 228, 253
Green, Mary Jean 199, ch5n18
Grimshaw, Jean ch10n8
Grunberger, Béla 15

Hamm, Jean-Jacques ch9n1
Harel, Simon 241, 261, ch12n3
Hébert, Anne 199–200
Hébert, Pierre 7, 54, 86, ch1n5, ch4n1
Heidenreich, Rosmarin 63, 64, 70, 72, 234

Hertel, François 8, 12, ch6nn2, 4, 5, 7; *Le Beau Risque* 86–8, 135; *Journal d'Anatole Laplante* 8, 89–95, 136; *Journal philosophique et littéraire* 92, 94
Hutcheon, Linda 14, ch10n7

Imbert, Patrick ch5n6
Iqbal, Françoise Maccabée 173, 174, 176, 177, 240, ch8n12
Irigaray, Luce 189, 190, 242, 261–2, ch7n9, ch11n3

Jakobson, Roman 257
Jameson, Fredric 3, 14, 26, 33, 40
Juhasz, Suzanne 46, 201

Kafka, Franz ix, 5
Kamboureli, Smaro 276–7n7
Kernberg, Otto F. 20
Kofman, Sarah 15, 23
Kohut, Heinz 20
Kristeva, Julia 7, 15, 17, 71–2, 76–7, 106, 110, 115, 117–18, 223, 229, 253, 260, 261–2, ch12n3
Kwaterko, Joseph 139, 176, 177, 185, 261, ch1nn5, 8, ch9n2

Lacan, Jacques 16, 110–11, 138, 219, 223, 225, 238, 241, 245
Lamarche, Claude: *Je me veux* 200, 208–10
Lamonde, Yvan 7, ch4n1
Larose, Jean 13, 32, 34, 35–9, 225, 230, 244–5, 248, ch6n6, ch7nn1, 2
Lasch, Christopher 262
Laurent, Françoise 144
Layton, Lynne 22
Lazaridès, Alexandre 179, 180, 182, 183, 185
Leduc-Park, Renée 229, 232

Leigh Hagan, Kay ch10n9
Lejeune, Philippe 58, ch4n4
Le Moine, Roger ch5nn1, 2, 3, 5, 7, 12
Lemoine-Luccioni, Eugénie 183, 188, 189, 190, 192, 193, 201, 202, 255, ch9n14
Lensink, Judy Nolte 46, 201
Le Poulichet, Sylvie 15, 16, 24
Leroux, Normand ch8n6
Lewes, Kenneth 137, 161, 178, 242, ch8n5
Lewis, Paula Gilbert 199
Loranger, Françoise 12; *Mathieu* 9, 112–21, 200

Maccabée Iqbal. *See* Iqbal
Mailhot, Michèle: *Le Passé composé* 12, 200, 211–13, ch11n7
Maillet, Andrée: *Lettres au Surhomme* ch11n1
Major, Jean-Louis 47–8, 49, ch4n3, ch5n5
Major, Robert ch6n2
Marcotte, Gilles 143, 144, 145, 171, 177, 227, 231, ch8n8
Marks, E. 139, 149, 221, ch9n3
Martens, Lorna 3, 47, 80, 199, ch7n8, ch10n6
Meissner, W.W. 19
Mélançon, Robert 127
Memmi, Albert 27–34, 234–5
Meyer Spacks, Patricia 197, 205
Michon, Jacques 102, ch6n8
Miller, Nancy K. 58
Minh-ha, Trinh T. 29, 30
Monette, Madeleine: *Le Double Suspect* 10, 162–6, 203, 237
Morrison, Andrew 15, 20, 22

Neuman, Shirley ch10n7

Noël, Francine: *Babel: Prise deux* 13, 225, 249, 254–63

Ouellette-Michalska, Madeleine 29, 30, 34, 39–40
Ouvrard, Hélène: *L'Herbe et le varech* 200, 214–17

Paradis, Suzanne ch5n3
Pavlovic, Diane 232, ch11nn5,6
Pelletier, Jacques 148, 185, ch1n8
Pinsonneault, Jean-Paul: *Les Abîmes de l'aube* 10, 140–3
Plante, Raymond 184–5
Pontalis, J.-B. 136, 161, ch9n7
Poulin, Gabrielle 184, ch8n11
Poupart, Jean-Marie: *Angoisse Play* 185–6; *Terminus* ch10n6

Raiche, Joseph: *Journal d'un vicaire de campagne* 8
Rainer, Tristine ch10n9
Randall, Marilyn 231, 234, 242
Raoul, Valerie 3, 4, 14, 46, 55, 58, 63, 85, 177, 201, 222, ch9n8
Reich, Annie 22–3, 54
Richard, Jean-Jules: *Journal d'un hobo* 10, 149–55
Richard, Robert 238
Robidoux, Réjean 5, 176, ch9n8
Rosenblatt, Paul C. 71, 74, 76, ch5n9
Ross, Michael J. 135
Roy, Gabrielle 6, 121, 199, ch8n4

Sainte-Marie-Eleuthère, Soeur 36, 110, ch7n3
Saint-Martin, Lori 234, 237, ch3n5
Saint-Onge, Paule 11, 200; *Ce qu'il faut de regrets* 200–3; *La Saison de l'inconfort* 203–5, ch8n4

Sarde, Michèle 35
Showalter, Elaine 131
Silverman, Kaja 138
Simard, Jean 12; *Mon Fils pourtant heureux* 6, 9, 101–9, 111
Simoneau, Pierre ch7n5
Simpson, Anne ch5n16
Smart, Particia 13, 37, 39, 61, 62, 67, 68, 72, 74, 75, 199, 234, 235, ch5n13
Smith, André 182, 185
Smith, Sidonie 200
Spender, Dale 23, 29, ch11n3
Stambolian, George 139, 149, 221, ch9n3
Stanford Friedman, Susan 167, 169, 170, 190
Stolorow, Robert D. 19, 20,

Taschereau, Yves ch11nn4, 6
Tétu, Michel 185
Théoret, France 219, 248, ch9n3
Thériault, Yves: *Le Grand Roman d'un petit homme* 6
Thompson, Dawn ch5n11
Tremblay, Michel 36; *Des Nouvelles d'Edouard* 10, 155–62, 168
Tremblay, Victor ch8n9
Trokimenkoff, Susan M. ch3n4
Turcotte, Raymond 8, 85, 95, 98

Vachon, R. 32, ch12n3
Vallières, Pierre 30, 32
Vanasse, André 187
Van Herik, Judith 85, 86
Van Roey-Roux, Françoise 7, 94–5, ch4n1
Verthuy, Maïr 80, 214
Villemaire, Yolande 248–9
Vincenthier, Georges 31, ch6n1

Weedon, Chris 17
Whitfield, Agnès 139, ch1nn3, 7, ch9n2
Winnicott, D.W. 15, ch7n4, ch10n3
Woolf, Virginia 23, 75, 182

# General Index

alcohol 78, 92, 111 119, 121, 142, 172–3, 210
America and Americans 35, 38, 88, 92, 99, 116, 172, 174, 179–80, 184–5, 199, 206–7, 210, 224–5, 232, 260, ch3n1, ch6n6, ch7n1
appearance, physical 79–80, 104, 113, 116–17, 121, 157, 163, 201–2, 204, 217, 258; *see also* specularity/mirrors
assimilation/engulfment 13, 19, 123, 254, 256, 261
author-narrator relationship 4, 58–9, 61, 77, 81, 87–8, 95–6, 100–1, 106, 112, 115, 169, 185–7, 200–1, 208, 212, 214, 217, 227, 239, 244, ch4n4, ch5n3, ch6n9

Blacks 27, 30–3, 40, 225, 234–40, 259

Canada 38–9, 92, 99, 150–3, 180, 197, 220, 224, 232–3, 238, 260–3
celibacy/chastity 67, 73, 88, 91, 101, 123, 125, 149, 198–9, 209–11, 229, ch5n12

death 17, 52, 55, 61–2, 68, 72, 76, 88, 104, 116–17, 126, 128, 131, 144, 155, 162, 164, 181, 201, 207, 233–4, 237, 240, 256; *see also* suicide
diaries: as fetish 22, 75–6, 165–6, 170, 178, 228, 241, 248; by women 6–8, 11, 13, 45–7, 56, 60, 63, 81, 148, 193, 199–201, 254, ch4n6
diary model (real/fiction) ix, 4–8, 45–50, 58–61, 80, 85, 102–3, 106, 114, 130, 136–7, 139–41, 143–5, 148, 150, 155–6, 159–60, 163–4, 168, 173, 175–7, 179, 187, 201, 205, 211–12, 222, 240, 244, ch1n3, ch4nn1, 2, 3, 6, ch5nn7, 9, ch10nn6, 7, 9, ch11n1

English Canadians 52, 56, 61, 79, 153–4, 180, 234–6, 239, 258, 260
English language and culture 88, 93, 99, 153–4, 180, 203–4, 207, 224–5, 232–6, 258–61

father 11–12, 16–17, 25, 37, 50, 56, 61, 65–6, 68–9, 72, 74, 78, 86–7, 90, 97, 101–4, 107–11, 116–19, 121, 129, 131, 136, 142, 145–6, 151, 161, 168, 172, 178–83, 187, 199, 201, 206–7, 210, 212, 238, ch9n1; *see also* mother
femininity/masculinity 17, 35, 54, 87–8,

90, 92, 94, 103, 106, 109, 111, 116, 119–20, 130, 160, 162, 170, 177, 180–1, 183, 188–90, 192, 203, 209, 215, 219, 223, 226, 230, 241, 260, ch5n1, ch9n3, ch10n8

fragmentation 19, 22, 72, 94, 112, 186, 222, 243, 257, 261

France and French culture 74, 91–3, 96, 99–100, 107–8, 119, 139, 155–9, 171, 175, 180–1, 210, 212, 224, 232, 235, 257, ch3n6

God/religion 7, 47–8, 51–2, 55, 59–61, 66, 68, 70–5, 81, 85–8, 91, 98, 100–3, 107–8, 113, 115, 118, 120, 125, 141, 145, 149, 171, 174, 179, 183–4, 191, 209, 211, 219, 224, 254, ch5nn19, 20, ch10n5

guilt/shame 17–18, 69–71, 73, 79, 88, 105–6, 141, 157

history ix, 28, 31–2, 64, 74, 138–40, 167, 171, 224

homosexuality/bisexuality 10, 12, 15, 17, 23–4, 35–8, 51, 54, 59, 67–8, 87, 89, 106–7, 131–2, 135–66, 173, 180, 182, 186–8, 192, 200, 206–7, 209, 220, 228, 232, 237, 243, 245, 248, 255, ch8nn1, 5, 9

illness 52, 60, 71, 88, 97, 107, 122, 128, 206, 210, ch5n15; *see also* madness

impotence 12, 19, 25, 38, 85, 91, 97, 100 105, 107, 110–12, 126, 130, 156, 172, 176, 186, 197, 203–4, 207, 214, 216–17, 220–1, 236, 241

incest 10, 66, 68, 72, 104, 128, 130–1, 148, 182–3, 206, 242, ch5nn7, 10

Jews 27, 92–3, 100, 210, 258, 260

language and self-esteem 22–3, 27, 29–33, 46, 103–4, 131, 153, 156–9, 168, 174–5, 179–80, 188, 198, 204, 210, 211–16, 220, 232, 240, 253, 257, 260, ch9n12

letters/epistolary model 7, 62–3, 89, 107, 129, 187–9, 224, 256

madness 9, 12, 19, 20, 109, 112, 115, 121, 124–32, 136, 146, 165, 200, 206, 222, 230, 231, 240, ch7nn2, 9, ch10n2

marriage 11–12, 38–9, 50, 52, 57, 62, 65, 67, 70, 77–8, 80, 98, 104, 116, 121–2, 139, 145, 147, 172, 181, 200–9, 215–16, 231, 245, 255, 262, ch3n7, ch4n6, ch5n20

masturbation 15, 17, 54, 68, 88, 91, 107, 109, 119, 136, 141, 156, 165, 177, 186, 227–8, 236, ch8n2

mirrors. *See* specularity/mirrors

misogyny 13, 37, 85–6, 89, 95–6, 104, 109, 111, 135–6, 171, 184, 229–30, 237, ch3n5, ch6n4

moral narcissism 11–12, 20–1, 28, 60, 72–3, 81, 90, 110–11, 138, 206

mother 10–12, 16, 24–5, 36–7, 49, 54–6, 61, 68–9, 72, 74, 78, 80, 86–7, 90, 103–11, 115–17, 120–7, 131–2, 136, 140–5, 151, 156, 165, 170–3, 178–9, 182–3, 187, 190–1, 193, 197–203, 205, 207, 209, 214, 217, 220, 229–30, 238, 242–3, 245, 247–8, ch8nn6, 9, ch9n14, ch10n1; *see also* father

narcissistic injury 19, 24, 69–73, 116, 145, 201

Narcissus/Echo 12, 21, 27, 82, 90, 94, 105–6, 137, 145, 209, 219, 228–9

narratee/reader 5, 22, 48, 53, 62–3, 69, 76–7, 87, 94–7, 107, 112–14, 118, 121–

2, 126, 141, 143–6, 154–5, 160, 162–3, 177–9, 184–5, 188, 203, 206, 208, 210–11, 214–15, 217, 221–2, 230, 232, 240, 244, 254
nationalism ix, 20, 30–4, 36, 56, 74, 85–6, 92, 96, 167–8, 184–5, 198, 200, 206, 209, 214–16, 218, 247, 258, ch3n3, ch6n1, ch9n2
Natives 40, 153–4, 228, 258–9
neuter 17, 33, 73, 90, 138, 165, 172, 192

primary narcissism 10, 16–17, 24, 66, 86, 123, 128–30, 185, 223

rape. *See* sexual intercourse/rape
récit/discours 38, 49, 101, 106, 149, 160, 168, 175–6, 201, 212–13, 223
refuge values 28, 30–1, 33–4, 73–4, 108–10, 167, 174, 198, 209, 220, 233, 262
reproduction/rebirth 11–12, 21–2, 32, 39, 55, 58, 68–9, 76, 89, 91, 96–7, 100, 105–6, 108, 111, 117, 119, 126, 129–30, 132, 139, 151–3, 159, 166, 168–70, 174–8, 181–6, 188–94, 197–8, 201–4, 207, 209, 213–14, 216, 233, 237–8, 240, 241, 255, 259–60, ch8n4, ch9nn5, 6, 10, 11

scopophilia 22, 94, 102, 125, 173, 240, 256
self-other confusion / double 10, 12, 15, 17, 19, 54, 65–7, 86–7, 89, 96–7, 111, 118, 121, 125, 127, 136, 142, 145, 158, 160, 163, 175, 182, 187, 209–10, 214, 218, 222, 228–9, 233–4, 241, 255, 258–9, 260–1
sexual intercourse/rape 90, 116, 119, 124, 128, 138, 141, 147, 151–3, 172, 178–9, 181, 199, 202, 204, 206, 212, 234, 236–8, 240–1, 256, ch10n1, ch11nn7, 8,
specularity/mirrors 14, 16, 50, 65, 70, 90, 94, 106, 108, 115, 117, 119, 124–5, 137, 146, 163, 200, 209, 215, 223, 228, 231, 248, 255, 260, ch7n4; *see also* appearance, physical
suicide 72, 109, 112, 115, 121–2, 124, 127, 147–8, 162–5, 182–3, 201–3, 229–31, 238–9; *see also* death
survival 11, 13, 32, 55–6, 75, 99, 108–9, 115, 132, 150, 182, 185, 193, 198, 203, 205, 213, 237, 239, 241, 262

time/memory ix, 5, 22, 29, 64–5, 72–3, 76, 82, 87, 89, 94, 96–7, 101, 112, 129, 149–50, 171, 175–7, 182, 187, 208, 212–13, 222, 238, 243, 246–8, 256, ch5n8, ch9n8, ch10n6

withdrawal/separation 13, 20–1, 47, 55, 71–2, 92, 117, 122–4, 142, 153, 165, 171–2, 178, 181–2, 187–8, 217, 222, 228
writing 5, 9, 46, 58, 61, 75–6, 88, 91, 95, 97, 99, 106, 109, 114, 120, 125, 129, 141, 146, 149–50, 154, 159–60, 163–4, 177–9, 186–90, 191–3, 197, 202–6, 208, 210–13, 215, 219, 225, 231, 236, 240–1, 247, 255–6

www.ingramcontent.com/pod-product-compliance
Lightning Source LLC
Chambersburg PA
CBHW071150070526
44584CB00019B/2729